D1614590

THE IRISH STAGE: A LEGAL HISTORY

The Irish Stage
A Legal History

W.N. OSBOROUGH

FOUR COURTS PRESS
in association with
THE IRISH LEGAL HISTORY SOCIETY

Typeset in 10.5pt on 12.5pt EhrhardtMt by
Carrigboy Typesetting Services for
FOUR COURTS PRESS LTD
7 Malpas Street, Dublin 8, Ireland
www.fourcourtspress.ie
and in North America for
FOUR COURTS PRESS
c/o ISBS, 920 N.E. 58th Avenue, Suite 300, Portland, OR 97213.

A catalogue record for this title is available
from the British Library.

ISBN 978–1–84682–528–6

Printed in England,
by Antony Rowe Ltd, Chippenham, Wiltshire.

Contents

Contents

Illustrations

Preface

There is an impressive library of books devoted to the history of the Irish stage. And there is a no less impressive series of essays tackling individual facets of that history in the periodical literature – in pages of journals such as *Irish Historical Studies, Eire-Ireland, Eighteenth-century Ireland* and *Dublin Historical Record*.

Given the wealth of coverage, a justification for yet another volume focusing on the fortunes of theatre in Ireland needs to be found. The title says it all. *The Irish stage: a legal history* is an attempt to explore the legal dimensions to entertainments that members of the public have over the years paid good money to come and see. The identity of topics to be covered in the planned inventory is hardly a surprise. These embrace such matters as riots and censorship, neither of which, as students of the history will be aware, is ignored in the existing literature. The synthesis offered here furnishes the excuse to visit afresh ground that is admittedly well-covered. But, in addition, there are other topics calling equally for attention that, curiously, have remained relatively neglected: the institution of the office of Master of the Revels; the regime of theatre patents for Dublin which lasted from the 1780s to less than a generation ago; the introduction of the dramatic author's performing right. A miscellany of residual matters calls out for attention as well: health and safety, liquor licensing and labour law issues (dealt with here under the heading 'Performers and managers'), among others.

The text kicks off with a quotation that establishes the close link that has existed, and continues to exist, between theatre in England and theatre in Ireland. Differences emerged even so, which demand extended treatment, differences such as the lack of a Lord Chamberlain for Ireland and Ireland's legislative lacuna as regards the provincial stage.

If, for comparative purposes, England makes a frequent appearance, this by no means exhausts the list of foreign jurisdictions where personalities and developments are incorporated into the present narrative. This is not an attempt to compose a legal history of the stage in global terms, but it is not too fanciful to suggest that, by putting foreign flesh and bones on the native story, the arguments and the picture that the author has sought to convey are both improved and enhanced. No apologies, therefore, for including mention of the unlikely characters that the reader who persists will encounter in his or her journey through 300-odd pages: Herodotus, Molière, Ibsen, Diaghilev, the Kaiser and Joseph Goebbels. Nor for including images of the disastrous theatre fire in Vienna in December 1881.

A trawl of writings, not reckoned to be immediately germane, bequeathed to us by literary figures, can also, I believe, add a dash of colour to this survey with its all too obvious legal bias. Charles Dickens has left an account of a London theatre gutted by fire (p. 135). As regards the breed of hack dramatists that it was hoped, perhaps too sanguinely, the concession in the 1830s of the dramatic author's performing right would do nothing to encourage (see p. 255), I did not, to my regret, find room, at the appropriate place, to recall Vincent Crummles' offer to Nicholas Nickleby to become a playwright-in-residence with a mandate to frame novel theatrical pieces around recently acquired stage props such as 'a real pump and two washing-tubs' (*Nicholas Nickleby*, ch. 22) – a conversational exchange that calls to mind Mr Toogood's assertion, conveyed to Mr Harding in Anthony Trollope's *The last chronicle of Barset* (ch. 42), that 'there have been many theatrical managers … who have usually made up their pieces according to the dresses they have happened to have in their wardrobes'. Chapter 15 is the place where such tendentious flourishes might have made an entry. That chapter, as it happens, appeared originally in the pages of the *Dublin University Law Journal* ('Chapters from the history of the dramatic author's performing right', *DULJ*, 10 (2011) 33). I am grateful for permission to reprint it here.

The assistance of the staff at the various institutions that made images available for reproduction – in Dublin, both the National Gallery and the National Library, Trinity College Dublin and University College Dublin, and in London, the British Museum, the National Portrait Gallery, the Victoria and Albert Museum, and the Wallace Collection – is gratefully acknowledged. My thanks too, to Dáire Hogan, Richard Barrett, Conor O'Malley, Ronan Smith, Christopher Murray, Robert Clark and Sarah Ravell (my daughter) for their assistance; to Miriam Walsh for the fair copy she produced from my manuscript; to Julitta Clancy for the general index. In the last weeks of the production of *The Irish stage: a legal history* I owed a particular debt of gratitude to Caroline Fine of the UCD Sutherland School of Law, to Robert Marshall of the Legal History Society and to Martin Fanning of Four Courts Press. Finally, I should like to thank all three.

May 2015

CHAPTER ONE

The Irish mastership of the revels, 1638–1830

LA TOURETTE STOCKWELL, in her pioneering survey of Dublin's theatres and theatre customs,[1] first published in 1938, boldly declared that

> The history of dramatic representation in Ireland belongs to the history of the English in Ireland, and its progress has been in a line which parallels the evolution of the theatre in England.[2]

Alan Fletcher, in no less ground-breaking a text,[3] has shed light on the early history of drama and performance in the country, reaching further back in time and taking in evidence from the Gaelic Ireland of the seventh century onwards. Intriguingly, this historical reassessment had been anticipated by one of the earliest historians of the stage in Ireland, the well-travelled W.R. Chetwood. The latter, in his *General history of the stage* of 1749,[4] recalled that in his youth he had seen

> a Chinese performance at Canton, where the scenes, machines, and habits were surprising and magnificent, but not understanding the language, the glare growing familiar, as Addison says by beauty, faded on the eye, and pall'd upon the sense.[5]

It is not impossible that the experience of foreign travel led Chetwood to adopt an open mind as regards the dating of public performance in Ireland. That he had such an open mind is demonstrated in the following remarks. 'This kingdom of Ireland,' Chetwood writes,[6]

> is one of the last in Europe where establish'd theatres were erected; yet I am assured one of the first, whose bards, or poets have celebrated in verse, the illustrious actions of their monarchs, nor any nation in the world, where

1 La Tourette Stockwell, *Dublin theatres and theatre customs, 1637–1820* (Kingsport, TX, Kingsport Press, 1938, repr. New York, B. Biom, 1968). References hereafter are to the 1968 reprint.
2 Stockwell, *Dublin theatres*, p. xv.
3 Alan J. Fletcher, *Drama, performance and polity in pre-Cromwellian Ireland* (Cork, Cork UP, 2000).
4 W.R. Chetwood, *A general history of the stage (more particularly the Irish theatre) from its origin in Greece down to the present time* (Dublin, E. Rider, 1749).
5 Chetwood, *General history of the stage*, p. 13.   6 Ibid., p. 49.

poetry and poets were in such high esteem. Every antient and noble family had one in their household, and their kings their poet laureats, as we have in England, but long, long before the English invaded Ireland.

There can be debate over the dating of the origin of drama in Ireland, but it would have to be conceded that this does not apply in the case of the history of the regulation of the Irish stage. Here it is plain that the practice is to be dated to the year 1638 – 28 February – when Thomas Wentworth, the lord deputy, the future earl of Strafford, created of his own volition the office of the Master of the Revels in Ireland.[7]

In England the post of Master of the Revels had been established in the reign of the second of the Tudors, Henry VIII.[8] His role was to facilitate the staging of masques and other entertainments intended to amuse the monarch. In the reign of Elizabeth I the issuance of a royal patent in 1574 bestowed upon the then holder of the office the power to vet plays intended for public performance. The exercise of the powers of the Master of the Revels in England came within the purview of another crown appointee, the Lord Chamberlain. In later years both office-holders purported to exercise identical functions – up until the major legal change adopted in 1737. One very obvious difference as regards the office of Master of the Revels as between England and Ireland was that in Ireland there was no equivalent to the more senior office of Lord Chamberlain.

The Irish post conferred by Wentworth in 1638 was given to a Scot, John Ogilby (1600–76), something of a jack of all trades, for, apart from his links with theatre in Ireland, he had been a dancing-master in London, became a publisher there too, and was later credited as a cartographer.[9] Heralded by Clark as 'the true founder of the Irish stage',[10] Ogilby was to open his first theatre in the vicinity of Dublin's Werburgh Street, close both to Dublin Castle and Christchurch Cathedral, probably in 1636, in other words as much perhaps as two years before Wentworth made him Master of the Revels.[11] This Werburgh Street venue, Morash has written,[12] 'was a versatile, intimate performing space … in some respects … a typical court theatre'.

7 Stockwell, *Dublin theatres*, pp 24–6; W.S. Clark, *The early Irish stage: the beginnings to 1720* (Oxford, Clarendon Press, 1955); Fletcher, *Drama, performance and polity*, p. 262.
8 David Thomas, David Carlton and Anne Etienne, *Theatre censorship from Walpole to Wilson* (Oxford, Oxford UP, 2007), pp 6–7.
9 His entry in the *Oxford DNB*, xli, 566, is content to describe him exclusively as a 'publisher and geographer'. See further K. Van Eerde, *John Ogilby and the taste of his times* (Folkestone, Kent, Wm Dawson & Son, 1976).
10 Clark, *Early Irish stage*, p. 27.
11 Historians of the Irish theatre (such as Stockwell and Fletcher) have expended considerable effort on fixing the date. For an up-to-date overview of the problem, see Christopher Morash, *A history of Irish theatre, 1601–2000* (Cambridge, Cambridge UP, 2002), p. 4.
12 Morash, *History of Irish theatre*, p. 6. See, too, Stockwell, *Dublin theatres*, pp 1–23; Van Eerde, *John Ogilby*, p. 23; and Fletcher, *Drama, performance and polity*, pp 261–77.

There was to be an outbreak of plague in London in May 1636, an outbreak which lasted until October 1637. This had brought a small number of performers to Ireland, and Ogilby was able to capitalise on their presence for his early productions. At this juncture it is worth observing that Ogilby's recruitment drive, when involved with a different Irish theatre after the Restoration, would involve him in considerable trouble then.[13]

Another arrival in Ireland in the 1630s was James Shirley (1596–1666), revered at the time both as a dramatist and a poet,[14] and best known today, perhaps, for these lines from his 'The contention of Ajax and Ulysses':

> The glories of our blood and state
> Are shadows, not substantial things;
> There is no armour against fate;
> Death lays his icy hand on kings:
> Sceptre and crown
> Must tumble down
> And in the dust be equal made
> With the poor crooked scythe and spade.

However talented Ogilby's troupe of performers may have fancied themselves to be, the omens for the future of theatrical productions in the country were far from encouraging. Shirley went out of his way to stress the lack of support that the new venture appears to have encountered:[15]

> When he did live in England, he heard say
> That here were men lov'd wit, and a good play …
> This he believed, and though they are not found
> Above, who knows what may be underground?

Shirley repeated the complaint in the prologue to his *The Irish Gentleman*:[16]

> We know at first, what black and general curse
> Fell on the earth; but shall this isle be worse?
> While others are repair'd, and grow refin'd
> By acts, shall this only to weeds be kind?

Shirley went still further, predictably deploring the taste audiences could display for alternative forms of entertainment to legitimate drama. In another prologue, Shirley wrote:[17]

---

13 Below, p. 157.
14 See further James Shirley, *Dramatic works and poems …*, *now first collected*, 6 vols (London, J. Murray, 1833); Eva Griffith, 'James Shirley and the earl of Kildare: speculating playhouses and dwarves à la mode' in Michael Potterton and Thomas Herron, *Dublin and the Pale in the Renaissance, c.1540–1660* (Dublin, Four Courts Press, 2011), p. 352.
15 Quoted, Clark, *Early Irish stage*, p. 34.   16 Quoted, Stockwell, *Dublin theatres*, p. 6.
17 Ibid., p. 7.

> Were there a pageant now on foot, or some
> Strange monster from Peru or Afric come,
> Men would throng to it; any drum will bring
> (That beats a bloodless prize or cudgelling)
> Spectators hither; nay the bears invite
> Audience, and bag-pipes can do more than wit.

At the Restoration when, as we are about to discover, Ogilby was to resume his career as a theatre manager, the auspices had by no means magically improved, at least not to judge from a note by a Dublin Castle official on the difficulty of attracting audiences. This is what the official in question confided to an acquaintance in January 1662/3:[18]

> Mr Ogilby gets money, and his actors reputation; though nothing but the conspiracy of foul weather and good company can betray the writer to see the inside of his new-mended theatre.

Rebellion broke out in Ireland in 1641 and the Werburgh Street theatre was closed on the instructions of the two lords justices, William Parsons and John Borlace.[19] (A similar fate befell all Dublin's theatres – admittedly for rather shorter periods of closure – both in 1798 and after Emmet's rebellion in 1803.) The 1640s, in fact, ushered in a period when drama was frowned on by the puritan elements in politics, soon to be in the ascendant.[20] Ogilby was to say of the period later, that his theatre in Dublin had been 'spoyled and a cow-house made of the stage'. It had fallen 'to utter ruin by the calamities of those times', a disaster in which he had lost at least £2,000. He himself at one point had been lucky to escape death.[21] As for the Werburgh Street venue, it simply disappeared.

At the Restoration the office of Master of the Revels was revived in England, the post going to Sir Henry Herbert in June 1660. In the following August, theatre patents were bestowed on Thomas Killigrew and William Davenant that led eventually to the opening in London of both Drury Lane and Covent Garden.[22] Davenant was destined to play a role in the developments that now occurred in Ireland. Succeeding to the post of court poet on the death of Ben Jonson in 1637, Davenant was a veteran dramatist (*The Tragedy of Alborine* (1629)) and poet, as well as a reputed godson of William Shakespeare and a staunch royalist. Davenant

---

18 Col. Ed. Cooke to Will. Legge, 10 Jan. 1662/3: H.M.C., *rep 10* (1887), app V, p. 11.
19 Morash, *History of Irish theatre*, p. 10.
20 See further, below, ch. 14.
21 From his petition to be restored as Master of the Revels in early 1661. *Cal. S.P. Ire., 1669–70 and addenda, 1625–70*, pp 416–17; Clark, *Early Irish stage*, appendix A, p. 180; Van Eerde, *John Ogilby*, p. 24.
22 Clark, *Early Irish stage*, p. 43; Andrew Saint, B.A. Young, Mary Clarke, Clement Crispi and Harold Rosenthal, *A history of the Royal Opera House, Covent Garden, 1732–1982* (London, Royal Opera House, 1982), p. 11.

moved quickly to secure the office of Master of the Revels in Ireland, and in
November 1660 he appeared to have succeeded when a royal warrant was made out
conferring the post on him and, in consequence, empowering him

> To erect or provide a Theater in Our Citty of Dublyn ... noe more Theaters
> or Play Houses [to] be permitted in Our Citty of Dublin than that One
> Theater or Play house to be erected or provided by the said Sir William
> Davenant.[23]

The prospect of the confirmation of this grant stirred John Ogilby into action.
Ogilby had helped to plan the pageants for Charles II's coronation in April 1661,
and around this time he had consulted the astrologer Elias Ashmole for advice on
a propitious time to start the learning of Greek – he was among his other
accomplishments an early translator of Homer.[24] More to the point perhaps, like
Davenant, Ogilby had friends in high places. The representations he then made,
in which he emphasised that he had been appointed Master of the Revels in
Ireland by Wentworth in 1638, plainly prevailed, for in March 1661, any grant in
favour of Davenant was revoked,[25] and arrangements made instead to bestow the
office on Ogilby.[26] This was done by a patent dated 8 May 1661, under which the
Scot was empowered

> to build upon such grounds by him to be purchased ... in Dublin or
> elsewhere in Ireland such Theatre or Theatres, as to him shall seeme most
> fitt ... and therein to represent Comedyes Tragedyes and Operas and other
> Enterludes decent and not obnoxious with a prohibition to all persons to
> performe ye same without License first obteyned from him.[27]

The patent at the same time alluded to the circumstance that Wentworth, the late
earl of Strafford, had named Ogilby Master of the Revels in Ireland in 1638, in
pursuance of which Ogilby

> did at his owne greate costes and charges ... erect a publick Theater in our
> Cittie of Dublin and did effectually reduce the publick presentacions of
> tragedies and comedies to the proper and harmeles use whereby those

23 The text of this warrant is reproduced in appendix A of Clark, *Early Irish stage*, at pp 179–80.
24 See Morash, *History of Irish theatre*, p. 12; Keith Thomas, *Religion and the decline of magic* (London, Penguin Books, 1978), p. 380. An accomplishment by which John Dryden for one was not impressed. There are two mentions of Ogilby at lines 102 and 174 in Dryden's poem, 'Mac flecknoe', *The works of John Dryden, vol. 2 – Poems, 1681–1684* (Berkeley and Los Angeles, CA, and London, Univ. of California Press, 1972).
25 See *Cal. S.P. Ire., 1669–70 and addenda 1625–70*, p. 416; Clark, *Early Irish stage*, p. 44.
26 Van Eerde claims that Davenant and Killigrew at this juncture were too preoccupied with Sir Henry Herbert's assertion of rights as Master of the Revels in England to care very much about Ogilby's lobbying to have the Irish post confirmed to him: *John Ogilby*, p. 160, n.
27 Clark, *Early Irish stage*, pp 44–5; appendix A, pp 180–1.

recreacions formerly obnoxious were made inoffensive to such of our
subjectes and other strangers voluntarily resorting thereunto.[28]

This grant of 8 May 1661, however, was not to represent the end of the immediate
post-Restoration changes.

Ogilby sensed the need to secure extra capital for the enterprise upon which for
the second time he had embarked, and a partner was found for him, through the
agency of Shirley, in the person of one Thomas Stanley, junior, son and heir of a
man of the same name, of Cumberloe in Hertfordshire. The decision was reached
that a new patent was required naming both men, which, while reserving the
designation of Master of the Revels for Ogilby alone, would enable any profits to
be shared. Ogilby surrendered his original patent, and in the spring of 1663 a fresh
patent was issued, describing the office in question as that of the Master of Revells
and Masques in Ireland.[29] This lengthy patent is curiously worded but it is quite
plain that, whatever position Stanley had enjoyed, it was scarcely the equal of
Ogilby, and it would be wrong to talk in terms of the new authority creating joint
or co-patentees. The text, transcribed originally by Lawrence and printed by Clark,
merits being set down *in extenso*:[30]

> Charles the second by the grace of God King of England, Scotland and
> Ireland, defender of the faith &c, To all to whom these presents shall come
> greeting. Whereas wee having thought fit that all masques, operas, interludes,
> tragedies and comedies and other things of that nature to be presented in our
> Kingdome of Ireland should be represented as innocently and inoffensively
> as might be, and that our Subjects of our said Kingdome of Ireland should
> enjoy the like privileges in that kind as our subjects in our Kingdome of
> England, by our letters pattents under our Great Seale of England bearing
> date the eight day of May in the thirteene yeare of our Reigne did declare our
> will and pleasure to be that from thenceforth there should be the office of
> master of Revells and masques in our said Kingdome of Ireland and thereby
> for us our heires and successors did erect and establish the said office to be
> for ever called and knoune by the said name of master of our Revells and
> Masques in our said Kingdome of Ireland. And wee, reposeing especiall trust
> and confidence in the loyalty, integrity and ability of our wellbeloved subject
> John Ogilby, gent, by our said letters patents did constitute and appoint the
> said John Ogilby to be master of all and every our playes, Revells, Masques
> and Interludes in our said Kingdome of Ireland during his natural life as by

28 Quoted, Fletcher, *Drama, performance and polity*, p. 442, n. 42.
29 Clark, *Early Irish stage*, pp 45–7, appendix A, pp 186–8; Rowley Lascelles, *Liber munerum
    publicorum Hiberniae*, 2 vols (London, 1852), vol. I, pt 2, pp 92–3. For the sequence of
    governmental decisions, see *Cal. S.P. Ire., 1660–2*, pp 416, 500, 576.
30 Clark, *Early Irish stage*, appendix A, pp 186–8. Lawrence transcribed the patent from the original
    enrolled in the Irish Chancery rolls held in the Irish Public Record Office before that office's
    destruction in 1922.

the said letters patents doth more at large appeare. And whereas the said John Ogilby hath voluntarily surrendered unto us the aforesaid letters patents and the said office thereby granted upon him, KNOW yee therefore that wee still reposeing the like special trust and confidence in the loyalty, integrity and ability of the said John Ogilby of our especial grace, certaine knowledge and meere motion by and with the advice and consent of our right trusty and right intirely-beloved Cousin and Counsellor, James, Duke of Ormond, our lieutenant-generall and Governor generall of our said Kingdome of Ireland and according to the tenor and effect of our letters under our privy Signett bearing date at our Court att Whitehall the twenty third day of January in the thirteenth yeare of our Reigne and now inrolled in the Rolls of our Chancery of Ireland have given and granted and by these presents for us our heires and successors do give & grant unto the said John Ogilby the said Office of Master of our Revells and Masques in our said Kingdome of Ireland, TO have, hould, exercise and enjoy the said office of Master of our Revells and masques in our said kingdome of Ireland unto him the said John Ogilby his executors and assignes for and during the naturall life of him the said John Ogilby and of Thomas Stanley Junior sonne and heire of Thomas Stanley of Cumberloe in the County of Hertford in our Kingdome of England Esquire, and the life of the longer liver of them, together with all fees, profitts, privileges, advantages and emoluments whatsoever in as ample manner and forme as the now Master of our Revells in our Kingdome of England or any other person or persons formerly enjoying the said office have received, taken and enjoyed, or ought to have taken and enjoyed, the said office to be executed by the said John Ogilby his executors and assignes or his or their sufficient Deputy or Deputys during the lives of the said John Ogilby and Thomas Stanley aforesaid. AND further know yee that wee of our more abundant grace, certain knowledge and mere motion have given and granted and by these presents for us our heires and successors do give & grant unto the said John Ogilby his Executors and Assignes full and sole power, license and authority to erect and build one or more theatre or theatres in whatsoever places to him shall seeme most fit and convenient either in our Citty of Dublin or elsewhere in our said kingdome of Ireland on such ground as the said John Ogilby his heires or Assignes shall purchase to himself or themselves in fee and in such Theatre or Theatres so built and erected as aforesaid at all lawfull times publiquely to present, Act or cause to be presented and acted all comedies, tragedies, operas or other enterludes of what kind soever decent and becoming and not profane and obnoxious. To have, hould and enjoy the said Theatre or Theatres so to be erected and built as aforesaid unto him the said John Ogilby his heires and Assignes for ever, AND further wee doe hereby for us our heires and successors streightly charge and comand, inhibite and forbid all person and persons whatsoever that they nor any of them presume to erect or build any theatre or theatres, stage or stages whatsoever and therin to present or act any comedies, tragedies, operas or other enterludes whatsoever without license from the said John Ogilby his Executors or Assignes in writeing under his or their hands or seales or hand and seale first had and obtained. AND wee doe hereby streightly charge and command all mayors, sheriffes, bailiffes, constables, head burroughs and all others our officers and ministers within our said Kingdome of Ireland that they cause all stage playes and enterludes which shall at anytime be presented or acted by any person or persons contrary to the meaneing of these presents to be suppressed from time to time, and that they be from time to time aiding, helping and assisting unto the said John Ogilby his Executors and Assignes in the suppressing thereof and apprehending of all such common players as shall presume to act any stage playes or enterludes without license as aforesaid as they and every of them will answeare the contrarie att their perlle. AND our further will and pleasure is and wee doe hereby declare our will and pleasure to be that all former grant or grants obteined by any person or persons from us under our Signett or Signe mannuall for, touching or concerning the premises or any part or parcell thereof shalbe from henceforth void and of none effect and the same and every of them we do revoke, determine, annihilate and make void by these presents. AND lastly our will and pleasure is and wee doe by these presents declare that these our letters patents or the Inrollment thereof shalbe in all things firme, good and effectuall in the law according to the true intent and meaning of the same any law, statute, act, ordinance, proclamation or provision or any other matter, cause or thing whatsoever to the contrary kind in any wise notwithstanding, although expresse mention of the true yearly value or certainty of the premisses or of any part thereof or of any gifts or grants by us or any of our progenitors to the said John Ogilby heretofore made in these presents is not made. Any statute, act, ordinance or provision or any other thing, cause, or matter whatsoever to the contrary or in any wise notwithstanding. IN witness whereof we have caused these our letters to be made patents, witness our aforesaid lieut generall and Governor Generall of our said Kingdome of Ireland at Dublin the fifth day of April in the fifteenth year of our Reigne.

Ogilby's determination to return to Ireland was in one sense a curious move for a man who had just earned praise for his translation of *The Iliad* and who was already embarked on a translation of *The Odyssey*. As Van Eerde, his biographer, has expressed it,[31] there was 'a distinct element of hazard for Ogilby in the decision to leave the metropolis of London for the provincial barrenness of Dublin'. An intriguing detail that Van Eerde managed to unearth was Ogilby's assertion that, as Master of the Revels, he was entitled to license lotteries in Ireland.[32] Nowhere in the two patents is there any clear authority for this.

The same year that Ogilby received his second patent, we know that a performance at his new theatre was put on at the express wish of Sir Nicholas

31 Van Eerde, *John Ogilby*, p. 63.   32 Ibid., p. 89.

Armourer, the head of the King's Guard in Dublin Castle – military men that were unusually supportive of the theatre in these Restoration years.[33] It is perhaps no coincidence that Joseph Ashbury, one of Ogilby's successors, also served in the King's Guard.[34]

The new theatre itself was located on a portion of the Blind Quay at the foot of Cork Hill and close to the River Liffey.[35] Sheldon furnishes a description of the neighbourhood at the point – in 1745 – when Thomas Sheridan became the theatre's manager.[36] The street the theatre was on was known as Orange Street, but it is better known as Smock Alley, the name that was to be attached to the theatre itself. Chetwood relates that the street, and thus the theatre, was named after

> Mother Bungy of infamous memory, and … in her days a sink of sin; but a man being found murdered in these bottomless pits of wickedness, the sheds were pulled down by the populace, and unclean vermin were banished, the place purged of its infamy, handsome dwellings now show their faces in a modest garb, and entertain modest, and reputable inhabitants.[37]

In the light of all this, Chetwood, writing in 1749, contended that the street 'ought to lose its old stained name'.[38] Smock Alley Theatre was to close down towards the end of the eighteenth century. Eventually, in 1813, the site was to provide a home for the Roman Catholic church of St Michael and St John. Today's Smock Alley Theatre Studio is adjacent. Morash has ventured a description of the theatre that Ogilby inaugurated. 'Even before the stage was fully operational', he was to write,[39]

> the fineness of the original Smock Alley theatre was evident in the decoration of the auditorium. The pit contained rows of cloth-covered benches, where the 'lords and ladies' sat. Above them were 'three stories of galleries', in which 'those of the greatest quality' sat lowest. Those next in quality sat the next above; and the common people in the utmost gallery.

The year 1669 ended on a note that presaged the difficulties that could still lie ahead. Ogilby returned to England, and a new lord lieutenant, Lord Robarts, who was a Presbyterian, closed the theatre. On Robarts' replacement the following year it reopened, but disaster struck at this juncture during a performance in December of Ben Jonson's *Bartholomew Fair*, when the upper gallery collapsed on to the middle gallery, which then splintered and collapsed as well.[40] There were fatalities,

33 *Cal. S.P. Ire., 1663–5*, p. 87; Clark, *Early Irish stage*, p. 65.
34 Entry in *Oxford DNB*, ii, 612.
35 J.T. Gilbert, *A history of the city of Dublin*, 3 vols (Dublin, McGlashan and McGlashan and Gill, 1854–9), ii, 68; Clark, *Early Irish stage*, pp 52–3; Morash, *History of Irish theatre*, p. 13.
36 E.K. Sheldon, *Thomas Sheridan of Smock Alley, recording his life as actor and theatre manager in both Dublin and London* (Princeton, NJ, Princeton UP, 1967), p. 34.
37 Chetwood, *General history of the stage*, p. 72 n.   38 Ibid.
39 *History of Irish theatre*, p. 14.   40 Morash, *History of Irish theatre*, p. 17.

but an absence of agreement over the exact number.[41] The theatre itself at this period, in Morash's words,[42] 'was still locked into a dependence on the court at Dublin Castle'.

A proclamation, issued in 1672/3 in the name of the earl of Essex, the then lord lieutenant, testified to the nature of the struggle Ogilby, when he held the reins, must have faced to make both ends meet. At the same time, the proclamation supplies evidence for the acceptance, and an assertion, of the all-Ireland responsibilities of the Master of the Revels. The proclamation recites Ogilby's first appointment of 8 May 1661; his authority to license persons to act tragedies, comedies, etc.; the ukase that unlicensed plays were to be suppressed; and then continues:

> Several men of good behaviour travelling with licensed masters, motions, shows and other plays and interludes have not been allowed to exhibit in some towns, and afterwards other unlicensed persons, rope-dancers, etc., have been tolerated.

The proclamation then instructed that 'all officers, mayors, etc. are to aid the Master of the Revels and his assigns'.[43]

William Morgan, Ogilby's nephew, had been made Deputy Master of the Revels in 1669, and Clark claims that the terms of the proclamation enabled Morgan to secure broader acceptance of the Master's licensing authority.[44] Ogilby was to die in 1676 and seven years later, in 1683, his partner of 1663, Thomas Stanley, relinquished such rights as he enjoyed in favour of Morgan. A fresh patent was issued on 11 August 1684[45] in favour of Morgan and two new arrivals on the scene, Joseph Ashbury (1638–1720) and Charles Ashbury, his son. Morgan's title to the Smock Alley venue, now dubbed the Theatre Royal, was confirmed as was the monopoly enjoyed by the holders of the Mastership in regard to the building of the theatres and theatrical performances generally in the country. Provisions comparable to those set out in the English grants of August 1660 to Killigrew and Davenant and in the Irish of 1663 to Ogilby were repeated. The Theatre Royal, it was laid down, could take from the public such payments 'as shall be reasonable in regard of the great expence of scenes, musick, and such new decorations as hath not formerly been used'; women's parts might be played by women 'so long as nothing scandalous is performed'; and any actor engaged by the patentee was forbidden from acting elsewhere save by permission given, to which the corollary

---

41 Chetwood, *General history of the stage*, p. 53 (2 deaths); Stockwell, *Dublin theatres*, p. 33 (3 or 4 deaths and other casualties not expected to survive); Van Eerde, *John Ogilby*, p. 16, n. 49 (3 deaths and many injured); Morash, *History of Irish theatre*, p. 17 (1 death).

42 Morash, *History of Irish theatre*, p. 17.

43 *The proclamations of Ireland, 1660–1820*, i (Dublin, Irish MSS Comm., 2014), pp 299–301; Clark, *Early Irish stage*, p. 71.

44 Clark, *Early Irish stage*, p. 72.   45 Ibid., p. 92.

was attached that if they chose to do so, they might not be re-engaged in London (the customary destination for the delinquent thespian). In 1701, Morgan died,[46] leaving the elder Ashbury, Joseph, in charge, a position he had in fact filled for several years, from 1675 onwards, and was to continue to do so for several years to come.[47]

Highlights of Ashbury's management were the tour of his Smock Alley troupe to Oxford in the summer of 1677 and a similar tour to Edinburgh in the summer of 1681.[48] The latter was not without incident when the Scottish customs at the port of Irving [Irvine] seized the troupe's wardrobe. Ashbury and his players applied to the Scottish privy council for relief, as the council's register tells us.[49] 'Upon notice of their Royal Highnesses being in Scotland and of the meiting of the ensueing Parliament', the petitioners, 'a company of players from Ireland', declared that they

> are come from Ireland to sett up a playhouse for the diversion and recreation of such as shall desire the same, and being now landed at the port of Irving in the West and brought alongst with them cloathes necessar for their imployment mounted with gold and silver lace, but no other thing which may anywayes be breach of the late proclamation.

It was these clothes which had been seized. Ashbury and company then pleaded that,

> seing by the late act of Parliament anent apparel there is a particular exception of trumpeters and stage players, which by the late act anent trade can never seem to be ane incroachment thereupon,

they therefore 'crave warrant as follows'.

On 19 July 1681, the privy council granted the relief sought, with a caveat (or 'provision') attached that is both striking and suggestive. 'The Lords', the register records,[50]

> find that by act of Parliament anent apparel 'comedians are particularly excepted, and that they are not comprehended in the late act of trade', so that they give warrant to the magistrates of Irving or collector of the customs to suffer the petitioners' clothes and apparel to pass without molestation, with

46 Morgan, in his will of 24 Feb. 1689–90, it is worth noting, had purported to bequeath his post of Master of the Revels to his wife Elizabeth: Van Eerde, *John Ogilby*, p. 92.
47 On Joseph Ashbury, see, in particular, Robert Hitchcock, *An historical view of the Irish stage from the earliest period ... with theatrical anecdotes*, 2 vols (Dublin, R. Marchbank, W. Folds, 1788–94), i, 20–1, 34–8.
48 Clark, *Early Irish stage*, pp 78, 86.
49 *The register of the privy council of Scotland, 3rd series, vii: 1681–2* (Edinburgh, 1915), pp 111–12.
50 Ibid.

the provision that it be inspected to see if under colour thereof any contraband goods are imported, to stop the same.

Reaching Edinburgh, the troupe, consisting of about thirty players, put on a performance of Nathaniel Lee's *Mithridates* at Holyrood House;[51] this was the same play in which the future Queen Anne was to take part in a production in London.[52]

There was the inevitable disruption during the conflict between James II and his son-in-law William III, but the Theatre Royal was finally to reopen in Dublin in March 1691/2. Five years later, Ashbury was prosecuted and fined for swearing on stage,[53] the preferment of the charge perhaps owing something to the Lord Chamberlain in London having issued the very same year an order to prevent the Prophaneness and Immorality of the stage. William Prynne, celebrated for his attack on the stage in his *Histrio-Mastix* of 1631, which earned him from Star Chamber the order to crop his ears, would doubtless have approved. As it happens, two years before, in 1695, the Irish parliament had passed an Act for the more effectual suppressing of Profane Cursing and Swearing,[54] labelled 'detestable sins', which earlier Irish legislation of the 1630s, it was claimed, doubtless unsurprisingly, had failed satisfactorily to tackle. Ashbury survived the episode to take his troupe to Kilkenny in 1698,[55] an excursion which served as the harbinger of a routine involving visits by the Dublin actors to provincial centres which seem to have started in earnest in the 1730s.[56] It is from this period that John Dunton was to credit Ashbury with having attracted a more cosmopolitan audience into Smock Alley. 'The Play-house', he wrote in 1699,[57] 'is free for all Comers, and gives Entertainment as well to the Broom man, as the greatest Peer'.

Several years later – at some point between 1704 and 1708 – an actor, one William Bowen, sought to wrest the office of Master of the Revels away from Ashbury, dwelling on the argument that Ashbury was now too old, and that his son, Charles, had already died. Bowen's petition was met with no success.[58] In 1713 Ashbury managed to face down another rival who sought to engineer the same outcome. On this occasion Ashbury's successful defence of his office only came after representations he made personally in London proved fruitful.[59] Chetwood,

51 Morash, *History of Irish theatre*, p. 18.   52 Below, p. 13.
53 Stockwell, *Dublin theatres*, p. 40; Clark, *Early Irish stage*, p. 105.
54 William Prynne, *Histrio-Mastix* (London, E.A. & W.I. for Michael Sparke, 1631) (see below, p. 208), 7 Will. III, c. 9.
55 Clark, *Early Irish stage*, pp 108–10.
56 W.S. Clark, *The Irish stage in the county towns: 1720 to 1800* (Oxford, Clarendon Press, 1965), chs 2–10.
57 *The Dublin Scuffle* (London, 1699), p. 339.
58 Stockwell, *Dublin theatres*, pp 46–7; Clark, *Early Irish stage*, p. 120.
59 Ashbury's letter to his wife, written in Chester, and telling of what had been this second unwelcome development is frequently reproduced: Chetwood, *General history of the stage*, p. 84; Stockwell, *Dublin theatres*, pp 50–1; Clark, *Early Irish stage*, p. 120.

who served a stint as Ashbury's assistant manager, 1714–15, adds the detail that it undoubtedly rebounded to Ashbury's advantage that he had coached the then Princess Anne in the part of Semandra in the play *Mithridates, King of Pontus*,[60] which was performed in the Banqueting Hall in Whitehall prior to Anne's accession to the throne.

A challenge from a rather different quarter came two years later, and here Ashbury was unable to claim victory. Indeed, what then occurred foreshadowed a number of later developments, including difficulties faced by the Irish legislature in 1779 and 1785 when major changes were debated.

In 1715 one Tony Aston petitioned the lord mayor of Dublin to permit him to offer public entertainment. The lord mayor, James Barlow, approved the application. 'I do hereby', Barlow recorded,[61]

> give Liberty and Licence to Anthony Aston, gent., with his wife and son, and musick to exhibit and represent within this City and the Liberties thereoff, such lawfull Diversions as may tend to the innocent Recreation of all those who are willing to see the same, they behaving themselves faithfully and honestly, as becomes His Majesty's subjects. In testimony whereoff I have hereunto subscribed my name, and affixed the Seal of Mayorality, this 10th day of September 1715.

A criticism of Aston's entertainment, which he denominated a medley, and was regularly put on in Patrick's Close, and which has come down to us, was not exactly enthusiastic:[62]

> His Medley, as [Aston] call'd it, which consisted of some capital Scenes of Humour out of the most celebrated Plays …; between every Scene, a Song or Dialogue of his own Composition fill'd up the Chinks of the Slender Meal.

Joseph Ashbury, at the helm for 45 years, finally died in 1720, to be succeeded as manager at Smock Alley by his son-in-law, Thomas Elrington,[63] who was able to supplement his income from a post in the Quit Rent Office and, as an inheritance from Ashbury, the position of steward at King's Inns.[64] Elrington, however, did not obtain the post of Master of the Revels, that post having gone to one Anthony Twyman under a reversionary grant in the latter's favour of April 1719.[65] On Twyman's death a few months later, the post passed, in October 1722, to Edward

---

60 The play Ashbury's company had put on in Edinburgh in 1681.
61 Clark, *Early Irish stage*, p. 156.   62 Quoted, Clark, *Early Irish stage*, p. 157
63 Hitchcock, *Historical view of Irish stage*, pp 37, 64–70.
64 Stockwell has an excellent note on other sources of income for persons involved in the Dublin theatre around this time: *Dublin theatres*, p. 317, n. 11.
65 Clark, *Early Irish stage*, p. 168.

Hopkins, secretary to the lord lieutenant, the duke of Grafton, and from 1721 to 1727 an MP for Trinity College.[66] Neither of these individuals had any connection with the theatre in either Dublin or London and the Mastership of the Revels was, in consequence, transformed into a purely nominal position, a sinecure in truth, which from 1720 on carried an annual reward of £300. The office of Deputy Master, on the other hand, could, as we are about to discover, play some role in shaping the fortunes of Irish theatre both in Dublin and in the provinces. But there was to be one last notorious exercise of jurisdiction by the Master himself – in this case Hopkins – which had far-reaching consequences. In 1722, at the start of his holding of the office, Hopkins sought to exploit his position as Master by billing Elrington, the new manager at Smock Alley, for the sum of £300, the price of a licence to put on plays at that venue. As we will learn later, Richard Daly, granted the first theatre patent under the 1786 Act, sought in 1792 equally to avail of the role he retained as Deputy Master to make things difficult for a manager at a provincial theatre – Michael Atkins in Belfast.[67]

To return to the episode involving Edward Hopkins and recorded for 1722, it would appear that eventually some kind of compromise was reached, involving the contested sum being reduced to £100, but Elrington in the interval had approached the lord mayor of Dublin for a licence enabling the Smock Alley company to act as 'strollers'.[68] It was not to be the last occasion upon which Dublin's lord mayor was invited to involve himself in the legalities of dramatic representations in the capital. Nor was it, of course, the first (as we have seen in the case of Aston's application of 1715).[69] The altercation between Elrington and Hopkins, it should be recorded, was to inspire a piece of satirical writing from Jonathan Swift – his 'Billet to a Company of Players sent with the Prologue'.[70] Here Swift presupposed that, following the prohibition imposed by the Master of the Revels as a result of Elrington's rejection of the Master's 'offer', a company of country strollers came and hired the Smock Alley playhouse:

> Our set of strollers, wand'ring up and down,
> Hearing the house was empty, came to town;
> And, with a license from our good Lord May'r.
> Went to one Griffith, formerly a play'r:
> Him we persuaded, with a mod'rate bribe,
> To speak to Elrington, and all the tribe,
> To let our company supply their places
> And hire us out their scenes, and cloaths, and faces …

Later in Swift's 'Billet', there is an allusion to Hopkins' precise 'offer':

66 Ibid., p. 169 n.; E.M. Johnston-Liik, *History of the Irish parliament*, 6 vols (Belfast, Ulster Historical Foundation, 2002), iv, 438.
67 See below, p. 80.   68 Stockwell, *Dublin theatres*, p. 51.   69 Above, p. 13.
70 *Swift: poetical works*, ed. Herbert Davis (London, Oxford UP, 1967), p. 234.

> Stay! Let me see – Three hundred pounds a-year
> For leave to act in town! – 'tis plaguy dear.

Further verses devoted to this particular incident and entitled 'To Mr Hoppy's benefit night, at Smock Alley' furnish evidence that Hopkins later reduced his demand to £100 – but with what immediate consequence it is not entirely clear. This later piece of versification was rejected by Herbert Davis as attributable to Swift as author, a rejection accepted by Rogers.[71] Browning, in his edition of Swift's poems brought out in 1910, harboured doubts as well, but, in the end, accepted 'To Mr Hoppy's benefit night' as coming within the canon.[72]

Reproducing from Browning's edition the poem's first six lines entails that we are furnished with a contemporaneous note that the Master of the Revels had indeed reduced his demand from £300 to £100:[73]

> To Mr Hoppy's benefit night, at Smock Alley
> …
> Thus, for Hoppy's bright merits, at length we have found
> That he must have of us ninety-nine and one pound
> Paid to him clear money once every year:
> And however some think a little too dear,
> Yet, for reasons of state, this sum we'll allow,
> Though we pay the good man with the sweat of our brow ….

It is worth noting that Edward Hopkins does not appear to have been sufficiently embarrassed by the rebuff his money-grabbing enterprise had received on this occasion to forego repetition of presenting such demands, for, a little later, as Helen Burke has recalled, Hopkins sought to impose a licence fee on one Randall Stretch, a puppeteer who had set up his booth in Dame Street.[74]

It is at this juncture that there were to come into existence a number of other playhouse or entertainment venues – a development that posited considerable competition and the loss inevitably of Smock Alley's effective monopoly.[75] By the time Chetwood took up his post a few years later, in 1749, it was possible to claim, as Chetwood himself was to do, that Dublin, whatever about the rest of the country, catered for every conceivable diversion, with, as Chetwood expressed it,[76]

---

71 Jonathan Swift, *The complete poems*, ed. Pat Rogers (London, Penguin Books, 1983).

72 *The poems of Jonathan Swift*, ed. W.E. Browning, 2 vols (London, G. Bell & Son, 1910). And Stockwell, writing of course before Davis' rejection of this 'epilogue' as Swiftian, follows Browning and actually reproduces the entire poem: *Dublin theatres*, pp 52–3.

73 *Poems of Swift*, ed. Browning, i, 128.

74 Helen M. Burke, *Riotous performances: the struggle for hegemony in the Irish theater* (Notre Dame, IN, Univ. of Notre Dame Press, 2003), pp 170–2.

75 J.C. Greene and G.L.H. Clark, *The Dublin stage, 1720–45: a calendar of plays, entertainments and after pieces* (London and Toronto, Association UP, 1993), passim.

76 Chetwood, *General history of the stage*, p. 77.

just one exception – 'Italian opera, which can neither produce mirth, or sorrow, pity or compassion' – quite a staggering put-down!

The first to arrive, late in 1729, was Madame Violante, 'the most famous rope-dancer now living together with her company of entertainers'.[77] She boasted a considerable reputation. In London, in October 1726, she had apparently performed with 'two pails of water tied to her legs without letting a drop fall on the ground'.[78] She and her company, on their arrival in Dublin, put on a show at Smock Alley, but she soon set up on her own, first in Dame Street (and not, as Hitchcock claimed, in Fownes' Court), and then, in 1731, in a new 'booth' in George's Lane.[79] The featured performances, apart from that of M. Lalauze, who did a peasant dance in wooden shoes,[80] were those of tumblers and rope-dancers. Violante herself was 'celebrated for her strength and agility', but Chetwood, for once, was unimpressed, as he made clear in a savage piece of criticism. 'The strength of the limbs, which these sort of undertakers expose', he observed,[81]

> in my opinion, is shockingly indecent, but hers [i.e., Madame Violante's] were masculinely indelicate, and were of a piece with the features of her face,

a description that fostered the rumour that Signora Violante was in fact a signor.[82]

Rope-dancing was dangerous as well, Chetwood warned, recalling the case of a pregnant 'Lady Isabella', who had an accident on her rope, fell and killed both her unborn baby and herself. These diversions, he was entirely satisfied, were 'below the dignity of the stage or humanity'.[83] The entertainment, if such it can be called, was not unknown in Dublin. Earlier in the century, the governors of the Blue Coat School had sanctioned the letting out of their Great Hall for sundry amusements as a means of increasing their income. In 1703, however, they decided to make an exception in the case of rope-dancing. 'Such diversions', they decreed,[84] 'were prejudicial to good government, causing the boys to be disorderly, to break the glass windows and cause scandal'.

Some months later, Madame Violante herself, 'finding her tumbling tiresome, fell into playing and pantomime'.[85] It was not a turn of events that endeared her to the management at Smock Alley who protested, not, one might have thought, to the Master of the Revels, but rather to Dublin's lord mayor. The latter accepted

---

77 Chetwood, *General history of the stage*, p. 59; Stockwell, *Dublin theatres*, p. 66; Grainne McArdle. 'Signora Violante and her troupe of dancers, 1729–32', *Eighteenth-Century Ireland*, 20 (2005), 55.
78 McArdle, 'Signora Violante', at 63–4.
79 Greene & Clark, *The Dublin stage, 1720–1745*, pp 25, 27–9; Hitchcock, *Historical view of Irish stage*, i, 47.
80 Greene & Clark, *The Dublin stage, 1720–1745*, p. 25.
81 Chetwood, *General history of the stage*, p. 59.
82 Greene & Clark, *The Dublin stage, 1720–1745*, p. 25.
83 Chetwood, *General history of the stage*, pp 62–3.
84 T.J. Walsh, *Opera in Dublin, 1705–1797* (Dublin, Allen Figgis, 1973), p. 15.
85 Greene & Clark, *The Dublin stage, 1720–1745*, p. 61.

the protest and proceeded to prohibit Violante's dramatic initiatives, ruling that she had 'no sanction or proper authority, to exhibit such entertainments'.[86]

The Violante interlude found an appreciative critic in McArdle.[87] In the latter's estimation, the Signora's impact on theatre in the Dublin of the period could not be understated nor underestimated. Her arrival shocked Dublin's theatre world for three seasons. She set up a viable and popular rival theatre to that of Smock Alley; she introduced new forms of theatrical entertainment, whetting the appetite for pantomime and dancing; and inaugurated a new system of lower priced seating.

The suppression of the Violante company of players was not welcomed, and the upshot was that a fresh venue for dramatic presentations was unveiled – in a geographical location outwith the jurisdiction of the lord mayor. Similar difficulties had once arisen in London; late in the reign of Elizabeth I the city of London's adoption of a package of draconian laws targeting actors had occasioned a not-dissimilar geographical exodus that resulted in the new public playhouses being erected outside the city's boundaries.[88] In Ireland, as a result of the lord mayor's stance, there thus came into existence the Rainsford Street theatre situated within the earl of Meath's liberty, one of the Dublin liberties. The street itself was located within what is now part of the Guinness Brewery complex. Before Violante's ex-troupe took up residence, their front man, Thomas Walker, had secured from the earl of Meath the right to put on theatrical performances for £40 per annum, that sum being distributed among the poor of the liberty.[89] The Rainsford Street venue, 'a very neat, compact building',[90] opened in February 1732/33 with a performance of William Congreve's *Love for Love*. The managers were a Mr Husband, who had made his debut in Dublin under Ashbury at Smock Alley in 1696, and Lewis Duval, a dancer, who had been a member of Madame Violante's company.

Thomas Elrington, the manager at Smock Alley, scored a major success in 1728 with no less than 40 performances of John Gay's *The Beggar's Opera*, an accomplishment that compares very favourably with the run of 63 performances at Lincoln's Inn Fields in London the previous year.[91] Thomas Elrington died in 1732 and was succeeded by his brother Francis. Francis Elrington and his company of actors responded to this unprecedented challenge presented by the Rainsford Street venture in an extraordinary fashion. The old Smock Alley Theatre was to be abandoned and a new theatre built in its stead. A contract was entered into with Sir Edward Lovett Pearce for the construction of this brand new building, which was

86 Hitchcock, *Historical view of Irish stage*, i, 77; Stockwell, *Dublin theatres*, p. 68; Greene & Clark, *The Dublin stage, 1720–1745*, pp 26–7.

87 Grainne McArdle, 'Signora Violante and her troupe of dancers, 1729–32', *Eighteenth-Century Ireland*, 20 (2005), 55; see at p. 77.

88 Thomas, Carlton & Etienne, *Theatre censorship*, p. 7.

89 Chetwood, *General history of the stage*, p. 64; Hitchcock, *Historical view of Irish stage*, i, 78.

90 Chetwood, *General history of the stage*, p. 66; Greene & Clark, *The Dublin stage, 1720–1745*, p. 28.

91 *An annual register of all the tragedies, comedies, farces that have been acted in the Theatre Royal in London from 1712 to 1760* (London, 1761), pp 153–4.

planned for Aungier Street at its junction with Longford Lane. The foundation
stone was laid in 1733, and a year later, on 9 March 1733/34, the new theatre was
opened[92] with a performance of George Farquhar's *The Recruiting Officer*.[93]
Benjamin Victor, who was to serve as Thomas Sheridan's manager back at Smock
Alley a dozen or so years later, was lavish in his praise of the support the plan had
received. Among the large number of noblemen and gentlemen who had
subscribed money, Victor tells us,[94] he had seen in the subscription list

> the names of Men of the first Fortunes, and most distinguished
> Understandings in the Kingdom; which fully demonstrates of what Utility
> to a flourishing Nation, they esteemed the Improvement of the public
> Diversions.

A little later, the Rainsford Street company, now effectively managed by Duval
alone, having decided the venue was 'too remote to be supported',[95] made their
peace with the lord mayor, who sealed the deal by then granting a licence.[96] Duval's
company then proceeded to secure the now vacant Smock Alley site, upon which
they erected a brand-new Theatre Royal on the very spot where Ogilby had set up
in business at the Restoration.[97] In London, it deserves to be mentioned in passing,
that when Samuel Foote was granted a patent for a new theatre in 1766, he was
similarly to avail of a site previously occupied by another theatre.[98] Thus, where
there had once stood the old Haymarket, the new Haymarket rose, again like some
phoenix from the ashes. In Dublin, with the opening of the new Smock Alley
building later in 1735, the theatre in Rainsford Steet was abandoned, and for the
next several years two principal rival companies graced Dublin's theatrical scene:
the old Smock Alley company at Aungier Street and the former Rainsford Street
company, managed by Duval, at the old Smock Alley site. Duval at this juncture,
for his part, is thought to have aimed to protect his position by securing, possibly
by purchase, the office of Deputy Master of the Revels.[99] Even so, the evidence is
incontestable that the two companies appear to have faced considerable difficulty
in making both ends meet: for several periods actors were not being paid[100] – a state
of affairs that horrified a significant theatre manager of the not too distant future,
Thomas Sheridan, and was to influence the latter's thinking on whether Dublin
could support two theatres competing against each other.[101] Duval appears to have

92 Stockwell, *Dublin theatres*, pp 70–2.   93 Chetwood, *General history of the stage*, p. 71.
94 Benjamin Victor, *The history of the theatres of London and Dublin, from the year 1730 to the present
     time*, 2 vols (London, T. Davies, 1761), i, 15.
95 Chetwood, *General history of the stage*, p. 69; Hitchcock, *Historical view of Irish stage*, i, 97.
96 Gilbert, *History of Dublin*, ii, 74.
97 Hitchcock, *Historical view of Irish stage*, i, 97; Stockwell, *Dublin theatres*, p. 74.
98 Benjamin Victor, *A history of the theatres of London from 1760 to the present time* (London,
     T. Davies, 1791), p. 184.
99 Greene & Clark, *The Dublin stage, 1720–1745*, p. 33.   100 Stockwell, *Dublin theatres*, pp 78–9.
101 Below, p. 24.

faced particular financial difficulties. In 1736, he was obliged to take out two fresh mortgages, and it can scarcely be accidental that that same year he lost the post of Deputy Master of the Revels, Luke Gardiner, Hopkins' successor as Master of the Revels, having declined to reappoint him.[102] (In the circumstances, what money, if any, Duval had paid Hopkins for the office the year before, would certainly be good to know.) Two years later, in 1738, Duval conveyed away his proprietorial interests in Smock Alley and, in tears, we are told,[103] three years later, in 1741, relinquished his management entirely.

That year Luke Gardiner had made James Worsdale from the Aungier Steet theatre Deputy Master of the Revels.[104] But it would be wrong to infer from this that the future prosperity of the stage in Dublin depended on Aungier Street.

The auditorium at Aungier Street, for a start, had not proved entirely satisfactory. Far from it: acoustics and sight lines were both regarded as poor.[105] Victor, as we have seen, had praised the initiative, but was compelled to endorse the opinion that Aungier Street was 'a very sumptuous but a very bad theatre'.[106] 'In a crowded audience', he wrote, 'a great part in both galleries can neither see, nor hear'.[107] Chetwood somewhat earlier had been the first to deliver a damning verdict. 'The architecture' at Aungier Street, he declared, 'had more view to the magnificent than the theatrical'.[108] And he had a riposte for any contemporary critic who considered he was not qualified to pronounce on the subject. 'Thrusting my own opinion in this manner', he was to continue,[109]

> might have the air of presumption if my employment and observation had not taken up full thirty years of my time. In other buildings, I would not pretend to give my judgment on a pidgeon-house, or a centry box, or give directions in erecting a thatched cabin or a turnpike.

As Victor was to recall in 1761, there was another reason why the venture did not prosper quite to the extent anticipated. 'The subscribers (called Proprietors)', he tells us,[110] 'chose their Chairman for a limited Time, and met in a Committee-Room in the Theatre every Saturday, to settle the Business, and to appoint the Plays for the following week.' The arrangement raised Victor's hackles, and he let fly:[111]

> Now, if any Gentleman, or Set of Gentlemen unskill'd in the Art of Navigation, were on board a Ship, and were called to conduct and steer the Vessel into her destined Port, I dare say they would singly and unanimously acknowledge their Incapacity, and for their own Sakes decline the

102 Greene & Clark, *The Dublin stage, 1720–1745*, p. 32.
103 Stockwell, *Dublin theatres*, pp 79–81. 104 Greene & Clark, *The Dublin stage, 1720–1745*, p. 32.
105 Stockwell, *Dublin theatres*, p. 77. 106 Victor, *History of theatres of London and Dublin*, i, 16.
107 Ibid. 108 Chetwood, *General history of the stage*, p. 71. 109 Ibid.
110 Victor, *History of theatres of London and Dublin*, i, 16. 111 Ibid., i, 16–17.

Employment! And yet how many Instances have we seen, both in Dublin and London, of Persons who have undertaken the Direction and Steering of a Theatre-Royal, (that First Rate Man of War!) without any one necessary Qualification for so arduous a Task! But those Gentlemen soon found their Error, and assigned the Conduct of the Business to the Actors, not doubting but they had Judgment and Honesty enough to support it for their own Sakes.

It was no surprise then that in 1739 it was suggested that the two companies should combine in some way. And in 1743, this came about, it then being agreed that the new Smock Alley should be made available for performances by a union of the two companies and that Aungier Street should be reserved for 'concerts, ridottos[112] and grand entertainments', a development facilitated by the flooring over of the pit at Aungier Street.[113]

We have now entered a period that witnessed a growth in countrywide tours to a number of provincial centres. A Smock Alley troupe had been to Cork in 1713; they were there again in 1733. An Aungier Street company followed in their footsteps in 1735 and 1736.[114] A Smock Alley troupe was in Drogheda in 1728 and there again in 1740.[115] They visited Waterford in 1737.[116] The year before, Duval had taken his company to Derry and Belfast – a jaunt repeated in 1741.[117] Clark commented sagely on the peregrination that had taken Duval to Belfast:[118] 'The hundred-mile journey from Dublin by horseback or by cart must have severely taxed the players' spirits'. A touring company also visited Limerick in 1736. Travel did not perceptibly become any easier as the century wore on. Willoughby Lacy, writing to David Garrick in London in the 1770s, about a theatrical tour that had taken him from Dublin to Cork (where he had played Hamlet), after a 12-hour crossing from Holyhead to Dublin, complained that the part of the journey in Ireland had been 'very tedious, having the same horses all the way'.[119]

Duval we know was to give up his licence of acting by permission of Dublin's lord mayor.[120] Before finally abandoning his post, however, he moved decidedly down market, as is plain from a Smock Alley poster for 1742 that Hitchcock was farsighted enough to transcribe.[121] The poster advertised an entertainment sanctioned by 'the Rt. Hon. Luke Gardiner', who had been appointed Master of the Revels jointly with his son Charles in 1736:[122]

---

112 A ridotto was a form of entertainment consisting of a performance of singing and of instrumental music, followed by a supper and communal dancing.
113 Stockwell, *Dublin theatres*, pp 81–2, Sheldon, *Thomas Sheridan of Smock Alley*, p. 77.
114 Clark, *Irish stage in county towns*, p. 70. 115 Ibid., p. 2. 116 Ibid., p. 147.
117 Hitchcock, *Historical view of Irish stage*, i, 97, 114. 118 *Irish stage in county towns*, p. 217.
119 Lacy to Garrick, 24 July 1778: *The private correspondence of David Garrick with the most celebrated persons of his time*, 2 vols (London, H. Colburn and R. Bentley, 1835), ii, 309.
120 Hitchcock *Historical view of Irish stage*, i, 104 121 Ibid., i, 122–3.
122 Lascelles, *Liber munerum publicorum Hiberniae*, vol. I, pt 3, p. 109; Stockwell, *Dublin theatres*,

By permission of the Rt. Hon. Luke Gardiner, esq.,
At the Theatre Smock Alley

This present evening, Tuesday, December 7th 1742 will be presented by the
celebrated company of Germans, Dutch, Italian and French, several feats of
activity, consisting of Rope-dancing, Tumbling, Vaulting, Equilibres, and
Ground Dancing. Madam Garman performs on the Rope with Stilts, (never
done here) and will also perform on the Slack Rope. Monsieur Dominique
will perform the surprising equilibres of the Circle, never attempted by any
but himself in which he is drawn up forty feet high on his head, fires off two
pistols, and is let down again in the same posture. Monsieur Dominique and
Monsieur Guiltar perform the surprising tumble over the double Fountain.
Monsieur Dominique tumbles through an Hogshead of Fire in the Middle,
and a lighted Torch in each Hand, etc.[123]

Hitchcock expressed his horror, albeit from a distance of over forty years:
'O shame, where is thy blush!'[124] Contemporaries too were critical. Mr Swan, in a
long prologue recited at a performance of *Othello* put on at Aungier Street a month
or so later,[125] uttered sentiments which he would have expected his audience to
endorse:

> Let other nations boast this senseless art
> Ours raise the genius, and improve the heart.

When Hitchcock added the observation that 'Every person of sense lamented the
disgrace and decline of the stage, now perverted from its noblest uses',[126] we could
be overhearing the remonstrances that Richard Daly would be directing at Philip
Astley in the battle over Astley's claim for an Irish theatre patent to be granted
under the Act of 1786.[127] Swan in his prologue had invited his audience to stand
up and be counted:[128]

> To lend the tragic muse your gen'rous aid
> And rescue sense from folly's wid'ning shade.

p. 309, n. 7. Johnston-Liik, describes Gardiner as Receiver-general to the Master of the Revels,
a designation not otherwise recorded: *History of Irish parliament*, iv, 257. Gardiner was to build
his country house in the Phoenix Park, which is now the headquarters of the Irish Ordnance
Survey. This house boasted a private theatre: *DIB*, iv, 26.
123 Hitchcock intimates that Gardiner had previously sanctioned similar entertainments in 1739 and
1740: *Historical view of Irish stage*, i, 104, 109.
124 Ibid., i, 123.   125 Reproduced, ibid., i, 124–5.
126 *Historical view of Irish stage*, i, 123.   127 Below, p. 88.
128 Hitchcock, *Historical view of Irish stage*, i, 124.

But to no avail. His efforts were ineffectual, since as was generally understood, however much it may have been cause for regret, the Dublin of the times could not really support two venues devoted to serious theatre.

The recent reconstruction of a Dublin directory for 1738 furnishes invaluable detail on the troupes at the two key Dublin theatres of the period – at Smock Alley and at Aungier Street. Smock Alley boasted 10 actors and 7 actresses; 2 dancers and one Irish harpist; and, in addition, apart from the manager (Duval), a dancer director, a prompter and a scene painter. The Aungier Street company was certainly different, 13 actors but only 3 actresses and a 'French comic dancer'; and, on the administrative side, a dancing director, a box keeper and a pit office keeper.[129]

Greene and Clark constitute our authority for a range of other developments. A theatrical booth opened in Dame Street was linked by Hitchcock to one Ward;[130] they, on the other hand, associate it in the alternative to one Stretch, and suggest it may have come into existence as early as 1721, lasting until 1736.[131] If the speciality here was puppet-shows – as seems possible – these were later moved to Capel Street north of the Liffey, where we know by 1745 a fresh venue altogether had been established – William Phillips' new Capel Street theatre.[132] More celebrated perhaps than any of these developments was the music-hall in Fishamble Street, which opened in 1741.[133] This was where Handel's oratorio 'The Messiah' was first performed in April 1742, and it is in its neighbourhood that regular performances of the oratorio are given annually today.

The union in 1743 of the former distinct companies associated with Smock Alley and Aungier Street presaged other developments of which it is right to take note. Legal difficulties linked to matters of finance resulted eventually in transfers of interests held by individuals such as Duval and Elrington. In return, they were ensured annuities 'to the amount of £400 per annum'[134] – a species of financial liability that was destined to haunt Dublin's theatre managers in the future. Again, not all the actors of the two former companies were taken on board by the new single company but, as smitten thespians, they were not prepared to abandon their profession. Banded together, early in 1745, they moved to the new theatre in Capel Street, alluded to above, and managed by William Phillips. The lord mayor, however, was first asked to sanction the venture.[135]

The management of the new united company was soon to be entrusted to Thomas Sheridan (c.1719–88), the son of the Thomas Sheridan, Swift's friend, and the father of Richard Brinsley. He had first appeared on the stage at Smock Alley in the role of Richard III in 1743, and was to become the dominant force in

---

129 *A directory of Dublin for the year 1738* (Dublin, Dublin Corporation Public Libraries, 2000), pp 200 and 108.
130 Hitchcock, *Historical view of Irish stage*, i, 96.
131 Greene & Clark, *The Dublin stage, 1720–1745*, p. 27.   132 Ibid., p. 35.
133 Hitchcock, *Historical view of Irish stage*, i, 96.   134 Stockwell, *Dublin theatres*, pp 85–6.
135 Ibid., pp 86–8.

Dublin theatre from 1745 to 1758.[136] Named Deputy Master of the Revels, he thus possessed the only royal patent throughout the period. He was to become responsible for reforming a number of Dublin theatre customs which, unchecked, made a night at the theatre not necessarily an enjoyable experience. He adopted a stance against 'odd money' admissions – letting late-comers in for a reduced fee[137] – and precipitated two major convulsions by the audience at Smock Alley,[138] as a result of the second of which the lords justices ordered the Master of the Revels to close both theatres in existence at the time – Capel Street as well as Smock Alley. This was in 1747. Both theatres protested, and the closure order was soon reversed.[139]

Peter Thomson, in his entry on Sheridan in the *Oxford DNB*, was to summarize his subject's endeavours to raise the standard of Dublin theatre in language that is far from laudatory. 'It is', Thomson wrote,[140] 'a mixed history of honest endeavour, social and intellectual snobbery, wise economy, extravagance and paranoia'.[141] A contemporary critic, Edmund Burke, originally a supporter of Sheridan's, came over time to share some of these implied criticisms of the man. He was also to take issue with Sheridan's 'personal appearance, acting style and literary taste, accusing him of being effeminate and ludicrous'.[142] Whether such attacks were in any way connected to Sheridan's rejection of a play submitted by Burke for possible performance at Smock Alley is, of course, impossible to say. As we are about to discover, the actor Charles Macklin evinced little regard for Sheridan either.[143] Differences of opinion concerning Sheridan were conspicuously acute, inspiring Sheldon's considered judgment that 'throughout his life Sheridan evoked the strongest feelings in others – of devotion or of animosity'.[144]

Among the devotees was Benjamin Victor who most certainly would have protested against the criticisms of Edmund Burke or Charles Macklin. Victor's career was unusual – a barber who became a linen merchant and Sheridan's right-hand man at Smock Alley and who ended his life in the theatre as treasurer at Drury Lane in London for Sheridan's son, Richard Brinsley. Smock Alley, on the eve of his joining it in the late 1740s, Victor was later to recall,[145] 'was then in a very low, distressed Condition'; but was later, he claimed, 'raised to a Magnificence that vies with the Theatres in London'.

Sheridan was notionally in charge of the Aungier Street venue as well as Smock Alley, but the theatre at the former venue went into gradual decline. By the late 1760s it was said to have been shut up for several years. In the end, demolition took place, and in 1825, the Carmelite Church (still there) was erected on the site.[146]

136 Stockwell, *Dublin theatres*, pp 88–120.   137 Ibid., pp 103–4.
138 See below, ch. 13.   139 Stockwell, *Dublin theatres*, pp 100–1.   140 *Oxford DNB*, l, 306.
141 And see further Sheldon, *Thomas Sheridan of Smock Alley*.
142 Quoted, Fintan O'Toole, *A traitor's kiss: the life of Richard Brinsley Sheridan* (London, Granta Books, 1998), p. 254.
143 Below, p. 25.   144 Sheldon, *Sheridan of Smock Alley*, p. 46.
145 Victor, *History of theatres of London and Dublin*, i, 73.
146 Stockwell, *Dublin theatres*, pp 88–9.

Smock Alley, too, was to be replaced by a church, and this, as it happens, was to be the fate of an early theatre in Limerick.[147] At Capel Street performances appear to have continued until 1750. Its closure was brought about by the simple expedient resorted to by Sheridan of acquiring the lease so that it could be shut down – a practice that speaks eloquently of the lengths to which the would-be monopolist was prepared to go.[148] It signified a precedent that later Dublin theatre managers, invariably concerned by falling receipts and the existence of rival auditoriums, looked back on both fondly and with envy – a precedent which, as it chanced, one successor manager, Thomas Ryder, in 1776, did manage to copy.

Sheridan published pamphlets on the problems of the Dublin stage, and he spoke with some authority as manager of Smock Alley from 1745 on. In the last of these pamphlets,[149] he argued forcefully for but a single proper theatre in Dublin, and when, contrary to his wishes – and as Deputy Master of the Revels he may have considered that these should count for something – the new Crow Street theatre was erected and opened, he abandoned his managership at Smock Alley and withdrew to England. There he continued to act (for a while) and to assist with the management at Drury Lane after his son, Richard Brinsley, became a co-patentee there in the 1770s. There were a number of return visits to Ireland, but, in the wake of the abandonment of his managing Smock Alley, Thomas Sheridan sought above all else to excel in a new career as an orthoepist – a switch that should encourage a rush on the part of readers for the dictionary.

It was in the spring of 1758 that the prospect of a rival theatre to Smock Alley was seen by Sheridan to be very real indeed. Alarmed at this turn of events, Sheridan despatched his associate Victor to London in a forlorn endeavour to come to some accommodation with Spranger Barry, who was behind the project.[150] Victor was to explain to Barry that Sheridan was prepared to offer him a partnership and also the position of sole manager of the united theatres of Aungier Street and Smock Alley. At first, Barry responded that the approach had come too late – the plan for the new theatre to be opened in Crow Street were too far advanced. Later, he seems to have contemplated acceptance, but in the end, this did not materialise. Victor concludes his account of these critical negotiations by noting that Sheridan's proposals had first been relayed to Barry 'above two years' before Victor's own visit to London in April 1758.

Barry's eventual stance – *aut Caesar aut nullus* – was not, of course, welcome to Sheridan, but the prevarication that had occurred persuaded the latter that Macklin, with whom he had crossed swords in the quarrel of 1747, furnished the true explanation for Barry's opposition. 'One of the worst of Men, but of great Plausibility', Sheridan was later to assert,

---

147   Above, p. 9; below, pp 26, 82.   148   Stockwell, *Dublin theatres*, pp 107–8.
149   *An humble appeal to the publick, together with some considerations on the present critical and dangerous state of the stage in Ireland* (Dublin, G. Faulkner, 1758).
150   Victor, *History of theatres of London and Dublin*, i, 222–6.

was the chief instrument in the Plot. The Manager, wholly attentive to his own Business, knew little of what passed in the World; or had he attempted to look abroad, there were some Iagos about him who would have sealed his Eyes as close as oaks.

At this juncture, Macklin did not exactly conceal what he thought of Sheridan. 'Let any person', he urged,[151]

> but observe [Sheridan's] confidence, his sophistry, his haughtiness, his peremptoriness, and his utter inattention to what others advance in argument, and, I think, they will conclude that he will die in a mad house![152]

The new theatre that Sheridan had fought unavailingly to oppose was housed in a building that was to long outlast the Smock Alley put up by Duval. Its construction was finished by a scheme of subscriptions – a scheme which concealed financial perils which would only become evident as the years passed.[153] The entire enterprise, in fact, was to be deemed 'a financial disaster' for Spranger Barry (1717–77), the prime mover.[154]

This theatre, in Crow Street, was, like Smock Alley, also located within today's Temple Bar quarter, and occupying a site that, towards the end of the nineteenth century, was to become the home of the medical school of the Catholic University. The occasion was marked by the then Master of the Revels, Robert Wood, appointed in 1756, with the transfer to Crow Street from Smock Alley of the official designation of Theatre Royal. The co-managers of the new venue, Spranger Barry and Henry Woodward, acceded to the post of Deputy Master of the Revels,[155] an elevation which, as we shall see, Barry was to seek to capitalise upon in difficulties he faced with the authorities in Cork when he took a troupe of performers there a few years later.[156] Smock Alley in more senses then one had a difficult year, for in October 1758 it fell victim to a serious maritime disaster off the Scottish coast. This was very different from the difficulties Ashbury had faced with the customs officials at Irvine the previous century.[157] A ship, *The Dublin*, captained by a Captain White, had left Parkgate only to encounter an appalling storm in the Irish Sea.[158] The vessel was driven past the Isle of Man and eventually foundered on the south-west coast of Scotland. 'She was an old ship', Victor tells us, 'new vampt, and had but three sailors and one boy' besides the captain. Among the seventy-odd passengers, all of whom were drowned, was to be counted the actor Theophilus Cibber, who, ironically, according to Chetwood, had also been born

151 Quoted, W.W. Appleton, *Charles Macklin: an actor's life* (Cambridge MA, Harvard UP, 1961), p. 111.
152 Compare this list of Sheridan's supposed failings with that set out above: p. 23.
153 Stockwell, *Dublin theatres*, pp 120–2.   154 *Oxford DNB*, iv, 151 at 152: see, too, *DIB*, i, 348.
155 Gilbert, *History of Dublin*, ii, 186.   156 See below, ch. 7.   157 Above, p. 11.
158 For this account, see Victor, *History of theatres of London and Dublin*, i, 249–51; Hitchcock, *Historical view of Irish stage*, i, 309; Stockwell, *Dublin theatres*, p. 125.

during a storm.[159] Victor had specifically invited Cibber to return to the Dublin stage: 'a Chest of Cloaths and Books' belonging to Cibber was washed up, also 'some Papers of no worth', belonging to him, 'and a Part in a Play, with his Name wrote on it'.[160] Another casualty was Maddox, 'our Harlequin', a loss that was 'almost irretrievable' because with him 'went the Music, and the Business and Plot of the [projected] Pantomime'.[161]

The arrival of Spranger Barry to take charge of Crow Street was soon followed by the arrival of another key actor-manager of the period, Henry Mossop (1727/8–74),[162] to take charge at Smock Alley, and the commencement of fierce rivalry between the two theatres that was to engage the talents not just of these two men but also of such successors as Thomas Ryder (1735–91),[163] Tottenham Heaphy, Richard Daly (1758–1819)[164] and Thomas Crawford.

The spoils over the years were shared between these two theatres, with the exception of a period around 1770 when an entirely different Capel Street theatre secured, for a short interval, recognition as the Theatre Royal.[165] It had previously been redesigned to mount puppet-shows, but, unlike in today's Prague for example, this species of entertainment attracted little enduring support. Mossop throughout his time as manager at Smock Alley defended the status of the theatre through reliance on yet another licence emanating from Dublin's lord mayor.[166]

In 1773, Thomas Ryder became the official lessee of Smock Alley, but three years later, emulating a ploy of Sheridan's, when he secured the lease of Crow Street as well, 'to prevent further competition', he closed Smock Alley down.[167] Improvements then made at Crow Street did not contrive to inspire Ryder's troupe of actors, and later in 1776, a number of them banded together to lease the music-hall in Fishamble Street and open it as a theatre. The lord mayor, applied to for yet another playhouse licence, graciously obliged.[168]

The music-hall venture did not immediately prosper, and the difficulties of operating theatres in Dublin, which such a set-back illustrated, caused people's minds to turn once more to a plan, sedulously promoted by the likes of Thomas Sheridan, that an attempt be made 'to procure an Act for the regulation of, and exclusive right for one Theatre only in Dublin'.[169] The public outcry that greeted this proposal ensured that it would be shelved at least for the moment.

Lascelles, in his *Liber munerum publicorum Hiberniae*, enables us, with the listing he there furnishes, to follow the succession to the post of Master of the Revels after the reign of the Gardiners, Hopkins' successors, came to an end in 1756.[170] One

159 Chetwood, *General history of the stage*, p. 119.
160 Victor, *History of theatres of London and Dublin*, i, 250, n.   161 Ibid., i, 251.
162 See entries in *Oxford DNB*, xxxix, 486 and in *DIB*, vi, 722.
163 See entries in *Oxford DNB*, xlviii, 462 and in *DIB*, viii, 705.
164 See entries in *Oxford DNB*, xv, 5 and in *DIB*, iii, 31.
165 Stockwell, *Dublin theatres*, p. 137.   166 Ibid.
167 Stockwell, *Dublin theatres*, pp 143–4.   168 Ibid., pp 144–5.
169 Ibid., p. 146.   170 Vol. 1, pt 3, p. 109.

Robert Ward, as we have seen, was appointed in 1756, and he held office until 1771. Ward was

> to have the same privileges as the Master of Revels in England, with exclusive power to erect a theatre and act plays, to hire and dismiss actors, all actors dismissed, or quitting voluntarily his service, not to be received without his licence into any other company.

The patent thus continued language to be found in Ogilby's patent of nearly a century earlier. There was, however, one variation, the patent adding that 'women performers are to act the female characters'.

Samuel Dash succeeded Ward in 1771, and held office for twenty years.[171] He was entrusted

> To erect a theatre in Dublin, or elsewhere in Ireland, on such ground as he can purchase in fee; there to exhibit all manner of plays not profane, at all lawful times, except otherwise forbidden.

From 1771 to 1783 Dash also doubled as Director of State Music, on a retainer of £860 per annum, the sum to be used to pay his musicians and for the purchase of trumpets, kettle-drums and music books.[172]

Dash's successor in 1791 was an English lawyer, William Meeke (1758–1830) who two years before had come over to Ireland with a new lord lieutenant, the earl of Westmoreland, and served principally as steward of the vice-regal household.[173] In 1790 Meeke also became the MP for Callan. Meeke's original appointment as Master of the Revels was expressed to be 'at pleasure', but in 1794 this was altered to read a grant for life.[174] William Meeke was to be the last holder of the office, the post itself being abolished by act of parliament in 1817,[175] after the last existing office-holder died.

None of the above appointees seem to have had links in any capacity with the two principal theatres of the later eighteenth century, Smock Alley and Crow Street. A little paradoxically, however, when Richard Daly obtained the first theatre patent under the legislation of 1786, he was still said to be possessed of the office of Deputy Master of the Revels. The co-existence of the Mastership or even the Deputy Mastership of the Revels with the regime of Dublin theatre patents introduced in 1786, was, unsurprisingly, dubbed incongruous by Dublin Corporation in their opposition to the statutory initiatives of 1779 and 1785.[176] They, of course, had also their own particular axe to grind, seeking quite predictably to preserve the licensing jurisdiction they claimed was possessed by the

---

171 Ibid.   172 Ibid.   173 Johnston-Liik, *History of Irish parliament*, v, 241.
174 Lascelles, *Liber munerum*, vol. 1, pt 3, p. 109.
175 An Act to abolish certain offices, and to regulate certain other offices in Ireland: 57 Geo. III, c. 62.
176 See below, chs 3 and 4.

lord mayor. That this jurisdiction had been exercised as frequently as it had may
have been denied by some, but the evidence nonetheless is compelling. Let us
rehearse it here:

1715	licence to Tony Aston to offer public entertainment
1722	licence to Thomas Elrington for his company to act as strollers
1731/2	prohibition of dramatic entertainments put on by Madame Violante
1745	licence for opening of theatre in Capel Street
1770	licence to Henry Mossop in respect of Smock Alley
1776	licence to ex-Crow Street players to open theatre in the music-hall at Fishamble Street.

To return to the Mastership of the Revels and the Deputy Mastership, it is not
altogether clear what the precise function of the holders of either post amounted
to. Edward Hopkins in 1722 involved himself in a battle of wits with Thomas
Elrington at Smock Alley – the episode that engaged the attention of Jonathan
Swift. In the 1740s the then Master of the Revels exercised censorship powers in
the case of Henry Brooke's *Jack the Giant Queller*, but seems only to have acted
when instructed to do so by the lords justices. And there is no evidence that when
that adverse verdict was overturned by a new administration and performance of
the play received the green light, the Master of the Revels was in any way
involved.[177] Again, in 1792 Richard Daly attempted to exercise some form of
control over the theatre in Belfast and its manager there, Michael Atkins. Under
Ogilby's patent the powers of the Master – and thus, presumably, the Deputy
Master – were considerable. But the impression such evidence as is extant would
appear to confirm is that these powers down the years became of diminishing
significance. True, the power to transfer the designation of Theatre Royal from one
theatre to another, and that to confer the designation on assorted provincial venues,
may have been regarded by some contemporaries as the conferment on the
succession of office-holders of something that mattered, but other observers may
not have been impressed at all. Spranger Barry's 'swinging of the lead' in 1761
when the authorities in Cork took umbrage at his plan to put on performances
eschewing the courtesy of asking permission first[178] is an eloquent piece of
evidence regarding the conduct pursued by one Deputy Master – but no other
comparable incidents appear to be recorded. In retrospect, one can hardly doubt
the wisdom of the rebuff delivered J.W. Calcraft, the mid-nineteenth-century
Dublin theatre manager, when in 1830, after the death of William Meeke, the last
holder of the office of Master of the Revels, and the formal abolition of the post
itself, Calcraft had sought unavailingly to secure its immediate resuscitation.[179] The
critical legislative provision, section 3 in the act of 1817,[180] an act which helped to

177 Victor, *History of theatres of London and Dublin*, i, 140–200. See, too, below, p. 229.
178 See below, p. 83.   179 Stockwell, *Dublin theatres*, p. 309, n. 7.   180 57 Geo. III, c. 62.

implement a programme of determined parliamentary opposition to all sinecures extending over a decade, left one in no doubt that that had to be the outcome. The key section listed nine offices in Ireland, including that of Master of the Revels, which were to be abolished 'from and after and upon the respective terminations of the respective existing interests in each and every of [those] offices'. It went on to provide – so as to make doubly sure as it were – that

> the said offices shall not, nor shall any of them from and after the passing of this Act, be granted to any person or persons whomsoever; and the said offices are thereby, from and after the respective times when the same shall respectively become vacant, wholly abolished.

Stockwell made an imaginative attempt to explain the role of these two offices in her history of the eighteenth-century Irish stage.[181] The Mastership, she argued, did in fact become essentially a sinecure. The order of the lords justices to close the theatres following the riot at Smock Alley in 1747, and transmitted through the then Master (which would have been Luke Gardiner), in no real sense detracts from that interpretation. The Deputy Master, on the other hand, conventionally acquired management responsibilities at the sole Dublin theatre designated the Theatre Royal. Convention equally allowed the other Dublin theatres to remain in business if sanctioned by the lord mayor. This is all very ingenious but it needs to be remarked that the evidence in support of this picture is tenuous enough. Whether, in fact, holders of either post had any role to play in the growth of provincial theatre in the eighteenth century needs surely to be teased out.

181 Stockwell, *Dublin theatres*, pp 25–6.

CHAPTER TWO

Regulation in Britain, 1737–1843

DEVELOPMENTS IN THE LAW RELATING to the stage in Britain that were to occur early in the reign of George II in the 1730s left their mark in Ireland as well, as we shall soon enough discover.[1] The employment of vagrancy legislation to punish actors drew attention to the unreformed state of the law, as did continuing controversy over the role of England's Master of the Revels in sanctioning new drama, particularly after the Drury Lane theatre from 1715 onwards declined to submit new scripts to him for his approval. At the time there existed the two patented theatres in London – Drury Lane and Covent Garden – but a number of other unpatented venues had opened for business, of which the Haymarket (1720) and Goodman's Fields (1729) were the most conspicuous, and this development had spawned a number of lawsuits launched for the express purpose of closing them down.

The momentum for reform was initiated by Sir John Barnard's playhouse bill of 1735.[2] This was designed to shut down the non-patented theatres and to enshrine in law the conventional understanding that no performances on stage were to be obscene or offensive to piety. It had been a common complaint that 'loose and scandalous performances' were *de rigueur* in the London theatres of the period. Goodman's Fields was an especial target, the theatre there being viewed by its critics as a 'public nuisance'. Barnard, however, was to lose all interest in his project when Sir Robert Walpole moved a key amendment to bestow upon the Lord Chamberlain the power of licensing individual plays, what in later days would be termed a regime of prior censorship. The conferment of such power we shall soon discover was to be expressly omitted from the Irish parliamentary statute of 1786.[3] To this specific power of prior censorship or licensing Sir John Barnard was resolutely opposed.

Events in England in 1737 led finally to the adoption of a measure that contained rudiments of Barnard's bill with the major addendum insisted upon by Walpole. Between January and May that year 100 performances of plays were put on that were hostile to Walpole and his government. Singled out, at a remove of some 150 years, by James Williams, in his introduction to Geary's *Law of*

1 See below.
2 See David Thomas, David Carlton and Anne Etienne, *Theatre censorship: from Walpole to Wilson* (Oxford, Oxford UP, 2007), p. 24ff. and R.D. Hume, *Henry Fielding and the London theatre, 1728–37* (Oxford, Clarendon Press, 1988), pp 192–9.
3 See below, ch.5.

theatres,[4] as attracting Walpole's particular ire was Henry Fielding's political extravaganza, *The Golden Rump*.[5] A contemporary critic, Colley Cibber, a supporter of censorship, agreed with this analysis, as did Benjamin Victor, a stalwart of the stage on both sides of the Irish Sea. 'The late Justice F – g (when he was in the dishonest Employment of an Incendiary Writer)', Victor wrote in 1761,[6]

> was, at this Time, in the Possession of the Little Theatre in the Haymarket, where he dealt about his Satires most unmercifully against the first Minister, as Cibber justly observes in Page 231, 'Knocking down all Distinctions. – Religion, Laws, Government, Priests, Judges, and Ministers, were all laid down by this Herculean Satyrist!'[7] These were the Proceedings that brought on this Beginning of a Distress upon the Stage.

Modern researchers have continued to highlight the impact of Henry Fielding's *oeuvre* on the changes introduced in 1737. 'In 1731', say Thomas, Carlton and Etienne,[8]

> Fielding's *Welsh Opera* and *The Fall of Mortimer*[9] set alarm bells ringing in government circles. In *The Welsh Opera*, the royal family was mocked in the figures of Squire Shinkers (George II), who has to cope with a shrewish wife (Queen Caroline), an awkward son, Owen (Frederick, Prince of Wales), and the machinations of Robin, the Butler (Walpole).[10] In *The Fall of Mortimer*, set in the time of Edward III [*sic*], Mortimer (Walpole) was shown conspiring with his brother, Horatio (Charles Townshend, Walpole's bother-in-law) and the Queen to deceive King and country.

Others again have opted rather to stress the role of John Gay's *The Beggar's Opera*[11] in contributing to the change in the public mood upon which Walpole was not slow to seek to capitalize. In the late nineteenth century there was to be an apt allusion to Gay's masterpiece in a case concerned with the interpretation of a complex will,[12] but the play itself in later years continued in certain quarters to be

---

4 W.N.M. Geary, *The law of theatres and music-halls including contracts and precedents of contracts* (London, Stevens & Sons, 1885).

5 Ibid., p. 9.

6 Victor, *The history of the theatres of London and Dublin from the year 1730 to the present time*, 2 vols (London, T. Davies, 1761), i, 50–1.

7 The reference is to Colley Cibber's *Apology*: see below, n. 20.

8 *Theatre censorship*, pp 21–2.

9 '*The Fall of Mortimer* at the Little Haymarket (12 May 1731) would turn out to be the most incendiary outgrowth of this season of partisan stage innuendo': Thomas Lockwood in his introduction to *The Welsh Opera*, in Henry Fielding, *Plays: vol. 2, 1731–34*, ed. Lockwood (Oxford, Clarendon Press, 2007), p. 9.

10 For the text, see conveniently Fielding, *Plays: vol. 2, 1731–34*, p. 31.

11 John Gay, *Dramatic works, vol. 2*, ed. John Fuller (Oxford, Clarendon Press, 1983), p. 1.

12 *In re Pickworth* [1899] 1 Ch. 642; see, too, W.N. Osborough, *Literature, judges, and the law* (Dublin,

regarded with considerable disdain. J.W. Calcraft, the manager of Dublin's Theatre
Royal in the early nineteenth century (whom we will meet again later),[13] recalled the
furore *The Beggar's Opera* had occasioned at the time of its original performance,
before expressing, in his tract on defence of the stage, brought out in 1839, his
disagreement with Jonathan Swift, who found the play harmless, and with the
archbishop of Canterbury who berated it for encouraging criminality.[14] Calcraft
made it plain even so that he did not care for *The Beggar's Opera* one bit. He could
have been unaware of a successful run of *The Beggar's Opera* at Smock Alley under
Thomas Elrington's management in 1728.[15]

   Back in 1737, news of the promulgation of a new bill dealing with the stage was
leaked in the month of February, but in the end this measure dealt only with the
regulation of theatrical performances in Oxford and Cambridge and in the vicinity
of both. In a sense, though, it foreshadowed what was to come. The long title of this
particular measure,[16] while it did not quite conceal what it was immediately about,
confused the reader as to its main thrust by dealing at the same time with
completely different subject-matter altogether (a far-from unprecedented legislative tactic for the period); or, to put it another way, as Geary phrased it,[17] the title
of the bill was 'remarkable as illustrating the English tendency to indirect
legislation'.

   This first measure introduced in 1737 was described as

> An Act for the more effectual preventing the unlawful playing of Interludes
> within the Precincts of the two Universities, in that part of Great Britain
> called England, and the Places adjacent; and for explaining and amending so
> much of an Act passed in the last Session of Parliament, intituled, An Act for
> laying a Duty upon the Retailers of Spirituous Liquors, and for licensing the
> Retailers thereof, as may affect the Privilege of the said Universities, with
> respect to licensing Taverns, and all other Publick Houses within the
> Precincts of the same.

As enacted, this new Act recited the letters patent and charters in favour of the two
universities, going on to express a doubt as to whether the several chancellors, vice-
chancellors, their deputies and others were 'sufficiently impowered to correct,
restrain or suppress common Players of Interludes, settled, residing or inhabiting

Four Courts Press, 2008), pp 93–5. The specific reference in *In re Pickworth* was to Air xxxv, as
   performed by Macheath: 'How happy could I be with either, / Were t'other dear Charmer away!
   / But while you thus teaze me together, / To neither a Word will I say?'. Gay, *Dramatic works*, vol.
   2, at p. 40.
13 Below, ch. 8.
14 J.W. Calcraft (pseud. of J.W. Cole), *A defence of the stage, or an enquiry into the real qualities of
   theatrical entertainments, their scope and tendency. Being a reply to a sermon entitled 'The evil of
   theatrical amusements stated and illustrated' … by the Revd Dr John B. Bennett, including an
   examination of the authorities an which that sermon is founded* (Dublin, Milliken & Son, 1839), p. 93.
15 Above, p. 17.   16 10 Geo. II, c. 19.   17 Geary, *Law of theatres and music-halls*, p. 9.

within the Precincts of either of the said Universities and wandering abroad.' As a motive for legislative intervention, the preamble went on to advance a contentious justification, in language that notoriously failed to be specific. 'And whereas', it was added, 'the Erection of any Playhouse within the Precincts of either of the said Universities, or Places adjacent, may be attended with great Inconveniences ...'

There was little left to chance, or to the imagination, in the critical provision in the legislation that targeted producers and performers alike. 'All persons whatsoever', this provision stipulated,

> who shall for Gain in any Playhouse, Booth or otherwise, exhibit any Stage Play, Interludes, Show, Opera, or other theatrical or dramatical Performance, or act any Part or assist therein, within the Precincts of either of the said Universities, or within five miles of the City of Oxford, or Town of Cambridge, shall be deemed Rogues and Vagabonds.

Such individuals it was lawful for the respective university authorities to commit to some house of correction or common gaol for one month, 'any licence of Chancellors, Masters and Scholars, of either University to the contrary notwithstanding'.

A second, more general, and equally draconian legislative initiative was announced by the *Daily Post* on 23 May. 'A bill is ordered into Parliament', the newspaper reported,

> for suppressing the great number of playhouses, so justly complained of, and for the future no Persons shall presume to Act any play, etc. without first obtaining a licence from the Lord Chamberlain of his Majesty's Household for the time being, any persons acting without such licence to be deemed vagrants and punished as such, according to the Act of the 12th of Anne.

The next day Walpole made it crystal-clear that the government through the office of Lord Chamberlain would indeed be assuming what Sir John Barnard all along had objected to, a power to censor. The long title to the measure, as enacted, stressed neither that a regime of prior censorship was being inaugurated – a regime that would last in Britain until 1968 – nor that the long-standing practice of issuing theatre patents under the prerogative would henceforth enjoy statutory sanction. This key enactment of the statute-book possesses a long title, in fact, that can only be regarded as positively misleading.[18] It tells us that the measure requires to be regarded as

> An Act to explain and amend so much of an Act made in the twelfth Year of the Reign of Queen Anne, intituled, An Act for reducing the Laws relating to Rogues, Vagabonds, sturdy Beggars and Vagrants, into one Act of

18 10 Geo. II, c. 28.

Parliament; and for the more effectual punishing such Rogues, Vagabonds, sturdy Beggars and Vagrants, and sending them whither they ought to be sent, as relates to common Players of Interludes.

Section 1 of the Act obliged producers to procure either a patent from the Crown or a licence from the Lord Chamberlain. The Act was passed into law on 21 June 1737, coming into effect on 24 June. Since it was well known that part of the object of the entire exercise was to close a number of the unauthorised theatres in London, it came as no surprise that the Little Haymarket theatre where Henry Fielding had had the majority of his plays performed was one of the first to shut down, a development that effectively put Fielding out of business.[19] The penalty for an actor performing at either kind of unauthorised theatre (unpatented or unlicensed) was twofold. Section 1 deemed such a performer a rogue and vagabond, and all that that entailed; and section 2 imposed a fine of £50. Section 2 targeted the entrepreneur as much as the performer, it providing that the fine attached to anyone choosing 'to act, represent or perform or cause to be acted, represented or performed for hire, gain or reward' any play in a theatre lacking either a patent or a licence.

Section 3 inaugurated the system of prior censorship that was destined to endure until 1968. It stipulates

> that no Person shall, for Hire, Gain or Reward, act, perform, represent or cause to be acted, performed or represented any new Interlude, Tragedy, Comedy, Opera, Play, Farce or other Entertainment of the Stage, or any Part or Parts therein; or any new Act, Scene or other Part added to any old Interlude, Tragedy, Comedy, Opera, Play, Farce or other Entertainment of the Stage, or any new Prologue or Epilogue, unless a true Copy thereof be sent to the Lord Chamberlain of the King's Household for the time being, fourteen Days at least before the acting, representing or performing thereof, together with an Account of the Playhouse or other Place where the same shall be, and the Time when the same is intended to be first acted, represented or performed, signed by the Masters or Managers of such Playhouse or Place, or Company of Actors therein.

Colley Cibber, as has already been noted, was to be counted among contemporary observers who reckoned legislative intervention was a good thing, indeed overdue. Writing in 1740, he took specific issue with the objection 'that to bring the stage under the restraint of a licenser was leading the way to an attack upon the liberty of the press'. Nonsense, he proclaimed:[20]

---

19 Hume, *Fielding and London theatre*, p. 243.
20 Colley Cibber, *An apology for the life of Mr Colley Cibber, comedian, and late patentee of the Theatre Royal, with a material view of the stage during his own time*, 4th ed. (Dublin, Geo. Faulkner, 1740), p. 165.

This amounts but to a jealousy at best, which I hope, and believe all honest Englishmen have as much reason to think as groundless, as to fear it is a just jealousy.

The stage, he was satisfied, stood in need of 'a great deal of discipline and restraint':[21]

Was it not as high time, then, to take this dangerous weapon of mimical insolence, and defamation out of the hands of a mad poet, as to wrest the knife from the lifted hand of a murderer?

A final flourish furnishes the clearest evidence on what it was that worried Cibber and those who felt like him. 'It cannot sure be a principle of liberty', he added,[22]

that would turn the stage into a court of enquiry, that would let the partial applauses of a vulgar audience give sentence upon the conduct of authority, and put impeachments into the mouth of a harlequin.

There was a single concession Cibber was prepared to allow. The text of a banned drama could still be published. That was permissible, for a printed satire was far from as bad as an acted one.

Naturally, there was criticism of the 1737 change as well and it was not slow to materialise. Twenty-one years after Cibber had set down his thoughts, Benjamin Victor explored the issue too. Writing in 1761,[23] Victor conceded that 'the Reasons for urging the Necessity' of passing the measure – an oblique reference to the amount of political satire on the London stage – 'were notorious', and, as such, 'it met with a Majority in both Houses'. In such fashion, had Fielding's foolhardiness brought on what Victor terms 'this Beginning of a Distress upon the Stage'.[24]

There had been opposition to the change, apart altogether from that expressed by Sir John Barnard. In the House of Lords a forceful speech from Lord Chesterfield warned against either chamber agreeing to the measure. 'Do not', Chesterfield urged,[25] 'let us subject [authors] to the arbitrary will and pleasure of one man'. It was a speech to which all those who had an interest in the well-being of the stage would regularly return;[26] and in 1966 it was quoted by Lord Birkett in a celebrated 5-hour-long debate in the House of Lords,[27] which led to the establishment of a parliamentary commission of enquiry and thus in due course to the abolition of prior censorship achieved by the Theatres Act of 1968.[28] That the measure produced 'a profound and constraining effect on the theatre' is one

---

21 Ibid., p. 167.   22 Ibid.   23 Victor, *History of theatres of London and Dublin*, i, 51.   24 Ibid.
25 *Cobbett's parliamentary history of England from the earliest period to the year 1803*, x (London, Longman & Co., 1811), col. 328 at col. 335.
26 Thomas, Carlton & Etienne, *Theatre censorship*, pp 38–9.
27 *Hansard, 5 (lords)*, cclxxii, col. 1202 ff.   28 1968, c. 54. See further below, ch. 14.

modern verdict.[29] For Hume, being more specific, what irked was that the measure 'effectively removed political and social controversy from the British stage'.[30]

In the immediate aftermath of this significant legal change, an aftermath explored by the authors of *Theatre censorship: from Walpole to Wilson*,[31] it is worth pointing out that the first play to be prohibited by the Lord Chamberlain exercising his new powers was Henry Brooke's drama *Gustavus Vasa*.[32] Brooke's work, we will later be showing, was also to cause political ripples in Ireland.[33] As regards the veto on *Gustavus Vasa*, it was understandable enough, the text implying whiggish sympathy for parliamentary sovereignty at the expense of the royal prerogative – an approach plainly anathema to both Walpole and George II.

The furnishing of a statutory bulwark to buttress the system of theatre patents was a feature of the 1737 legislation that merits more than a passing mention. Within thirty years of its enactment there occurred one officially sanctioned grant of a new London theatre patent that is distinctly curious, but which nevertheless was to serve as a precedent in the very different circumstances of the stage in Dublin later in the eighteenth century and early in the nineteenth.[34] In July 1766 Samuel Foote was given a patent enabling him to put on a summer season of drama at the Little Theatre in the Haymarket, technically in the city of Westminster.[35] The authors of *Theatre censorship: from Walpole to Wilson* expand on the background to this unusual seasonal authorisation. 'The patent', they write,[36]

> was granted by the Lord Chamberlain (the duke of Portland), apparently at the request of the duke of York. It seems that the latter felt a keen sense of personal responsibility for a riding accident in which Foote was seriously injured and subsequently had one of his legs amputated. The grant of a patent was therefore viewed as a means of compensating the actor for the loss of a limb.

The question of whether a third permanent patented London theatre should be permitted became a matter of political controversy in the early years of the nineteenth century.[37] Lack of choice and the poverty of the repertoire at Covent Garden and Drury Lane were the sorts of argument utilised by opponents of the existing duopoly. The rights of the existing patentees, including Richard Brinsley Sheridan in respect of Drury Lane, were stoutly defended, and the extreme financial difficulties both of those theatres encountered after the disastrous fires of 1808 and 1809 when the cost of replacements had to be faced, contributed to the shelving of this key question for several years to come. O'Toole tells us that in

29 Thomas, Carlton & Etienne, *Theatre censorship*, p. 256.
30 Hume, *Fielding and London theatre*, p. 243.
31 Thomas, Carlton & Etienne, *Theatre censorship*, pp 24–53.
32 Victor, *Annual register of all the tragedies*, pp 116–17.   33 Below, ch. 14.
34 Below, p. 90.   35 Victor, *History of theatres of London*, pp 183–4.
36 Thomas, Carlton & Etienne, *Theatre censorship*, p. 51.

Sheridan's case, he was to make 'ruthless use of his political position – the issue was decided by the Privy Council of which he was a member'.[38] In the end, major change under this particular heading was to be deferred until 1843 following specific parliamentary scrutiny, which had linked the questions of the London theatre patents and of the lack of protection for the dramatic author's performing right.[39]

As a future chapter will point out,[40] statutory reforms of various sorts – principally affecting provincial theatre in Britain – were introduced later in the eighteenth century, but the next major legislative innovation only took place in 1843, when the so-called Act for regulating theatres was adopted.[41] This was both a reforming and a consolidation measure. Dealing with the question of pre-censorship – a regime which remained intact – it was provided that the requirement of advance notice to be given the Lord Chamberlain was reduced from 14 days to 7.[42] At this juncture it is worthy of notice that in 1799, as recounted by O'Toole,[43] Richard Brinsley Sheridan submitted the text of his new play, *Pizarro*, to the Lord Chamberlain as late as a mere 24 hours before the play's première at Drury Lane. Section 12 of the new legislation went on to stipulate what precisely had to be forwarded to the Lord Chamberlain within the revised time-frame – a section that thus replaced section 3 in the Act of 1737. This was to be

> one copy of every new stage play, and of every new act, scene, or other part added to any old stage play, and of every new prologue and epilogue, and of every new part added to an old prologue or epilogue intended to be produced and acted for hire at any theatre in Great Britain.

Section 14 of the new Act was set to replace another section of the Act of 1737 – section 4. This had given the Lord Chamberlain the express power to prohibit any performance at any time. In the volatile political atmosphere of 1794, as O'Toole had recalled,[44] it was employed to shut down a production of Thomas Otway's *Venice Preserv'd* (1682), which Sheridan had chosen at the time to put on at Drury Lane. Newspapers supportive of the government were to complain that the play was being put on in order to inspire rebellion – not too far-fetched a notion, for the play treats of civil discontent, suspicion and betrayal. When, on the third day of the play's 'run', there was a show of violence in the streets of London, the Lord Chamberlain intervened: the licence for the play was withdrawn and future performances were banned for seven years.[45] Section 4 of the 1737 measure expressed the Lord Chamberlain's powers in very broad terms; the replacement provision in the Act of 1843 was seemingly more specific. The power to ban

37 Ibid., p. 52.
38 Fintan O'Toole, *A traitor's kiss: the life of Richard Brinsley Sheridan* (London, Granta Books, 1998), pp 431–2.
39 Below, ch. 15.   40 Below, ch. 7.   41 6 & 7 Vict., c. 68.   42 S. 12.
43 *A traitor's kiss*, p. 343.   44 Ibid., p. 296.   45 Ibid.

performances was henceforth exercisable whenever the Lord Chamberlain was of opinion that such was 'fitting for the preservation of good manners, decorum or of the public peace'.[46]

Of the other major changes introduced by the 1843 Act, one – undoubtedly the change of the most practical significance – was to bring to an end the theatrical monopoly enjoyed in London by the patent theatres such as Covent Garden and Drury Lane.[47] And outside the geographical limits of the Lord Chamberlain's jurisdiction in and around London and Westminster, justices of the peace were given full power to license houses for the performance of stage works.[48]

The precarious legal position of new theatre enterprises in the London area prior to the general reforms of 1843 is excellently illustrated by William Ewing's unsuccessful suit against David Webster Osbaldiston heard by Lord Chancellor Cottenham in 1837.[49] Here Cottenham declined to give effect to a draft partnership agreement concerning the Surrey Theatre on Blackfriars Road in Surrey.[50] Osbaldiston had acquired the lease of the theatre and, seeking a partner to share in the venture, wrote to Ewing who was based in Edinburgh. Ewing was tempted to become involved, and was to forward to Osbaldiston two separate sums of £500, part of which was employed to pay for the lease of the theatre. How well-versed Ewing was in the applicable law is not immediately clear, but he was right to seek assurances from Osbaldiston that everything in the draft partnership agreement would pass muster. That was because the Surrey Theatre was one mile distant from both London and Westminster and one-and-a-half miles distant from the patent theatres, and in the absence of obtaining a patent, the only way forward was to obtain a licence from justices under the Act of 1788,[51] but that was not possible according to the statute, in the case of any theatre within 20 miles of London or eight miles of a patent theatre.

Osbaldiston sought to reassure Ewing in a letter sent to him in December 1831, on the 23rd, three days in fact before the theatre was to open under his management. 'We open', Osbaldiston wrote,[52]

> with a new drama called *The Sorcerer* or *The Two Brothers of Catonia*; *Cinderella*; and a new pantomime called *Old King Cole*, or *Harlequin and the Fiddlers Three*. Don't alarm yourself about any notices from the patent theatres; I have the best authority for stating they will not annoy us if we don't play their pieces called the regular drama, which I had before resolved not to do.

46 1843 Act, s. 14.   47 Ibid., s. 3.   48 Ibid., s. 5.
49 *Ewing v. Osbaldiston* (1837) 2 My & Cr 53, 40 Eng Rep 561.
50 It was destined to be burnt down in 1865: see below, p. 135.
51 28 Geo. III, c. 30. This Act enabled JPs in general or quarter sessions to give licences for 60-day runs of plays in the provinces but not within 20 miles of London, Westminster or Edinburgh, or 8 miles of any patented theatre: see further ch. 7, below.
52 Quoted, 2 My & Cr at 61.

A further letter sent on 19 January 1832, and again designed to reassure and not lead to the loss of a potential partner, was perhaps rather more equivocal. 'We played *Othello*', Osbaldiston confided,[53]

> Monday and Tuesday, to £77 2s. and £58. The town is on my side, and the march of intellect and reform has progressed too far to be stopped by the aristocratic hand of monopoly.

'Should the patents bring an action against me', he added, 'I can defend it by public subscription'.[54] Ewing nevertheless pressed for an article to be included in the partnership agreement to ensure that nothing would ever be put on at the theatre that might be construed to interfere with the two patent theatres of Covent Garden and Drury Lane. One sum of £150 from the profits of the theatre was paid over to Ewing by Osbaldiston, but relations between the two men soured, even after Ewing was to travel to London, and in July 1833 he moved his bill to have the draft partnership agreement given effect to. He sought at the same time to have Osbaldiston removed as manager. Vice-chancellor Shadwell dismissed Ewing's bill, and Ewing's appeal to Lord Chancellor Cottenham was similarly unsuccessful. Osbaldiston, for his part, had opposed both manoeuvres on the entirely un-meritorious ground that all performances at the Surrey Theatre were illegal, and that the projected contract between himself and Ewing was for an illegal purpose, and thus void. That interpretation Cottenham upheld. The lord chancellor went on, however:[55]

> It is undoubtedly a case of great hardship upon the plaintiff to have parted with his money, and now to be denied the fruits of it; – but this hardship is common to all cases of contract which cannot be enforced, from their illegality.

Cottenham added that he had been advised that Osbaldiston was planning to return to Ewing his money. The lord chancellor commented:[56] 'As an honest man, this was, and clearly is, his duty'. But he could not enforce it.

The next year, *Ewing v. Osbaldiston* was followed in a case involving another new theatre, the Victoria, which was described as being within 2 miles of both London and Westminster.[57] Here once again no licence could have been obtained from justices because of the stipulation contained in the Act of 1788. The decision of the defendant, Yates, to renege on the deal to open at the theatre with a play on Whit Monday, 15 May 1837, thus left the plaintiff, one Levy, remediless and, probably too, out of pocket. The Queen's Bench (Lord Denman, chief justice, and Littledale, Patteson and Coleridge JJ) agreed that the contract was clearly illegal.

53 Quoted, 2 My & Cr at 62–3. 54 At 63. 55 At 88. 56 Ibid.
57 *Levy v. Yates* (1838) 8 Ad & El 129, 112 Eng Rep 785.

As already explained, all these difficulties were set aside with the abolition, introduced by the Theatres Act of 1843,[58] of the monopoly enjoyed by London's patent theatres. The change was achieved by the bestowal upon the Lord Chamberlain of the supplementary power of licensing. Section 3 of the Act explained. 'The authority of the Lord Chamberlain for granting licences', it prescribed,

> shall extend to all theatres (not being patent theatres) within the parliamentary boroughs of the cities of London and Westminster, and of the boroughs of Finsbury and Marylebone, the Tower Hamlets, Lambeth and Southwark, and also within those places where her Majesty, her heirs and successors, shall, in their royal persons, occasionally reside.

58 6 & 7 Vict., c. 68.

CHAPTER THREE

Regulating the Dublin stage: the abortive plan of 1779

THE REGIME OF PATENTED THEATRES for Dublin city and county, finally sanctioned by the act of the Irish parliament passed in 1786, is believed to have been inspired, at least in part, by the views of Thomas Sheridan, the manager of the theatre in Smock Alley in the 1750s. Returning to the managership of Smock Alley in 1756, Sheridan was disconcerted to learn of the existence of a project, linked principally with the name of one Spranger Barry, to unveil an entirely new theatre in Crow Street – disconcerted because Sheridan had long been of opinion that Dublin could support but a single proper theatre.[1] His purchase of the Capel Street theatre lease, to which reference has already been made,[2] stood testimony to the force of the conviction. In 1758, as the erection of the new Crow Street venue continued, Sheridan put pen to paper, urging in effect lovers of the theatre in Dublin to take action to avoid what he regarded as an all but certain catastrophe: *An humble appeal to the Publick together with some Considerations in the Present critical and dangerous State of the Stage in Ireland*[3] was the result.

An humble appeal set the tone for the discussion that continued for the next twenty odd years, and it is likely Sheridan's unqualified support for a Dublin theatre monopoly helped drive the campaign for the adoption of the first proposed legislative measure in 1779, a campaign, however, which was to prove abortive. That the legislative measure finally adopted in 1786 did not, on the surface at least, threaten the imposition of any kind of monopoly cannot, however, be cited to demonstrate that Sheridan's overweening concerns for the health of the Dublin stage had not influenced some at least of the legislators of 1785 and 1786. As it happens, the true motivation that drove the legislation adopted in 1786 remains obscure; and it certainly deserves to be emphasised that within a very short space of time indeed the resultant act was interpreted so as to preclude the prospect of endorsing any theatrical monopoly at all.

Sheridan's *An humble appeal* starts with a potted history of the changes he had personally wrought in what he regarded as the civilising of the Dublin theatre audience. Apart from the episodes with which we are already familiar, or are to be visited again in the chapter on theatre disruption and riot,[4] we are told of the patron who, after a performance, brazenly walked on stage and started to cut up

1 See further, above, ch. 1, at p. 24.   2 Above, p. 24.   3 Dublin, G. Faulkner, 1758.
4 See above p. 23 and below, ch. 13.

the scenery, and of another patron who, with equal equanimity, indecently assaulted Peg Woffington when acting the part of Cordelia in *King Lear*.[5] The emphasis in the coverage is not so very different from that to be found in his 1747 pamphlet dealing with the Kelly-inspired disruptions, *A full vindication of the conduct of the manager of the Theatre Royal*.[6] 'One part of the house', Sheridan wrote,[7] he had found 'a bear garden, the other a brothel.' The abuse to which he had been exposed, the property losses as well, prompted him to glance over his shoulder, or at least across the Irish Sea:[8]

> Happy Managers of London Theatres! You are really possessed of lordly Villas, which you visit in splendid Equipages; you enjoy all the Elegancies as well as Comforts of Life.

Turning finally to the theme that dominates the remainder of *An humble appeal*, Sheridan first cites Chetwood's *History of the stage*.[9] Dublin theatre, Sheridan paraphrases,[10]

> never was on a tolerable footing when there was more than one. It made a shift to subsist in the Time of old Ashbury, and afterwards of Tom Elrington; but the instant two were set up, they destroyed each other.

Financial difficulties even afflicted managers in London – who had been obliged to pay their actors only half what was their due,[11] a state of affairs that prompted him to press this observation on critics who claimed that now that Dublin was bigger and wealthier it might indeed manage to support two theatres – 'There ought to be first some Proof given, that it [Dublin] is, at this day, well able to support <u>one</u>, at the present advanced Prices paid to Performers.'[12] Having mentioned in passing the welcome given to union of the Aungier Street and Smock Alley troupes back in 1743/44,[13] Sheridan went on to express the fear for proponents of the idea of two theatres that they might

> share the same Fate with the old Woman, who having a good Hen that regularly laid her one Egg a Day, thought that, if she gave her twice that Quantity of Food, she would lay two; but the Consequence was, that she left off laying entirely.[14]

Sheridan then passes from fable to sarcasm. 'It would be proof of the blindest Ignorance and highest Stupidity', he proceeds to argue,[15]

---

5 *An humble appeal*, p. 14.　　6 Dublin, S. Powell, 1747.　　7 *An humble appeal*, p. 15.
8 Ibid., p. 28.
9 W.R. Chetwood, *A general history of the stage (more particularly the Irish theatre) from its origin in Greece down to the present time* (Dublin, E. Rider, 1749).
10 *An humble appeal*, p. 51.　　11 Ibid.　　12 *An humble appeal*, p. 53.　　13 Ibid., p. 56.
14 Ibid.　　15 *An humble appeal*, p. 60.

to wish for another Theatre, on any other Condition than one; which is, that the present Stage should be allowed to be at so low an Ebb in point of Conduct, Decency, and Regularity, and that the Entertainments, exhibited there, should be so very wretched, and in so slovenly a Way, that no change whatsoever could possibly make things worse.

Having rejected the contention that his opposition to a second theatre was based on his jealousy of other actors and linked to his own supposed financial meanness (he would have had to pay more to his actors in a competitive environment),[16] Sheridan repeated his central conviction. 'If the two theatres', he hypothesised,[17]

> should open in Opposition to each other, the Stage will not only be speedily reduced to Poverty and Distress, but, in all human Probability, will never be able to raise its Head again in the Kingdom.

In a final direct appeal 'to the public', Sheridan reiterates his concern:[18]

> As you regard the future Peace and Quiet of this City as you value the best of your Entertainments, listen to my Request; for remember (hereafter if you neglect the Warning, you will have woeful Cause to remember) I now assert that if two Theatres should open next Winter in this City the Stage must in a short time Sink, never to raise its Head again in this Kingdom.

At this precise juncture in 1758, Sheridan adds his own recipe for the avoidance of disaster. 'The Constitution of the Stage of Paris', he writes,[19]

> where the Theatre is the property of the Public, and give a certain Portion of the Profits to charitable Uses, seems to him [Sheridan] the only one that would place that of Dublin on a good and durable Foundation.

He recommended, accordingly, that a parliamentary bounty should be procured to buy out what remained of his own lease at Smock Alley; that construction work on the new Crow Street theatre should cease at once; and that Spranger Barry, the guiding light behind the Crow Street venture, should have made available to him the Smock Alley venue. This extraordinary proposal, from the man who signed himself not only the manager of the Theatre Royal but also Deputy Master of the Revels, made no headway at all, and seems to have been immediately forgotten or ignored.

That this must have been a disappointment to Sheridan is quite plain. In the epigram for *An humble appeal*, derived from the Greek orator Demosthenes' *First Philippic*, Sheridan stressed both the gravity of the matter and the need for urgent action. Demosthenes, in his speech to the Assembly in Athens, delivered probably

16 Ibid., p. 61.   17 Ibid., p. 74.   18 At p. 85.   19 *An humble appeal*, p. 86.

early in 351BC, chided his fellow citizens for failing to detect the menace that Philip of Macedonia represented. Philip was challenging the power of Athens with his interference in the affairs of Thrace and his intrigues in Euboea; he had also seized ships transporting corn to Attica. And yet no effective counteraction had been taken or was even planned. This is the passage from Demosthenes' oration that Sheridan repeats:[20]

πότ᾽ οὖν, ὦ ἄνδρες Ἀθηνῖοι, πόθ᾽ ἃ χρὴ πράξετε; ἐπειδὰν τί γένηται; ἐπειδὰν νὴ Δί᾽ ἀνάγκη τις ᾖ. νῦν δὲ τί χρὴ τὰ γιγνόμεν᾽ ἡγεῖσθαι; ἐγὼ μὲν γὰρ οἴομαι τοῖς ἐλευθέροις μεγίστην ἀνάγκην τὴν ὑπὲρ τῶν πραγμάτων αἰσχύνην εἶναι. ἢ βούλεσθ᾽, εἰπέ μοι, περιιόντες αὐτῶν πυθάνεσθαι ᾿ ῾λέγεταί τι καινόν;᾽ γένοιτο γὰρ ἄν τι καινότερον ἢ Μακεδὼν ἀνὴρ Ἀθηναίους καταπολεμῶν καὶ τὰ τῶν ῾Ελλήνων διοικῶν;

[When, Athenians, will you take the necessary action? What are you waiting for? Until you are compelled, I presume. But what are we to think of what is happening now? For my own part I think that for a free people there can be no greater compulsion than shame for their position. Or tell me, are you content to run round and ask one another, 'Is there any news today?' Could there be any news more startling then that a Macedonian is triumphing over Athenians and settling the destiny of Hellas?]

    Whether enough of those who made it their business to read *An humble appeal* knew classical Greek sufficiently well to appreciate the force of the allusion in its relation to the plight of the Dublin stage (or the depth of Thomas Sheridan's feelings) must naturally remain a matter of some doubt.

    The Crow Street enterprise, to Sheridan's dismay, went ahead, and he himself gave up the managership at Smock Alley and withdrew to England. Nevertheless, he did not immediately throw in the sponge, for a few years later, back in Dublin, he sought once again to galvanise opinion at a public meeting. At this he repeated his conviction that progress along the lines he had earlier supported constituted 'the only means of restoring the stage to a proper degree of credit and respectability'. But to no avail. 'The meeting', Hitchcock tells us,[21] 'was attended with very little effect, a contrariety of opinions which could not be reconciled, prevented the embracing so salutary a scheme'.

    It is noteworthy that Gilbert, in his account of the fortunes of the Smock Alley theatre at this critical juncture, besides furnishing a number of details not repeated elsewhere, has Sheridan at one point contemplating, not perhaps with total equanimity, Smock Alley and Crow Street in a species of friendly rivalry – one

20 Demosthenes, *First Philippic*, 10.
21 Robert Hitchcock, *An historical view of the Irish stage from the earliest period ... with theatrical anecdotes*, 2 vols (Dublin, R. Marchbank, W. Folds, 1788–94), ii, 214.

good company of actors performing tragedies in Crow Street and comedies in Smock Alley, alternately.[22]

As Sheridan had plainly anticipated, financial difficulties confronted both Smock Alley and Crow Street in the years ahead, intermittently becoming very serious indeed, and it was only in 1779 that his plan for restoring order out of chaos was revived, if not entirely along the lines he might have supported. Unsurprisingly, perhaps, this new initiative did not immediately prosper. On 7 December 1779 the House of Commons granted leave for the introduction of heads of bill to regulate the Dublin stage.[23] The prime instigators of the movement that achieved this remarkable step La Tourette Stockwell identified as having been two contemporary dramatists, almost, if not quite, lost from view today – Robert Jephson and George Colman.[24] Jephson, who was Irish, held at the time the post of Master of the Horse at Dublin Castle.[25] Colman had theatrical interests in London.

In the Irish House of Commons, two MPs, Denis Daly, a member for Co. Galway, and George Ogle, a member for Co. Wexford, appear to have been made responsible for the text of the draft heads of bill, formally introduced by Daly in the Commons on 12 February 1780.[26] That text itself, sadly, does not appear to be extant. On 8 December 1779, the day after the legislative process had been initiated, the Commons were presented with a motion for them to consider which was clearly linked to talk of an act of parliament: a motion to appoint a committee to inquire into the state and management of the theatres in Dublin.[27] As the *Commons' journal* phrases it, this motion was 'passed in the negative', that is, was lost on a vote of 16 for and 43 against. No record of the arguments for and against is known to be extant, but the episode itself served as a harbinger of what was to come: the complete collapse at this juncture, early in 1780, of the single legislative proposal that so far had been canvassed. Several individuals and Dublin Corporation between December 1779 and February 1780 had petitioned the Commons against the projected heads of bill, and this combined assault, it is safe to assume, killed off the initiative for the time being, a conclusion Gilbert endorses.[28]

None of this augured well for the success of Jephson and Colman's plan. In addition, the opponents of the plan had been swift off the mark, utilising the resources of the press to heap ridicule both on it and its sponsors.[29] The prospect

---

22 J.T. Gilbert, *A history of the city of Dublin*, 3 vols (Dublin, McGlashan and McGlashan and Gill, 1854–9), ii, 94–5, 181.

23 *Commons' jn., Ire.*, x, pt 1, p. 52: 7 Dec. 1779.

24 La Tourette Stockwell, *Dublin theatres and theatre customs* (Kingsport, TX, Kingsport Press, 1938), p. 146.

25 See, too, T.J. Walsh, *Opera in Dublin, 1705–1797: the social scene* (Dublin, Allen Figgis, 1973), p. 251.

26 *Commons' jn., Ire.*, x, pt 1, p. 64: 12 Feb. 1780.   27 Ibid., p. 53: 8 Dec. 1779.

28 Gilbert, *History of Dublin*, ii, 201–2.   29 Stockwell, *Dublin theatres*, pp 147–8.

of the creation of a monopoly was raised; and a deterioration in the quality of productions, productions it was averred, sarcastically, 'instead of those antiquated performances of Shakespeare and Congreve', specifically warned against. The attack on Jephson in particular was merciless. 'At a time', a correspondent wrote in the *Hibernian Journal* in November 1979,[30]

> that even our Legislature is telling all Europe that we are all moneyless and starving, an upstart minion of the Castle, who has wriggled himself into Parliament by the Spaniel Arts of Adulation, looks for an exclusive Act for regulating a playhouse in the city.

'With language of freedom and redress' in the mouths of members of the Lords and Commons, the same correspondent went on to demand,

> can they for the pecuniary advantage of a petty scribbler adopt, themselves, the measure of tyranny? The obscure subaltern ... should not be an object of encouragement to a patriotic Parliament, especially when he dares to demand their assent to an act of injustice.

A correspondent, writing to the *Freeman's Journal*, was equally forthright. He railed against control of the theatre being bestowed on 'half-starved courtiers or obsequious players'.[31]

The petitioners whose claims helped to defeat the Jephson-Colman plan were people with existing financial interests in either Smock Alley or Crow Street. First to air his concerns was Thomas Ryder, who had acquired a 21-year lease on the Smock Alley theatre in 1773. Ryder's petition was received by the Commons on 8 December 1779.[32] He had moved fast. In the petition, Ryder claimed that he had embarked his whole property in providing for the nobility and gentry 'the best entertainment and the most eminent dramatic performers who could be procured'. The planned legislation, he contended, was a device to establish an 'exclusive right for one theatre only in Dublin', and was brought forward by individuals who,

> situate as the stage is now in both Kingdoms, can promise no additional entertainments, but seem rather stimulated merely by an interested view of monopoly which if obtained will be the ruin of the petitioner.

This was not to be the last occasion when opposition was expressed to the possibility of the creation of a monopoly, even though no details as yet were to hand

---

30 *Hibernian Journal*, 17 Nov. 1779; quoted in Stockwell, *Dublin theatres*, p. 147.
31 *Freeman's Journal*, 4–6 Jan. 1780, quoted in Helen M. Burke, *Riotous performances: the struggle for hegemony in the Irish theatre, 1712–1784* (Notre Dame, IN, Univ. of Notre Dame Press, 2003), p. 247.
32 *Commons' jn., Ire.*, x, pt 1, p. 53.

as to what precisely was being planned. The same day that the Commons voted against establishing a general committee to review theatre management in Dublin, they also voted against referring Ryder's petition to a committee as well.[33] This was on a vote of 20–11, but since a quorum, set at 40, had not been present, the speaker treated that vote as a nullity. On 19 February 1780, the Commons seems to have reversed its stance, sanctioning on that date an appearance by counsel to present Ryder's objections on the floor of the chamber.[34] There is no record, however, in the *Commons' journal* that such an appearance ever occurred.

The Revd Thomas Wilson, a senior fellow of Trinity College, was the author of a second petition from an individual with a financial stake in Smock Alley.[35] Wilson had made the acquaintance of the actor-manager, Henry Mossop, while the latter was still a student in Trinity, and either lent money directly to Mossop or rescued him from his creditors. None of this money seems to have been paid back, as Mossop, launched on his career, sank further and further into financial difficulty. In 1777 Wilson found himself in the unenviable position of having incurred a liability to pay £500 on the strength of some engagement entered into by Mossop. Earlier, Wilson had agreed to take out a mortgage on Mossop's then leasehold interest in Smock Alley by way of security for a further advance to him of £1,200. Wilson had then found out, doubtless to his horror and by way of considerable embarrassment, that Mossop had already mortgaged this interest. This prior interest Wilson had then bought out for £475. The plot was set to thicken. The owner of the ground on which the Smock Alley theatre had been built, a Mrs Lucy Herbert, brought a successful action in the courts on an ejectment for non-payment of rent, as a result of which she obtained actual possession. To protect his interest in the theatre, such as it was, Wilson considered that he had no alternative but to satisfy the decree in Mrs Herbert's favour. This involved him in a further outlay of £175, made up of accumulated rent, renewal fines and costs. In April 1773, Mrs Herbert then made a new lease of the theatre in favour of Wilson himself. Wilson had then sought to recoup part of his losses by means of the sub-lease made to Ryder the same year. The total moneys Wilson had expended over the year on Smock Alley came to the grand total of £3,615. Concluding, Wilson said he dreaded, from the imminent threat of the enactment of the projected legislation, the loss of any return at all in the future on 'his only savings in the space of twenty-seven-years, employed by him in education and in superintending the education of youth'. He had been reduced, he claimed, to a situation where he possessed no property of any value, 'save only his fellowship and his books'.

The same day, 19 February 1780, the House of Commons received the first petition against the threatened legislation to emanate from individuals, linked to the other principal theatre in Dublin, Crow Street, a petition from William Chaigneau, the principal agent to most of the regiments on the Irish establishment, and from other subscribers who had advanced the moneys that in 1759 enabled the

33 Ibid.   34 Ibid., p. 72.   35 Ibid., pp 71–2; Gilbert, *History of Dublin*, ii, 104.

new Crow Street theatre to continue in business.[36] The two impresarios, Spranger
Barry and Henry Woodward, who two years before had taken leases of the property
on which the theatre had been built, found that they had overreached themselves
financially, after spending in excess of £20,000. Chaigneau and two others came to
their rescue by taking a mortgage on the various leasehold interests, and the
theatre's 'wardrobe and particulars'; in return they advanced £3,000. It was then
sought to spread the risk by the issuance of a number of £100 subscriptions. Under
the terms of a special deed of trust each subscriber became entitled to one ticket to
be present at, and to view, all dramatic performances put on at the theatre, Barry
and Woodward guaranteeing the arrangement. Chaigneau and the others believed
that the avowed intention of the projected new law would be to strip them of their
property interests without any compensation. They accordingly looked for
provision to be first made for payment of what was due to them all 'for principal
and interest'.

In 1766 Spranger Barry had negotiated a quite separate transaction to help
him over his financial difficulties. The upshot was that one William Benson, 'a
merchant', took out a mortgage that year on the Crow Street theatre as security for
advancing Barry the sum of £400. By 1779, by which time Benson was dead, his
widow, Frances Benson, claimed there was due to her £400 plus a large amount of
accumulated unpaid interest. She brought these matters to the attention of the
House of Commons in a petition of 26 February 1780.[37]

Further insight into the financial side of theatrical management in the Dublin
of the period and, necessarily, into the uphill struggle that Spranger Barry of the
Crow Street theatre faced throughout is obtained from the last of this group of
petitions, that presented to the Commons a few days earlier, on 21 February 1780,
by Barry's widow, Anne Crawford.[38] This was the former Anne Dancer, in her day
regarded, apparently, as a handsome tragic actress and by no means inferior in
talent to Mrs Siddons: 'superior in the pathetic … inferior to her in the terrific'.[39]
Survival on the Dublin stage had become a precarious business, and Anne Dancer
had profited from her experiences by becoming extremely careful in matters
pertaining to money. Gilbert tells us, for instance, that, as an actress, Anne Dancer
acquired the reputation of usually declining actually to appear on stage until she
had received payment, to furnish which theatre managers were often obliged to
collect the money for her as it was taken from patrons by the doorkeepers.[40]

In her petition to the Commons, Mrs Crawford – she had married again after
Barry's death in 1778 – repeated much of the information regarding Barry's affairs
contained in William Chaigneau's petition. A few details are added. Thus Barry's
leases of plots of ground – in Crow Street, Dirty Lane, St Cecilia Street and
Fownes Street – taken out in 1757, which enabled the Crow Street theatre to be
built, had involved an outgoing for him of £188 per annum. He had had to buy out

36 *Commons' jn., Ire.*, x, pt 1, p. 72.   37 Ibid., p. 79.   38 Ibid., p. 74.
39 Gilbert, *History of Dublin*, ii, 200.   40 Ibid., pp 204–5.

the existing leasehold interests, incurring further outgoings. The removal of existing buildings and the construction of what became the Crow Street theatre involved expenditure of over £22,000 – some £2,000 higher a figure than that mentioned by Chaigneau. Over 100 individuals, Mrs Crawford claimed, had subscribed the £100 each, as envisaged in the arrangement negotiated between Barry and Chaigneau, but even this had not been enough to cover Barry's continuing indebtedness, and in 1767, one year after the mortgage in favour of Benson, Barry let the theatre, arranging for the profit from this, aside from a sum earmarked for his own support, to be made over in favour of his many creditors. By 1778, the year of Barry's death, £8,000 had been paid back to his creditors, but more was still owing. By his will, therefore, it was understandable that he should have charged the theatre with a continuing responsibility to pay his debts, that is aside from two small annuities amounting to £180 per annum, and a sum in support of his widow – the petitioner. Anne Crawford then averred that while Barry had himself managed Crow Street, she had given every assistance to ensure that the 'said theatrical amusements [were] carried on with as much elegance as possible', and that she had 'received a very small gratuity for her labour'. As regards more recent events, she sought to assure the Commons that she had not received 'any emolument ... as yet from the said bequest [of Barry], having devoted every shilling from the said [Crow Street] theatre for the benefit of [Barry's] creditors'.

Disaster would strike everyone if the projected Stage Regulation Bill went ahead in its present form. As Chaigneau had pointed out in his petition, the 100 or so subscribers would suffer, being deprived 'not only by the original contract of their interest on their subscription but also of their amusements'. The two annuitants mentioned in Barry's will would suffer as well. The long list of creditors would also be deprived of the only means left for the payment of their demands.[41] Nor did life hold out an attractive prospect for Mrs Crawford herself. Closing the theatre or transferring the interests in it elsewhere would cause the various ground landlords to descend on her for their annual rents. Furthermore, she would be totally deprived of the financial maintenance that Spranger Barry had fully intended to bestow upon her.

As we have had occasion to note, there had been a long-running dispute between Dublin Corporation and the government as to who had responsibility for dealing with theatre in Dublin: the corporation laid claim to a right to issue licences to theatrical companies, a claim which the government had long refuted.[42] Unsurprisingly, a further, final petition against the anticipated legislation emanated from this quarter.[43] The corporation's petition, sanctioned on 21 February 1780[44] and presented three days later, argued that the projected measure would be

---

41 *Commons' jn., Ire.*, x, pt 1, p. 74.   42 Above, p. 14.   43 *Commons' jn., Ire.*, x, pt 1, p. 77.
44 *Cal. anc. rec. Dublin*, xiii, 108.

highly derogatory to the rights and privileges of the city of Dublin, by depriving their chief magistrate of a power to license plays, interludes and pastimes within his liberty, for the entertainment of the public.

It was just within living memory – in the year 1715 to be precise – that Dublin's lord mayor had first exercised this assumed power to license theatres, when such a licence had been granted to Tony Aston 'to offer public entertainment'.[45] And there had been all the other licences bestowed, for example, that in respect of Smock Alley in the days of Elrington.[46] The prohibition pronounced by the lord mayor in the 1730s, on Madame Violante's dramatic endeavours, which led to a new theatre being opened in Rainsford Street within the earl of Meath's liberty,[47] furnished further evidence to buttress the belief in the validity of this licensing power. The corporation's second argument touched on a somewhat different point, the fact that the office of Master of the Revels was there for government to avail of, in terms of any licensing it wanted introduced. 'Nor', the corporation averred,[48] does there

> appear any apparent necessity for the said law as his Majesty exercises a power by his patentee, the Master of the Revels, to license a royal theatre wherever he may think proper.

As we will soon discover, the Corporation would again enter their protest when fresh efforts would be launched in 1785 to regulate the stage in Dublin.[49]

---

45 Above, p. 13.   46 Above, p. 14.   47 Stockwell, *Dublin theatres*, pp 68–9; above, pp 16–17.
48 *Commons' jn., Ire.*, x, pt 1, p. 77.   49 Below, ch. 4.

CHAPTER FOUR

The Bill of 1785: the opposition outflanked

BY THE TIME THE Dublin Stage Regulation Act became law in the spring of 1786[1], it is plain that considerable efforts had been made to answer most of the objections raised when the earlier bill had been introduced in 1779. Richard Hely-Hutchinson, the MP for Sligo, one of the movers of the bill in 1785, thus went out of his way to reassure the House of Commons that opposition to the bill on the grounds that it violated private property had been met. No person's property interests, he sought to convince the house, were being interfered with.[2] What the arrangements were that were introduced to protect the financial interests of those who had protested in 1779 and 1780 are nowhere detailed in any official source. Gilbert, however, who can be expected to have been well informed on the matter, indicates very clearly what happened. Conditions were attached to the first theatre patent granted under the new Act, that in favour of Richard Daly, under which the patentee agreed to settle annuities on those with financial claims antedating the new regulatory regime. Dr Thomas Wilson, for instance, we learn from Gilbert, received an annuity of £232, and Anne Crawford one of £100.[3] Doubtless, a calculation was made as to the extent of the claims Wilson, Mrs Crawford and any others actually possessed and the level, the amount and the duration of the annuities determined accordingly. The charge on the income of Daly as the first patentee will not, naturally, have been inconsiderable; rather the reverse. Whether this had a bearing on the price that had to be paid for the obtaining of the first patent cannot, in the absence of the critical information, be either affirmed or denied. One immediate consequence of the new system of regulation cannot at the same time but have contributed to the solvency of the holder of the first patent. The theatre in Smock Alley was closed, leaving the theatre in Crow Street with a virtual monopoly in the sphere of serious theatre. Very shortly afterwards, the old theatre was to be converted into a warehouse for the storage of whiskey and flour.[4] It was an advantage that, as we are about to discover, Daly was not long to enjoy.

---

1 The Act received its royal assent on 8 May: *Commons' jn., Ire.*, xii, pt 1, 141; *Lords' jn., Ire.*, v, 753.

2 *Parl. reg. Ire.*, v, 288.

3 J.T. Gilbert, *A history of the city of Dublin*, 3 vols (Dublin, McGlashan and McGlashan and Gill, 1854–9), ii, 110–11, 206.

4 Gilbert, *History of Dublin*, ii, 111.

In 1785 and 1786 the principal, if not the sole, objection to the Stage Regulation Bill emanated from Dublin Corporation. In 1779, as may be recalled, the corporation had protested rigorously, arguing that the proposed legislation trenched on the rights and privileges of the lord mayor, and that the measure itself was superfluous. On this occasion, they added a third complaint: the vesting of such a power to license theatres in officers of the crown would tend to create a monopoly in public entertainment and 'become an Instrument of Restraint on the Exertions of dramatic Genius'.[5] Dublin Corporation had its defenders in the House of Commons, as is clear from the account of the heated debates that took place there on 20 and 22 July 1785, and probably also in the House of Lords where the bill itself, as we have seen, was finally approved, by a vote of 22–5 on 1 April 1786.[6]

It is self-evident that a majority in parliament were determined to override the wishes of Dublin Corporation. One line of attack, mounted on 20 July 1785, and repeated two days later, was to question the validity of the corporation's petition in protest. Several meetings to secure backing for the petition had been convened, but no quorum had been present, Richard Hely-Hutchinson claimed in the Commons, when an apparent approval had been registered.[7] Dudley Hussey, the recorder of Dublin and MP for Taghmon, Co. Wexford, was to retort that even so the petition had been valid,[8] rejecting Hely-Hutchinson's description of the petition as 'smuggled' and of dubious worth. Richard's brother, John, the MP for Cork at the time as well as being the provost of Trinity College and secretary of state, supported his brother's stance, labelling the attitude of the corporation and that of the Recorder astonishing and unacceptable.[9] Returning to the fray on 22 July, Richard Hely-Hutchinson challenged outright the contention advanced on behalf of the corporation that the lord mayor was legally entitled to license theatrical performances in Dublin.[10] Luke Gardiner, the MP for Co. Dublin, soon to be ennobled as Baron Mountjoy, wholeheartedly agreed: the lord mayor's claim to do any such thing was 'as groundless as his late claim of right to compel the weighing of corn'.[11]

In light of this, it is important to know something of the basis upon which the corporation sought to justify the exercise by the lord mayor of this power. A petition the corporation drew up at the time[12] claimed that

> the chief magistrate of Dublin has, since the establishment of the chartered rights of your petitioners, been the civil and military governor of this metropolis and as such has licenced all plays, interludes, and pastymes within his liberty.

The petition went on to assert that the lord mayor as chief magistrate had acquired this privilege along with many

5 *Commons' jn., Ire.*, xi, pt 1, 472: 22 July 1785.   6 *Lords' jn., Ire.*, v, 733.
7 *Parl. reg. Ire.*, v, 275.   8 Ibid., 275–6.   9 *Parl. reg. Ire.*, v, 276.
10 Ibid., 287.   11 Ibid., 289.

Ancient grants from the Crown and several Franchises, Priviledges and Immunities, received as Rewards for the long and faithful services of your Petitioners' predecessors, exerted upon many occasions against English and Irish enemies.

Travers Hartley, the MP for Dublin City, a successful merchant and a Presbyterian to boot, introduced into the debate a different topic altogether. He feared, as a number of others did, a monopoly but there was something worse than this – the possibility of censorship. The administration, Hartley contended, might render such control of the stage as was

injurious to liberty, by preventing any piece from being acted which breathed the sentiments of freedom, and on the other hand encourage only the representation of such plays as served to extinguish the sacred fire of patriotism.[13]

In sum, it was

dangerous to put such a power in the hands of the crown, as it might at will grant or disannul patents and thereby keep managers under its controul.

Talk of damping down or even of extinguishing Hartley's 'sacred fire' did not impress Hely-Hutchinson. A further reason for rejecting the corporation's petition, he believed, was the nonsensical talk of one member of the corporation, as relayed to him:[14]

What, shall our lips be sealed in the theatre – no groaning any tyrant viceroy – no hisses – no clapping of hands for the Volunteers and Lord Charlemont?

Hely-Hutchinson, for his part, was adamant even so that it was not intended to support censorship or introduce any system of prior restraint. 'It was no part of his scheme', he said,[15]

to lay any such restraint upon the liberty of the press, or to subject dramatic exhibitions in this kingdom to any sort of revision or control.

Both he and his brother John, the secretary of state, freely conceded that the system of stage regulation introduced for England in 1737 did include such an element, but that was because of circumstances that were uniquely English. John proffered a short historical *aperçu* that contained an explanation concentrating

---

12 *Cal. anc. rec. Dublin*, xii, 435 (petition recorded 22 July 1785).   13 *Parl. reg. Ire.*, v. 289.
14 Ibid., 287.   15 *Parl. reg. Ire.*, v, 288.

correctly, as was known at the time and exhaustively confirmed since,[16] on the career of Henry Fielding. Mr Fielding, 'whose merits as an author', John Hely-Hutchinson added, 'deserved to be highly commended', had prevailed on the manager of one of the London theatres to put on plays that were

> very licentious and improper, as they were abusive satires on the crown, royal family and the whole administration.[17]

As Richard Hely-Hutchinson had earlier explained, English law had thus gone on to provide for the imposition of a £50 fine in respect of the performance of a play that had been banned by the Lord Chamberlain, and, where the performance had been put on in a patented theatre, forfeiture of the patent.[18] Luke Gardiner was to endorse the Hely-Hutchinson brothers' assurance that it was not intended to dictate what was to be performed.[19]

The main thrust of the attack on the corporation was to the effect that it had done nothing to guarantee a solid foundation for the development of permanent serious theatre in Dublin. Sir Boyle Roche, the MP for Portarlington, criticised the lackadaisical approach of the corporation which had resulted in 'adventurers and strolling companies' being attracted to Dublin. Disgrace had been brought on the stage, and bankruptcy and ruin had flowed from the encouragement extended to give such adventurers 'credit upon speculation'.[20] Luke Gardiner's attack was even more telling. There were fatal flows, he told the House of Commons, in how the corporation went about issuing a licence:[21]

> It was usual, on the application of any set of players, were they ever so wretched performers, on complying with the terms of appropriating a box to the lord mayor and family, and putting up the city arms over it, and paying a twenty guinea fee to his lordship's secretary (alias to his lordship) to have a licence granted them.

Gardiner continued that there had been innumerable occasions where the audiences at performances licensed in this fashion had been ludicrously low. Many of the companies were 'a disgrace to the stage, and an insult to all admirers of the drama in the metropolis of this kingdom'.[22]

Earlier, in the House of Lords, in April, Earlsfort, the chief justice of King's Bench, had also taken a broader view when welcoming the bill.[23]

---

16 See especially R.D. Hume, *Henry Fielding and the London theatre, 1728–1737* (Oxford, Clarendon Press, 1988).
17 *Parl. reg. Ire.*, v, 292.   18 Ibid., 288.   19 *Parl. reg. Ire.*, v, 290.   20 Ibid., 289.
21 Ibid., 289–90.   22 Ibid., 290.   23 *Morning Chronicle*, 11 Apr. 1786.

CHAPTER FIVE

The passing of the Dublin Stage
Regulation Act, 1786

ON 13 JUNE 1785 leave was given by the House of Commons for the introduction of a bill to regulate the stage in the city and county of Dublin.[1] Where the initiative of 1779 had failed, this fresh one was destined to succeed. Four members of the Commons were associated with the bill's introduction and its successful progress through parliament, one of them, Denis Bowes Daly, the member for Co. Galway, the sole survivor from the earlier attempt at legislative reform in 1779–80. The others were Richard Hely-Hutchinson, the member for Sligo, Luke Gardiner, the member for Co. Dublin, and James or Robert Uniacke, the member for Youghal, Co. Cork. The measure made reasonably swift progress. On 22 July 1785 agreement was reached to instruct the committee conducting hearings on the projected bill to insert a clause exempting the Lying-in Hospital (the Rotunda), from the regulatory regime that was being planned.[2] Section 3 of the Act as eventually passed thus made provision to this effect. Another intervention that occurred on 22 July did not however have any lasting impact: this was a proposal to include a provision to appoint a person or persons to superintend the conduct of managers and to settle differences between managers and performers.[3] That this proposal was not proceeded with recalls the adverse vote recorded in the Commons on 8 December 1779 on a plan to appoint a committee to inquire into the state and management of the theatres in Dublin.[4] Further consideration of the bill was postponed until March 1786 when one other change was proposed and adopted,[5] and which became section 4 of the Act as passed: a second broad exemption from the projected regulatory regime, expressed in the following terms – 'provided also', this amendment proposed in the Commons stipulated,

> that nothing herein contained shall extend or be construed to extend to prevent the Exhibition of any Feats of Horsemanship, Puppet Shew; or such like Species of Entertainment.

The Act of 1786 was to target performances for gain in venues lacking a patent. What was meant by a performance for gain had been defined in section 7 of the British Act of 1737; this definition was borrowed and is set out in section 5:

---

1 *Commons' jn. Ire.*, xi, pt 1, p. 460.   2 Ibid., p. 471.   3 Ibid., p. 472.
4 Above, p. 45.   5 *Commons' jn., Ire.*, xii, pt 1, p. 114: 21 Mar. 1786.

That if any interlude, tragedy, comedy, etc. ... shall be acted, represented, or
performed in any house or place where wine, ale, beer or other liquors shall
be sold, or goods of any kind retailed, or any kind of entertainment exhibited,
for which any money shall be paid, the same shall be deemed to be acted,
represented, or performed for gain, hire, and reward, and liable to the
penalties aforesaid.

By 21 March 1786 the Commons had completed passage of the new legislation
and on that date they sought the concurrence of the Lords.[6] Passage of the measure
through the Lords was swift, it receiving its third reading and being deemed
approved, though only on a vote of 22–5 on 1 April.[7]

Two speeches in opposition are recorded for the critical third reading debate in
the Lords.[8] Lords Mountmorres and Farnham objected to the level of the penalty
proposed for putting on a play in an unlicensed theatre. The penalty was fixed at
£100 in England; the Irish bill proposed a level of £300 (which indeed was
retained in the enacted statute) – a discrepancy which, in the reported language of
Lord Mountmorres,[9] 'was not congruent to the relative abilities of the two
countries'. Mountmorres also queried the need for the measure at all, rehearsing
the conviction of others besides himself that the crown already possessed the power
of granting patents. Mountmorres concluded by expressing the view which, it
would seem, was commonly, if erroneously, entertained at the same time, that the
legislative intention was to have but one authorised theatre in Dublin – a grievous
mistake in his estimation, as it 'might prove an obstruction to the labours of
dramatic writers of ability who ... ought, he thought, to meet with every encouragement'.[10] Mountmorres then read out for the benefit of his fellow peers pages
from the critical speech of Lord Chesterfield on theatre censorship in England.[11]

Supporting the measure, Thomas Barnard, the bishop of Killaloe, upbraided
Mountmorres for the recital of Chesterfield's remarks. The purpose of the present
bill was very different from that espoused by the legal regime in England. There,
due to 'the great immorality and licentiousness of the stage', it had been judged
'expedient to introduce a regulation that no play should be presented on the British
stage, until it had previously received the perusal and gained the approbation and
fiat of the Lord Chamberlain'.[12] Lord Earlsfort, the chief justice of King's Bench,[13]
in his contribution, echoed the bishop's understanding of the background to the
introduction of pre-censorship under Walpole's administration. 'Mr Thompson
[*sic*], the celebrated author of "The Seasons"', Earlsfort began,

6 *Lords' jn., Ire.*, v, 715.   7 Ibid., v, 733.
8 *Proceedings of the Irish House of Lords, 1771–1800*, ed. James Kelly, 3 vols (Dublin, Irish MSS
   Comm., 2008), i, 376–9.
9 *Irish Lords' Proceedings*, i, 376.   10 Ibid.
11 As Lord Birkett was to do in the British House of Lords in the important debate there on theatre
   censorship in 1966, see below, p. 225.
12 *Irish Lords' Proceedings*, i, 376–7.

and other eminent writers of that day, had turned their pens and their abilities against the ministry, and when some of the most scandalous as well as mischievous productions were exhibited on the stage. This gave the … minister [Walpole] the opportunity of curbing such unwarranted and licentious dramatic productions, by causing a bill to be brought in, subjecting all plays to the previous inspection and approbation of the Lord Chamberlain.[14]

Earlsfort's allusion to the part that James Thomson (1700–48), the poet and dramatist, had played in inducing Walpole's administration to introduce pre-censorship for the British theatre merits some comment: most observers have identified rather the impact of Henry Fielding or John Gay. Thomson, a Scot by birth, and best known today, not for 'The Seasons', but as the versifier who gave us 'Rule Britannia', only emerged relatively late in his short career as one of Walpole's critics. In Thomson's play *Agamemnon* (1738), the evil counsellor is all too clearly intended to represent Walpole – an ironic turn-around, given that Thomson's 'Poem in memory of Sir Isaac Newton' (1727) had been dedicated to Walpole, who had responded with a gift of £50 to Thomson. In 1739, two days before another play of Thomson's, *Edward and Eleonora*, was due to open at Covent Garden, its performance was prohibited. This last-minute ban by the Lord Chamberlain, after the actors and theatre management had invested a good deal of time and money, was, in the words of Thomson's biographer, James Sambrook, both 'admonitory and vindictive'.[15] For long after his death Thomson was, indeed, as Earlsfort's mention of him illustrated, primarily remembered as the poet of 'The Seasons'.

In the third reading debate in the Irish Lords, Bishop Barnard of Killaloe, having, as we have seen, upbraided Mountmorres, went on to confess his total disinterest in the matter under discussion. 'Although', as he phrased it, 'he had formerly gratified himself with [theatrical] entertainments, he did not know that he should ever in the future attend them'[16] – an indication of his intentions which plainly intrigued Earlsfort, and to which the chief justice, in his own remarks, was to return. 'A well-regulated theatre' in the metropolis, the bishop condescended to add,[17] was, however, 'salutary and good'.

Bishop Barnard's expression of disinterest is, to say the least, a mite difficult to entertain. Archdeacon Cotton, in his short sketch of the prelate's character, refers to Barnard as the friend of Goldsmith, Dr Johnson, Edmund Burke, Sir Joshua Reynolds and Bishop Percy among others.[18]

13   The former John Scott, who was later advanced through the peerage to become in 1793 the earl of Clonmell.
14   *Irish Lords' Proceedings*, i, 377.   15   *Oxford DNB*, liv, 516 at 520.
16   *Irish Lords' Proceedings*, i, 377.   17   Ibid.
18   Henry Cotton, *Fasti ecclesiae Hibernicae: the succession of the prelates and members of cathedral bodies in Ireland: vol. 1 – The province of Munster* (Dublin, Hodges & Smith, 1847), pp 407–8.

Barnard, in his remarks, alluded to the advantages of improvements in the regulation of Dublin theatre. In the opinion of members of the House of Lords who contributed to the debate, there would appear to have been two aspects to this. Charles Agar, the archbishop of Cashel, highlighted both. 'The bill', he argued first, 'was not only politic, but absolutely necessary to keep our people of fortune and fashion from roving to foreign cities for amusement'.[19] Earlsfort agreed. 'Sound national policy' was involved: 'establishing entertainment at home' would 'prevent so many of our country from seeking it abroad, and spending so many hundred thousand pounds at Bath, etc.'[20]

'The security and stability of the Irish stage', in Agar's view, constituted a no less compelling consideration. 'As matters now stood', he contended,[21]

> Any person could hire a common room and exhibit plays in, from the opening of which, as people in general are fond of every species of novelty, of however subordinate a degree, a manager, after embarking large sums of money in the cause of public entertainment, might be greatly injured.

Earlsfort had earlier concurred. 'There was an absolute necessity for [the bill's] passing', he had argued:[22]

> Before and since Mr Sheridan's management of the Irish stage, there had been almost one uninterrupted series of ruin and distress, occasioned in this city by theatrical oppositions.

'To his own knowledge, during his practice at the bar', Earlsfort continued,[23]

> such opposition had repeatedly tended to the impoverishment of all parties, managers and actors, indentures, etc. and ultimately ending in the ruin of all concerned, besides involving the public in numerous heavy losses from the extensive credits that had been given adventuring managers.

Earlsfort went on to heap praise on Richard Daly, then the manager of the Crow Street theatre, for his 'unwearied diligence', as a result of whose management 'the Irish stage had risen to real consequence'. There was lavish praise, too, for Daly's wife: 'an actress of the most distinguished brilliant abilities'.[24]

Turning finally to the bishop of Killaloe's confession of his abandonment of the theatre, Earlsfort observed

> that from a well-conducted stage, and the times growing more enlightened, he hoped soon to see the prelate entertained with the representation of

19 *Irish Lords' Proceedings*, i, 379.   20 *Irish Lords' Proceedings*, i, 378.
21 *Irish Lords' Proceedings*, i, 379.   22 *Irish Lords' Proceedings*, i, 377.
23 Ibid.   24 *Irish Lords' Proceedings*, i, 377–8.

elegant moral pieces, for that he knew of no law, either of God or man, why the bench of bishops may not frequent a properly regulated theatre.[25]

Following the endorsement by the Lords of the bill on 1 April, Viscount Ranelagh was deputed to advise the lord lieutenant, the duke of Rutland, that the bill was now fit to be certified to London for purposes of receiving the royal assent. That assent was then pronounced on the last day of the current parliamentary session on 8 May.[26]

Section 2 of the Act, as enacted, attempted to list the kinds of performance to be put on in Dublin that would render the impresario responsible under an obligation to seek a patent and, in the absence of the latter, liable to a financial penalty. What is in the nature of an interpretation provision will be examined shortly.

For the moment it is requisite that we set down the precise delineation of the crown's power to issue theatre patents, a delineation to be found in section 1 of the Act which incorporates the measure's preamble as well. It can be safely assumed that the language of this key section was well-known to the parliamentarians who discussed the measure as it passed through the Commons and whose contributions to the debates, as recorded in the *Irish parliamentary register*, add significantly to the bland coverage of the passage of the legislation as noted in the *Commons'* and *Lords' journals*.

'Whereas', this key section reads,

> the establishing a well regulated theatre in the city of Dublin, being the residence of the chief governor or governors of Ireland, will be productive of publick advantage, and tend to improve the morals of the people, be it therefore enacted
>
> …
>
> That it shall and may be lawful to and for his Majesty, his heirs and successors, to grant under the great seal of this Kingdom, for such term not exceeding twenty-one-years, and under such restrictions, conditions, and limitations as to him or them shall seem meet from time to time, and when and as often as he or they shall think fit, one or more letters patent, to one or more person or persons for establishing and keeping one or more well-regulated theatre or theatres, play-house or play-houses in the city of Dublin, and in the liberties, suburbs, and county thereof, and in the county of Dublin.

Contemporary comment on the adoption of the Act to regulate the Stage in the City and County of Dublin is relatively sparse. Robert Hitchcock was one of the

---

25 Ibid., i, 378. Earlsfort also dismissed the notion that any conferment of a monopoly would tend to distress poor players (ibid.).

26 *Lords' jn., Ire.*, v, 752–3.

few who committed their thoughts to print.[27] He was enthusiastic, extolling the circumstance that

> the good guardian of our laws and liberties have lately interposed their authority, to rectify its [the theatre's] abuses, correct its errors, and direct its future efforts to the original design of the drama – TO MAKE THE STAGE THE SCHOOL OF VIRTUE.

The legislation itself, as we have just seen, talked in terms of a properly regulated theatre tending 'to improve the morals of the people'. The self-same language had been employed in a piece of journalism from earlier in the century focusing on the purpose of the theatre besides amusement and instruction, which Walsh tracked down if only to comment, and comment wryly, that 'this sentiment' – 'to improve the morals of the people' – 'must have come as a surprise to eighteenth-century Dublin theatre-goers who up to then had hardly realised that a visit to the theatre was expected to correspond with a visit to church'.[28] Without necessarily aligning oneself with the tone of scepticism that Walsh for one was induced to adopt at this point, it is nevertheless undeniable that with the enactment of the Dublin Stage Regulation Act, and the establishment of the regime of control that it initiated, a further milestone in the regulation of theatre in Ireland had been attained.

27 Robert Hitchcock, *Historical view of the Irish stage from the earliest period ... with theatrical anecdotes*, 2 vols (Dublin, R. Marchbank, W. Folds, 1788–94), i, introduction.
28 T.J. Walsh, *Opera in Dublin, 1705–1797: the social scene* (Dublin, Allen Figgis, 1973), p. 124.

CHAPTER SIX

Performances within the reach of control

LAWYERS AND CENSORS DOWN the centuries, irrespective of the regulatory regime applicable to the stage, confronted one identical problem: understanding the reach of the control aimed at stage performances by the salient regulatory regime. In the modern Irish Republic the decision on the categorisation of a performance can, as we shall subsequently discover, have a bearing on, of all things, the entitlement of the venue in question to host a bar for the sale of alcohol to patrons.[1] As it happens, there has been a long history of this need to wrestle with the problem of definition. When in 1648 parliament in London issued a draconian ordinance directed at the stage, declaring stage-players to be 'rogues' and punishable as such, it aimed at 'the utter suppression and abolishing of all stage-plays and interludes'.[2] Not specifically targeted on the occasion was opera, a loophole capitalised upon by Sir William Davenant (who, we may recall, fought with Ogilby over the Irish Mastership of the Revels at the Restoration),[3] which enabled him to present the first opera seen on the London stage in 1656, *The Siege of Rhodes*.[4] This particular definitional lacuna – if that is how it is to be regarded – was not, as we are about to find out, to be repeated.

The regulatory regime for theatre in Britain, initiated by the Act of 1737 which authorised the issuance of a patent from the crown or a licence from the Lord Chamberlain, and complemented by Acts of 1751 and 1788 sanctioning the issuance of a licence by local justices, was designed to capture within its embrace a considerable variety of kinds of theatrical performance. Whilst the Act of 1737 targeted 'any interlude, tragedy, comedy, opera, play, farce or other entertainment of the stage',[5] that of 1788 was content to employ the broad, unspecific category of 'theatrical representation'. A return to a more specific listing was the feature of the consolidating measure of 1843, which brought the two strands of regulation within a single statute. A stage play for purposes of the issuance of a patent or either kind of licence was now defined as a 'tragedy, comedy, farce, opera, burletta, interlude, melodrama, pantomime or other entertainment of the stage'.[6] The Irish Act of

---

1 See below, ch. 11.
2 C.H. Firth and R.S. Rait (eds), *Acts and ordinances of the Interregnum, 1642–1660, vol. 1: 1642–1649* (London, HMSO, 1911).
3 Above, ch. 1.
4 David Thomas, David Carlton and Anne Etienne, *Theatre censorship: from Walpole to Wilson* (Oxford, OUP, 2007), pp 15–16.
5 S. 1.   6 S. 23.

1786 differed from the British Act of 1737 by adding to the definition contained in the latter 'prelude ..., burletta [and] pantomime'.[7] This legislation also made it clear, as we have seen, that the obligation to obtain a patent did not extend to feats of horsemanship, puppet-shows or such like species of entertainment.[8] 'Burletta' and 'pantomime', it is worth repeating, first make their appearance in any British legislation many years later, in the consolidating statute of 1843. Statute law in the two islands was to differ in one other respect over the significance, so far as possible regulation was concerned, of the venue hosting the theatrical performance. The Irish Act, dealing, it is to be remembered, solely with theatre patents for Dublin city and county, insisted a patent would be requisite for performances put on for gain in any 'theatre, house, booth, tent or other place'.[9] This rule is in marked contrast with the exclusion from the regulatory regime of the consolidating British statute of 1843 of any 'theatrical representation in any booth or show lawfully allowed in any fair, feast or customary meeting'.[10]

A body of case-law was to grow up over the interpretation to be placed on all these words and phrases that brought stage entertainments under licensing control. But before this collection of cases is examined, it is well to set down, from among the papers sent in by Mr Spencer Ponsonby to the select committee of 1866, the intriguing document entitled 'Various entertainments licensed by the Lord Chamberlain from 1628 to 1866':[11]

1628	Comedyes, Historyes, Interludes, and other Stage Playes
1635	Fresh Comedians to act Interludes and Stage Playes
1666	Rope Vaulting on a Stage
1672	Drolls and Interludes
1695	Licence to Betterston and others for Tragedyes, Comedyes, Playes
1731	Interludes, Opera, and all other theatrical and musical Entertainments whatever
1738	A Puppet Show
1745	Pantomime Entertainments and Concerts
1749	French and Italian Comedies and Comic Operas
1755	Burlettas or Italian Comedies
1759	Scott's Musical Pastoral, 'The Gentle Shepherd'
1760	Concert of Music at Mr Cock's Great Room in Spring Garden
1773	Concerts and Assemblies
1781	Masquerades
1792	Dibdin's 'Recitation, Singing, and Music' by himself alone
1794	Astronomical Lectures
	Public Music and Dancing
1795	Readings and Music

7 S. 2.   8 S. 4.   9 S. 2.   10 S. 23.
11 *Report from the select committee to inquire into the working of Acts of Parliament for licensing theatres*, HC 1866, xvi, 1, appendix B, p. 286.

1799	Oratorios
1805	Juvenile Entertainment of Burlettas, Operatic Ballets, Pantomime and Action Songs, by Children under 12.
1806	Dancing, Song, Recitations, Optical and Mechanical Exhibitions, at Adelphi
1807	Music, Dancing, Pantomime and Horsemanship
1810	Mechanical Exhibitions, Hydraulic Equipment, and Artificial Fireworks
1811	A Ballet Performance
1816	Fantoccini, with Music and Singing
	Music, accompanying an Exhibition of Mechanical and Picturesque Views
1818	Melodrama and Comic Pantomime
1821	Ventriloquism, Music, Dancing and Experimental Philosophy
1822	Fancy Dress Ball
1823	Horsemanship and Rope-dancing
1824	Extempore Recitation
1825	Music, Dancing and Assemblies
1828	A Dramatic Concert
1833	Monodramatic Entertainment
1839	Promenade Concerts
1840	Magical Experiments, and Legerdemain
1842	Equestrian Performances and Trained Animals

Ponsonby's document adds a footnote. 'The word "Spectacle"', we are told, 'also issued in some of the Licences.'

The sorts of performance reckoned by presenters to fall foul of these various prescriptions generated a small body of case-law which is worth revisiting. It does not seem that any difficulties under this head surfaced in Ireland – at least there are no recorded instances of this. It is otherwise with the concept of 'other place of entertainment' for purposes of the liquor licensing laws.[12] In England, it was to be different, theatre managers proving unusually adept at mounting spectacles which they, or at least their legal advisers, argued fell outside the prohibited list. That the legislation was difficult to enforce, especially when the stage entertainment relied little, if at all, on the written word, can scarcely be doubted. And as the years rolled by, this certainly proved to be the case in London, where, as Kwint was to express it, 'An indiscriminate blend of lyrical genres, cheerfully disrespectful of cultural hierarchy, persisted within London's expanding opportunities for commercialised leisure and pleasure'.[13] Even Lords Chamberlain could express unease at the hand it was theirs to play. In evidence to the 1866 select committee Lord Sydney, Lord

12 See below, ch. 11.
13 Marius Kwint, 'The legitimization of the circus in late Georgian England', *Past & Present*, 174 (2002), 72 at 80.

Chamberlain, 1859–66 and 1868–74, confessed that he found it unclear what was a 'stage play'.[14]

Dion Boucicault, in evidence to the same committee, confessed to a degree of bewilderment as well. The singing of a song by one man attired in simple evening dress and accompanying himself on a piano could be viewed, Boucicault seems to have argued, as the representation of a dramatic piece, and thus violative of the copyright entitlements bestowed under the Dramatic Authors Act.[15] But would it, he inquired, be within the species of entertainment for which a licence was required under the 1843 Act?[16] Boucicault attempted to shed further light on this vexed question in further testimony. 'Taking a soliloquy out of Shakespeare's plays, and delivering it at a literary institution', he was satisfied, 'would not be an infringement of the 6 & 7 Victoria.' He went on:[17]

> Anybody may read a play, even in costume, and read it with a scene behind him, with all the appliances of a theatre; but if, instead of reading the character, he gesticulates, and pretends to be the character, immediately he begins to act, and the drama is constituted.

Ballet performances at the King's Theatre in the Haymarket in London in the early 1790s posed the critical question: did they or did they not fall within the range of the kinds of performance listed in the legislation? In *Gallini v. Laborie*, decided in 1793,[18] the King's Bench, presided over by Lord Kenyon, the lord chief justice, reckoned that they did. The matter arrived before the court in an oblique way: a dispute over the non-fulfilment of a contract. The manager of the theatre, Gallini, sought to avoid liability on the basis that Laborie's agreement to dance ballets was an illegal contract since no patent was in force for the King's Theatre at the time.

A verdict in favour of Gallini was pronounced after a trial before Lord Kenyon and a jury, and this was upheld when the matter was reviewed by the full court (Lord Kenyon, Ashurst, Buller and Grose JJ). At this review the leading judgment was given by Lord Kenyon who, unsurprisingly, backed the stance he had adopted earlier. For him there was no doubt that a patent was requisite, since ballet indubitably fell within the notion of an 'entertainment of the stage'. 'The intent of the Legislature', he argued, 'manifestly was to put all places of public diversion under the controul of the magistracy'.[19] It was a complete misapprehension to believe that the legislation had only been aimed at dramatic performances. An allusion to the circumstances in which the statute of 1737 was adopted then follows. 'Possibly', the chief justice continued,

14 *1866 select committee report*, p. 268.
15 3 & 4 Will. IV, c. 15 (Bulwer Lytton's Act). On this Act, see below, ch. 15.
16 *1866 select committee report*, p. 153.   17 Ibid.
18 5 Term Rep 242, 101 Eng Rep 136. See further W.N.M. Geary, *The law of theatres and music-halls* (London, Stevens, 1885), pp 79–80.
19 5 Term Rep at 243, 101 Eng Rep at 137.

the notion of the statute's being confined to such productions [dramatic performances following a script] may have arisen from the occasion which is supposed to have given birth to it; and which was, some plays by Mr Gay and others, levelled against the existing administration, with the intention of bringing it into disrepute with the public.[20]

Two years later, in a review of a conviction under the statute of 1737, arising from a performance at the Amphitheatre in Birmingham, Lord Kenyon distanced himself from the remarks he had uttered in *Gallini v. Laborie*. *The King v. Handy*[21] focused on the classification to be accorded a performance of 'tumbling'. (The tumbling is not described in the report, but it sounds like a protracted display of acrobatics.) Handy's conviction and fine of £50 was reviewed on *certiorari*. Counsel, in supporting the conviction, relied on the two great objects which they claimed had been behind adoption of the 1737 Act:[22]

> The one was to suppress the representation of any play, farce or interlude, that might injure the morals of the public; the other was to prevent the assembling together of a large number of the lower orders of the people in places of public entertainment without regard to the particular thing to be represented.

The consequence followed, as surely as night the day:[23]

> And those objects cannot be attained unless the Act is held to extend to every species of stage entertainment.

Counsel for Handy argued simply that 'tumbling' was not an 'entertainment of the stage'. For good measure, he added the contention that there was no evidence whatsoever that the object of the statute had been to prevent numerous assemblies.[24]

Without, on this occasion, entering into the question of the exact purpose that the Act of 1737 was thought to serve, Lord Kenyon observed that he had gone much too far in *Gallini v. Laborie* in arguing that every species of stage entertainment came within the prohibition. Tumbling did not meet the criteria, no more than would have fencing on stage.[25] The chief justice added two further points. In *Gallini v. Laborie* he had argued that it was possible to entirely disregard the prior censorship provisions of the 1737 Act which required 'a true copy' of what it was intended to perform to be furnished in advance to the Lord Chamberlain when the central question was simply whether ballet was an

20 Ibid. There was to be another case where a contract to perform in an unlicensed theatre was held unenforceable: *De Begnis v. Armistead* (1833) 10 Bing 107; 131 Eng Rep 846 (the Amphitheatre, Liverpool). See Geary, *Law of theatres*, pp 81–4.
21 6 Term Rep 286; 101 Eng Rep 556.   22 Ibid.   23 Ibid.
24 6 Term Rep at 287; 101 Eng Rep at 556.   25 Ibid.

'entertainment of the stage'. Here, then, the censorship provision was an irrelevancy. Now in *Handy*'s case he elevated the point into something of real substance: how could 'a true copy' of a tumbling performance be drawn up and forwarded? It could not.[26] Lord Kenyon's final point, in retrospect, may not appear too convincing either. The Act of 1737, he observed, was a penal statute, 'and we cannot extend it to entertainments not existing when the statute was made'.[27]

One wonders what Kenyon and his colleagues would have made of *Une Étoile*, one of the 'lost' Ballets of Covent Garden known to have been performed there in June 1854.[28] It was described at the time as a new 'Divertissement of a very gay and sparkling character' in which the action was carried on 'through a variety of choreographic forms, as a grand Pas de Fascination, a Beechanalian Waltz, etc., by Stella and her sister Stars.' Perhaps it would have passed muster, in the light of the rethink represented by *The King v. Handy*.

Inadequacies in the definition section in the consolidating Act of 1843 were cited by justices in Margate in dismissing an information against a local impresario in 1860, a decision which was reversed by the Queen's Bench: *Thorne v. Colson*.[29] Thorne, the licensee of the Theatre Royal in Margate, a theatre patented under Margate's local Act of 1786,[30] moved an information against Colson on the grounds that the latter had kept a place of public resort for the public performance of stage plays unpatented and unlicensed – the offence as set out in section 2 of the Act of 1843.

Colson owned the 'London Bazaar' in the High Street in Margate, an emporium that sold toys and assorted fancy goods. In August 1860 a stage had been put in place for performances of a drawing-room entertainment, entitled *Not Quite So Fast, or Errors Redeemed, a Story of the Heart*, an entertainment in four scenes acted by a Rosina Pennell and a Mr Reginald St Clair. The law report furnishes a brief account of a performance. After the curtain opened and the playing of the piano ceased, the two actors appeared and throughout the four scenes played different characters – 14 in total – in different costumes. Sometimes the actors uttered soliloquies, sometimes there was dialogue. Among parts played by Mr St Clair was that of Ms Pennell's lover, sometimes behaving honourably, sometimes not. Seats at the Bazaar ranged from 3s. to 2. Bills of performance handed out included reviews of the entertainment. The Margate justices termed the whole a 'duologue', and dismissed the information brought by Thorne largely on the grounds that 'duologue' was not listed in the definition section of the 1843 Act. The Queen's Bench was to disagree. This was a 'stage play', they held, and unpatented or unlicensed performances were against the law. The matter was returned to the justices with orders to convict, subject to their being satisfied that

26 6 Term Rep at 287; 101 Eng Rep at 556.
27 6 Term Rep at 288; 101 Eng Rep at 557.
28 Saint et al., *A history of the Royal Opera House Covent Garden, 1732–1982* (London, Royal Opera House, 1982), p. 65.
29 (1861) 25 JP 101.   30 26 Geo. III, c. 29.

Colson could be treated as the keeper of the venue when the performance occurred. (He had, it would seem, been in London at the time, and it was his wife who had sanctioned the arrangements.)

A somewhat similar case brought at the same time, and which resulted in another conviction, was referred to in the evidence to the 1866 select committee by Mr F. Stanley, the solicitor for the London Music Hall Proprietors Protection Association.[31] A prosecution had been brought under the 1843 Act against the proprietor of the London music-hall known as Canterbury Hall. At a Christmas show two people appeared on a stage acting no less than 17 or 18 different characters and adopting successive quick changes of dress. Fines of £5 were imposed. What irked Stanley most of all, however, was that the application by the music-hall in question to procure a licence for this and comparable shows had been turned down – impresarios were thus obliged to function in a 'catch 22' environment – 'damned if you do, damned if you don't'.

A variety show produced at the same venue some years later did, however, pass muster. This show, dubbed *Robin Hood*, consisted in the main of impromptu dialogue. Matter forming the sketch was written from time to time on slips of paper and passed between the two actors and then destroyed. Any plot was not at all well connected. There was a great deal of extraneous detail brought into the performances with allusions to passing events. Every now and then the actors would burst out into popular song. There was no conviction.[32]

Two separate cases that came before the courts in England in 1865 afforded yet further opportunities for classification on the kinds of performance where a patent under the 1737 Act or a licence by local justices under the statute of 1788 (on which more anon) was to be deemed necessary. In *Day v. Simpson*[33] the examination of the spectacle in question concerned an entertainment, *Pepper's Ghost*, put on by James Day, described as a licensed victualler, in a concert hall he occupied in Birmingham. Mercer Hampson Simpson, the Younger, was the proprietor of a licensed theatre in Birmingham, and he had initiated the prosecution of Day for violating, as he, Simpson, saw it, the relevant rules. Day's concert hall was licensed under a clause in the Birmingham Improvement Act. But such licence did not cover any stage play (the 1737 Act) or any theatrical representation (the 1788 Act), if that indeed was what Day had presented.

Patrons entering the concert hall paid 6*d*., which entitled them to a seat and drink up to the value of 3*d*. Seats were provided at tables around the auditorium and also in a gallery. When the curtain rose, the scene revealed a storm at sea. The representation of a man, not a live person, but in theatrical parlance, a 'double', was seen to be swimming. The storm subsides to disclose a drop scene with a clear lake in the background. A character, dressed as a Greek prince, appears, and, seemingly emerging from a shipwreck, speaks a few lines, to which an attendant

---

31 *1866 select committee report*, p. 100. 32 Geary, *Law of theatres*, p. 23.
33 10 CB (ns) 680, 144 Eng Rep 612, 1 Bar Reports 386.

responds. In due course, a king, a princess and a chorus emerge, and the 'entertainment' proceeds to explore themes of love, courtship and matrimony. What was remarkable about the production was that, with the exception of two of the dramatis personae mentioned, all the others performed from a chamber below the stage – a complicated pattern of lenses and mirrors being employed to reflect all of these on to mirrors at the back of the stage. There was a great deal of dancing, music and singing. No changes of scenery or of dress occurred. Day, in his appeal, was to argue that *Pepper's Ghost* was no entertainment of the stage, but rather an entertainment below it.

The Queen's Bench affirmed the conviction. While saying so, Chief Justice Erle went out of his way to declare that he was 'desirous of not laying down anything calculated to prevent the exhibition of ingeniously contrived spectacles for the amusement of the public'.[34] For Mr Justice Byles even a lecture on stage with scenery and footlights would have been caught by the relevant legislation.[35]

A dancing extravaganza produced at the Alhambra theatre in London, which possessed neither a patent nor a licence for 'stage plays', only a licence for music and dancing under legislation of 1751 (25 Geo. II, c. 36), engaged the attention of the courts also in 1865.[36] Here we are fortunate in being given by the law report a fairly detailed description of this extravaganza. There were, it would appear, various platforms at the back of the stage that enabled performers to come down from a considerable height. A cascade of water descended from a place some thirty feet high. There were palm trees and rocks and the whole represented an oriental landscape. The law report continues with this graphic description of what happened once the performers made their entrance. The description is included in 'the facts' proved before the London police court on 2 June 1865:

> Sixty to seventy females dressed in the ordinary costume of theatrical ballet-dancers, came down through a large opening at the top of the platform painted as rocks, and danced down them to the stage. They were not dressed alike. Some had gold-tissue skirts over white. Those who first descended danced on the stage in a serpentine figure, so as to occupy the whole front of the stage, till all had come down. When all were down, they defiled to the right and left. Four were placed on each side in front of the proscenium, with property, viz., sham musical instruments, in their hands, supposed to be played by them to the dancers. The dancers began to dance the pas des piognards, each lady armed with two daggers, charging through each other's ranks, striking right and left with the daggers in mimic warfare, then in front as far as the foot-lights.
> This performance of the dagger-dance ended in several of the females standing over others as if in triumph, and retiring, when others came forward

34 10 CB (ns) at 691, 144 Eng Rep at 616.   35 Ibid.
36 *Wigan v. Strange* (1865) LR 1 CP 175. The case is alluded to in the *1866 select committee report*: see p. 14. See, too, Geary, *Law of theatres*, pp 20–2.

holding property, viz., sham palm-leaves, in their hands, and danced waving them, and formed an avenue, as expecting an arrival. Then, a lady dancer, who at regular theatres would be called *la première danseuse*, passed down the avenue formed by the other dancers, who retired while she performed a pas seul with gestures. The other dancers then formed groups, placing the palm-leaves so as to represent the opening of a flower. Others had a property called a pallisade, and danced with it so as to represent a basket of flowers. Several more pas seuls having been executed by the *première*, the rest went through other evolutions, and the performance concluded.

The police magistrate who had furnished the Court of Common Pleas with this description of the 'entertainment' had, in the end, declined to convict. In the Common Pleas, all four judges agreed that the authority of Strange's music and dancing licence had not been overstepped. There issued, therefore, no order to the police magistrate to convict. That the court did not find it easy to adjudicate on the question that had been brought before it is best brought out in the judgment of Mr Justice Willes who, it will be seen, did eventually place considerable reliance on the sense of the relevant definition section (that in the 1843 Act). 'One cannot help being struck', the judge began,[37]

> with the justice of the remark ... as to the difference between an entertainment <u>of</u> and an entertainment <u>on</u> the stage.

'It must at once be acknowledged',[38] he continued,

> that we cannot construe the statute by reference to what has ordinarily been represented on the stage. In our own times, we have seen exhibited on the stage of theatres of the highest class entertainments having nothing of a dramatic character, such as the wonderful performance of Paganini on the violin, and that of Van Amburgh and his lions.

He went on:[39]

> We cannot, therefore, construe this section by ascertaining whether the 'ballet divertissement', as here described, was represented ordinarily or occasionally on the stage at the time when the 6 & 7 Vict., c. 68 [the 1843 Act] passed, and then come to the conclusion, that, because it was, therefore it is an entertainment of the stage within the meaning of the interpretation clause, s. 23. Those words must be construed to mean entertainments such as those before expressed, viz., tragedy, comedy, farce, etc., which are all of a dramatic character. No doubt, a ballet representing a connected story by acting would properly be called an entertainment of the stage, though not a

37 LR 1 CP at 183.   38 At 183–4.   39 At 184.

word was spoken. On the other hand, mere dancing on a stage, without a story, would not.

These decisions of the courts in 1865 inevitably attracted the attention of the select committee that sat a year later, one witness being content to observe then that the litigation that had taken place over new kinds of entertainment put on at music-halls was due 'to the obscurity of the definition of the word "stage plays" in 6 & 7 Victoria, c. 68 and of "music, dancing and public entertainment" in 25 George II, c. 30'.[40]

Despite the force of these various precedents, it continued to be asked whether certain kinds of stage entertainment and, in particular, ballets and groups of sketches, were properly or advisedly caught by the regulatory regime that insisted on the possession of a theatre licence. The matter was taken up by a later select committee who in a report of 1892 made it plain that they favoured reform – a reform that would enable shows of that limited character to be exempted from the requirement of obtaining a theatre licence. 'In that class of music halls ... referred to as theatres of varieties', the committee urged that it should

> be made lawful, without the possession of a licence for stage plays, publicly to present ballet, ballet divertissement, or ballet of action, and those performances commonly called sketches, if the duration of each such performance shall not exceed forty minutes, and no more than six principal performers take part therein, and if there shall be an interval of at least twenty minutes between any two such sketches, and no two sketches performed on the same evening at such place of public entertainment shall have a connected plot.[41]

This recommendation, applicable as much to Ireland as to Britain, was not, however, to be acted on, for nothing was done.

It has already been remarked that no disputes over the reach of the requirement to possess a theatre licence, such as are recorded for England, appear to have surfaced in Ireland or at least to have become notorious. It is hard to accept even so that they did not occur. Entertainment – if that is what it can be called – furnished by a succession of stage hypnotists is part of the history of theatre in Dublin as elsewhere.

Further research necessarily would have to be carried out to establish whether anyone the likes of the Memory Man in Hitchcock's film of John Buchan's *The Thirty-nine Steps* kept them company.[42] Venues for performances of this sort were, of course, at a premium, and the explanation for the absence of controversy may lie not so much in officialdom turning a blind eye, but rather in the performances

40 *1866 select committee report*, p. 282.
41 *Report from the select committee on theatres and places of entertainment, 1892*, HC xviii, 1 at p. vi.
42 He makes no appearance in the dénouement in Buchan's novel of 1916.

themselves being restricted to theatres that already possessed a patent or licence. In *Ulysses*, Leopold Bloom is made to recall a circus performance in the context of what he recognised as 'the irreparability of the past'. 'Once', we are told,[43]

> At a performance of Albert Henzler's circus in the Rotunda, Rutland Square, Dublin, an intuitive particoloured clown in quest of paternity had penetrated from the ring to a place in the auditorium where Bloom, solitary, was seated and had publicly declared to an exhilarated audience that he (Bloom) was his (the clown's) papa.

Any legal difficulty linked to Henzler's circus may have been cancelled out once notice was taken of the venue. More likely, since this could well not have been a charity performance (and thus exempted from regulation under section 3 of the Irish Act of 1786), officialdom would have been prepared to treat the circus as within the contemplation of the second exempting section in the Act of 1786, section 4, with its reference to 'feats of horsemanship, puppet-show or such like species of entertainment'. On the other hand, as we are shortly to discover, one of the earlier Irish theatre patents was requested, and was obtained, for a circus entertainment, Astley's.[44]

So long as prior censorship existed in Britain, finding the right category into which to place the particular performance on stage remained a not inconsiderable legal challenge. And the precedents such as they were, were by no means dead letters. This is plain from one of the last prosecutions to be undertaken against a theatre manager and producer – a prosecution involving a revue entitled *Folies Strip-Tease* put on at the Royal Pavilion in Blackpool.[45] The script of a revue *Nite Life, New York* had been submitted to the Lord Chamberlain for his approval. Changes called for occasioned a delay, and in the interval the new revue *Folies Strip-Tease* was put on in its place. The police reported that the script of the new revue was largely the same as that submitted for *Nite Life, New York*, with certain innocuous variety acts being replaced by a series of striptease performances. A prosecution followed at which the defendants pleaded not guilty on the grounds, inter alia, that *Nite Life, New York* was not a stage play and that *Folies Strip-Tease* was a completely different entertainment. The casuistry, if such it was, availed them not at all. A conviction and fines resulted.

43 James Joyce, *Ulysses* (London, The Bodley Head, 1960), p. 816.   44 Below, ch. 8.
45 J. Johnston, *The Lord Chamberlain's blue peril* (London, Hodder & Stoughton, 1990), p. 185.

CHAPTER SEVEN

Theatre in the provinces

THE PREOCCUPATION OF BOTH THE British Act of 1737 and the Irish Act of 1786 was with the regulation of the stage in the two capital cities of London and Dublin. The question of legal provision for theatres in provincial centres was not immediately addressed, constituting a lacuna in the statute-book that contributed, as we shall see, to no small amount of legal uncertainty.

PROVINCIAL THEATRE IN GREAT BRITAIN

In Britain the Act of 1737 envisaged that theatrical performances of the various kinds described, and where the obtaining of a patent from the crown or a licence from the Lord Chamberlain was made mandatory, would be restricted to the city of Westminster, its liberties and to such places where the monarch chanced to reside.[1] This severe geographical restriction was first modified some fourteen years later in the so-called Disorderly Houses Act,[2] but the focus was still metropolis-centred, since the powers conferred by this later legislation on justices of the peace to grant licences of the sort that was germane were restricted to the cities of London and Westminster and within a radius of twenty miles of the two. Section 1 of this cumbersome piece of legislation targeted 'the advertising a reward with no questions asked, for the return of things which have been lost or stolen' – a practice condemned as 'one great cause and encouragement of thefts and robberies'. The next section, section 2, which is relevant in the present context, needs to be set out *in extenso*. 'And whereas the Multitude of Places of Entertainment', the section begins,

> for the lower Sort of People is another great Cause of Thefts and Robberies, as they are thereby tempted to spend their small Substance in riotous Pleasures, and in consequence are put on unlawful Methods of supplying their Wants, and renewing their Pleasures: In order therefore to prevent the said Temptation to Thefts and Robberies, and to correct as may be the Habit of Idleness, which is become too general over the whole Kingdom, and is productive of much Mischief and Inconvenience; Be it enacted by the

1 10 Geo. II, c. 28, s. 5.
2 An Act for the better preventing Thefts and Robberies; and for regulating Places of publick Entertainment; and punishing Persons keeping disorderly Houses, 1751: 25 Geo. II, c. 36.

Authority aforesaid, That from and after the first Day of December one thousand seven hundred and fifty two, any House, Room, Garden or other Place kept for public Dancing, Musick or other publick Entertainment of the like Kind, in the Cities of London and Westminster, or within twenty Miles thereof, without a Licence had for that purpose, from the last preceding Michaelmas Quarter-Sessions of the Peace, to be holden for the County, City, Riding, Liberty or Division in which such House, Room, Garden or other Place is situate (who are hereby authorized and impowered to grant such Licences as they in their Discretion shall think proper) signified under the Hands and Seals of four or more of the Justices there assembled, shall be deemed a disorderly House or Place.

All such licensed venues had to display a notice intimating that they were licensed under the Act;[3] and the venues themselves were prohibited from opening before 5p.m.[4] It was made plain by another section[5] that the legislation was not to be construed to affect the standing of the two theatres royal, Drury Lane and Covent Garden, or that of 'the King's Theatre in the Hay Market'.

As we are about to discover, a succession of *ad hoc* exemptions from the ban laid down in section 5 of the 1737 Act ensured the growth of provincial theatre in England and Scotland, but before the first of these enabling statutes was adopted in 1767, what happened at Bath in 1754 conveyed a salutary lesson: that year saw the successful prosecution of the Orchard Street Theatre in the spa town.[6]

The city of Edinburgh was the first place to benefit from the adoption of the new liberal approach. Section 19 of the general statute dealing with the Scottish capital[7] briefly recited that 'a licensed Playhouse is much wanted in that part of the United Kingdom called Scotland', went on to repeal section 5 of the 1737 Act 'so far as the same respects the City of Edinburgh', before confirming

that it shall and may be lawful to His Majesty, his Heirs and Successors, to grant Letters Patent for establishing a Theatre or Playhouse in the City of Edinburgh, or Suburbs thereof, which shall be entitled to all the Privileges and Subjected to all the Regulations, to which any Theatre or Playhouse in Great Britain is intitled and subjected.

Between 1768 and 1807 a succession of cities and towns benefited from the same strategy: a statutory measure in their favour, containing an exemption from the

3 S. 3: 'licensed under 25 Geo. III, c. 36', and not, understandably, 'licensed under the Disorderly Houses Act'.
4 Ibid.   5 S. 4.
6 David Carlton, David Thomas and Anne Etienne, *Theatre censorship: from Walpole to Wilson* (Oxford, Oxford UP, 2007), p. 41.
7 An Act for extending the Royalty of the City of Edinburgh over certain adjoining lands; and for giving Powers to the Magistrates of Edinburgh for the Benefit of the said City; and to enable His Majesty to grant Letters Patent for establishing a Theatre in the City of Edinburgh, or Suburbs thereof: 7 Geo. III, c. 27.

ambit of section 5 of the 1737 Act, and confirming the entitlement of the crown accordingly to grant a theatre patent in the city or town in question. The statutes in question took on a standard form, some employing the term 'playhouse', others the term 'theatre'. The legislation for Margate in 1786 was a trifle different. For a start, the preamble struck a novel note.[8] 'Whereas', it began,

> the Town and Port of Margate and several of the Villages within the Vicinity of the same have of late Years greatly increased both in Buildings and Inhabitants, owing to the numerous Resort of Persons, who frequent the same on account of the Convenience of Bathing and Salubrity of the Air, And whereas the Inhabitants of the said Town and Port, in order to contribute to the rational Amusement of the Company for resorting thereto, or desirous of having a licensed Playhouse there ...

Second, the legislation restricted the opening of any Playhouse thereby sanctioned to the period between 14 June and 31 October in any year. Theatre in Margate was to be a seasonal summer or early autumn attraction. (We have met such seasonal restrictions, restrictions adopted for a somewhat different purpose, elsewhere.)[9]

The restrictions alluded to in the statutes of 1803 and 1807, dealing with Glasgow and Birmingham respectively, were of a different order altogether. In the case of Glasgow, exemption from the 1737 Act was predicated on the basis that a licensed playhouse there 'would be of convenience to the said city and to the persons resorting there',[10] the legislation itself proceeding to stipulate that the prospective letters patent would be

> subject to such Restrictions as to the Number of Persons to be interested therein [i.e., in the theatre or playhouse], and in the Profits thereof, and with such Privileges, and under such Provisions and Regulations for the due and orderly conducting and managing the same, as to His Majesty shall see fit.

Birmingham's statute of 1807[11] instructed the theatre's prospective proprietors to appoint a committee of management and required the names and addresses of the proprietors to be published in a Birmingham newspaper.[12] Questions of 'Control and inspection' for the theatres in neither centre were left at large. For Birmingham, the pertinent authority was the JPs for the County of Warwick,[13] and

---

8 An Act to enable His Majesty to license a Playhouse within the Town and Port of Margate, in the Isle of Thanet, in the County of Kent, under certain Restrictions therein limited: 26 Geo. III, c. 29.

9 Above, p. 36.

10 An Act to enable His Majesty to grant Letters Patent for establishing a Theatre, under certain Restrictions, in the City of Glasgow, 1803: 43 Geo. III, c. cxlii.

11 An Act to enable His Majesty, His Heirs and Successors, to grant Letters Patent for establishing a Theatre or Playhouse, under certain Restrictions, in the Town of Birmingham, in the County of Warwick, 1807: 47 Geo. III, sess. 2, c. xliv.

12 Ss. 2, 3.   13 S. 4.

for Glasgow 'the Lord Provost, Baillies, Dean of Guild and Deacon Convenor of the Trades of the City of Glasgow, and ... the Sheriff Depute of the County of Lanark for the time being'.[14]

The full list of provincial centres that benefited from this statutory approach was as follows:

1767	Edinburgh[15]
1768	Bath[16]
1768	Norwich[17]
1769	York, Kingston-upon-Hull[18]
1771	Liverpool[19]
1775	Manchester[20]
1777	Chester[21]
1778	Bristol[22]
1778	Margate[23]
1787	Newcastle-on-Tyne[24]
1803	Glasgow[25]
1807	Birmingham[26]

14 43 Geo. III, c. cxlii, s. 2.
15 An Act for extending the Royalty of the City of Edinburgh over certain adjoining Lands, and for giving Powers to the Magistrates of Edinburgh for the Benefit of the said City; and to enable His Majesty to grant Letters Patent for establishing a Theatre in the City of Edinburgh, or Suburbs thereof: 7 Geo. III, c. 27.
16 An Act to enable His Majesty to license a Playhouse in the City of Bath: 8 Geo. III, c. 10.
17 An Act for licensing a Playhouse within the City of Norwich: 8 Geo. III, c. 28.
18 An Act for enabling His Majesty to licence a Playhouse in the City of York; and in the Town and County of the Town of Kingston upon Hull: 9 Geo. III, c. 17.
19 An Act to enable His Majesty to license a Playhouse in the town of Liverpoole, in the County Palatine of Lancaster: 11 Geo. III, c. 16.
20 An Act for enabling His Majesty to license a Playhouse in the town of Manchester in the County Palatine of Lancaster: 15 Geo. III, c. 47.
21 An Act to enable His Majesty to license a Theatre in the City of Chester: 17 Geo. III, c. 14.
22 An Act to enable His Majesty to license a Theatre in the City of Bristol: 18 Geo. III, c. 8. For a few details on theatrical activity in Bristol in the 1760s, i.e., prior to the change authorised in 1778, see Victor, *History of theatres of London*, pp 149–52.
23 An Act to enable His Majesty to license a Playhouse within the Town and Port of Margate, in the Isle of Thanet, in the County of Kent, under certain Restrictions therein limited: 26 Geo. III, c. 29.
24 An Act to enable His Majesty to license a Playhouse in the Town and County of the Town of Newcastle upon Tyne: 27 Geo. III, c. 50.
25 An Act to enable His Majesty to grant Letters Patent for establishing a Theatre, under certain Restrictions, in the City of Glasgow: 43 Geo. III, c. cxlii. This was to be the first of the special statutes to be included not in the series of 'public statutes' but in that of the novel series of 'local and personal statutes'.
26 An Act to enable His Majesty, His Heirs and Successors, to grant Letters Patent for establishing a Theatre or Playhouse, under certain Restrictions, in the Town of Birmingham, in the County of Warwick: 47 Geo. III, sess. 2, c. xliv.

Concurrently with these developments, a more general sanctioning of dramatic performances throughout the provinces in Britain was authorised by statute in 1788[27] – the Act to enable justices of the peace to license theatrical representations occasionally under the restrictions therein contained – a statute only finally superseded in 1843.[28] 'Whereas divers acts of parliament [i.e., those in the list set out above stretching from 1767 to 1787]', it is recited in the Act of 1788,

> have since [the 1737 Act] been solicited and obtained for divers cities, towns and places for exempting them respectively from the provisions of said law, And whereas it may be expedient to permit and suffer, in towns of considerable resort theatrical representations for a limited time and under regulation; in which, nevertheless, it would be highly impolitick, inexpedient and unreasonable to permit the establishment of a constant and regular theatre,

the statute then proceeds to bestow a general licensing power on local justices of the peace. Authorisation extended to such plays, etc. as were acted at patent and licensed theatres in the city of Westminster or as had 'in the manner prescribed by law' ... been submitted to the inspection of the Lord Chamberlain.

There were other important constraints. Thus, applicants for such a licence had to give three weeks notice. Licences could not exceed sixty days, and only one licence could be granted in the appropriate administrative area. Other restrictions followed.

No such provincial licensed theatre could be located within 20 miles of London, Westminster or Edinburgh, within 8 miles of any patented or other licensed theatre, within 10 miles of any residence of his majesty, or within 14 miles of Oxford or Cambridge – stipulations the focus of attention in a key lawsuit of 1837 examined above.[29]

Manchester became eligible for the grant of a theatre patent under legislation of 1775, but John Garside Neville, when he put on a production of *Il Barbiere di Seviglia* in December 1829, possessed neither patent under the 1775 Act nor justices' licence under the Act of 1788. For this omission he was to be prosecuted and convicted. *Certiorari* having been obtained, the question of the correctness of that conviction in all the circumstances was strenuously canvassed.[30] Neville's conviction was under section 2 of the 1737 Act, which made it an offence to put on a stage entertainment in the absence of a crown patent or Lord Chamberlain licence. There was considerable force in the objection presented on Neville's behalf. 'As the statute [of 1737]', counsel declared,[31]

27 28 Geo. III, c. 30.
28 An Act for regulating Theatres, 1843: 6 & 7 Vict., c. 68.
29 *Ewing v. Osbaldiston* (1837) 2 My & Cr 53, 40 Eng Rep 561; above, ch. 2.
30 *The King v. Neville* (1830) 1 B & Ad 489, 109 Eng Rep 869.
31 1 B & Ad at 490.

only allowed a patent or license to be granted within a certain portion of the Kingdom [i.e., the city of Westminster], the penalty imposed by that statute for acting without such authority must be restricted to the same limits, and that a party could not be punished for acting without license, in a place where the Act had established no licensing power.

What counsel here omitted to mention, was the circumstances that since 1775 a theatre in Manchester was eligible for a patent. Even so, counsel's argument was a logical deduction from the Act of 1737 itself. It did not however impress the Queen's Bench presided over by Chief Justice Tenterden.[32] The prohibitions in section 2 and section 5 of the 1737 Act on acting without a patent applied everywhere. If Neville had obtained a local licence from the justices and showed it, that would, in the chief justice's estimation, have been assuredly a valid defence.[33] Tenterden's judgment is not without interest on other grounds, for in a short compass he produces his own potted history of theatre regulation in England.[34]

PROVINCIAL THEATRE IN IRELAND

Prior to 1898 when, as we will see, a modest increase was made to the lord lieutenant's licensing jurisdiction,[35] Irish legislation regulating the theatre did so by means exclusively of theatre patents. The legislation of 1786 and 1898 had this in common, however. Both had in contemplation merely Dublin city and county. For the provinces no general legislation was ever introduced either before the Union by the Irish parliament or thereafter by the parliament at Westminster along the lines of the British statute of 1788 to afford local justices the power to grant licences to enable plays to be performed locally – a power that was to be transferred to county councils and other local authorities a century later. In view of what is now known of the growth of theatre in sundry Irish provincial centres, this legislative lacuna is something of a surprise. As we shall soon discover, Northern Ireland alone was to rectify the situation so far as its jurisdiction was concerned in 1927.

Charting this growth was a specific concern of early historians of the Irish theatre. La Tourette Stockwell, basing herself, largely, it would seem, on the researches of W.J. Lawrence, arrived at the following conclusions.[36] Cork had its first theatre in 1713, in the great cellar or malt house and the upper part of the dwelling-house of John King, a 'joyner', but only its first permanent theatre in 1736. Belfast had its first *c*.1731, the evidence for which was found in an entry for that year in the burial records for the First Presbyterian Church (burial of Mrs

---

32 Who sat with Parke, Taunton and Pattesen JJ.
33 1 B & Ad at 495.   34 1 B & Ad at 494–6.
35 Below, p. 117.
36 La Tourette Stockwell, *Dublin theatres and theatre customs* (Kingsport TX, Kingsport Press, 1938), p. 359, n. 8.

Johnes from 'the play howse').[37] Drogheda witnessed its first performances in 1735 when Dublin's Smock Alley visiting troupe performed tri-weekly in the Crown and Thistle Inn. The same troupe visited Newry the same year, but the town opened its first permanent theatre several years later (1769). Limerick had its first visit from a different troupe, the Aungier Street company in 1736, but inaugurated its first permanent theatre in 1770. The Smock Alley troupe took in Londonderry on a northern tour in 1741, but the city opened up its first permanent theatre only in 1774. A company 'recruited by a widow, Mrs Parker' performed for the first time in Galway in 1741. The same year the playhouse in Waterford was advertised for sale.

Clark, in his monumental survey, *The Irish stage in the county towns*, furnishes further details for the early development of the theatre in a number of the venues listed by Stockwell – Cork, Belfast, Newry, Limerick, Londonderry, Galway and Waterford – and breaks fresh ground with information relating to Ennis and Kilkenny. Morash, in turn, is able to add details on theatrical performers recorded before the end of the eighteenth century in the following places, not previously documented – Antrim, Lisburn, Wexford, Sligo, Athlone, Castlebar, Clonmel, Tralee, Youghal, Bray and New Ross.[38]

As already remarked, there was to be no general legislation, but in two instances local acts of parliament sought to rectify the deficiency. The Cork Improvement Act of 1868,[39] though this was by no means to be anticipated from the verbose language of its long title –

> An act to enable the mayor, aldermen and burgesses of the borough of Cork to make a diversion in the line of the Cork, Blackrock and Passage Railway; to authorize Agreements with the Harbour Commissioners; to define and extend the Powers of the Corporation in reference to water supply; to raise further moneys; to alter and amend the existing Acts relating to the borough; and for other purposes –

introduced clarity in the matter so far at least as Cork was concerned. Section 172 of the Act thus cast an obligation to obtain a licence from the corporation on any person who had or kept

> any house or other place of public resort [within the city] … for the performance of stage plays or other theatrical representations, or any circus or any place for entertainments in the nature of dramatic entertainments, or for any place of public resort kept or used for public dancing, music, or other entertainment of a like kind … into which admission is obtained by payment of money.

37 J.C. Greene, *Theatre in Belfast, 1736–1800* (Bethlehem, PA, Lehigh UP, London, Associated UP, 2000), p. 20.
38 Morash, *History of Irish theatre*, p. 68.
39 31 & 32 Vict., c. xxxiii.

The succeeding three sections of the Act continued the focus on theatre in Cork. Section 173 dealt with the theatre licence as such; section 174 gave the corporation the power to prohibit smoking in theatres in their bye-laws; and section 175 conferred a power of entry into any unlicensed theatre. In a modern case, such Cork licences not being obtained from 'justices of the peace' entailed that the provisions of the Excise Act of 1835[40] did not take effect there: this had implications so far as liquor licensing was concerned – the legality of the sale of alcohol in the Cork Opera House bar.[41]

In Belfast's Improvement Act, adopted some twenty-three years earlier,[42] a section similar to Cork's section 172 of 1868 betrays an identical preoccupation with the unlicensed theatre. Section 242 of this Act of 1845 thus gave power to two justices of the peace to order the police

> to enter any house or room kept or used ... for stage plays or dramatic entertainment or for any public show or exhibition into which admission is obtained by payment of money, and which is not a licensed theatre or a building authorised by the mayor to be used for such purposes.

Keepers of such 'house or room' ran the risk of a £20 fine, or in default 2 months imprisonment with or without hard labour; and performers a 40s. fine. It is a sign of the times that the very next section in the Belfast Act is the proscription of 'the fighting, or baiting of lions, bears, badgers, bulls, cocks, dogs or other animals'.[43] Nowhere in the body of the Act is there to be found any clause casting a positive obligation on the theatrical impresario actually to obtain a licence. But the inference can certainly be drawn from the language of section 242 that that now had to be done. It was certainly the view of Mr Michael Gunn, the manager of the Gaiety Theatre in Dublin, who touched on the vexed question of the licensing of provincial theatre in Ireland in his evidence to the parliamentary select committee in 1892,[44] an account that was to be backed by that committee in their report.[45]

A little more detail regarding the authorisation for theatrical performances in Belfast is to be gleaned from Clark's account of the growth of provincial theatre in Ireland down to 1800. Hitchcock tells us of a trip to Belfast by Duval's Smock Alley troupe in 1736,[46] a reference that squares with Clark's assertion that some years before 1740 a playhouse, known as The Vaults, had been opened in Belfast at the bottom of High Street on the right-hand side close to the River Lagan.[47] Ten years later, there is a further reference to drama being performed, 'by', as it is put,

---

40 5 & 6 Will. IV, c. 39. See, too, below ch. 11.
41 *Cork Opera House plc v. Revenue Commissioners*, Hedigan J., 21 Nov. 2007.
42 An Act for the improvement of the borough of Belfast, 1845: 8 & 9 Vict., c. cxlii.
43 Ibid., s. 242.
44 *Report from the select committee on theatres and places of entertainment*, 1892, HC xvii, 1 at 233.
45 Ibid., p. iv (4).   46 Hitchcock, *Historical view of the Irish stage*, i, 97.
47 Clark, *Irish stage in the county towns*, p. 216. See now generally Greene, *Theatre in Belfast*.

'the Permission of the Worshipful Sovereign' (the office the equivalent of mayor).[48] In 1769, at the conclusion of a countrywide tour, that had already taken in Waterford, Kilkenny, Drogheda, Sligo and Derry, Thomas Ryder, then the manager at Smock Alley, planned an appearance by his troupe of actors in Belfast, and deputed the actor John O'Keeffe to seek permission in advance, again from Belfast's sovereign.[49] O'Keeffe, in his autobiography, furnishes an account of his mission.[50] In none of any of this is there a mention of a possible role being played by the Master of the Revels, despite the fact that successive patents expressly conferred on the office-holder countrywide responsibilities for theatres and performances at them. This was to change in 1792 when Michael Atkins who had been the manager at Belfast since 1773 successfully thwarted the attempt by Richard Daly, the holder of the first patent issued under the 1786 Act, and still, technically it would appear, the Deputy Master of the Revels, to add the theatre in Belfast to his existing empire of Theatres Royal at Cork, Limerick, Newry and Waterford as well, of course, to the Theatre Royal in Dublin.[51] Clark, in his account of the business, prints the letter of Dr Haliday, a local supporter of Atkins, to the earl of Charlemont, seeking his assistance in the campaign to defeat the machinations of Daly. Daly, Haliday wrote,[52]

> is a Tyrant eager to invade foreign Territories; the other [i.e., Mr Atkins] is a mild Monarch tender of his Subjects, and wishes only to defend himself – he has been known among us for a length of years and is universally esteem'd as a good and just man, and a humane, liberal manager – if your Lordship can help him and us in this business, I need not solicit you to do it.

Atkins, curiously, had sought the issuance of a patent to keep Daly at bay – something which under the then state of Irish law was scarcely on offer. He secured no patent, but, as Clark was to express it, 'his representations fully headed off whatever designs Daly might have intended'.[53]

The transition from sovereign to mayor as the source of permission for theatrical performances in Belfast is likely to have caused no hassle at all, but, as we are about to discover, inferring a power to license theatres from such oblique and opaque language as is to be found in the pertinent section of the Belfast Act of 1845, does indeed present a challenge that is not easily surmountable judicially.

Gunn's evidence to the select committee in 1892 merits further attention.[54] The situation in Cork was clear-cut, Gunn averred, because of the express authority

48 Clark, *Irish stage in the county towns*, p. 217.   49 Ibid., p. 228.
50 John O'Keeffe, *Recollections of the life of John O'Keeffe, written by himself*, 2 vols (London, Henry Colburn, 1826), i, 197, 200–1.   51 Clark, *Irish stage in the county towns*, p. 271.
52 Haliday to Charlemont, 26 Apr. 1792: R.I.A., Original correspondence of James, late earl of Charlemont, vi (2nd series), no. 16, quoted Clark, *Irish stage in the county towns*, p. 271. See too Greene, *Theatre in Belfast*, p. 29.
53 Clark, *Irish stage in the county towns*, p. 271; Greene, *Theatre in Belfast*, p. 29.
54 *Report from the select committee on theatres and places of entertainment*, 1892 HC xviii, 1 at 233.

conferred by the Improvement Act of 1868. Wexford he did not discuss, and the position in Limerick, Waterford and Londonderry, which he does, was not exactly clarity writ large. On Limerick Gunn observed:

> the theatre is stated to have been erected and still exists, by permission of the mayor; but the authority under which the same is licensed I have not been able to discover.

Nor have I. But it is worth noting that in the time of the Master of the Revels, a time that effectively ends in 1817, there is evidence to substantiate the claim that the likes of Richard Daly, in his role as Deputy Master, was in a position to legitimise the stage in Limerick. On Waterford, Gunn was content to remark that the theatre there had been erected under the authority of the corporation and was managed by a committee consisting of four members of that body. In Londonderry the new theatre there had been licensed by the corporation, but he was again unaware of the authority under which they had purported to act.

A little more information on the entire topic may be culled from two official inquiries. In evidence supplied to the royal commission on liquor licensing in 1898, the then Irish solicitor-general, Dunbar Barton, averred that outside Dublin the respective municipal authorities had control over the creation and erection of theatres. Barton asserted specifically corporation control existed in Belfast, Cork, Limerick and Waterford.[55] The matter is revisited by a parliamentary committee in 1909.[56] This committee was concerned with censorship and, in the case of Ireland, what it viewed as the absence of clarity regarding the licensing of Irish provincial theatres. They appear to have been prepared to accept that a power did exist in local justices to exercise the necessary jurisdiction, and this was to continue to be the received wisdom as the solution to the legal enigma. At the hearings held by the 1909 committee, Mr T.P. Le Fanu, the chief clerk at the Irish Office, did draw attention to one development that tended to confirm the existence of this local power of approval.[57] The Public Health Acts Amendment Act of 1890,[58] which recognised a system of licensing for places of public entertainment,[59] had been adopted in both Derry and Waterford. Control of sorts therefore existed there. The measure had not, by 1909 at least, been adopted for Kilkenny, Limerick or Wexford.[60]

Clark's survey of the growth of provincial theatre in eighteenth-century Ireland enables us to pursue the entire question in a little more details. As we have already

---

55 *Royal commission on liquor licensing laws: minutes of evidence with appendices and index*, 1898, HC xxxviii, 527 at 547 (13).
56 *Report from the joint select committee on stage plays (Censorship)*, 1909, HC viii, 451.
57 Evidence of Mr Le Fanu: ibid., p. 187 (677).   58 53 & 54 Vict., c. 59.   59 See s. 51.
60 For more on the power conferred by this Act, see below. In relation to Waterford, note should be taken of Le Fanu's reference in his evidence to the joint select committee on stage plays (censorship), at p. 189 (679), that its corporation had purported to adopt appropriate bye-laws respecting theatre under the Municipal Corporations Act 1840.

implied, involvement of the Master of the Revels despite his seemingly extensive jurisdiction was slight indeed. The successful rebuff of Daly by Belfast's actor-manager Michael Atkins carries the implication that neither the Master nor any of his Deputies possessed any effective authority at all. What Clark tells us about the growth of theatre in the municipal centres he deals with – Galway, Ennis, Limerick, Cork, Waterford, Kilkenny, Newry, Derry as well as Belfast – admits of no other conclusion. There is no involvement at all of State money in the erection or opening of the bewildering array of playhouses to which Clark in his survey introduces us. As Gunn reported in 1892, the corporation at Waterford did indeed bear the cost – some £200 – for the erection in 1784 of a new playhouse and assembly room, a building that still stands.[61] Otherwise, the principal source of backing for the various theatres built or converted in the eighteenth century was the private subscriber. Innumerable subscription lists for playhouses were the order of the day as they were, too, for books. In Limerick, for instance, the new Cornwallis Street theatre, opened in 1770, had cost £600 which had been contributed by 24 gentlemen who, in return, were given free tickets.[62] Tottenham Heaphy, the actor-manager with a base at the time in Limerick,[63] who, one presumes, oversaw the raising of this amount, like other provincial actor-managers of the era, was heavily involved in fund-raising, and striving, sometimes against considerable odds, to make both ends meet. Audiences in Limerick, as elsewhere, could remain unpredictable. In 1824, for a production of *Richard III* at the Assembly House on Charlotte's Quay, the celebrated Shakespearean actor Edmond Kean had been booked for 12 performances; he walked out after 5 nights, citing the sparseness of the audiences.[64] As is clear, the gentry proved the main buttress, but the merchant class could be supportive too, for not all of the latter manifested the 'puritanical indifference' to the stage which Clark found at Kilkenny on the eve of the Union.[65]

What is well documented is the extent to which mayors of towns and cities were brought 'on side' by impresarios seeking local support. It was to be commonly advertised that a particular production or season of drama occurred 'by permission of the mayor'. Newspapers and flyers alike contained that comforting intelligence, which furnishes proof that, largely by default on anyone else's part, the mayors were effectively to establish their own unique licensing jurisdiction. (There was no formal statutory authority for this – a deficit which doubtless mystified both Gunn and the select committee of 1892.)

On one notorious occasion the failure of one prominent actor-manager, travelling with his troupe of actors, to observe local convention and obtain the permission of the mayor before putting on any play did make something of a stir.

---

61 Clark, *The Irish stage in the county towns*, p. 153.
62 Maurice Lenihan, *Limerick, its history and antiquities, ecclesiastic, civil and military, from the earliest ages* (Dublin, Hodges, Smith & Co., 1866), p. 364.
63 For more on Heaphy, see Stockwell, *Dublin theatres*, p. 141.   64 Lenihan, *Limerick*, p. 465.
65 Clark, *The Irish stage in the county towns*, p. 189.

In 1761 Spranger Barry took his Crow Street troupe to Cork, but omitted to seek the customary permission from the mayor, at the time one Joseph Wetherall. Members of the corporation were not amused, and on 3 July they adopted the following resolution:[66]

> Whereas a set of players have lately come to this City, and have printed bills for acting on Monday night next, without asking the Mayor's permission, it is the opinion of this Council that Mr Mayor ought to prevent their acting until they apply for his permission and publish same in their bills.

Barry was not impressed. Two years before, the then Master of the Revels, Robert Ward, had transferred the Theatre Royal patent from Smock Alley to Crow Street, arranging at the same time for the co-managers there, Barry and Henry Woodward, to become Deputy Masters of the Revels. That entailed, as Barry was swift to point out to the authorities at Cork, armed as he was with physical proof of the warrant of deputisation, that he did not need permission of anyone in the country to put on a dramatic performance anywhere. In consequence, Barry threatened to take matters further: perhaps an action at law. This, understandably, concerned the Council, and they agreed on further action on their part in October, in support of the stance of Wetherall's successor as mayor, Andrew Franklin:[67]

> Whereas it is apprehended a suit is intended to be brought against Mr Mayor, for preventing the players from acting in this City, on account of their putting up bills without the Mayor's permission, ordered, that in such case, the Mayor's costs be paid out of the Corporation revenues.

In the end, no lawsuit appears to have been launched and, like a number of Irish controversies both then and later, the heat generated died down, and the conflict between the two sides simply fizzled out. It is possible that the express conferring of a theatre licensing jurisdiction on the Cork authorities in the Act of 1868 may have owed something, however, to these altercations of a century earlier: somebody was in a position to recall the history of the matter and press for the legislative bestowal of an unvarnished, unchallengeable legal authority.

   We must now revert to the situation following the demise of the office of Master of the Revels in 1817, and examine once more the precise status of the theatre in Belfast. Whether section 242 of the Belfast Act of 1845 could in fact be interpreted to confer an actual authority to license theatres represents an historical conundrum which it is not necessary today to resolve. But the general question arises, regarding our ability to deduce any such thing from statutory provisions that are similarly oblique. And that question refuses to go away.

66 *The Council Book of the Corporation of the City of Cork, from 1609 to 1643, and from 1690 to 1800*, ed. Richard Caulfield (Guildford, J. Billing & Sons, 1876), p. 747 (3 July 1761); Hitchcock, *Historical view of the Irish stage*, ii, 41; Clark, *The Irish stage in the county towns*, pp 85–6.
67 *Cork Council Book*, p. 752 (28 Oct. 1761).

The lack in Ireland of any counterpart to Britain's legislation of 1788 bestowing an express power on local justices to license theatres has been responsible for the degree of uncertainty that has attached to the lawfulness of theatrical performances in the Irish provinces. One view – by no means the only one that can be held – is that the matter was indeed clarified by an Act of 1835 which, however, did not deal directly with theatres as such. This was the Excise Act of that year which exempted licensed theatres from the customary requirements of a drinks licence.[68] Section 7 of this measure reads:

> It shall be lawful for the Commissioners and Officers of the Excise ... to grant retail licences to any person to sell beer, spirits, and wine in any theatre established under a Royal Patent, or in any theatre or other place of entertainment licensed by the Lord Chamberlain or by Justices of the Peace, without the production by the person applying for such licence or licences of any certificate or authority for such person to keep a common inn, alehouse, or victualling house.

This section was the subject of interpretation by the Northern Ireland High Court in 1926, following the refusal of the commissioners to grant a drinks licence to the then proprietors of the Londonderry Opera House: *Morrison v. Commissioners of Customs*.[69]

The recorder of Londonderry had previously given those proprietors a licence to put on plays, etc. at the Opera House, but the commissioners, in resisting an order of *mandamus* that a drinks licence should also now issue, argued that the recorder had acted without and in excess of jurisdiction.[70] Their contention was that the Act of 1835 conferred no such power that the recorder had sought to avail of. Counsel for the proprietors of the Opera House argued that ever since the 1835 Act had been passed, the existence of an implied power in local Irish justices to licence theatres had been acted upon, and with this interpretation of the 1835 Act the High Court was to concur. The upshot was an order to the commissioners to issue the drinks licence. It deserves to be noted that in 1993 Mr Justice Geoghegan of the Dublin High Court refused to accept that the 1835 Act had conferred on justices the implied authority that the Northern Ireland High Court in the Morrison case claimed they had: *Point Exhibition Co. Ltd v. Revenue Commissioners*.[71] If it had, the judge argued, there would have been no need for the conferment of an express power to license theatres in the Theatres Act 1843[72] on justices of the peace in England.[73]

Unease in official circles may well have been expressed in Northern Ireland too over the decision in the *Morrison* case, for action was swiftly taken by the legislature

68 5 & 6 Will. IV, c. 39.   69 [1927] NI 115.
70 For earlier difficulties over plans to open a bar at the venue, see below, ch. 11.
71 [1993] 2 IR 551.   72 6 & 7 Vict., c. 68.   73 [1993] 2 IR at 558.

to remove all doubt. A section in liquor licensing legislation of 1927[74] thus, a little unusually perhaps, created an express power to license theatres, a power which was reposed in the local licensing court, described as 'a court of quarter sessions constituted of the county court judge or recorder sitting alone'.[75] Section 12(1) provided:

> A building, hall, room or other premises shall not be used primarily and ordinarily as a theatre or music hall without a licence for such purpose first obtained from the licensing court ... and for the registration of such licence a fee of five shillings shall be paid by the person applying therefor.

Rules on publicity and on the consequence of failing to secure a theatre licence were also laid down.[76]

These arrangements introduced in 1927 were replaced when the licensing of theatres throughout Northern Ireland was placed on a more modern footing by the Theatres (N.I.) Order of 1980.[77] Premises were not to be primarily and ordinarily used as a theatre unless duly licensed. Failure to secure such a licence would lead to the premises being dubbed a 'disorderly house' and to the occupier being rendered liable to a maximum fine of £200.[78] First licences were obtainable from the county court, renewals and transfer from a court of summary jurisdiction.[79] If planning to apply, advance notice was to be given to the clerk of the relevant court, to the appropriate district council, and to the police. Objections were receivable from the council and the police.[80] Were a licence granted, an inscription in large capital letters stating this was a licensed theatre had to be erected in a conspicuous place on the premises. A further condition dictated that the theatre could only be open at the times specified.[81] Other conditions not particularised, could be attached. Licences were made valid for one year. Any breach of conditions could lead to the imposition of a maximum fine of £200 and revocation of the licence.[82]

The Theatres Order of 1980 was superseded by comparable provisions in the Local Government (Miscellaneous Provisions) (N.I.) Order of 1985,[83] a measure that brings together rules on camping sites for travellers, regulations on acupuncture, tattooing and ear-piercing, as well as those that are our immediate concern – licences in respect of all places of entertainment.[84] These latter relate to theatrical performances; dancing, singing and music of all kinds; circuses; and sundry indoor events (mainly sporting). The definition here reads:

> Any entertainment which consists of, or includes, any public contest, match, exhibition, or display of
> (i) Boxing, wrestling, judo, karate or any similar sport,

74 Intoxicating Liquor and Licensing Act (N.I.), 1927: 17 & 18 Geo. V, c. 21.   75 Ibid., sch. 2.
76 Ibid., sch. 2; s.12(2).   77 S.I.1980, no. 190 (N.I. no.1).   78 Art. 3 (1), (2).
79 Art. 4 (1), (2).   80 Art. 4 (3), (4).   81 Art. 5 (2).   82 Art. 5 (3), (4).
83 S.I. 1985, no. 1208 (N.I. no. 15).   84 See Art. 3 and sch. 1.

(ii) Billiards, pool, snooker or any similar game,

(iii) Darts,

(iv) Any other sport or game prescribed for the purposes of this paragraph by an order made by the Department subject to affirmative resolution.

Fearing overreach, the order in council goes on to make it clear that the rule requiring a licence would not apply to 'any music or singing in a place used wholly or mainly for public religious worship or performed as an incident of a religious meeting or service'. Separate arrangements were made to apply in the case of outdoor musical entertainments, but here, too, important caveats were made to apply.[85] The obligation to secure a licence was not mandatory therefore in the case of 'a garden fete, bazaar, sale of work, sporting or athletic event, exhibition, display, etc. whether lasting one day or two or more days.' Nor was it mandatory in the case of a religious meeting or service merely because music or singing was incidental thereto.

The licensing of cinemas, of course, remains governed by the Cinematograph Act 1909.[86]

The twentieth century, it is worth noting, had of course witnessed a virtual expansion in theatrical activity outside centres such as Dublin and Belfast. In 1925 Anew McMaster brought his McMaster Intimate Theatre Co. on an Irish tour, which took in Wicklow, Arklow, Enniscorthy, Wexford, Mallow, Youghal, Cobh, Clonmel and Waterford.[87] The amateur theatre movement took hold at much the same time, leading in 1932 to the establishment of the Amateur Dramatic Association.[88] By 1946 there were amateur dramatic festivals outside Dublin and Belfast in places as far apart as Bundoran, Enniskillen, Sligo, Tubbercurry, Cavan, Dundalk, Athlone, Bray, Limerick, New Ross, Waterford and Killarney.[89] And from the 1970s onwards there were to be established professional companies such as The Druid in Galway and the Red Kettle in Waterford,[90] which were quick to establish their own unique reputations – a state of affairs, in short, very different from what obtained before 1730 and indeed for many years after that.

85 Ibid., cl. 2.   86 9 Edw. VII, c. 30.   87 Morash, *History of Irish theatre*, p. 177.
88 Ibid., p. 192.   89 Ibid., p. 194.   90 Ibid., p. 253.

CHAPTER EIGHT

Dublin theatre patents: the first hundred years and more

RICHARD DALY RECEIVED the first patent to be issued on the strength of the 1786 Act in the autumn of that year. The patent, dated 25 November 1786, was stated to last for 14 years.[1] It authorised Daly to purchase or rent ground for purposes of building a theatre; enabled him to receive such sums as were customarily given at theatrical performances, to pay the actors and to remunerate himself out of moneys made; instructed him to eject all disorderly people out of the company of performers, whose salaries were thenceforward to cease; and to avoid 'giving scandal to morals, to the police, to religion, or to the characters of clergymen which are hereby termed sacred'. If he offended in the latter particular and did not cease so offending, on notice given by the lord lieutenant, the grant, and the privileges and immunities attaching, were to be deemed null and void. The patent itself makes no mention of the financial liabilities Daly also undertook, and to which Gilbert refers: liabilities effectively to compensate the various individuals with investments in Dublin theatres and who had previously petitioned against the introduction of any legislation.[2]

One London newspaper, *au fait* with news across the Irish Sea, commented on the likely confirmation of Daly's patent that the moment Daly was established in it, 'his first provision must be a wardrobe. The apparatus at present under that name would disgrace a barn'.[3] Walsh's claim that, concurrently with Daly being awarded his patent, he was appointed Master of the Revels for 14 years cannot be supported.[4] In 1786 the Master was Samuel Dash, and Dash was succeeded in 1791 by William Meeke, the last holder of the office.[5] What is thought to have been the case is Daly's appointment as Deputy Master, an office which Daly believed, but believed wrongly, gave him the right to lord it over Michael Atkins, the actor-manager prominent in theatrical affairs in Belfast late on in the eighteenth century.[6]

---

1 *Liber munerum publicorum Hiberniae*, vol. 1, pt iii, p. 109. For details of the draft letters patent, see '*A volley of execrations': the letters and papers of John FitzGibbon, earl of Clare, 1772–1802*, ed. D.A. Fleming and A.P.W. Malcomson (Dublin, Irish Manuscripts Commission, 2005), p. 50. On Daly's early career see, inter alia, Claire Tomalin, *Mrs Jordan's profession* (London, Penguin Books, 1995), ch. 1, and Gilbert, *History of Dublin*, ii, 105.
2 Above, chs 3, 4.   3 Quoted, Walsh, *Opera in Dublin, 1705–1798*, p. 260.   4 Ibid.
5 Above, ch. 1.   6 See above, ch. 6.

Within sixteen months of receiving his patent Daly found himself in court arguing against the issuance of a second Dublin patent.[7] In these proceedings, heard in the Court of Chancery in April 1788, Daly urged the lord chancellor to withhold the great seal from this second patent. The patent was designed to accommodate Philip Astley and to permit him during certain months of the year to put on feats of horsemanship, musical pieces, dancing, tumbling and pantomimes. He was not, however, to exhibit 'any regular tragedy, comedy, opera, play or farce' – an exclusion doubtless designed to protect, to some extent at least, the viability of Daly's Theatre Royal. Daly and his counsel mounted a multi-pronged attack. For Astley the legal snares now besetting his plan to set up shop in Dublin were nothing new; from as early as 1773 he had faced prosecution and other forms of harassment over his circus enterprises in England.[8] Daly argued, first, that the granting to Astley of the projected patent would be of considerable prejudice to him 'after the expence [*sic*] he had been at in fitting up and supporting the theatre'.[9] He contended, second, that the form taken by the projected patent was not warranted by the 1786 Act.[10] That Act had in view 'the establishment of a well regulated theatre, to improve the morals of the people'. But the theatre being sanctioned for Astley was 'to become a theatre to exhibit every species of buffoonery, and distortion of the human figure, learned pigs, monkeys and dancing dogs.' 'Such', argued Daly,

> cannot be called a regular theatre, or contribute to improve the morals of the people. It would defeat the purposes of the Act, by withdrawing the people from the rational and instructive entertainment of a well regulated theatre.

Smock Alley, it might be observed in parentheses, was notable, after 1767, for putting on comedies and rope-dancing. And Daly himself, in the 1784–5 season, was reputed to have brought performing dogs from France to appear at the same venue.[11]

A third argument addressed to the lord chancellor was no less sophisticated, even if the supposed rationale for the issuance of any second or subsequent theatre patent which counsel in the case rehearses lacks any kind of corroboration.[12] It was conceded that the crown could issue divers patents but that power, it was alleged, was given it 'only to punish a patentee for neglect or misconduct, by granting another patent'. There was, however, no evidence at all that Daly had been guilty either of neglect or of misconduct. A fourth and final argument touched on the

---

7   *Ex parte Daly* (1788) Vernon & Scriven 499.

8   Marius Kwint, 'The legitimization of the circus in late Georgian England', *Past & Present*, 174 (2002), 72, at 82.

9   Vernon & Scriven, at p. 500.   10   Ibid., at p. 501.

11   Gilbert, *History of Dublin*, ii, 100; T. Mooney and F. White, 'The gentry's winter season' in David Dickson (ed.), *The gorgeous mask: Dublin, 1700–1800* (Dublin, Trinity History Workshop, 1987), 1, at 7; Walsh, *Opera in Dublin, 1705–1797*, p. 253.

12   Vernon & Scriven, at p. 502.

supposed inconsistency in the words of the projected patent for Astley.[13] The patent expressly forbade Astley from exhibiting entertainments such as had been presented at the Theatre Royal before proceeding to sanction 'the exhibition of musical pieces and pantomimes' which, as a matter of notoriety, *had* been put on at the Theatre Royal.

As the keeper of the King's conscience, the lord chancellor, Viscount Lifford, was urged to withhold the great seal. This, however, Lifford was disinclined to do.[14] The lord lieutenant, the marquis of Buckingham, had granted the patent and there was no suggestion that the patent itself was illegal. That Astley's patent would to an extent infringe on Daly's, Lifford was prepared to accept. It would clearly tend to diminish Daly's profits. A final throw of the dice furnished little comfort for Daly. 'Certainly', remarked Lifford,[15] 'the more places of entertainment there are, it will make some difference to all. Perhaps it is better there should be more'. Kwint says of the decision to grant Astley his patent, that in Dublin 'the British authorities were less concerned to protect existing culture' and of Astley's growing reputation in England and France as well as in Dublin that it 'represented the advance of the artisan classes into the mass consumer market'.[16] Astley's legal triumph in Dublin in 1788 is likely to have been recalled by him with considerable fondness when faced, later in his career, with developments very much less to his taste:[17]

> loss of amphitheatres to revolution in Paris and rebellion in Dublin; internment and escape as an enemy alien in France; and fires that twice razed his underinsured London circus buildings.

Counsel supporting Astley's patent included John Fitzgibbon, the attorney-general, who in a year's time was to succeed Viscount Lifford as lord chancellor. In a case that came before Fitzgibbon as lord chancellor in 1794,[18] where he was urged once again to uphold a monopoly – albeit a monopoly of a very different sort: the printing of the Bible – the language in the report of his judicial pronouncement on the issue that had arisen is markedly biased yet again in favour of competition, whatever the price. 'If ever', wrote Fitzgibbon, now ennobled as Viscount Fitzgibbon,[19]

> there was a time which called aloud for the dissemination of religious knowledge it is this; and, therefore, I should with very great reluctance determine in favour of such monopoly as this, which must necessarily confine the circulation of this book.

13 Ibid.   14 Ibid., p. 504.   15 Ibid.
16 Entry on Astley in *Oxford DNB*, ii, 778 at 780 (Kwint).
17 Kwint, 'The legitimization of the circus', at 93.
18 *Grierson v. Jackson* (1794): Ridgeway, Lapp and Schoales, 304.   19 At 307.

Lifford's decision rejecting the challenge to the patent for Astley was handed down on 19 April 1788. Four days later, on the 23rd, Astley's patent was sealed.[20] As Daly had complained, it authorised the representation by Astley of 'feats of horsemanship, musical pieces, dancing, tumbling and pantomimes of any nature', with the proviso that all were to be 'decent and becoming and not profane or obnoxious'. These shows could only be held between 29 October and 29 January inclusive in each of the years of the 7-year period for which the patent had been granted. Such time restrictions were not unknown in the case of theatre patents issued in England. In July 1766, for instance, when a patent was granted to Samuel Foote to build a theatre in the city of Westminster and 'to exhibit dramatic performances' – the origins of the new *Haymarket Theatre* opened in May 1767 – the patent restricted such 'exhibition' to the period between 14 May and 14 September each year.[21] In Astley's case, no regular tragedy, comedy, opera, play or farce was to be put on at Astley's venue, his amphitheatre, 'as shall have been exhibited at the theatre royal'. No one was permitted 'to erect or rent amphitheatres for the same purpose', unless duly licensed or authorised. One financial obligation was attached: Astley secured his patent on condition he paid £100 to the Lying-in Hospital on each 20 January over the 7-year period. Astley's patent was renewed for a 14-year term in 1794.[22] The conditions were the same, and there was one new power bestowed: to take of persons resorting to his amphitheatre such money as Astleys or his assigns 'shall think reasonable in respect of expenses incurred'. In a further 14-year renewal in 1808, Astley's winter season was extended by a month, to the last day of each February.[23] Astley himself died in Paris in 1814. He is buried in Père Lachaise.

Philip Astley had been no stranger to Dublin. He had first brought his 'equestrian extravaganza' to the capital in 1773.[24] In 1787, shortly before his successful bid for a patent, Astley had erected his amphitheatre on a plot of land bordering Peter Street, the street parallel to Bishop Street, the home today of the National Archives, but to the north. A contemporary description of the venue is extant.[25] The Peter Street location was not perhaps the ideal choice, but Astley had had little alternative for Daly, faced by the impending competition, had 'with the object of obstructing his proceedings, taken every other vacant place in the city suitable for a circus'.[26] Even after the amphitheatre was unveiled, and for a number of months, Daly suffered seriously from its opening, until, as was made clear by the terms of Astley's patent, he was forced by law to discontinue the performance

20 *Liber munerum publicorum Hiberniae*, vol. 1, pt iii, p. 109.
21 Benjamin Victor, *The history of the theatres of London, from the year 1760 to the present time* (London, T. Becket, 1771), pp 183–4.
22 Ibid.   23 Ibid.   24 Stockwell, *Dublin theatres*, p. 346, n. 44.
25 *Dublin Post*, 20 Oct. 1791, cited by Stockwell, *Dublin theatres*, p. 351, n. 5.
26 Gilbert, *History of Dublin*, i, 45. On the difficulties faced in Belfast by the Lyric Players in securing a site for the planned new Lyric Theatre in the 1960s (eventually established on Ridgeway Street in Stranmillis), see Conor O'Malley, *A poet's theatre* (Dublin, Elo Press, 1981), p. 26.

of dramatic pieces.[27] Forced to concentrate on his circus entertainment, Astley thrived. 'Immense numbers', Gilbert tells us,[28] flocked to his amphitheatre off Peter Street, 'to witness the feats of horsemanship, and all the approaches to the circus were densely thronged from six to seven o'clock in the evenings'.

There is a description of an Astley circus entertainment in the visit paid to it by the Nubbles family, Kit included, in chapter 39 of *The Old Curiosity Shop* by Charles Dickens:

> Dear, dear, what a place it looked, that Astley's! with all the paint, gilding and looking-glass; the vague smell of horses suggestive of coming wonders; the curtain that hid such gorgeous mysteries; the clean white sawdust down in the circus; the company coming in and taking their places; the fiddlers looking carelessly up at them while they tuned their instruments, as if they didn't want the play to begin, and knew it all beforehand! What a glow was that, which burst upon them all, when that long, clear, brilliant row of lights came slowly up: and what the feverish excitement when the little bell rang and the music began in good earnest, with strong parts for the drums, and sweet effects for the triangles! …
>
> Then the play itself! The horses which little Jacob believed from the first to be alive, and the ladies and gentlemen of whose reality he could be by no means persuaded, having never seen or heard anything at all like them – the firing, which made Barbara wink – the forlorn lady, who made her cry – the tyrant, who made her tremble – the man who sang the song with the lady's maid and danced the chorus, who made her laugh – the pony who reared up on his hind legs when he saw the murderer, and wouldn't hear of walking on all fours again until he was taken into custody – the clown who ventured on such familiarities with the military man in boots – the lady who jumped over the nine-and-twenty ribbons and came down safe upon the horse's back – everything was delightful, splendid and surprising!

Intriguingly, in the pages of English fiction there had been an earlier allusion to the entertainment Astley's afforded. In Jane Austen's *Emma* (1816), Robert Martin and Harriet Smith – the match that Emma Woodhouse had done so much to prevent – accept the invitation accorded them by the Weston family to join them in an excursion to Astley's, and it is there that they resume their courtship.[29]

Frederick Edward 'Buck' Jones, who emerged on the Dublin scene in 1793, turned out, in the end, to prove a much more serious competitor for Daly. With the earl of Westmeath in tow, Jones opened the former Music Hall in Fishamble Street (where the first performance of 'The Messiah' had been given in 1741) as a private theatre.[30] In a production of *The Rivals* as part of the opening season, Jones himself

27 Gilbert, *History of Dublin*, ii, 213.   28 Ibid.   29 *Emma*, ch. 54.
30 Gilbert, *History of Dublin*, i, 85–6. Lady Morgan's father, Robert Owenson, had previously put on drama at the Fishamble Street venue: Morash, *History of Irish theatre*, p. 67.

played the part of Sir Lucius O'Trigger.[31] An application for a patent under the Act of 1786 was made, and proved successful. It was granted for a 7-year period in March 1794; Jones was named the patentee. There were three remarkable features: restrictions on the size of any theatre opened by Jones; the use of amateur actors; and a prohibition on theatre-goers paying at the door. The terms of this singular patent as reproduced by Lascelles merit being set forth at length. Jones had conferred on him, the words of the patent began,[32]

> full power to open a theatre wherever he shall think fit, in the city and county, unless government shall direct otherwise, to act all interludes, tragedies, comedies, preludes, operas, burlettas, plays, farces, pantomimes, of what nature soever, decent and becoming, and not profane or obnoxious; with a proviso that he shall not permit any person to be present for money; saving to him a power to receive subscriptions to defray the necessary expences from such patrons as he may think fit, and that such subscribers may be present upon such terms as he and they shall agree upon; and that he shall not employ any male actors for hire, further that he may employ such female performers as he may think fit; but if any immoral or improper play, etc. be performed and be not discontinued, on receiving notice in the name and authority of the Chief Governor, that then this grant, immunity and privilege shall cease, determine and become void; such allowances to be issued to the female performers as he shall think fit, with power to eject all scandalous, disorderly, (or other) persons as he thinks proper; then the clause that these letters patent shall from the inrolment or exemplification, be firm, valid, etc., with favourable interpretation, etc.

The Fishamble Street venture having proved a success, Jones was urged to open a second public play-house. Dissatisfaction with Daly's management of the Theatre Royal in Crow Street seems to have acted as the trigger.[33] The contemporary verdict on Crow Street by a French traveller speaks for itself:[34] 'La salle de spectacle public est assez laide, le théâtre étant peu suivi, les acteurs ne sont pas meilleurs que dans une petite ville de province'. Jones accordingly presented a memorial in 1796 to the lord lieutenant, Earl Camden, soliciting a patent to open a fully fledged theatre. Daly was apprised of what was afoot and, unsurprisingly, remonstrated in the strongest of terms. Dublin, he protested, had but indifferently supported one theatre; the opening of a second would render the ruin of both inevitable.[35] Camden then referred the whole question to the attorney-general, a move that serves as the harbinger of the greater formality that was about to surround future applications for a patent. Arthur Wolfe, the attorney-general,

31 Gilbert, *History of Dublin*, i, 98.
32 *Liber munerum publicorum Hiberniae*, vol. 1, pt iii, p. 109. See, too, the précis in Gilbert, *History of Dublin*, ii, 214.
33 Gilbert, *History of Dublin*, ii, 215.   34 Quoted, ibid.   35 Gilbert, *History of Dublin*, ii, 215.

in his report verified the complaints against Daly, whereupon Camden intimated he was prepared to issue a second patent in favour of Jones.[36] What happened next is traced in a series of exchanges reproduced by Gilbert.[37] The upshot was that Daly offered to dispose of his existing patent to Jones, and Jones agreed to inherit a number of Daly's financial obligations, to pay annuities to Daly himself and to Daly's nine children and to pay Daly profit rent on theatres the latter had established in Cork and Limerick.[38] Daly then withdrew from the fray. Jones commenced his management of the Theatre Royal in January 1798.

Both Morash and Greene place a somewhat different interpretation on events.[39] Daly, who everyone agreed was 'compulsively quarrelsome', fell out with John Magee, the editor of the *Dublin Evening Post*, against whom a number of controversial law suits were to be launched. Recourse to the law of libel was scarcely a surprise since Daly had been subjected to a long and vicious campaign in print orchestrated by Magee.[40] In the key contest of 1789, which came before the chief justice of King's Bench, the earl of Clonmell, the latter attached his imprimatur to a total of four writs or *fiats* marked £7,800 against Magee in a sequence of libel suits. To secure his liberty pending the hearing of the cases in question, Magee had to post this sum of money. It being beyond his means, he was to remain incarcerated for several months.[41] Magee sought his revenge against Clonmell by organising his Olympic pig hunt in Blackrock, Co. Dublin, close to Clonmell's residence.[42] And against Daly by dispersing supporters among the audience at the Crow Street theatre to create an amount of disruption.[43] There is some evidence that Daly was successful in the introduction of countermeasures,[44] but it is a plausible explanation for Daly's quitting of the Dublin theatrical scene in 1798 that the dispute with Magee had been a factor, as much as the competition from Astley, the grant in favour of Jones at the Fishamble Theatre, the civil tensions brewing before the 1798 Rising, as well as the death in 1795 of his wife – the four other factors identified by Greene.[45] As Greene's further researches have revealed, two other matters can scarcely be left out of the equation – Daly's 4-month sojourn in gaol in 1792–3 for assaulting a trouble-maker and the flight with his family to the Isle of Man in 1797 to escape his creditors.[46]

---

36 Ibid.   37 Gilbert, *History of Dublin*, ii, 216–18.
38 Ibid., ii, 218. Daly had also gained control at an earlier stage of his career of theatres in Newry, Drogheda and Waterford.
39 Morash, *History of Irish theatre*, p. 75; J.C. Greene, 'The trials of Richard Daly and John Magee, involving the Sham Squire, the Lottery Swindle of 1788, the Billiard Marker's Ghost, and the Grand Olympic pig hunt', *Eighteenth-Century Ireland*, 24 (2009), 135.
40 Greene, ibid., describes Magee as a 'bookseller, stationer, newspaper owner, lottery office keeper, and political reformer.'
41 Brian Inglis, *The freedom of the press in Ireland, 1784–1841* (London, Faber & Faber, 1954), p. 76.
42 Ibid., pp 76–7.
43 Thomas Bartlett, *Revolutionary Dublin, 1795–1801: the letters of Francis Higgins to Dublin Castle* (Dublin, Four Courts Press, 2004), p. 204.
44 Ibid.   45 Greene, 'Trials of Daly and Magee', 135.   46 Ibid., 157.

Jones' fresh patent passed under the privy seal in London on 25 June 1798[47] – not, of course, the most auspicious of times. It is worthy of notice that this was a new patent. There is scant evidence in Ireland that tyro impresarios sought to gain entry into the world of the theatres by purchasing rights under an existing patent – something, however, that appears not to have been uncommon in England. In 1767, for example, four individuals, Messrs Colman, Harris, Rutherford and Powell, paid a total of £60,000 to purchase the patent in respect of Covent Garden theatre.[48] Jones' 21-year patent of 1798 (the longest granted so far) enabled Jones to erect a theatre in the city or county of Dublin and gave him the power 'to keep as many players as he shall think fit; the usual power to allow them what he shall think fit, and to collect for that purpose the customary prices'. No performances were to be permitted 'reproachful to the Christian religion in general, or to the Church of England in particular, nor any abuse or misrepresentation of sacred characters'. Jones complained of losses he sustained as a result of the proclamation of martial law on the occasion of the rising of the United Irishmen in the spring of 1798; this had prohibited people from appearing in the streets of Dublin after 8p.m. A petition presented to the House of Commons on 25 February 1799, stressing the consequences in financial terms of an 8-week closure, yielded a recommendation from the house's Committee of Supply that Jones be compensated to the tune of £5,000. The suggestion, however, was voted down by the Commons itself and the government, according to Gilbert, induced Jones to press his claims no further.[49] Jones was to suffer further losses in the aftermath of Emmet's rebellion in July 1803, when there was introduced a curfew extending from 8p.m. to 6a.m.[50] Jones' management at Crow Street is celebrated above all for his support of opera in Dublin;[51] but notably there had long been critics as well.[52] Whatever the reason, he was destined to fall out with the Dublin Castle administration, and when, in 1819, his patent came up for renewal, in a deliberate snub, no renewal took place, the patent for the Theatre Royal at Crow Street being transferred to Henry Harris, in the tortuous circumstances explained by Gilbert.[53] Harris made immediate changes. A new Theatre Royal, designed by Samuel Beazley and costing £50,000, was erected in Hawkins Street, close to where today's Screen Cinema is to be found, and the Crow Street theatre, like Smock Alley before it, was to be demolished.[54] It was at this new theatre that George IV saw Sheridan's *La Duenna* on 22 August 1821.[55]

47 *Liber munerum publicorum Hiberniae*, vol. 1, pt iii, p. 109; Gilbert, *History of Dublin*, ii, 218.
48 Victor, *History of London theatres*, pp 114–15.
49 *Commons' jn., Ire.*, xviii, 37 (25 Feb. 1799), 57 (6 Mar. 1799).
50 Gilbert, *History of Dublin*, ii, 219–20.
51 T.J. Walsh, *Opera in Dublin, 1798–1820: Frederick Jones and the Crow Street theatre* (Oxford, 1993).
52 J.W. Croker, *Familiar epistle to Frederick Jones, Esq. on the present state of the Irish stage* (Dublin, J. Barlow, 1804).
53 Gilbert, *History of Dublin*, ii, 248–54.   54 Morash, *History of Irish theatre*, p. 77.   55 Ibid., p. 79.

The government would appear to have accepted that Jones had been hard done by, for, in 1829, a patent for a further theatre in Dublin was issued to Jones' sons, Richard Talbot Jones and Charles Horatio Jones.[56] This gave the right to put on 'concerts, feats of horsemanship, fantoccini,[57] ballets, melodramas, pantomimes, operatic pieces' and such other exhibitions as were customarily put on in named minor theatres in London. The patent expressly forbade the performance of regular drama, the liberty of the performance of which had been conferred by the patent in favour of Harris. The Jones brothers opened their theatre north of the River Liffey on Abbey Street,[58] but from 1833 appear to have been content to let others effectively manage the new theatre, John and James Calvert from 1833 and M. West from 1844. The Calverts and West were to ignore the terms of the 1829 patent by putting on performances of regular drama, a move that was to attract the ire of J.W. Calcraft, the manager at the Theatre Royal since 1822.

Calcraft, as we are about to discover, jealously defended his rights as the possessor of the theatre patent for the Theatre Royal in Hawkins Street. He did not thus hesitate to resort to the law to protect his supposed prerogatives. But there was more to it than this. In a spirited defence of the stage which he published in 1839,[59] the background to the composition of which will shortly be explained, Calcraft saw fit to employ in his battery of arguments key excerpts from the Theatre Royal's patent of the period. He thus reproduced the passage where the wish was expressed 'that the Theatre in future may be instrumental to the cause of virtue and instructive to human life'.[60] Also, a much longer passage where the Theatre Royal was expressly forbidden from authorising productions that could be perceived as critical of religion. 'We have thought fit hereby to declare', the relevant part of the patent portentously recounted,[61]

> that from henceforth no representations be admitted on the Stage, whereby the Christian religion in general, and more especially the Church of England, may in any manner suffer reproach, and we do hereby strictly inhibit all and every degree of *abuse* or *misrepresentation* of sacred characters, which may in any degree tend to expose religion or bring it into contempt. And that no such character be introduced or placed in any other light than such as may increase the just esteem of those who answer the end of their sacred function.

Not to be ignored either, as Calcraft also recalled in his defence of the stage, were the sentiments set forth in the preamble to that Act of 1786 that laid the statutory foundation for Dublin's theatre patents:[62]

56 Gilbert, *History of Dublin*, ii, 254.   57 Marionette shows.   58 Gilbert, *History of Dublin*, ii, 254.
59 J.W. Calcraft, *A defence of the stage, or an inquiry into the real quality of theatrical entertainments, their scope and tendency, being a reply to a sermon entitled 'The evil of the theatrical amusements stated and illustrated by the Revd Dr John Bennet'* (Dublin, Milliken & Son, 1839).
60 Calcraft, *A defence of the stage*, p. 32.   61 Ibid., p. 158.   62 26 Geo. III, c. 57, s. 1.

> Whereas the establishing a well regulated theatre in the city of Dublin … will be productive of publick advantage and tend to improve the morals of the people.

No other holder of a Dublin theatre patent is thought to have placed himself on record in quite this fashion.

John William Calcraft, as lessee and manager of the Hawkins Street Theatre Royal, was to dominate the world of Dublin theatre down to the 1840s, his 'able and efficient' management earning in 1842 the special praise of the Halls.[63] On the death of William Meeke in 1830, Calcraft, as we have seen,[64] had sought, unsuccessfully, to be appointed Master of the Revels. Legislation adopted in 1817, as we have also previously had occasion to point out, had abolished the office on the death of the then incumbent, and Calcraft was predictably rebuffed. Calcraft even so might be reckoned to have earned his spurs, while failing to gain the office of Master of the Revels, with the justification he mounted of the theatre in a long pamphlet he produced in 1839 – his *Defence of the stage*, to which allusion has just been made. Calcraft's *Defence* was by way of being the reply to an extraordinary, but well-argued attack on the theatre as such, shortly before furnished by a Methodist minister in Dublin, the Revd Dr John Bennett – an attack of a sort with a not undistinguished pedigree that we examine elsewhere.[65] Bennett nowhere pleads for legislation to outlaw theatre, much as such a course of conduct might have appealed to him, but Calcraft probably read the public mood aright when he judged it fell to him as the holder of the Theatre Royal's patent to present as staunch a defence of the drama as he could muster.

Bennett had previously produced an anonymous tract on the evils of the theatre. He returned to the theme in a sermon preached at the Methodist chapel in Dublin's Lower Abbey Street, in the autumn of 1838. An expanded version of this sermon was then published late in the year under the title *The evil of theatrical amusements, stated and illustrated in a sermon, preached in the Wesley-Methodist Chapel, Lower Abbey Street, on Sunday, November 4, 1838, with an appendix*.[66] Though Gladstone was later to alter his stance, it is worth recalling that at this period in the 1830s he was no friend of the theatre either. In his diary entry for 19 December 1832, he thus wrote that races and the theatre 'involve the encouragement of sin'.[67] When, in 1757, the Edinburgh Presbytery issued an Admonition and Exhortation against the play *Douglas*, written by John Home, the Presbyterian minister of Athelstaneford, and performed at Edinburgh's Canongate Theatre, they went into rather more detail as to why they reckoned the stage dangerous. 'The Presbytery', the Admonition began,[68]

63 Mr & Mrs S.C. Hall, *Ireland: its scenery, character, etc.*, 3 vols (London, How & Parsons; Jeremiah How, 1841–3), ii, 336.
64 Above, p. 28.   65 Below, ch. 14.   66 Dublin, John Fannin, 1838.
67 *The Gladstone diaries*, 14 vols, i, ed. M.R.D. Foot (Oxford, Clarendon Press, 1988), p. 595.
68 *Edinburgh Courant*, 7 Jan. 1757, quoted in, Alan Bold, *Modern Scottish literature* (London and New York, Longman, 1983), p. 279.

taking into serious consideration the declining state of religion, the open profanation of the Lord's Day, the contempt of public worship, the growing luxury and levity of the present age – in which so many seem lovers of pleasure more than lovers of God – and being particularly affected with the unprecedented countenance given of late to the Playhouse in this place, when the state of the nation and the circumstances of the poor, make such hurtful entertainments still more pernicious, judged it their indispensable duty to express in the most open and solemn manner, the deep concern they feel on this occasion. The opinion which the Christian Church has always entertained of stage plays and players as prejudicial to the interest of religion and morality is well known, and the fatal influence which they commonly have on the far greater part of mankind particularly the younger sort is too obvious to be called into question.

Bennett's *The evil of theatrical amusements* recalls previous well-known attacks on the theatre. Jeremy Collier, the non-juror High Church clergyman (1650–1726), gave us in 1698 *A short view of the immorality and profaneness of the English stage*. Best known of all perhaps is the lengthy tract written by the leading Puritan and lawyer of an earlier generation, William Prynne (1600–69), of whose *Histrio-Mastix* (1631), at over 1,000 pages, we postpone consideration for the moment.[69]

Collier, it is worth noting, was not content to bequeath to us a single text attacking the theatre. His *A short view of the immorality and profaneness of the English stage*, for all its vitriol – and thus in lineal descent from *Histrio-Mastix* – earned for its author a favourable impression. 'There is a vigour', it has been asserted,[70] 'a verbal resilience, a clarity and directness of invective which is missing from his other moralizing, solemn pieces'. A like encomium can justifiably be applied to Bennett's *The evil of theatrical amusements*. Whatever about Collier, Bennett, for his part, did not fail to advance a particularly bold claim for his venture into print targeting the theatre. 'I have', he writes,[71]

the gratification of knowing that several individuals who, up to the time of their hearing this Sermon, were play-goers, have been led, through its instrumentality, to a renunciation of the evil and dangerous indulgence.

'The glory be', he then adds, 'to Him who can clothe with energy the humblest effort made in His name, and for the promotion of His cause!'

Bennett immediately concedes that to attack what he chooses to term 'theatrical amusements' was to embark on 'a task of much difficulty': 'the passions and prejudices of those who favour the stage are so strongly arrayed upon its side, as to cloud their judgment'. He then goes into some detail:[72]

69 Below, ch. 14.   70 Entry on Collier in *Oxford DNB*, xii, 640.
71 *The evil of theatrical amusements*, p. iv.   72 Ibid., p. 8.

To the enthusiastic play-goer (and there are many such) the theatre is a major circle of delight. Compared with its thrilling enjoyments the common-place transactions of life are tame, flat, and uninteresting – dull *Waking* realities, from which his mind turns away, anxious to dream again – longing once more to tread the enchanted ground, and submit himself to a spell which, while it lures him into tumultuous excitement, suffers little of either recollection of the past or anticipation of the future, to cast a gloomy shade over the brightness of the present.

Another early passage in Bennett's forty-plus page diatribe supplies further evidence of his impressive style and range of content.[73] He hypothesises the existence of some individual totally ignorant of the theatre,

> now enquiring, what are these dramatic exhibitions which excite so much interest, attract crowds to sacrifice time and money in their enjoyment, engross so large a portion of the conversation in what is called fashionable society and occupy so much of the attention of the conductors of the public press?

This somewhat tendentious answer is then provided. Would such an individual, Bennett continues,[74]

> not at first be astonished to hear that the amusement consists in seeing a number of persons dressed in gaudy tinselled costume, and with their faces painted, pretending to do certain acts, and to feel certain passions – sometimes affecting to be in love with one another, sometimes to be angry, or to kill each other or themselves, – which feigning of passion, with fictitious dialogue and gesture, constitutes a play?

Bennett predictably takes issue with the argument that theatre could constitute a force for moral good – to be sure, an argument that had prevailed with legislators in the past. It was nonsense, he asserted, that the drama had served to elevate from barbarism to refinement; it was, rather, 'a dispenser of almost unmixed evil':[75]

> a character, either male or female, formed on the model [the stage] presents, would be a blot on the face of society here, and totally disqualify for admission into the society of the saints in light.

Bennett leaves us in no doubt as to his conviction

> that the patronage which the theatre has received, has arisen, *not* from a conviction of its excellency as an instrument for the diffusion of either moral or intellectual truth, but, on the contrary, from the love of the ungenerate

73 Ibid., p. 9.   74 Ibid., p. 9.   75 Ibid., pp 11–12.

heart for that which gratifies its passions, panders to its lusts, extenuates its crimes, and invests the creations of man's polluted imagination with a glittering garb of sentiment and poetry that conceals their hideousness from his associates and victims, if not from himself.[76]

Historical references abound. The 'low buffoonery and obscenity' of Aristophanes was contrasted with the achievements of Aeschylus, Sophocles and Euripedes.[77] 'One of the principal causes of the decline, corruption, and degeneracy of the Athenian state' was the passion for representations of the theatre, quoting the French historian Rollin. Athens was destined to 'lose the spirit of liberty and independence', in consequence, 'and sink deeper and deeper still in lethargic indolence.' Nero on stage spoke eloquently, as well, of how low Rome, too, was to stoop.[78] As for the Chester mystery plays of the Middle Ages, no one should ignore the additions deliberately introduced to placate assorted audiences – the additions 'to make sport' and to 'glad the hearers'.[79] The indulgence by Shakespeare in profaneness and obscenity made his plays 'altogether unfit for general perusal'.[80] The Restoration period predictably came in for attack.[81] The 'audacious ribaldry' of Wycherley and Congreve attracts Bennett's particular venom, and the decision at this juncture to let women perform women's parts in plays he dubs 'one of [theatre's] most powerful instruments for the overthrow of public morals'.[82] A similar disavowal of Restoration drama was also to issue from the pen of Calcraft.[83]

In Bennett's book the managers of theatres were unlikely to escape censure either. And so it turns out. 'Managers', he was to write,[84]

open theatres, it is notorious, not as philanthropists and patriots to diffuse the blessings of morality and education, but as commercial speculators to promote their own pecuniary gain. And in pursuit of this end, they know how to cater in accordance with the taste of their patrons.

Returning to his central theme, Bennett boldly avers that he was unaware of a single acted play in which there were not to be found 'serious moral faults, the Bible being the standard of appeal'.[85] This observation leads Bennett to concede that neither in the Old Testament nor in the New is there to be found any explicit criticism of the drama (which was, admittedly, in existence at the pertinent periods). But then, Bennett adds,[86] nor does the Bible specifically inveigh against gambling, the exposing of infants, gladiatorial fights with beasts of prey, or suicide. But there exist sentiments to be found in the New Testament which are there nonetheless to be called in aid of critics of the stage:[87]

76 Ibid., p. 12.   77 Ibid., p. 13.   78 Ibid., p. 14.   79 Ibid., p. 15.   80 Ibid., p. 16.
81 Ibid., pp 16–17.   82 Ibid., p. 16.   83 Below, p. 105.
84 Bennett, *Evil of theatrical amusements*, p. 22.   85 Ibid., p. 21.   86 Ibid., p. 23.
87 Bennett quotes from the *Authorised Version* throughout.

Ephesians 4, v. 29 and v. 4
Let no corrupt communication procured out of your mouth, but that which
is good to the use of edifying, that it may minister grace to the hearers.
Neither filthiness, nor foolish talking, nor jesting, which are not convenient;
but rather giving of thanks.
Matthew 12, v. 36
Every idle word that men shall speak, they shall give account thereof in the
day of judgment.
Romans 14, v. 21.
It is good neither to eat flesh, nor to drink wine, nor any thing whereby thy
brother stumbled, or is offended, or is made weak.
1 Corinthians 8, v. 9 and v. 13
Take heed lest by any means this liberty of yours become a stumbling block
to them that are weak.
If meat make my brother to offend,
I will eat no flesh while the world standeth,
Lest I make my brother to offend.

Having reached the unsurprising conclusion that young females were most at risk
from attendance at 'theatrical amusements',[88] Bennett ends with his heartfelt plea.
'All who desire the coming of the Saviour's Kingdom', he writes,[89]

> should pray, with increasing earnestness and perseverance, for that effusion
> of the Holy Spirit by which this and all the other strongholds of Satan shall
> be overthrown, and a religious joy, equally pure and permanent, be
> universally brought in.

In *A defence of the stage*, Calcraft's 175-page reply to Bennett's *The evil of
theatrical amusements*, its author strove to occupy the middle ground. Not for him
an encounter designed to degenerate into a fist fight. The choice of epigrams taken
from the Bible tells us what we can expect. Where Bennett had highlighted an
injunction from *Exodus* – 'Thou shalt not follow a multitude to do evil'[90] – Calcraft
found comfort in the words of St Paul to the *Philippians*[91] – 'Let your moderation
be known unto all men' – as well as to *Titus*[92] – 'Speak evil of no man'. Intellectual
arrogance, a grave enough offence being levelled at his adversary, Calcraft was
aware was anathema to the author of *Ecclesiastes*. 'Be not', it was there written,[93]
'righteous over much; neither make thyself over wise: why shouldest thou destroy
thyself?' Calcraft's choice for his first epigram, again taken from *Ecclesiastes*,
demonstrated among this welter of biblical quotation that he had not lost sight of

88 Bennett, *Evil of theatrical amusements*, p. 31.   89 Ibid., p. 42.
90 *Exodus* 23, v. 2: see *The evil of theatrical amusements* at p. 5.
91 *Philippians* 4, v. 5: *A defence of the stage*, p. 1.
92 *Titus* 3, v. 2: *A defence of the stage*, title page.
93 *Ecclesiastes* 7, v. 16: *A defence of the stage*, title page.

the mission he had set himself – to reject Bennett and to defend the stage. 'To every thing', it is said in *Ecclesiastes*,[94]

> There is a season, and a time to every purpose under the heaven.
> ...
> A time to weep, and a time to laugh: a time to mourn and a time to dance.

In summary, his was to be a 'softly, softly' rejoinder. 'Literary warfare', Calcraft averred,[95]

> has often rendered men, otherwise amiable, callous and uncharitable on a favourite question. Milton expressed no compunction for the death of Salmasius, nor has the *Quarterly* recorded any penitence for the article that put an end to Keats.

These two extraordinary literary allusions on Calcraft's part merit a word of explanation. Salmasius, Claude de Saumaise, a learned French protestant, published in 1649 a defence of the executed Charles I and thus an attack on the English administration of the day: *Defensio regia pro Carolo I*. The council of state the following January, alarmed at the possibility of damage to trade resulting from Salmasius' tract, ordered John Milton to pen a reply. Milton was to sacrifice what remained of sight in his one remaining 'good' eye (the right) in rising to the occasion and complying with the council's wishes. The result was *Joannis Miltonii Angli defensio pro populo Anglicano contra Claudii Anonymi, alias Salmasii, defensionem regiam*. This piece of prose from Milton was notable for its vitriol and the ferocity of its personal attack on Salmasius, who is referred to as 'a lying hired slanderer', 'a brute beast' and a 'blockhead', and even on Salmasius' wife who is labelled a 'barking bitch'.[96]

Salmasius died in 1653, and it was soon claimed that his death was as a consequence of rough treatment at the hands of Milton. In 1839 in Dublin Calcraft repeats the story. Kathryn A. McEven, having reviewed the question, while not denying the possibility, was to maintain that other factors were involved – gout, 'taking the waters' at a polluted spa, etc. – and argued accordingly that 'one may reasonably assume Salmasius died of natural causes'.[97]

Keats died in Italy in February 1821. In September 1818 the delayed spring issue of the *Quarterly Review* contained a criticism of Keats' 'Endymion' by J.W. Croker. Other critics of the period issued similar unfavourable reviews. Croker

---

94 *Ecclesiastes*, 3, vv.1, 4: *A defence of the stage*, title page.
95 *A defence of the stage*, p. iv.
96 See *Complete prose works of John Milton*, vol. 4, ed. D.M. Wolfe (New Haven, Yale UP and London, Oxford UP, 1966), pt 1, 'Introduction' by Wolfe at pp 114–15.
97 'Salmasius: opponent of Milton' in *Complete prose works of John Milton*, vol. 4, pt 2, p. 962 at p. 979.

seized the opportunity to attack Keats' low origins and his medical training as well as his supposed skill as a poet. As in the case of Salmasius, it began to be bruited abroad that the savagery of Croker's attack precipitated Keats' early death – the report that was to find favour with Calcraft twenty-one years later. It is possible to discern in Byron's comment on the business in 'Don Juan' (canto 2, stanza 60) that he, for one, may not have been entirely convinced:

> 'tis strange the mind, that very fiery particle
> Should let itself be snuffed out by an article.

To return to Calcraft's preface and the immediate matter in hand, the Theatre Royal's lessee and manager moved swiftly to explain his choice of strategy.[98] He would object to the manner in which Bennett had marshalled the arguments in the latter's favour, and he would emphasise the strength of the defences to be found in the host of authorities in support of the stage. Calcraft kept his word.

Bennett got the reasons for the decline of Athens plain wrong.[99] It was less to do with an over-indulgence in theatre, and more to do with the eclipse of her political nous and military power. The downward trajectory from the failed Sicilian expedition of 415BC to Demosthenes' despair at the pusillanimity of Athens' politicians of 351BC (a despair, it might be recalled, Thomas Sheridan had had occasion to note in a different context)[100] was proof positive of that decline. Calcraft also mounted a defence of Aristophanes: there was a great deal of 'sound political advice' in the dramatist's 'comedies of peace' – *The Acharnians* and *Lysistrata*.[101] The drama in ancient Rome had not been fairly assessed either. There had been much that was wrong, but, Calcraft continued,[102]

> If … any portion of Roman degeneracy arose from the Stage, let it be ascribed to an extreme indulgence in its illegitimate accessories, rather than to a fair cultivation of its purer components.

The philosophical point he was craving to make was worth emphasis. 'If', Calcraft continued,[103]

> we cry down an art as evil, because vicious spirits have degraded it, or derive the causes of national degeneracy from the excesses of such monstrous exceptions as Nero and Commodus, we may as safely argue that a bush is always dangerous because there was once a tiger in it; or pronounce a city uninhabitable because it has once been visited by the cholera or the plague.

Bennett's translation of key passages in Tacitus and in Livy was grievously at fault.[104] And staying with the topic of the drama in ancient Rome, note needed to

---

98 *A defence of the stage*, p. iii.   99 Ibid., pp 43–8.   100 Above, p. 44.
101 *A defence of the stage*, p. 40.   102 Ibid., p. 51.   103 Ibid., p. 53.   104 Ibid., pp 58–60.

be taken of Cicero's panegyric in celebration of the actor Roscius (W.R. Chetwood had made similar obeisance to Roscius in recalling Cicero's words in his *General history of the stage*, of 1749):[105]

> Fraudavit Roscius! Est hoc quidem auribus animisque hominum absurdum
>
> (Roscius has committed a fraud! This must indeed appear absurd to the ears and minds of all men.)[106]

The background to the charge – which, it was argued, was groundless – was that Roscius had been accused by his agent Fannius of withholding from the latter his share in a rural property. The farm in question had been awarded by way of a court settlement in other proceedings initiated by the actor.

In a different oration,[107] in a passage again quoted verbatim by Calcraft,[108] the acting talents of Roscius receive Cicero's express praise. In this oration, Cicero was to argue in favour of the Greek poet Archias' entitlement to Roman citizenship.[109] It encompasses a once-celebrated passage on the value of literature. Reading, Cicero contended, broadened the sympathies and enlightened the understanding.

> Quis nostrum tam animo agresti ac duro fuit, ut Roscii morte nuper non commoveretur? Qui cum esset senex mortuus, tamen propter excellentem artem, ac venustatem, videbatur omnino mori non debuisse.
>
> (Which of us was possessed of a bosom so rude, and so devoid of feeling, as not to have been moved by the recent death of Roscius? Who, although he died advanced in years, yet seemed on account of his surpassing skill and grace to have been worthy of living for ever.)

Turning to the impact of Christianity, Calcraft makes two critical points. First, it was far more significant than Bennett allowed that there was no mention at all of the stage in the New Testament: there was abundant evidence of the popularity of the drama in far-flung outposts of the Empire as well as in Rome at the time of Christ: places such as Jerusalem, Damascus, Ephesus, Antioch, Corinth, Athens, Thessalonica, Philippi and Alexandria.[110] Second, even if the early Christian Church was hostile because of the link between the drama and heathen superstition, things were soon to change. 'These pious men', Calcraft says of the early Fathers,[111]

---

105 W.R. Chetwood, *A general history of the stage … from its origin in Greece down to the present time* (Dublin, E. Rider, 1749), dedication.

106 Cicero, *Pro Quinto Roscio, comoedo*, vii; Calcraft, *A defence of the stage*, pp 66–7.

107 *Pro Archia, poeta.*   108 Calcraft, *A defence of the stage*, pp 12–13.

109 *Pro Archia, poeta*, viii.   110 *A defence of the stage*, p. 71.   111 Ibid.

in their zeal to withhold the impurities of the ancient dramatists from the community, do not appear to have carried their scruples, so far as to reject the aid of mistaken genius, when it could assist themselves or strengthen their arguments.

The role of St John Chrysostom, bishop of Constantinople and a doctor of the church (AD347–407), in rescuing Aristophanes from oblivion is noted, as well as the interest in the stage of such churchmen as Archbishop Gregory Nazianzan, Archbishop Theophylact and Bishop Apollinaris of Laodicea.[112]

Later Christian writers were supportive as well. For St Thomas Aquinas, 'Ludus est necessarius ad conversationem vitae humanae' (Amusement is necessary for the carriage of human life).[113] Cardinal Bonaventura (*c*.1250) gave plays his blessing, with the caveat that they should not be put on 'in times of sadness' or acted by members of the clergy.[114] Albertus Magnus (*c*.1320), too, relied on a detail in *Exodus*, where we read of Miriam the prophetess, the sister of Aaron, dancing to the sound of timbrels – action deemed praiseworthy.[115] Martin Luther, too, was a fan, stressing two educational arguments – the study of Roman dramatists facilitated the learning of Latin; in addition, he declared, 'of all amusements, the Theatre is the most profitable, for there we see important actions when we cannot act importantly ourselves'.[116] Likewise Philip Melancthon was an enthusiast:[117]

> Promitto etiam eis hoc eventurum, ut quo legent saepius, eo magis admiraturos et amaturos et lecturas eas avidius
>
> (... the oftener the young read [dramatists], the more they will admire them and turn with the greater eagerness to their re-perusal.)

Borromeo's reversal of his edict as archbishop of Milan to outlaw play-houses,[118] a reversal dictated by the deleterious consequence that ensued on the prohibition, prompted Calcraft to contemplate – with dismay – one other possible consequence of such a draconian step. 'Is', he asks,[119]

> there not danger in this extreme severity of doctrine, lest, in rooting out from the heart every inclination to gaiety, we should, at the same time, expel from it the kindly feelings of charity, and supply the void with narrow and gloomy selfishness?

---

112 *A defence of the stage*, pp 71–3.   113 Ibid., pp 73–4: *Summae Theolog.*, q. clx viii.
114 *A defence of the stage*, p. 75.   115 Ibid., pp 75–76, see *Exodus*, ch. 15, vv. 20–1.
116 Quoted, Calcraft, *A defence of the stage*, pp 76–8.
117 *Epistola de legendis tragoediis et comoediis*: see *A defence of the stage*, pp 78–81.
118 *A defence of the stage*, pp 39–40.   119 Ibid., p. 89.

Calcraft speaks highly of the drama in the France of the seventeenth and eighteenth centuries[120] – the *Polyeucte* (1641) of Pierre Corneille (1606–84); the *Athalie* (1691) and *Esther* (1689) of Jean Racine (1639–99); the 'mirth and pleasantry' of Molière (1622–73); the *Zaire* (1732) of Voltaire (1684–1778). Nailing his colours very firmly to the mast, he manifested no liking whatsoever for the excesses of Restoration comedy – and none at all either for John Gay's *The Beggar's Opera*.[121] An expurgated version of Vanbrugh's *The Provoked Husband* Calcraft was prepared to admit into the canon,[122] but his dismissal of most Restoration drama is unequivocal. 'When', he writes,[123]

> we reflect on the great plague and fire of London, which occurred during the high season of debauchery, we discern in those tremendous visitings, as clear a manifestation of divine wrath to rouse the nation to repentance, as the pillar in the wilderness was a token of divine favour, to guide the Israelites to the Land of Promise.

It was plainly a matter on which Calcraft felt very deeply indeed, and here, of course, he was in total agreement with Bennett. The reign of Charles II, Calcraft wrote,[124] 'furnished a picture of national profligacy, which the historian blushes to record, and the reader sighs to believe'. An unflattering postscript of the monarch himself is gratuitously appended:[125]

> A libertine, unreclaimed by the misfortunes of his family, the fate of his father, or his own early years of banishment and adversity; in the full maturity of manhood, ascended the throne of his ancestors amidst the universal acclamations of the people;[126] and at once surrendered himself up to all the unbridled licence of a vicious temperament.

Calcraft was thus delighted to be in a position to report that so much Restoration drama had been 'driven from [the] boards for ever'.[127]

The manager of the Theatre Royal rejects with a show of considerable firmness the threat of the drama that this (to him) unfortunate period might be thought to have presented. It is a key passage in *A defence of the stage*: 'That', Calcraft writes,[128]

> there have been bad plays, as there have been bad every thing else, is a fact too palpable to be disputed; but that for that reason the Stage should be abolished, and its use denied, because of its abuse, would be almost as wise in practical legislation, as to denounce the pulpit, because there have been rebellious and heterodoxical preachers; to proscribe the bench, because there

120 Ibid., pp 55–6. 121 Ibid., pp 92–3. 122 Ibid., p. 27. 123 Ibid., p. 26.
124 Ibid., p. 25. 125 Ibid.
126 Amid celebrations, it may be recalled, partly engineered by John Ogilby, above, p. 5.
127 *A defence of the stage*, p. 26. 128 Ibid., pp 28–9.

have been unjust judges; to illegalize the art of printing, because there have been immoral books; to abolish penmanship because there have been forgeries; or to forbid wine because there have been drunkards.

Calcraft takes pains to rebut the rumour that a Mr Eustace Budgell had been driven to suicide after a visit to the theatre[129] – the true explanation was that Budgell had determined to avoid the disgrace of a conviction for forging a will. He equally rebuts another argument that persons with a disposition to vice gravitated towards the playhouse:[130]

> When Mr James informs us, that 'not many days ago, a venerable and holy man said to him, that he once robbed his father of a shilling, to go to the gallery.' I reply, that it is not many weeks since a friend of my own had his pocket picked in church; yet I am not going for that reason to argue that churches are immoral institutions, or principally frequented by 'the vicious and depraved.'

As previously recounted, Calcraft recalled that the Theatre Royal's patent expressly forbade attacks on religion.[131] This served as an incentive to the production of a long check-test of dramas composed by men of the cloth[132] – evidence of a kind to rebut the notion that religion and the theatre were antipathetic to each other. Another argument worth rehearsing, in this continuing struggle to convince critics of a puritanical cast of mind, was to point out that times of performances in theatres did not ordinarily or at all conflict with the carrying out of the citizen's 'professional or religious duties'.[133] Sundry other arguments were touched on as well – the importance of the theatre to the economy;[134] its importance as a source of livelihood for numerous families;[135] the circumstance that the profession of actor required 'temperate habits, and unremitting application';[136] David Garrick and the establishment of the Drury Lane Theatrical Fund, a charity.[137]

Returning to Bennett's assault on Shakespeare, Calcraft, in his defence of the man,[138] wrote that 'the coarse passages' in the plays 'impeach the taste and manners of the day more than the character of the writer, and affect the delicacy rather than the moral tendency of [Shakespeare's] works'.[139] Milton is called in aid: not just the preface to *Samson Agonistes*, but to the circumstance that in Milton's manuscripts in Trinity College, Cambridge, Milton made a list of 100 plans of subjects for tragedies based on incidents in the Bible or from British history.[140]

Early on in *A defence of the stage* Calcraft produced an account of dramatic performances attended by Elizabeth I and by James I and VI.[141] Performances at

129 Ibid., pp 110–12.   130 Ibid., p. 54.   131 Above, p. 95.
132 *A defence of the stage*, pp 100–7.   133 Ibid., p. 145.   134 Ibid., p. 159.
135 Ibid., p. 159.   136 Ibid., p. 166.   137 Ibid., pp 163–4.   138 Ibid., pp 120–6.
139 Ibid., p. 121.   140 Ibid., p. 108.   141 Ibid., pp 32–4.

colleges and universities are dealt with too, which stood as a testament to the educational benefit that such performances were believed to garner.[142] In a footnote, Calcraft introduced a personal detail: the enjoyment occasioned by the putting on of regular pre-Christmas dramatic entertainment at the school he had attended as a boy at Corsham, near Bath in Wiltshire.[143]

It was indeed this capacity of the theatre both to educate and to entertain that appears in Calcraft's book to have constituted the strongest argument in its support: 'All sorts and conditions of mankind', he was to write,[144] refresh their faculties 'by listening to the stirring energy of Shakspeare [*sic*], the sparkling wit of Sheridan, or the thrilling melody of Rossini'. Elsewhere Richard Brinsley is singled out for special praise. 'What reasonable objection', Calcraft demands to know,[145]

> can be urged against Sheridan's Comedy of *The School for Scandal*? The wit is brilliant, the language elegant and the moral purpose sound: extravagance is reclaimed, hypocrisy punished, and that detestable bane of society, scandal, lashed with an unsparing hand.

There is a passage in *A defence of the stage* which comes just a little later, which, perhaps, more than anything else, captures the essence of what Calcraft, and those who thought like him in the early days of Victoria's reign, sensed was at stake, and why it was important, nay crucial, that their views should be made known to the public. 'If the Theatre', Calcraft took leave to fancy,[146]

> be 'a mass of evil', its component parts must be of similar quality, and if we abolish the Stage, as a vicious institution, we must at the same time proscribe music, dancing, poetry, painting, sculpture, oratory and history, of which it is compounded. We thus, 'at one fell swoop', deprive society of nearly all that embellishes life, or softens manners, retaining little more than 'the carpenter's rule and the Bible', which, according to the expanded views of the Barebones parliament, comprise 'every thing that is necessary for the happiness or improvement of man'.

A criticism levelled at Samuel Richardson's novel *Pamela* (1740), by way of challenging any claim it may have presented to verisimilitude, has been to question how the eponymous 'heroine' ever found time as a servant girl to write such long letters of impeccable English to her parents, which constitute the germ of the novel, which indeed supply its *raison d'être*. How J.W. Calcraft found the time too to compose his lengthy rebuttal of Bennett's contentions it is not easy to fathom either, for he was obliged on a number of occasions to deal with much more prosaic matters: the arrival on the Dublin scene of rival impresarios and the establishment

142 Ibid., pp 33–5.   143 Ibid., p. 34 n.   144 Ibid., p. 142.   145 Ibid., pp 137–8.
146 *A defence of the stage*, p. 141.

of rival venues. Throughout, he manifested a pronounced disinclination to turn a blind eye when, as he saw it, the rights of his Theatre Royal were threatened. In 1829 another new venue opened:[147] the Adelphi, later known as the Queen's, in Great Brunswick Street, today's Pearse Street, and alongside Trinity College and across from Hawkins Street. Calcraft proceeded to secure the lease of this new venue – only then to shut it down – a ploy, it may be recalled, that Thomas Sheridan had initiated in the time of Smock Alley.[148] When the Adelphi reopened in 1835 Calcraft was to sue the manager there, W. Last, for debt, succeeded in the action, but recovered nothing. The Adelphi itself obtained its patent somewhat belatedly in 1844.[149] This was in the name of John Charles Joseph who, according to Morash, had managed to acquire a dormant patent.[150]

When under the Calverts, John and James, the Abbey Street theatre, in contravention of the express terms of the relevant patent, put on regular drama, Calcraft commenced proceedings under the 1786 Act, but, due to James Calvert's embarrassed circumstances, recovered nothing. When West, the successor manager at the theatre from 1844, continued to put on tragedies and other plays of regular drama, Calcraft, despite the legal reverses he had frequently suffered, mounted a major challenge. He filed bills against West himself, George Gray, an actor, and two actresses, M.A. Tyrell and E. Makenzie; he also sought an injunction. The lord chancellor of the day, Sir Edward Sugden, was thus fated to preside over the first major inquiry into the rights of a patentee claiming his rights had been violated.[151] Counsel for West at the outset identified a major obstacle in the way of Calcraft succeeding in his suit. 'Now there have been, since the time of Charles II', counsel began,[152]

> patent rights to hold theatres; the patentees under those patents had a property (if it be property) in the right to act plays; but though the right has been frequently invaded, there is no instance of the patentees having ever attempted to obtain redress by an action on the case, or by an injunction; but there are many instances of proceedings by indictment for a nuisance, and by action for penalties.

Lord Chancellor Sugden agreed, concluding that in the circumstances Calcraft could only sue for a penalty as a common informer.[153] Among the precedents Sugden relied on was an observation of Chief Justice Popham in the *Case of Monopolies* in the reign of Elizabeth I[154] that even if the playing-card monopoly challenged in that case had been adjudged lawful (which he denied), no action on the case could have been brought against any individual who had invaded it.[155]

147 Morash, *History of Irish theatre*, p. 81.   148 Above, p. 24.
149 Seamus de Burca, 'The Queen's Royal Theatre, 1829–1960', *Dublin Historical Record*, 27 (1973–4), 10 at 11.
150 Morash, *History of Irish theatre*, p. 81.   151 *Calcraft v. West* (1845) 2 Jo & La 123.
152 At 135.   153 At 140.   154 (1602) 11 Co Rep 84b, 101 Eng Rep 1260.
155 11 Co Rep at 88b, 101 Eng Rep at 1266.

The period contemporaneous with Calcraft's dominance of the Dublin theatre would spawn further legal problems linked to the rights of those who held theatre debentures,[156] and to a series of surrenders and reissues of patents and a succession of managers. Financial difficulties invariably furnished the context, and these were again to the fore when attempts were set in train in the 1850s and '60s to secure further issues of theatre patents.

In 1857 when but two Dublin theatres were actually functioning – the Theatre Royal in Hawkins Street and the Queen's in Great Brunswick Street, under the management of John Harris and J.C. Joseph, respectively – a memorial was presented to the lord lieutenant seeking a patent under the 1786 Act for a third theatre.[157] The applicant was a retired solicitor, one John Knight Boswell. The attorney-general J.D. Fitzgerald (later, as Lord Fitzgerald, the first Irish lord of appeal in ordinary) arranged for a hearing on the matter to be held in his own residence in October 1857. Notice of the application was given to both Harris and Joseph who were represented by counsel. Fitzgerald, in opening the proceedings, announced that he proposed to entertain Boswell's application 'on the only grounds he could do so with propriety' – the public requirements. Harris and Joseph furnished some statistical information: the Theatre Royal could hold 3,800 people with an average audience of 2,000; the Queen's 750 in the pit, 400 in the lower gallery, 600 in the upper gallery and 200 in boxes, but was, usually, only half-full. Fitzgerald announced he would be advising the lord lieutenant, the earl of Carlisle, not to grant the sought-for patent. The statistical evidence he adjudged conclusive. 'It must be remembered', he was to be reported as having observed,

> that in the Theatre Royal every entertainment of character produced in London is given in Dublin; and that, if between the two theatres, the public did not get all they required, it was beyond even the fertile brain of Mr Boswell to invent any attraction for them. If they did not rightly fill either, whence was Mr Boswell's audience to be gathered?

Ten years later, another application seeking a patent was presented in the name of the Winter Garden and Exhibition Palace Co.[158] They sought to exhibit plays in the smaller Concert Rooms. Hearings were commenced in Dublin Castle before the two law officers, Hedges Eyre Chatterton, the attorney-general, and Robert Richard Warren, the solicitor-general. The inquiry was adjourned whereupon the applicant company collapsed. The lack of success that met this application was greeted with approval by one contemporary observer who remarked:

---

156 Cf. *Malone v. Harris* (1859) 11 Ir Ch Rep 33.

157 See Anon., *The history of the Theatre Royal, Dublin, from its foundation in 1821 to the present time* (Dublin, Edward Ponsonby, 1870), pp 146–8.

158 Ibid., p. 148.

> We trust there is now an end of all such attempts which, proceeding on the specious ground of the public good, are merely speculations for individual benefit, or frantic efforts to sustain sinking projects.

It had been a hard-fought business even so, with counsel representing all the interested parties at the now traditional hearing in Dublin Castle before the Irish law officers.[159] Denis Heron, QC, represented the Winter Garden and Exhibition Palace Co.; Theobald Purcell, QC, Mr Bicknell, the holder of the patent for the Theatre Royal in Hawkins Street, and General Sir Frederick Smith and Mr Measure, trustees for the same theatre's annuitants; Richard Dowse, QC, Mr Joseph, the patentee of the Queen's Theatre; William Exham, QC, Mr Harris the sublessee and manager of the Theatre Royal; and, last but not least, Bartholomew Lloyd, QC, the provost and Board of Trinity College Dublin, the lessors of the Theatre Royal. At the adjournment of the proceedings, the attorney-general, Hedges Eyre Chatterton, soon to be elevated to the bench as vice-chancellor, had indicated that at the planned resumption of the hearing the Winter Garden and Exhibition Palace Co. would continue to face significant obstacles.[160] He demanded that they would have to convince him of the necessity for another theatre in Dublin and that they had a suitable building in mind. Even if such conditions were met, Chatterton was adamant that the company had to produce the names of individuals prepared to take any grant and to become responsible for the good conduct and management of the theatre. Neither a company nor a fluctuating body such as a committee was a proper recipient for a Dublin theatre patent. In the end the application failed.

The next theatre patent to be awarded was that awarded to Mr Richard Gunn and Mr John Gunn in respect of the theatre in South King Street, later denominated the Gaiety. The patent was awarded in 1871, and was preceded by the now customary hearing conducted by the law officers, at the time Charles Robert Barry, the attorney-general, and Richard Dowse, the solicitor-general, the latter of whom had had the experience of representing the patentee of the Queen's Theatre at the 1867 inquiry. This public hearing was unusually protracted, commencing in February 1870, resuming in April, and culminating in a decision favourable to the Gunns in June. In the process, a great deal of detail regarding the then state of the theatre in Dublin is brought into the public domain.

Counsel for Messrs Gunn, the applicants, introduced witnesses who detailed the plans for the theatre which had not yet been built. Mr John Gunn, in his evidence, explained that he had sought the advice of theatre managers in London: Messrs Boucicault, Sothern and Chatterton. He also took pains to repudiate the notion that would appear to have swayed the law officers in 1857 and 1867, that Dublin would not be in a position to support a third theatre. In towns of any considerable size, he argued, the ratio was one theatre to every 65,000 inhabitants.

159 *Irish Builder*, 9 (1867), 105–6.   160 Ibid., at 106.

He added, for good measure, that he had already to hand a considerable portion of the funds necessary for building the theatre.

Counsel for Mr Joseph, patentee of the Queen's Theatre, opposed the application. He relied on a memorial got up 'by most respectable citizens', in which the view was expressed that there was no necessity whatever in Dublin for more theatres than those already in existence. He detected in the stance of the law officers a mood of sympathy towards the applicants. In view of the struggle of his own client to secure renewal of his patent in the past, he (counsel) found that stance hard to stomach. He added that it would be a great calamity if the result of starting a third theatre was to create ruinous competition between them. Mr Joseph himself testified that he was perfectly certain that there was not in Dublin a sufficient number of play-going people to support three theatres.

Counsel for Mr Harris, the lessee of the Theatre Royal, surveyed the history of the theatre since its erection in 1820, emphasising the financial problems by which it had regularly been confronted. In 1820 it had cost between £80,000 and £90,000 to construct and the debentures on it amounted to about £10,000. All Harris' predecessors had lost largely by it – another Harris, the first lessee, then Abbott, followed by Gunn and Calcraft. In 1849 the theatre became vacant and remained so for two or three years. When the present Mr Harris came forward in 1851 to take it, a large sum was due on it for rent. Counsel asserted that the outgoings were enormous, and it continued to be extremely difficult to make ends meet. The rent was £1,100 a year; there were persons in London with annuities charged on it to the amount of £1,000 a year (the same annuitants, one assumes, who had raised objections to the plans of the Winter Garden and Exhibition Palace Co. three years before). Mr Harris himself explained that the annuities payable out of the revenues of the theatre amounted in total to £3,000 a year. There were, besides, 100 debenture-holders, of whom 60, he advised the law officers, availed themselves of their privileges when he took the theatre. His management having proved a little more successful than that of his predecessors, he found almost the entire 100 made their appearance. In his first years as lessee he had kept the theatre open until August, but regular losses, sometimes as much as £100 a week, occurring from May onwards had obliged him to alter his approach. The Theatre Royal could never exist, he insisted, unless it had an exclusive right. He had worked like a slave for twenty-one years, and made nothing by it. He had paid two cheques for £400 each to Patti for twelve nights, besides having to pay all the other artists, when the receipts were £130 a night. On redecorating the theatre he had spent £3,800 in 1858, £150 in 1859 and £1,000 in 1865. His total investment in the theatre came to around £10,000. During the opera seasons expenses varied between £1,200 and £1,500 a week. The auditorium could accommodate 6,380 persons, but only once, during a production of *A Midsummer Night's Dream*, a production graced by the presence of the viceroy, the earl of Eglinton, had he seen every seat taken. On average opera nights there was room in the dress circle for 100 persons more than it contained. The house had never been full for five years. During the last pantomime, on which he claimed he had expended £2,000 before he received a penny, there was room in every part of the theatre every night.

Two interventions by Richard Dowse, the solicitor-general, are recorded from the resumed hearing of April 1870.[161] Referring to a memorial supportive of the application which had been adduced in evidence, Dowse averred he had never seen a document so largely and respectably signed. But, he continued, the only signatory who had been produced was Sir William Carroll, and Carroll in his testimony had not pledged himself to the statement in the memorial, but, on the contrary, guarded himself against expressing a positive opinion. 'This only showed', Dowse is recorded as observing,[162]

> how easily people were induced to sign memorials, and how desirable it was that some of them should be produced for examination as to their opinions on the matter.

Dowse's second intervention was precise and to the point. 'It would materially increase the attractions of the Theatre Royal', he intimated, 'if backs and arms were added to the seats in the boxes.'

On 14 June 1870 Charles Robert Barry, the attorney-general, announced the decision of his colleague, the solicitor-general, and himself: that they would be recommending to the lord lieutenant that, subject to certain conditions, that he should exercise his powers under the 1786 Act to grant a patent to the Messrs Gunn.[163] An objection to the award of the patent had been advanced by the Exhibition Palace Co. (who had failed in their own application of 1867). This objection, Barry concluded, amounted to nothing more than a motion to seek postponement of the inquiry, which he had not been prepared to accept. Doubt was cast on the *bona fides* of the owner and lessee of the Queen's Theatre, in pressing their objections. Here Barry revisited recent history. 'In 1857', he chose to recall,

> an application for a third theatre was made by a Mr Boswell, and the owner of the Queen's Theatre having undertaken to make alterations and improvements in it, the application was refused; but the danger of competition being past, the undertaking seems to have been forgotten, and there is no evidence that the promised improvements in the Queen's Theatre have been carried out.

The expressed opposition of the Theatre Royal was a more serious obstacle, but, in the end, Barry and Dowse chose to override it. Invited to follow the precedent involving the Queen's Theatre in 1857, i.e., to deny the application for a third patent on condition that the Theatre Royal make structural improvements (to the ventilation and the seats), the two law officers declined to do anything of the sort:

161 *Irish Builder*, 12 (1870), 90.   162 Ibid.   163 *Irish Builder*, 12 (1870), 141–2.

once bitten, twice shy. Turning to the substantive problem, both law officers considered there was undoubted merit in the argument presented by Messrs Gunn that the current lessee of the Theatre Royal had failed to accommodate himself to the tastes of the day by persevering in the monotonous and unvarying production of 'regular' or 'legitimate' drama. The dismissal of similar applications back in 1867 and 1857 was a matter of equal concern. 'Another refusal now', argued Barry,

> to recommend that a patent should be granted would establish such a series of precedents for the refusal, that no law officer in this generation in all likelihood would depart from it, and a continuing monopoly would thus be established in favour of the present patentees.

Messrs Gunn had a site secured and a large proportion of the requisite capital; they also had a plan of the theatre prepared and an architect ready to enter on the work: none of this had obtained in the case certainly of Mr Boswell's application of 1857.

There would be conditions and limitations in the patent the law officers finally recommended that the lord lieutenant should award:

> The patent will be limited to dramatic performances, such as are specified in the heading of the memorial signed by the citizens in favour of the proposed theatre. It will authorise only the erection of a theatre upon the site named, and it will contain a clause enabling the Crown to revoke the patent if at any time, in the opinion of the Lord Lieutenant, the theatre became defective in its sanitary arrangements, in its means of ingress or egress, in its accommodation for the public; or if, in the class or conduct of its audience, the nature of its performances, or any other respect, it should prove, in his opinion, not to be a place of respectable entertainment to the citizens of Dublin.

The patent for the Gaiety, which issued in 1871, sanctioned the putting on at the venue of 'interludes, comedies, preludes' and other kinds of entertainment, but, for the time at least, prohibited the putting on of tragedies, the performance of which was reserved to the Theatre Royal in Hawkins Street. This restriction was short-lived, being removed following further proceedings in 1890.[164]

The plans for the new theatre, as the decision on the Gaiety's application pointed out, entailed that accommodation would be at a premium and it would not, in consequence, be in a position to stage Italian opera – a factor further indicative of the circumstance that this new entrant would not necessarily be as damaging as might have been reckoned at the time to the financial prospects of the Theatre Royal. Michael Gunn at the Gaiety had his own financial worries of course, and sought to deal with those by the adoption of a truly remarkable – and certainly

164 *Irish Builder*, 32 (1890), 178.

controversial – stratagem: the investment in 1874 of moneys that saw him become both lessee and manager of the Theatre Royal itself. This followed the assignment to him under the Theatre Royal's patent which had been renewed for a further twenty-one years in February 1861.[165]

One criticism that Gunn faced a few years before is unlikely to have caused him too many sleepless nights. The press covered the laying of the foundation stone for the Gaiety by Dublin's lord mayor in July 1871, and the banquet that was held thereafter to mark the occasion. The trade journal, the *Building News*, entered a sour note. 'At a time', the journal remarked, begrudgingly,[166]

> when so many people in Ireland are talking about 'Home Rule', it is a pity the people of Dublin were obliged or felt inclined to go to London for an architect [the Mr Phipps who had appeared as a witness at the hearing of the application for the patent], and to Paris for a name for the new theatre, and particularly as one by the same name has recently been erected in London.

One other development at this particular juncture may be briefly noted: the renewal in March 1872 for a period of twenty-one years of the patent enjoyed by the Queen's Theatre (the former Adelphi). This patent, again out of concern for the viability of the Theatre Royal, repeated the prohibition on the presentation at the Queen's of 'regular drama'.

Two years before the Theatre Royal's patent of 1861 was due to expire, disaster struck on 9 February 1880 when the theatre itself was destroyed by fire. It was not to be finally replaced by a new Theatre Royal on the same site until December 1897.[167] What occurred in the months and years following requires to be understood against this background. The theatre had been insured, and Michael Gunn, the manager, was not exactly out of pocket, and he still had the Gaiety to manage. But the lack of any provision for serious theatre – a lack that the Queen's was not permitted to rectify, nor the Gaiety itself, until the terms of its patent were modified in 1890 – grated with some, as an angry contributor to the *Irish Builder* in 1883 pointed out.[168]

A year later, when there was still no sign of any plan to rebuild the Theatre Royal, a James Dillon, described as an advertising contractor, appeared on the scene, seeking a patent for a new theatre on Great Brunswick Street, opposite the Queen's, a theatre to be called the Lyceum.[169] The attorney-general of the day, John Naish, having given notice to all the interested parties, conducted a hearing on the application on 30 January and 1 February 1884, announcing his decision on 15 March.[170] The attorney-general dwelt on the fact that no steps had been taken to replace the old Theatre Royal over the preceding four years. The fact that Gunn

165 *Irish Builder*, 26 (1884), 87.   166 Quoted, *Irish Builder*, 13 (1871), 188.
167 Morash, *History of Irish theatre*, p. 106.
168 'The Dublin drama and the old Theatre Royal', *Irish Builder*, 25 (1883), 16.
169 *Irish Builder*, 26 (1884), 32.   170 Ibid., p. 87.

had lately surfaced with a plan to do just that seemed to owe something to Mr Dillon having taken his initiative. The site chosen by Dillon for his Lyceum was central and there was a public interest in creating a state of affairs where there would be rivalry with the Gaiety. The attorney-general, while favourable to the granting of a patent, laid down a number of conditions: the new theatre should provide 2,900 seats (this meant the plans submitted would have to be revised); the theatre was to be completed within eighteen months to the satisfaction of a competent person appointed by the Board of Works who was to certify that the theatre had been completed in accordance with the rules regarding ingress and egress as per the regulations for theatres in London; conditions applicable to theatres in London were to be attached; and breach of any of these conditions would entail forfeiture of the patent. Dillon's project was not destined to prosper. The change to the plans increased the costs, and, although in the autumn he was confident building on the site would commence in the spring of 1885,[171] in mid-December 1884 the patent had still not been signed,[172] though in 1885 it was.[173] In the spring of 1887 there was still no progress, despite the circumstance that Dillon had memorialised Dublin Castle for an extension in the time allowed him to complete building. This delay, suggestive of the entire collapse of the project, earned a barbed comment from the *Irish Builder*. 'The ghosts of the old debenture-holders and free-passers', the issue of 15 October 1884 intoned,

> might have disturbed the dreams of some very interested today, but there were other reasons which can be better imagined on the part of citizen playgoers than described by us.

The collapse of Dillon's project may have been signalled by two developments recorded from the summer of 1890 – a further request for the extension under his patent of the time limited thereby for the erection of the theatre, and an associated request for permission to assign his rights under the patent to a Mr Paeton of London as trustee on behalf of a company not yet formed for acquiring the patent and the site for the construction of the theatre and for erecting and maintaining the latter.[174] Late in July 1890 the attorney-general, Hugh Holmes, gave extended consideration to Dillon's request for the assignment. He granted it, despite understandable concerns over the financial viability of the entire project. In so doing, Holmes gave this doomed project a new lease of life.[175] The amended patent was to name Mr Paeton alone.

Dillon's project finally galvanised Gunn into taking action himself, for in the spring of 1887 he applied for a patent for a new theatre, to be called Leinster Hall, to be opened on the site of the old Theatre Royal, the patent in regard to which had expired in 1882, two years after the fire.[176] Piers White, QC, Gunn's counsel, at the

171 Ibid., p. 303.   172 Ibid., p. 365.   173 *Irish Builder*, 27 (1885), 101.
174 *Irish Times*, 17 July 1890.   175 *Irish Builder*, 32 (1890), 178–9.   176 Ibid., 29 (1887), 130.

now predictably routine formal hearing, chose to dwell on the circumstance that Gunn had already spent £23,000 on the actual building, £15,000 of which probably presented what the insurers had made over for the loss of the Theatre Royal in 1880. Architects gave evidence on the adaptability of the present plans to make a much enlarged theatre. Gunn, in evidence himself, indicated that it was very likely Sarah Bernhardt could be booked to appear if a patent might be expeditiously granted. A Mr Hague, of a troupe known as the Hague Minstrels, may or may not have added to the chorus of enthusiasm when assuring the attorney-general, J.G. Gibson, that he would be able to put on a much better show on the larger stage of the Leinster Hall. Gibson was invited to consider the rights of debenture-holders in the Theatre Royal following its destruction, but declined to enter that minefield and adjourned his decision on the main issue. Gibson recommended the grant of a patent, which ensued, but with a restriction forbidding the performance of tragedy, a restriction that was to be removed in further proceedings in 1890.[177]

A grand new Theatre Royal was eventually erected on the Hawkins Street site, opening in December 1897. This, in turn, was replaced by another new building in 1934–5, a development, as it chanced, which provoked litigation over ancient lights.[178] This third Theatre Royal was to be finally demolished in 1962, some seven years before the Queen's (the Adelphi) suffered the identical fate.

Two further developments occurring before the end of the nineteenth century merit mention. First, a local Act specific to Dublin, enacted in 1890,[179] introduced tough new regulations to guard against the risk of fire in Dublin theatres.[180] As we shall see in a subsequent chapter,[181] this initiative fitted in with comparable developments throughout the then United Kingdom where fire hazards in all places of public resort, and especially in theatres, were now regarded as unacceptably high and requiring legislatively sanctioned remedial measures, such as those laid down in another statute of 1890, the Public Health Acts Amendment Act.[182] The Dublin Act of 1890, it is safe to assume, however, must have owed something to the memory of the Hawkins Street fire of ten years before which had destroyed the then Theatre Royal.

This flurry of concern left one legacy so far as future Dublin theatre patents were concerned. These would now make it incumbent on proprietors and managers alike to ensure that the buildings in which dramatic and other performances took place were structurally sound and that all practicable precautions against the outbreak of fire were put in place and maintained. There was one other consequence to note. Earlier patents had not forbidden smoking in the auditorium, e.g., the Gaiety's patent of 1879;[183] future patents would adopt a markedly different stance. This was the case, for instance, in the case of the patent

---

177 *Irish Builder*, 32 (1890), 178.   178 *Smyth v. Dublin Theatre Co. Ltd* [1936] IR 692.
179 Dublin Corporation Act, 1890, 53 & 54 Vict., c. ccxlvi.
180 See ss. 54–6.   181 Below, ch. 10.   182 53 & 54 Vict., c. 59.
183 Evidence of Mr Gunn to the select committee of 1892: HC 1892, xviii, 1 at p. 235.

for the Leinster Hall, the concert-hall venue, built on the site of the Theatre Royal in Hawkins Street.[184]

The second development witnessed an addition to the powers already possessed by the lord lieutenant. In 1898, legislation[185] endowed him with the power to issue occasional licences for the performance of any stage play or other dramatic entertainment.[186] But there were conditions. The profits generated, it had to be shown, were to be 'applied for a charitable purpose or in aid of funds of any society instituted for the purpose of science, literature or the fine arts exclusively.' There was a geographical limitation too. Applications for the issuance of such occasional licence would only be entertained if emanating from local authorities in the Dublin area (the council for the county of Dublin or the county borough of Dublin or any urban district within the county). The provinces once again were being studiously ignored by Parliament.

The background to this unusual addition to the statute-book has been established by Morash.[187] Early in 1898 the managers of the three patent theatres, the Theatre Royal, the Queen's and the Gaiety, issued a public warning threatening to prosecute anyone staging plays in Dublin. This caused consternation among those who at this very moment were planning the establishment of the Irish Literary Theatre – the likes of W.B. Yeats, Lady Gregory and Edward Martyn. Representations were made and section 89 of the 1898 Local Government (Ireland) Act was the result. There was a certain irony in the circumstance that what was to become the Irish National Theatre with its base at the Abbey Theatre (from 1904) should have begun its life under 'the patronage' of Dublin Castle. In a few short years, however, the legal basis upon which this new theatre continued to function would change: it was a case of a return to the Act of 1786. The patentees' threat of early 1898 was in line with warnings both before and after, targeting the performance of dramatic sketches in Dublin's emerging music-halls. Such performances, it would seem, were to be successfully opposed,[188] cases being brought at the behest of the attorney-general.

In the autumn of 1904 two new theatre patents were issued. Prior to announcing his recommendations to the lord lieutenant on these two patent applications – in respect of the Pavilion Theatre in Kingstown (Dun Laoghaire) and in that of what became known as the Abbey Theatre in Dublin – the solicitor-general, J.H.M. Campbell, KC, MP, prefaced his judgment with a few general remarks on the approach he sensed was properly to be employed in the operation of the Act of 1786. 'It was plain', he was to be reported as having declared,[189]

---

184 Ibid.   185 Local Government (Ireland) Act, 1898: 61 & 62 Vict., c. 27.   186 S. 89.

187 Morash, *History of Irish theatre*, pp 115–16.

188 *Report from the joint select committee of the House of Lords and House of Commons on the stage plays (censorship)*, HC 1909, viii, at p. 189.

189 Quoted, Anon., 'The law of the stage in Dublin', *ILT & SJ*, 43 (1909), 209 at 210. A contemporary account of Campbell's judgment will be found in *The New Irish Jurist and Local Government Review*, 4 (1904), 339.

that the object of the statute was to provide that the patents to be granted should not be of such a character as to render it impossible to grant further patents so long as the holders of existing patents were not hindered or prevented from conducting their own business on commercial and profitable lines.

As was not entirely unexpected, both these applications were to be opposed by the holders of the three existing theatre patents in Dublin – at the Theatre Royal, Hawkins Street; the Queen's (formerly the Adelphi), Great Brunswick Street; and the Gaiety, South King Street. At the hearing of the Kingstown Pavilion's application, Mr O'Shaughnessy, KC, counsel for the Gaiety, urged the solicitor-general to accept the argument that the 1786 Act only contemplated the granting of a patent for a theatre in the restricted sense of that term, namely a building continuously and exclusively devoted to the production of plays – an argument not unlike that which had been addressed to Lord Lifford by Richard Daly in the controversy in 1788 over the projected patent for Philip Astley. The solicitor-general refused to do anything of the sort. The terms of the first section of the 1786 Act, coupled with the provisos in the second and third sections, demonstrated that the word 'theatre' in the Act was used in the wider sense of a building devoted to spectacular entertainments of any kind; the intention of the Act had been, he was satisfied, merely to prohibit the performance of plays in any such theatre unless under the sanction of a patent.[190] He had been pressed to accept as the principal objection the fear that to grant a patent would unduly conflict with the legitimate interests of the existing theatres, reflecting a concern that Campbell, as we have seen, admitted was valid. But again, the solicitor-general was not persuaded: 'during the period when the Pavilion had been in full blast, the receipts in the Dublin theatres had not fallen off in a way that would support such an argument'. If the Pavilion put on first-class plays, the cost of producing them would not be less than in Dublin and members of the audience would, in addition to the payment for entrance, have to pay their fares to Kingstown. Furthermore, if, on the other hand, as was most likely, the Pavilion put on a lighter class of play, once again that would not really involve competition.[191] Aside from all these arguments, there were the interests of the public to consider, and the desirability of improving indoor entertainment for visitors to a booming tourist destination like Kingstown. Precautions against fire and the provision of better dressing-room accommodation at the Pavilion would be required, and the proprietors would be prohibited from selling intoxicating liquors, but subject to conditions in all these respects being imposed, the solicitor-general would be reporting to the lord lieutenant that a patent should be granted. The plans for the Pavilion being somewhat experimental, the operation of the patent would be limited to seven years.[192]

---

190 Ibid., 339–40.   191 Ibid., 340.   192 Ibid.

The application presented by Miss Horniman on behalf of the Irish National Theatre Society for the society's premises in Lower Abbey Street was also to succeed.[193] But, after doubt had been expressed over granting a patent to a person with residence outside the jurisdiction, the name of Lady Gregory was substituted as the applicant and she it was who received the patent. This first patent for the Abbey was granted for but six years, and was made subject to the receipt of a certificate from the Dublin city architect that structural improvements had been carried out to his satisfaction. Plainly, the shadow of the fire at the Theatre Royal in 1880 continued to influence decision-making.[194] Following discussions with the holders of the existing theatre patents, Miss Horniman's legal team agreed not to seek an excise licence for the sale of alcohol and not to enlarge the existing premises, so as to provide for a greater number of patrons than it was capable of holding at the time. A third plank in the agreement constituted a form of mission statement for the putative Abbey. It concerned the type of dramatic production that would be put on there – a somewhat unusual specification that was in fact inserted in the actual patent. 'The patent', the legal language of the document read,[195]

> shall only empower the patentee to exhibit plays in the Irish or English language written by Irish writers on Irish subjects, or such dramatic works of foreign authors as would tend to interest the public in the higher works of dramatic art; all foregoing to be selected by the Irish National Theatre Society under the provisions of Part 6 of its rules and existing and subject to the restrictions therein contained.

The patent, it was additionally prescribed, would cease if the Irish National Theatre Society was dissolved.

The earl of Dudley, the lord lieutenant, accordingly granted both applications. In the case of the Irish National Theatre Society (the Abbey), this patent of 1904 was thereafter to be regularly renewed, the first such renewal – for the more customary twenty-one years – occurring in 1911.[196]

---

193 The hearings were held in Dublin Castle on 5, 8 and 9 Aug. 1904: *NIJ & LGR*, 4 (1904), 270.
194 *NIJ & LGR*, 4 (1904), 339.   195 Ibid.   196 Morash, *History of Irish theatre*, p. 145.

CHAPTER NINE

Dublin theatre patents: countdown to abolition

IN THE LATE 1970s the Oscar Cinema in Sandymount was converted into a theatre and the lessees of the site memorialised the government for a grant of letters patent in June 1979.[1] These lessees were replaced a few years later by an entity known as Volkslied Ltd and the latter presented a fresh memorial in May 1984, no significant progress having occurred so far as the memorial of 1979 was concerned. An interesting question arose on the first memorial, presented in the name of the Ballsbridge Cinema Co.: did they hold under a lease or by means of a mere licence? More serious issues perhaps arose in regard to the application in the name of Volkslied. Put on notice, Dublin Corporation reported unfavourably on the safety of the building in which the theatre was housed: ventilation was poor, ditto in the case of exit routes. Electric wiring was defective and combustible material was stored where it ought not to have been. The theatre continued to put on performances and made much of its role as an 'educational theatre'. With seating restricted to 285 seats, income presented a major headache. An application in 1982 for a music and singing licence under the 1890 Public Health Acts Amendment Act[2] was designed to pave the way for the grant of an alcohol retail licence, but the corporation let it be known that they would object to the renewal of any such licence. The building in its view continuing to present a fire hazard, a prosecution under the Fire Services Act 1981[3] could not be ruled out either. A final stage in the history of the Oscar was reached in late 1984, a few months after Volkslied Ltd had presented its memorial. The company sought planning permission for the opening of a lounge bar on the premises. Dublin Corporation said 'yes', but An Bord Pleanála overturned that decision. Ironically, if the latter had not, and a formal inquiry over the application for letters patent had gone ahead, the corporation, wearing a different hat, would have continued to object or at least to lodge reservations. Following this reverse, Volkslied announced that it was disposing of its interest in the site, and the Oscar closed.

In the late 1980s and early 1990s inquiries concerning the granting of letters patent were received from a number of quarters, inquiries, however, that were not

---

1 This chapter is based very largely on information contained in old files relating to the regime of theatre patents held in the Office of the Attorney-General which I was permitted to consult, a permission for which I am most grateful.
2 53 & 54 Vict., c. 59: see s. 51. 3 No. 30 of 1981.

pursued: for example, for the Point Depot, for the deconsecrated Church of Ireland church of St George's in Hardwicke Place, and for the Grapevine Arts Centre on City Quay. Many other 'theatres' chose not to make application at all, and these included the Eblana in Store Street, the Focus in Pembroke Place and the Project Arts Theatre in East Essex Street (Temple Bar). Trinity College Dublin took its obligations under the 1786 Act rather more seriously, and in 1995 put in a lengthy and excellent memorial seeking (in the name of the then provost and secretary – T.N. Mitchell and Michael Gleeson) a grant of letters patent for the new Samuel Beckett Theatre opened on its centre-city campus. By this time, all the letters patent for Dublin's principal theatres – the Gaiety, the Olympia, the Gate, the Abbey with the Peacock – had all expired, and, although in some instances application had been made for renewals, nothing had been done, no inquiries under the 1786 Act had been undertaken by attorneys-general at the new venue where such inquiries had in the more recent past taken place, the appropriately designated Patent Office in Merrion Square. The bars in all these theatres continued to function, however, a matter over which the Revenue commissioners on several occasions chose to express their extreme disquiet.

The Theatre Royal in Hawkins Street, rebuilt after the disastrous fire of 1880, was itself demolished in the early 1930s, not long after a fresh patent, backdated to November 1928, had come into force, a sequence of events precipitating a new inquiry which led in due course to an entirely new patent, bearing date in the summer of 1935.[4] The replacement building of the same year lasted less than thirty years, the Theatre Royal closing for good at the end of June 1962. The writer Frank McDonald relates that it got 'an emotional send-off'.[5] As the auctioneers deputed by the Rank Organisation, the building's owners, he wrote,[6]

> were preparing to sell off the theatre's fittings, even its ticket kiosks and safety curtain, ordinary Dubliners filled every one of its 2,500 seats for the last time. The 'Royal Finale' featured a host of stars associated with the theatre since it first opened in 1935.

Hawkins House now stands on the site.

Another theatre had suffered a similar fate in the same decade. The Queen's had served as a temporary base for the Abbey since the fire at the latter's old home in 1951. With the return of the Abbey company to its brand new theatre building in 1966, the lease of the Queen's came on the market. In next to no time outline planning permission for an office block on the site was obtained. In due course, demolition occurred and an office block constructed on the site – 'five storeys high, with a bricked-in car park at street level' and called Áras an Phiarsaigh, and serving for years as a social welfare office.[7]

4   On the background to this inquiry, see the *Irish Times*, 10 Jan. 1935.
5   Frank McDonald, *The destruction of Dublin* (Dublin, Gill & Macmillan, 1985), p. 41.
6   Ibid.   7   McDonald, *Destruction of Dublin*, pp 44–5.

The two closures represented a significant break with the past. Both theatres had possessed letters patent stretching back for well over a century. Larger performance venues thenceforth were now in short supply. Others, of course, remained.

Along with the Gate, the Olympia was the only other theatre to be granted letters patent for the first time following Irish independence. This occurred in December 1937, and was testimony to the change in the tastes for which the Olympia considered it was best placed to cater. A renewal occurred for the customary twenty-one-year period in 1957 when the directors of the then owners, Olympia Productions Ltd, were given as Brendan Smith, Lorcan Bourke, Joan Grist, and Noel Pearson (as nominee for Richard Hillinan), the preceding memorial having given as the aim of the Olympia to present variety, concerts and pantomimes – all, of course, clearly within the definitions set out in the 1786 Act. Disaster struck at the Olympia in November 1974, four years before this renewal was due to expire, when, mercifully involving no loss of life, the proscenium arch in the theatre collapsed.[8] The letters patent of May 1957 had been made out in favour of Stanley Illsley and Leo McCabe as trustees for the Olympia Theatre Ltd. In occupation of the theatre at this critical juncture were a different concern, Olympia Productions Ltd, and it was by no means clear which entity should apply for fresh letters patent. A dispute ensued between the two companies over who was liable to repair the damage caused by the collapse of November 1974, no rent had been paid, and Olympia Theatre Ltd in consequence were refusing to grant Olympia Productions Ltd a fresh lease under the Landlord and Tenant Act 1931.[9]

Matters dragged on as regards the Olympia itself. In 1981, it was agreed that any letters patent now being applied for would be held by one of the directors of the landlord company, Mrs Joan Grist, and it was decided that a new lease in favour of Olympia Productions Ltd should be granted. As a result of the collapse of November 1974, Dublin Corporation had been put on notice that, on grounds primarily of public safety, inspection of the theatre likely to be ordered in advance of a letters patent inquiry would require to be especially rigorous. It would be essential to ensure in the case of an old building that no further deterioration in the soundness of the structure had taken place or was taking place. A cursory investigation indicated that means of escape from the bars and from the dressing-rooms would have to be improved. A full report by the Board of Works architect was finally received in February 1994. This highlighted the presence of wet rot in joists in the ceiling (which had then been replaced), collapsed plastering and unstable stair rails leading to the Upper Circle. The previous autumn it had apparently been agreed that all outstanding repairs and improvements would have to be carried out within two years, and the chief state solicitor had advised on 7 September 1993 that any letters patent, should these be about to be granted, should be backdated by as much as 15 years to May 1978 when the last letters

---

8 Ibid., p. 44.   9 No. 55 of 1931: see s. 25(i).

patent had expired. Once again, for a variety of reasons – the dispute over the lease, the concerns of Dublin Corporation and the Board of Works – a theatre had been retailing sales of alcohol when not apparently licensed to do so – a practice that continued to alarm the Revenue commissioners.

Renewals of the letters patent for the Gaiety in South King Street are recorded up until 1954. The original grant of 1871 was renewed in favour of Michael Gunn for a further twenty-one years in 1891. The theatre was sold to the Gaiety Theatre Dublin for £35,000 in 1909, and it was in their favour that the letters patent expiring in 1912 were renewed in the latter year. Fresh letters patent were sought in the name of David and David C. Telford, after the customary twenty-one years, in 1933, and when these were on the point of expiring, a fresh memorial was lodged in the name of Louis and Abraham Elliman on 7 July 1953. The inquiry that then took place, conducted by Thomas Teevan, the then attorney-general, raised issues that went to the heart of the entire process of allocating theatre patents, issues that will be gone into more detail later. In the end, following considerable delays, renewal of the Gaiety's letters patent was sanctioned on 1 May 1956, the twenty-one-year period of renewal being backdated to 9 March 1954, when the old letters patent had expired. On the expiry of the 1956/1954 letters patent in March 1975, steps had already been taken to secure another twenty-one-years grant in the name of William Sandys and Bartholomew O'Shea. But, as we will shortly discover, the process was to be dragged out, so much so in fact that in the end no grant of letters patent was made out prior to the abolition of theatre patents in the National Cultural Institutions Act in 1997.

The second theatre subsequent to Irish independence to be granted letters patent under the 1786 Act was the Gate, a theatre which in its early years was associated with its founders Micheál MacLiammóir and Hilton Edwards. It was granted its letters patent in the early 1930s. Renewals followed, one such occurring for the traditional twenty-one-year period as from 24 October 1952 in a grant dated seven years later on 20 October 1959. This grant was made in favour of the earl of Longford and Louis Jammet as trustees for the Dublin Gate Theatre Co. Ltd. These letters patent expired on 24 October 1973, but it was only nearly seven years later that a fresh memorial seeking a renewal was presented. This memorial of 16 April 1980 sought a grant of the patent for Hilton Edwards, Terence de Vere White and Mary Cannon as trustees for the Edwards MacLiammóir Dublin Gate Theatre Productions Ltd. Once again a theatre had operated for close on seven years without a patent. In this instance, that did not immediately betoken that alcohol had been retailed unlawfully, for under a clause in the letters patent of 1952/9 the condition had been imposed that

> No intoxicating liquor shall be sold or served or permitted to be sold or served in any part of the said premises in respect whereof these letters patent are granted.

Remarkably, however, a further clause enabled the named holders of the patent 'to apply to a member of the government to alter or modify' any of a number of conditions, including the one on the sale of liquor, and were such alteration or modification permitted, then the particular condition was 'deemed to be altered and modified accordingly'. At some point subsequent to 1959 this was done, for on the Revenue commissioners' blacklist of theatres operating without a theatre patent or licence and thus without a drinks licence, a blacklist drawn up in 1980, the Gate was to appear.

The Gate letters patent of 1952/9 constitute one of the last of the grants to go into detail as regards what was allowed to be done on stage or rather what was not allowed to be done.[10] Henceforth, it was recited,

> no representation shall be admitted on the stage by virtue or under cover of these presents whereby the Christian Religion or any other Religion recognised by the State by virtue of Article 44 of the Constitution may in any manner suffer reproach AND all and any degree of abuse or misrepresentation of sacred characters which may in any degree tend to expose religion or bring it into contempt are hereby strictly prohibited and no such characters shall be introduced or played in any other light than such as may increase the just esteem of those who answer the end of those sacred functions.

No less remarkable are two ensuing stipulations. First, that by way of

> the strictest regard to such representations as anywise concern the Civil Policy or the Constitution of the State [it] is hereby enjoined that these may contribute to support lawful authority and to the preservation of order and good government.

Second – a stipulation that, more typically, resonated with what had gone before –

> And so that for the future the said theatre may be instrumental in the promotion of virtue and instruction of human life it is hereby enjoined and commanded that no entertainment or exhibition whatsoever be acted or produced under the authority hereby granted which does or may contain any expression or passage or gesture offensive to decency piety or good manners until the same shall be corrected or purged by the Manager or Managers for the time being by expunging any such offensive expressions, passages and gestures.

This last stipulation was copper-fastened by detailed rules banning 'profanity or impropriety of language' and 'indecency of dress, dance or gesture' on stage. The theatre was to be kept in due and proper repair and to be duly ventilated. It was to

10 For the full text, see the Appendix.

be compliant with Dublin Corporation bye-laws of 1934 and other pertinent rules, regulations and bye-laws of the corporation currently in force. Woe betide the theatre too should it, for whatever reason, 'cease to be an orderly well-conducted and respectable place of public entertainment'.

The further following conditions were also made to apply:

2. Admission shall be given at all times to the authorised members of the Garda Síochána.
3. Admission to the interior of the theatre shall be given only to so many persons as there shall be seating accommodation for.
6. No offensive personalities or representations of living persons shall be permitted on the stage or anything calculated to give offence or to produce riot or a breach of the peace.
7. No women or children shall be hung from the flies nor fixed in positions from which they cannot release themselves.
8. No public masquerade shall be permitted in the theatre.
9. No encouragement shall be given to improper characters to assemble or ply their calling in the theatre.
10. All refreshments sold in the theatre shall be sold only in such positions as not to interfere with the convenience and safety of the audience.
11. All suitable and proper dressing rooms and accommodation shall be provided for male and female performers in the said theatre premises.

And last but not least:

12. On demand being made in that behalf by a member of the Government a full and accurate return shall be made showing the number and character of the performances and the length of time occupied by each of such performances in the theatre during any specified period.

Intriguingly, a number of these conditions are also to be found in the grant of letters patent in favour of the Theatre Royal made in 1909. There was one conspicuous omission. The Gate was thus excused from obeying the ukase that no exhibition of wild beasts or 'dangerous performances' were to be permitted on the stage.

The sequence of events relating to the Abbey Theatre and its successive grants of letters patent requires finally to be rehearsed. It will be recalled that the first grant, limited to six years, was made in favour of Lady Gregory in 1904. The renewal, in 1911, was expressed for the more customary twenty-one years and a second renewal, again for twenty-one years, was sanctioned in January 1932, the grant itself being expressed to run from 1 December 1931. This grant of January 1932 had but a year to run when, on 17 July 1951, disaster occurred when the Abbey was burnt down – a tragedy in the history of the Irish stage immediately on a par with the loss of the Theatre Royal in 1880. As is well known, the Abbey, however, following the conflagration, found a new home – in the Queen's Theatre on Pearse Street (the former Great Brunswick Street) and there it remained until 1966 when it returned to the new purpose-built theatre on the old site in Abbey Street.[11]

By way of preparation for the return to north of the Liffey, a memorial in the name of the National Theatre Society Ltd seeking a fresh grant of letters patent was lodged at the end of June 1966. Named as potential recipients of the patent were Riobeard Ó Farachain, Controller of Programmes in Radio Éireann, and Seamus Wilmot, the Registrar of the National University of Ireland. On 28 October 1966, advertisements were inserted in the press advising interested parties that the attorney-general was intending to hold an inquiry into the application for a patent under the provisions of the 1786 Act. Already put on notice were the chief state solicitor, the Garda Síochána, the commissioners of Public Works and Dublin Corporation. A novel feature in this particular memorial was a request for any resultant grant to be made to cover both of the theatres it was intended to unveil in the same new building – the larger Abbey itself and the smaller Peacock (a name chosen, one is led to suspect, because it, too, rose from the ashes). Completion of the Peacock was delayed, and Dublin Corporation refused to give it the 'all clear' until it was. The attorney-general inquiry was finally resumed in October 1967 with the attorney-general being in a position to announce his recommendation after January the following year. That recommendation was favourable, the attorney-general of the day, Mr Colm Condon, arguing that the letters patent should be backdated so as to run from 18 July 1966.

The majority of the conditions attached appear to have been based on those contained in other theatre patents of the period, such as those to be found in the grant in favour of the Gate made in 1959:

> compliance with Dublin Corporation bye-laws;
> right of entry for Gardaí;
> seats for every patron;
> sales of refreshments;
> suitable dressing rooms; and
> the conduct of a well-regulated theatre.

Where conditions attached to the grant in favour of the Gate stipulated that no women or children were to be hung from the flies or fixed in positions from which they could not release themselves, the grant in favour of the Abbey and the Peacock stated more simply that no actor was to be put in a position where he could not release himself.

In addition, however, there were to be two major variations. The first dealt with the constantly vexatious question of provision for the sale of alcohol. The condition read:

11 See Michael O'Neill, *The Abbey at the Queen's: the interregnum years, 1951–1966* (Nepean, Ontario, Borealis, 1999).

> No intoxicating liquor shall be sold or permitted to be sold in any part of either of the theatres save only in the bars therein as shown on the plans nor shall any such sale be permitted before 6 o'clock in the evening, except during matinee performances on Wednesdays, Saturdays or Bank Holidays when the hours during which such alcohol may be sold should not be earlier than 3 o'clock p.m. and in no case whatsoever shall such liquor be permitted to be sold earlier in the day than one half hour before the commencement of a performance or later in the day than one half hour after the termination of a performance and in any event after the hour of 12 o'clock midnight.

The other variation purported to control the character of the representations put on by management. The conditions had two prongs. The first never attracted any sort of criticism. 'Such proportion', the first of these read,

> of the aggregate of the performances in each of the theatres in any year as may, having regard to the circumstances, be reasonable shall consist of performances substantially within the meaning of the Act but not such exhibitions of sound or silent film.

The second prong dripped history, the history of what true believers sensed the Abbey was in business for. The original patent of 1904, it may be recalled, restricted

> the patentee to exhibit plays in the Irish or English language written by Irish writers on Irish subjects, or such dramatic works of foreign authors as would tend to interest the public in the higher works of dramatic art.

The memorial, citing the Abbey's memorandum of association and the language of the letters patent of January 1932, proposed a modification that would restrict the theatre to

> plays written by Irish authors, and plays by foreign authors (not including English authors) and English plays written prior to the year 1830, except that performers other than the Society's performing in the said theatre shall in addition be entitled in any one year to give up to a maximum of 100 performances of other dramatic works not coming within the limitations aforesaid.

As an afterthought as it were, the memorialists sought a further modification that would enable the Society itself to put on modern English and American plays for a maximum of 30 nights in the year.

The attorney-general, Mr Condon, harboured doubts over incorporating these several restrictions in any letters patent issued. He said as much in his advice to the government. In the letters patent eventually issued, the Abbey had had its way: the restrictions, as modified, were repeated.

To follow the story of the Abbey's letters patent, it is enough to know that a memorial presented in June 1987, in advance of the expiry of the 1966 letters patent on 16 July 1987, reworded these key restrictions so that they would henceforth read as follows:

> Save for the period of 30 days in any year the performances acted, represented and performed in the Abbey shall be limited to plays written by Irish authors, plays by authors of any nationality on Irish subjects, plays by foreign authors (not including English authors) and English plays written prior to the year 1830 provided that performers other than those employed by the trustees upon behalf of the Society shall be entitled in any year to give up to a maximum of 100 performances of other plays not coming within the aforesaid limits.

This memorial of 1987 led to no formal law officer's inquiry, abandonment of the entire system of regulating the stage in Dublin by means of the Act of 1786 now being on the cards. In a sense, one can only express regret over this state of affairs, for enlightenment on the meaning of key words in this memorial (as in previous letters patent) would have been welcome, and this must now be regarded as highly unlikely. What is a play on an Irish subject? Who are embraced by the term 'English authors'? Why should the year 1830 have been chosen as the cut-off date, dramas written before then being welcome, dramas written after decidedly not?

In a lengthy *aide-memoire* composed by Mr Condon in 1968, it is plain that he was far from convinced that it was appropriate to attach a formal *imprimatur* to these restrictions. Restrictions to plays of a particular type, he wrote, was hardly contemplated by the Act of 1786. There was no need for these restrictions to be incorporated in the patent, and it would be a simple matter for the Abbey to employ the Companies Act of 1963 to alter its memorandum of association. Another suggestion he threw out in his advice to the Department of the Taoiseach who would eventually sanction the issue of letters patent, was to the effect that if the government wished to influence the pattern of plays put on by the Abbey, they could easily do so via the terms of the subsidy given to the theatre. Only if the Abbey were insistent, should the government acquiesce in entertaining the various restrictions set forth in the memorial.

The Condon *aide-memoire* of 1968 is significant not just on account of the attorney-general's professionally expressed discontent over fixing the Abbey's only marginally modified mission statement in letters of gold in a patent. The entire document breathes dissatisfaction with the Act of 1786, the procedures associated with its implementation, and the need to persist with it at all. It provides us with the first clear evidence that in official circles at least a fresh look required to be taken. Remarkably, it was to take another three decades before the Act was repealed and the system tied to it abandoned, but from this point on it does indeed seem to be the case that the regime of Dublin theatre patents was clearly doomed. As we shall see, concerns other than those that weighed in 1968 with Mr Condon played a part. But those that weighed with him were far from unimportant.

From a wide-ranging critique of the entire system, Condon concluded abolition was an intelligent option. Patents were designed to deal with a variety of concerns linked to the theatre that were best dealt with in the modern world in a very different way. Patents down the years had increasingly highlighted the need for safety in the theatre: in the case of Dublin such matters were now regulated by Dublin Corporation's bye-laws for the Protection of Places of Public Resort. (Ensuring the safety of theatre buildings and the pressure this continued to place on planners, architects, surveyors and fire prevention experts, especially after such disasters as the fire at the Abbey in 1951 and the collapse of the proscenium arch at the Olympia in 1984, was to lead to very considerable delays in the conduct of inquiries under the 1786 Act, and thus, in a markedly different way, was to contribute to the move in the direction of repeal.) Patents, secondly, made it their business to insist on 'proper conduct' in theatres. This, Condon argued, signalled mainly an attempt to exercise a censorship over theatrical productions in the patented Dublin theatres that was not implemented in the contemporary world. The relevant rules were expressed in the existing patents in 'ludicrously archaic language'; nor did they apply in theatres outside Dublin or those in Dublin run as nominal club membership theatres. His recommendation was that the powers that be should use rather the general law and rely on police supervision for the preservation of the peace. Thirdly, possession of a theatre patent (unless any restrictions to the contrary applied) entitled the patentee to a liquor licence under the Excise Act of 1835. These matters were important, but it could be left to the general laws on liquor licensing to deal with the question.

A distinctive feature of the last batch of theatre patents to be issued was the frequency with which these were only sanctioned some time – indeed, in certain instances, some considerable time – after the grants they succeeded had expired. Many, indeed, were then backdated. Since most of the theatres entitled to retail alcohol relied on the Act of 1835 which granted automatic excise licences to holders of theatre patents, if no valid theatre patent existed, what the theatres continued to do – to retail alcohol in their bars – contravened the laws. That the hiatus in most instances occurred because the law officer's inquiry into a possible renewal of a patent, though usually commenced, had not concluded, reflected a state of affairs that was far from satisfactory. The Revenue commissioners would regularly complain about the situation, and prosecutions on several occasions were at least threatened.

Legal difficulties, such as those that arose at the Olympia following the collapse of the proscenium arch, were one source of delay, but very much more frequent was a dispute between the theatre owners and Dublin Corporation over safety measures that the latter deemed essential to have installed before they would agree to a fresh patent being issued. In the wake of the fire at the Abbey in 1951, it is no surprise that the inquiry conducted by Thomas Teevan, the attorney-general at the time, into a proposed new patent for the Gaiety in 1954 should have taken so long. The corporation on this occasion listed requirements for improvements to the building in South King Street, variously estimated at the period to cost £60,000 or £70,000. Counsel for the Gaiety said the theatre could only set aside £10,000 for this purpose; and if the corporation dug in its heels, the Gaiety would have no option but to close. The rights and wrongs of interference by local authorities in ensuring the safety of public buildings could involve counsel at these law officer's patent inquiries turning up legal authorities to justify their respective stances. One such precedent opened at the Gaiety inquiry of 1954 was a row at the turn of the century between the proprietors of St James' Hall in London and London County Council over the insistence by the latter of the construction of a staircase in the hall after the council's predecessor, the Metropolitan Board of Works, acting under the same powers, had officially acquiesced in the staircase being taken down.[12] This indeed was an era when London County Council was unusually proactive. In 1902, for example, they demanded that under new fire regulations alterations to the tune of £20,000 be carried out at Henry Irving's Lyceum Theatre. The syndicate running the Lyceum at the time was forced into receivership, as a consequence of which the Lyceum was sold, gutted and turned into a music-hall – 'the ultimate desecration of Irving's ideal'.[13]

Since, naturally, building and fire safety standards were unlikely to remain static over the twenty-one-year period of the standard theatre patent, it is easy to see why corporation officials, architects and others should opt for the observance of the best of standards by theatre proprietors before any new patent was granted. Henry Moloney, SC, counsel for the Gaiety in 1954, whilst conceding that his clients accepted they were subject to control in regard to matters of safety by the corporation, could perhaps be forgiven all the same for his snide observation that at the same time they begged to be excused from the obligation to observe regulations in regard to pigsties and cowsheds.

Even where application was made to the corporation in advance of the lodging of any memorial to secure a fresh patent, the delays could be considerable, thus exacerbating once again the situation where successive letters patent did not slot in seamlessly the very day after their predecessors had expired.

The end came finally, largely untrumpeted,[14] in 1997 when by section 6 of the National Cultural Institutions Act of that year[15] the Act of 1786 was repealed.[16] No constitutional challenge contributed to the burial of this eighteenth-century measure which had played its part in shaping the history of the stage in Dublin but

12 *St James' Hall Co. v. London Co. Council* [1901] 2 KB 250.
13 Jeffrey Richards, *Sir Henry Irving: a Victorian actor and his world* (London, Hambledon Continuum, 2005), p. 5.
14 But not entirely. Existing memorialists for new patents – on behalf of the Gaiety, the Olympia, the Gate, the Abbey/Peacock, and the Samuel Beckett Theatre in Trinity College Dublin – were all put on notice in November 1995 that repeal of the 1786 Act was then imminent.
15 No. 11 of 1997.   16 The section came into force on 2 April 1997.

which, plainly, had outlived its usefulness. But it could have done. The decision to repeal could to some limited extent at least have been influenced by the views of the anonymous official in the Attorney-General's Office in Dublin who wrote that the measure was vulnerable for its interference with freedom of expression and for its discriminatory treatment of Dublin. It is additionally worthy of note that, in 1991, in proceedings linked to the Tivoli Theatre's ultimately unsuccessful attempt to secure an ordinary seven-day publican's licence,[17] the constitutionality of the 1786 Act had been raised as an issue. In January 1992, Mr Justice Lynch, in his decision in this case, held that the matter did not yet fall for formal consideration.[18] With extinction of the Act in 1997, that moment would appear to have passed for good.

17 *In re Tivoli Cinema Ltd* [1992] 1 IR 412.   18 [1992] 1 IR at 422–4.

CHAPTER TEN

Health and safety

SAFETY IN PLACES OF PUBLIC RESORT IS, quite understandably, a contemporary preoccupation.[1] So far as theatres are concerned, there is a long history on the topic. In Dublin, this goes back at least to 1670 when, as previously recalled, the galleries collapsed at the Smock Alley Theatre during a production of Ben Jonson's *Bartholomew Fair*. There was to be another recorded collapse of the galleries thirty-one years later.[2] Indeed, concern over the stability of the building itself regularly manifested itself thereafter. In 1712, Ambrose Phillips was engaged to compose a few lines designed to satisfy patrons on the self-same score, and these were declaimed in front of the audience. His verse contained the scarcely reassuring couplet:[3]

> Nor shall the Crack of one disjointed Rafter
> Disturb the Scene, or interrupt your Laughter.

In February 1729/30 Thomas Elrington, in the last years of his management of the same theatre, and five years before the old Smock Alley Theatre was demolished, felt obliged to take rather more practical steps in the interest of reassuring the public. Rumours having circulated that the building was unsafe, Elrington engaged Captain Thomas Burgh, the director-general and overseer of fortifications and buildings in Ireland, to carry out a survey. The outcome was favourable, Burgh making out a certificate to the effect that, in the words of the *Dublin Journal*,[4] the building

> was safe and would bear any number of people who shall please to resort thither, nor is there likely to be the least failure for several years.

This guarantee was unwise, for in March 1734 part of Smock Alley did after all collapse, though, seemingly, there was on this occasion to be no loss of life.[5]

1 In other countries the same holds true: the devastating fire at the Ring theatre in Vienna on 8 December 1881 cost in excess of 500 lives.
2 See ch. 1. For confusion over the date, see Stockwell, *Dublin theatres and theatre customs* (Kingsport, Texas, Kingsport Press, 1938), p. 314, n. 63.
3 Quoted, Stockwell, *Dublin theatres*, p. 64.
4 Of 3 Feb. 1729/30; quoted, Stockwell, *Dublin theatres*, p. 65.
5 J.C. Greene and G.L.H. Clark, *The Dublin stage, 1720–1745, a calendar of plays, entertainments and after pieces* (Bethlehem PA, Lehigh UP; London, Associated UP, 1993), p. 15.

William Phillips, who opened a new but apparently short-lived theatre in Capel Street in 1745 – the one that along with Smock Alley was shut down by the lords justices in the wake of the Kelly-inspired riots of 1747[6] – had at the outset of his management sought to reassure possible patrons about the safety of the building housing his theatre. The theatre had been hastily built, and to still any criticisms there might have been, Phillips caused this advertisement to appear in *Faulkner's Dublin Journal*:[7]

> Mr Phillips, to remove any reflections or injurious aspersions calculated to prejudice him in this affair, will take care to obtain the judgment and certificates of the best master builders, as to its warmth, strength and security [of the new theatre].

Provincial theatres were as much at risk of structural failure as those in metropolitan centres. The eighteenth-century buildings that housed theatres in Belfast were no exception. In 1784, and in advance of the forthcoming season, Michael Atkins, the manager at the Rosemary Lane theatre, sought to allay the fears of patrons over the condition of the roof at the theatre, following reported storm damage. Messrs Dunlap and Mulholland, a firm of local architects were engaged to inspect the building, which they subsequently certified as 'perfectly secure'.[8]

Theatrical performances switched to the new Arthur Street theatre in February 1793, but the following year the flooring in the pit collapsed. In an editorial, the *Belfast Newsletter* rose to the occasion. 'One would think it advisable', a little pompously the editorial began,[9]

> for the manager after [the pit is rebuilt] to publish the opinion of an architect as to the strength both of it and of the galleries for the purpose of doing away the fears of any who will not themselves examine them.

The newspaper had a second suggestion: 'it is alleged that the present gloom of the boxes might be removed by sinking the chandeliers some inches lower than their present stations.' Dunlap and Mulholland visited again, but only after a second return visit were they prepared to certify that everything was hunky dory.

Concern for the safety of the performers has been a constant, and is even reflected in the conditions attached to some of the more recent theatre patents, and in particular, this one: 'No women or children to be hung from the flies nor fixed in position from which they cannot release themselves'. Even so, there were to be accidents, not all of which, it can safely be assumed, are recorded. An early

---

6   Above, p. 23.   7   15 Jan. 1745, quoted Greene & Clark, *The Dublin stage, 1720–1745*, p. 35.
8   J.C. Greene, *Theatre in Belfast, 1736–1800* (Bethlehem, PA, Lehigh UP; London, Associated UP),
    p. 27.
9   10 Nov. 1794, quoted Greene, *Theatre in Belfast*, p. 31.

exception occurred in Dublin in November 1741 when Mr Morgan, who was supposed to exit the stage flying on the back of a witch in a production of Thomas Shadwell's *The Lancashire Witches*, was allowed to fall as well as the witch.[10] Neither actor was seriously hurt, but it could easily have been otherwise. The theatre's *post mortem* – not that there had been any death – found that the team of stage hands working the machinery – wires of various sorts seem to have been involved – had been at fault. That there could be deaths is clear from Chetwood's account of what befell a rope-dancer, the 'Lady Isabella', and her unborn child.[11]

The risk of fire, perhaps, rather more than structural failure or dangerous stage props, in the end proved the major worry for theatre management. There was an outbreak of fire at Dublin's Smock Alley in 1764, which did not, however, prove lethal.[12] Management continued to resort to the offices of versifiers to reassure their clientele that safety was the priority. In 1794, for instance, when a new Drury Lane theatre was unveiled in London, words composed in a ditty by James Boaden were publicised as a comfort to patrons:[13]

> The very ravages of fire we scout
> For we have wherewithal to put it out.

Unfortunately, however, to judge from the conflagration that enveloped the building in 1809, the theatre's precautions (the 'wherewithal') did not in the end prove sufficient.

The lighting of theatres prior to the introduction of electric light was accomplished by means of candles, oil lamps and gas light. The actor John O'Keeffe recalls how on one occasion candles mounted on a chandelier had caused the headdress of some lady in the auditorium to catch fire.[14] Towards the end of the nineteenth century, the continuing hazard presented by gas light, coupled with the condition of the buildings that housed theatres, and often the lack to hand of fire-fighting equipment, was perceived to create a state of affairs where the risk of fire, with consequent damage to property and, more seriously, loss of life, was adjudged to be unacceptably high. Local history and assembled statistics told their own sombre tale.

Dublin's Theatre Royal in Hawkins Street was burnt down in February 1880 and, in more recent times, the Abbey was damaged by fire in July 1951. The select

10   W.R. Chetwood, *A general history of the stage; (more particularly the Irish theatre) from its origin in Greece down to the present time* (Dublin, E. Rider, 1749), p. 141; Stockwell, *Dublin theatres*, p. 375, n. 190; Greene & Clark, *The Dublin stage, 1720–1745*, p. 88.

11   Chetwood, *General history of the stage*, pp 62–3.

12   T.J. Walsh, *Opera in Dublin, 1705–1747* (Dublin, Allen Figgis, 1973), p. 121.

13   Fintan O'Toole, *A traitor's kiss; the life of Richard Brinsley Sheridan* (London, Granta Books, 1998), p. 429.

14   John O'Keeffe, *Recollections, of the life of John O'Keeffe, written by himself*, 2 vols (London, Henry Colburn, 1826), i, 162.

committee report of 1866[15] furnished details of all the fires at London's theatres between 1833 and 1866, including the cases of total destruction. There were six such cases: Astley's in June 1841, in which a girl died and twenty-three houses were destroyed; the Garrick in November 1846; the Olympic in March 1849, in which twenty houses were also damaged; the Pavilion in February 1856; Covent Garden the following month; and the Surrey Theatre in January 1865. Four days after the destruction of Covent Garden in March 1856, Charles Dickens, just returned from a sojourn in Paris, visited the blackened relics of the conflagration. As he was to remark, the scene was more than passing strange: there were the iron pass-doors, the chandeliers, and pieces from the men's wardrobe – 'the clothes in the *Travatore*', he believed.[16] The 1892 select committee report continues this grim inventory. In London, between 1866 and 1892 no less than ten theatres were said to have been gutted by fire.[17] And in Edinburgh, in the case of the thirty years prior to 1892, its Theatre Royal there had been burnt down on no less than three occasions.[18]

Accidents in two London theatres in the year 1864 caused the then Lord Chamberlain, Lord Sydney, to take a number of initiatives. In a horrific incident at the Pavilion Theatre a Miss Thorne, a performer, was burnt to death. A Middlesex coroner's jury at the ensuing inquest urged the necessity of ensuring articles of linen clothing worn by performers were fireproof by manufacturers and laundresses. Sydney agreed, sending a memorandum to all managers of theatres which asked them to make certain that 'in future the dresses of ballet dancers ... be rendered uninflammable, and that all ground lights ... be protected'.[19] Another accident occurring at the Princess' Theatre yielded a further suggestion passed on to Sydney from Dr Lankester who presided at the inquest there. This was the need for theatre managers to increase their vigilance, 'more especially during the extra-dangerous season of the Pantomimes, or Christmas, and Easter spectacular pieces'.[20]

On 5 February 1864 Sydney, as Lord Chamberlain, set his seal on an entirely new set of regulations that were then circulated to all theatres licensed by his office:[21]

> Regulations for the better Protection against Accidents by Fire at Theatres Licensed by the Lord Chamberlain
>   1.   All fixed and ordinary Gas Burners to be furnished with efficient Guards. Moveable and occasional lights to be, when possible, protected

15 *Report from the select committee to inquire into the working of Acts of Parliament for licensing theatres*, HC 1866, xvi, 1.
16 Peter Ackroyd, *Dickens* (London, Sinclair-Stevenson, 1990), p. 759.
17 *Report of the select committee on theatres and places of entertainment*, HC 1892, xviii, 1, at 521.
18 Ibid., p. 275 (J.B. Howard).
19 *Memorandum by the Lord Chamberlain transmitted to Managers of Theatres 1864*, HC 1864, l, 489.
20 *Copies of a Letter relating to Precautions against Fire, addressed by the Lord Chamberlain to the Managers of Theatres, 7 Feb. 1864*, HC 1864, l, 489.   21 HC 1864, l, 490.

in the same manner, or put under charge of persons responsible for lighting, watching and extinguishing them.

2. The Floats to be protected by a Wire Guard. The first Ground-Line to be always without Gas, and unconnected with Gas, whether at the Wings or elsewhere. Sufficient space to be left between each Ground-Line, so as to lessen risk from accident to all persons standing or moving among such lines.

3. The rows or lines of Gas Burners at wings to commence Four Feet at least from the level of the Stage.

4. Wet Blankets or Rugs, with Buckets of Water-pots to be always kept in the Wings; and attention to be directed to them by Placards legibly printed or painted, and fixed immediately above them. As to Rule 1, some person to be responsible for keeping the Blankets, Buckets, etc., ready for immediate use.

5. These Regulations to be always posted in some conspicuous place, so that all persons belonging to the Theatre may be acquainted with their contents; every Breach of Neglect of them, or any act of carelessness as regards Fire, to be punished by Fines or Dismissal by Managers.

Sydney

Lord Chamberlain

Lord Chamberlain's Office,
St. James' Palace,
5 February 1864.

The first survey of theatre buildings from the standpoint of public safety is reputed to have been carried out in London in 1812 at the behest of the then Lord Chamberlain.[22] This would have been either the earl of Dartmouth or the marquess of Hertford. The timing was no accident – a devastating fire at Covent Garden in 1808 had been followed the next year by the equally devastating conflagration we have already alluded to at Drury Lane.[23] The latter was of immediate concern to Richard Brinsley Sheridan, at the time both the manager and one of the theatre's co-patentees. The blaze that broke out at Drury Lane theatre on 24 February 1809 soon took hold of the entire theatre:[24]

> The treasurers managed to save the iron chest which contained the valuable patent, but little else survived. In less than a quarter of an hour after the blaze was noticed, a column of fire extended 450 feet across the entire facade.

O'Toole, in revisiting the episode in his biography of Sheridan, recalls that the day after the fire Sheridan told a meeting of the Drury Lane company 'that they must stick together and protect the most vulnerable of the ordinary workers in the

---

22 *1866 select committee report*, pp 281–2.
23 Above, p. 134; Thomas, Carlton & Etienne, *Theatre censorship*, p. 51.
24 O'Toole, *A traitor's kiss*, p. 429.

theatre'.[25] He also repeats the report that was in circulation at the period that only £40,000 of the total losses of £300,000 were covered by insurance.[26]

From 1852 onwards it became customary for the Lord Chamberlain's office to request district surveyors to furnish certificates regarding the safety of the structure of theatre buildings. The first annual inspections took place there years later. Information as to what was involved is contained in the select committee report of 1866:[27]

> (i) the means of egress in case of fire or other alarm, involving alteration of doors, removal of inconvenient barriers and awkward steps, and alteration of staircase;
> (ii) improvement of ventilation;
> (iii) means of extinguishing fire, state of water supply, force pumps, supply of buckets and state of gas burners;
> (iv) (aficionados of *The Phantom of the Opera* will appreciate this) the safe hanging of chandeliers;
> (v) cleanliness of the building, and state of urinaries and closets.

The reference here to the need to improve ventilation may serve to recall the controversial lack of it at Crow Street, as commented on in 1778. That year Spranger Barry had announced that plays would continue to be put on at the theatre throughout the summer. The announcement provoked a sarcastic comment from a Dublin newspaper, alluding to the lack of ventilation at the theatre and the likely spread of disease in consequence:[28]

> The doctors, apothecaries, nurse-keepers, undertakers, sextons and grave diggers of Dublin, return their sincere thanks (as in duty bound) to the manager of the Theatre Royal.

In due course, down the years, a variety of statutes and local authority bye-laws and regulations would be adopted to ensure the structural safety of buildings used as theatres (or, indeed, other places of public resort) and to guarantee ease of movement ('convenient means of ingress and egress') within such buildings. Typical of this regulatory regime is a key section in the Public Health Acts Amendment Act of 1890,[29] which was availed of in a successful prosecution in 1903 of the Olympia Theatre, known at the time as the Empire Palace Theatre, in Dublin's Dame Street.[30]

Section 36(1) in this Act of 1890 insisted that buildings of public resort within any urban district that had adopted the legislation had, to the satisfaction of the urban authority, to be

25 Ibid., p. 431.   26 Ibid.   27 *1866 select committee report*, pp 281–2.
28 *Dublin Evening Journal*, 28 May 1788.
29 53 & 54 Vict., c. 59. A local Act for Dublin of the same year has a similar focus: Dublin Corporation Act 1890, 53 & 54 Vict., c.ccxlvi, ss. 53–5.
30 *Corporation of Dublin v. Figgis* (1903) 37 ILTR 148.

substantially constructed and supplied with ample, safe and convenient means of ingress and egress for the use of the public, regard being had to the purposes for which such building is intended to be used, and to the number of persons likely to be assembled at any one time therein.

And sub-section 2 added:

The means of ingress and egress shall during the whole time that such building is used as a place of pubic resort be kept free and unobstructed to such extent as the urban authority shall require.

Dublin Corporation adopted the Act of 1890, and in January 1898 activated section 36(2), by passing a resolution to the effect that in no place of public resort within their jurisdiction should any person be permitted to stand in any of the passages or gangways.[31] In 1903, Arthur T. Figgis, then the manager of the Empire Palace Theatre, faced nine summonses before the Dublin Metropolitan District Court, alleging that on specified days in the months of January and February that year he had suffered a building, during the whole time it was used as a place of public resort, to be so used that the means of ingress to and egress from the building were not kept free and unobstructed as required. What had happened was that on the occasions in question more tickets had been sold to patrons than there were seats for, the upshot being that people had been allowed to stand in passages round the theatre's pit and the pit stalls. Ignatius O'Brien, a later Irish lord chancellor, argued, on Figgis' behalf, that the only sort of obstructions the legislation had in contemplation was a permanent obstruction. Mr Swift, the magistrate, was not convinced and counter-attacked with the observation that Figgis had done nothing to comply with the corporation's resolution by at least endeavouring to get his excess of patrons to sit down.

Figgis was convicted and fined 40s. on each of five of the summonses, and 20s. on each of the remaining four. The complainant, Dublin Corporation itself, was allowed 10s. costs on each of the summonses.

A preoccupation of the last series of Dublin theatre patents, as we have already demonstrated, has been this question of safety in the theatre – for performers as well as for members of the audience. Indeed, it is quite clear that in a number of instances a grant or a renewal of a patent was to become conditional on increasingly stringent standards on safety being met.

It is salutary at the same time to bear in mind that management could never be relied upon effectively to negate all manner of risks. The acid attack on Sergei Filin, artistic director of the Bolshoi Theatre in Russia, in January 2013 furnishes just such an instance. The attack was planned – so the resultant criminal prosecution maintained – by a leading male ballet dancer, Pavel Dmitrichenko,

---

31 See 37 ILTR at 149.

angered at Filin's failure to give leading roles to Pavel's girlfriend, the ballerina Anzhelina Vorontsova. In December 2013 Dmitrichenko was given a six-year prison term. An accomplice, who actually threw the acid in Filin's face, was given ten years, and the driver of the get-away car four years. Speculation at the time hinted that Dmitrichenko might have become emotionally unbalanced as a consequence of his recent role dancing the part of Ivan the Terrible.[32]

More run-of-the-mill self-evidently, the same month that Dmitrichenko and company were convicted and sentenced was an accident reported from London. This was the collapse of part of the ceiling at the Apollo Theatre in Shaftesbury Avenue.[33] The ceiling took parts of the theatre's balconies down with it. The collapse occurred not long after that evening's performance had commenced. This was *The Curious Incident of the Dog in the Night-Time*. Some eighty patrons were injured when the audience was showered with masonry and general debris.

32 *Irish Times*, 6 Mar. 2013; *The Guardian*, 4 Dec. 2013.   33 *Irish Times*, 20 Dec. 2013.

CHAPTER ELEVEN

Refreshments for patrons

THEATRE MANAGEMENTS WERE not long at their task before learning that their patrons, besides (hopefully) enjoying the performance, would relish the opportunity to partake of refreshments – even a little food – at intervals, or even before or after the curtain went up. Arrangements accordingly were set in train. A facility, destined to be introduced globally, did not want for critics whenever, in the eyes of some, it came to be abused. Alfred Döblin, for instance, had harsh words to utter on Berlin theatre audiences of the 1920s and 30s, though the abuse of which he sought to take note was not necessarily the fault exclusively of the management.[1] Before the play started, members of the audience would unwrap chocolates and sweets. Most irritating of all, papers would be noisily scrunched during the actual performance. A later visit by Döblin to the theatre brought no improvement. Even before the curtain went up, Döblin recalled, the audience

> were sucking pralinés right and left; in the intervals a crowd of people stood there; a gaggle of common faces, laughing, gossiping and shouting, their dewlaps stuffed with ham rolls; beer glasses in their hands.

The expression of exasperation is predictable:

> Art! Artistic achievements! God save the artist from coming into contact with his 'fans'.

Such irritation and worse that Döblin had experienced is possibly more likely today to be experienced in the cinema where popcorn is commonly on offer besides ice-cream and soft drinks. Everywhere, of course, there is nowadays the mobile phone.

In Ireland as in England theatre patrons, in the early days at least, had to make do with very different kinds of fare. Fare in the singular, as it turned out. In 1742 we learn that the management of the Smock Alley Theatre franchised to one Johnstone, described as a fruiterer of the city of Dublin, 'the liberty and privilege' of selling fruit in the theatre for the sum of £12 per annum.[2] That arrangements such as this one, the first that Stockwell's researches unearthed, could also in a

---

1 Giles MacDonagh, *Berlin, a portrait of its history: politics, architecture and society* (New York, St Martin's Press, 1997), pp 44–5.
2 La Tourette Stockwell, *Dublin theatres and theatre customs* (Kingsport, TX, Kingsport Press, 1938), p. 257.

limited way prove something of a money-spinner will not, naturally, have been lost on tyro managements, ever eager to make ends meet.

Risks even so could attend the invasion of any theatre by phalanxes of orange-sellers, as a news item in the *Dublin Post* in 1787 plainly demonstrated. During a performance of *Julius Caesar* at Crow Street, the *Post* reported,[3]

> Some fruit wenches were not only blasphemous and noisy, but violently abusive and immodest at the middle gallery and pit passages. Many persons were highly annoyed, but by the direction of the Manager they were secured by the Police Watchmen and lodged in the Watch house.

Irish history furnishes no counterpart to Nell Gwynn who we first hear of selling oranges in the King's Theatre, London, in 1663.

Cafes make an appearance before the end of the eighteenth century. There are references to a cafe at the Fishamble Street Theatre in 1784 and to one at Crow Street in 1798. On offer, apparently, would be tea, coffee, lemonade and orgeat.[4] A Mr Atwell of Dame Street is named as the franchisee at Crow Street.

We must now turn to theatre bars.

Special rules regarding drinks licences for theatres have their origin in Westminster legislation of 1835, in the Excise Act of that year.[5] Section 7 of this measure provided as follows:

> It shall be lawful for the commissioners and officers of excise, and they are hereby authorised and empowered, to grant retail licences to any person to sell beer, spirits, and wine in any theatre established under a royal patent, or in any theatre or other place of public entertainment licensed by the Lord Chamberlain or by justices of the peace, without the production by the person applying for such licence or licences of any certificate or authority for such person to keep a common inn, alehouse, or victualling house; any thing in any Act or Acts to the contrary notwithstanding.

This section in the 1835 Act, we have already had occasion to note, has been the focus of discussion in the context of the lack of an express power within the corpus of Irish legislation bestowing upon the justices of the peace a jurisdiction to license theatres – the legislative deficit to which Britain's Act of 1788 draws immediate attention. The 1927 Northern Ireland decision in *Morrison's* case[6] was to the effect that the 1835 Act had impliedly conferred such a power – an interpretation explicitly disavowed by Mr Justice Geoghegan in the Republic in 1993 in the *Point Depot* case,[7] and expressly too (without any allusion to *Morrison's* case) by Mr

3   *Dublin Post*, 18 Jan. 1787, cited in Stockwell, *Dublin theatres*, p. 258.
4   Stockwell, *Dublin theatres*, pp 258–9. Orgeat was a syrup or cooling drink made originally from barley and subsequently from almonds, and mixed with orange-flavour water.
5   5 & 6 Will. IV, c. 39.   6   *Morrison v. Commissioners of Customs* [1927] NI 115.
7   *Point Exhibition Co. v. Revenue Commissioners* [1993] 2 IR 551. See further, above, p. 84.

Justice Hedigan in the Republic in 2007 in proceedings involving the Cork Opera House.[8]

As the Commons select committee of 1866 was to hear, from evidence brought before them, the 1835 Act, and in particular section 7, encountered immediate opposition from publicans. And that opposition was sufficiently influential as to induce the Treasury not long after the Act had reached the statute-book to take the dubious constitutional step of instructing the Excise to suspend the operation of the Act. The Excise's order of 28 August 1835 then came under attack from managers of theatres in the face of the competition from the music-hall, as the latter grew in popularity at this juncture. The Treasury referred the entire matter to the law officers, and in 1859 the attorney-general, Sir Fitzroy Kelly, and the solicitor-general, Sir Hugh Cairns, ruled that the suspension lacked legal force and it was accordingly lifted.[9]

It was frequently pointed out in discussions occurring in the nineteenth century on the difference between the music-hall and the theatre that a principal attraction of the former was the availability to the patron of alcoholic refreshment. As one witness put it to the 1866 select committee, the music-hall was 'mainly for drinking, smoking and entertainment'.[10] In the case of the theatres, steps were taken to restrict the availability of alcohol to separate spaces called bars or refreshment rooms situated at the side or at the rear of the auditorium, and not, naturally, in the auditorium itself.[11] Unsurprisingly, there were always individuals prepared to damn the liberalism reflected in the Excise Act of 1835, who queried the need for the true supporter of drama to seek to quench his thirst via the imbibing of alcoholic beverages. Historians among this group might well have been prepared to go so far as to praise the availability of oranges from the orange-sellers in the eighteenth-century theatre. But they would not have been prepared to go much further than that.

By the end of the nineteenth century this opposition to the availability of alcohol for consumption by patrons in the Irish theatre was about to chalk up a major victory. As we have already remarked, both of the theatre patents granted in 1904 – to the Kingstown Pavilion and to what became known as the Abbey – contained conditions forbidding the patentees from seeking to avail of the provisions of the Excise Act of 1835.[12] Writing in 1952, P.J. Stephenson was to ponder whether, in the case of the Abbey at least, the prohibition was attributable to the influence of the Dublin Total Abstinence Society.[13] This could well have been the case, but it needs to be recalled that the patents of 1904 were issued but two years after the radical rehauling of liquor licensing in Ireland by the important Act

---

8   *Cork Opera House plc v. Revenue Commissioners*, 28 Nov. 2007: Mr Justice Hedigan.
9   *Report from the select committee on theatrical licences; together with the proceedings of the committee, minutes of evidence and appendix*, 1866, HC 1866, xvi, 1, at pp 5 and 282.
10 Ibid., p. 282.   11   Ibid.
12 Above, pp 118–19.
13 P.J. Stephenson, 'The Abbey Theatre', *Dublin Historical Record*, 13 (1952), 22 at 25.

of parliament of 1902,[14] itself a consequence of the major review of the entire subject undertaken by the royal commission on liquor licensing laws that sat from 1896 to 1899. The latter, in the case of Ireland, had reached the unremarkable conclusion that the country possessed too many public houses. In 1845, for a population of 8,295,061, the country had 15,000 pubs; by 1891, when the population had declined to 4,704,750 that number had soared to 17,000. Evidence was led before the commission to show what would happen if steps were taken to ensure that there was just one pub for every 100 families: in Dublin this would mean there should be 499 pubs rather than the current figure of 1,551; in Belfast, 416 rather than 1,110; in Waterford 44 rather than 232; and in Clonmel 18 rather than 113.[15] An equally startling feature of the commissioners' final report is a map for Longford town highlighting in red the location of all 63 of the town's licensed premises for a population of 3,789.[16]

A major interpretation of a key section in the Licensing (Ireland) Act of 1902,[17] which resulted in denying to holders of a spirit grocer's licence the right to apply for a full publican's licence, was handed down by the King's Bench Division in 1903. Mr Justice Madden in his concurring judgment in this case – *The King (Collins) v. Donegal Justices*[18] – conveys very well something of the mood of the times on the topic of the abundance of outlets for the purchase and consumption of intoxicating liquor. 'The interests', Mr Justice Madden wrote,[19]

> of the general public and of holders of existing publicans' licenses happened in the instance to point in the same direction. They were both interested in having some check placed on the reckless multiplication of licensed houses in Ireland which was taking place owing to the action of certain licensing authorities; a state of things the existence of which is a matter of common knowledge and to which we cannot shut our eyes in construing this Act of Parliament; for it is the mischief with which it deals. This mischief is remedied to some extent by stereotyping the existing state of things for a period of five years, due regard being had to existing interests, and to the legitimate interests of the public.

A noteworthy facet of the attachment of this critical condition to the two Irish theatre patents of 1904 is that the attachment of a similar condition to an English theatre licence had been scrutinised by the Queen's Bench Division in London in 1896 and pronounced valid.[20] It is almost certain that that decision would have

---

14 Licensing (Ireland) Act 1902: 2 Edw. VII, c. 18.
15 For a synopsis of the findings of the commission, see E.J.D. McBrien, *The liquor licensing laws of Northern Ireland* (Dublin, Gill & Macmillan, 1997), pp 9–14.
16 *Royal commission on liquor licensing laws: minutes of evidence with appendices and index: vol. 7 – Ireland*, C. 8980, HC. 1898, xxviii, 527 at 909 (320).
17 S. 2.   18 [1903] 2 IR 533.   19 [1903] 2 IR at 538.
20 *The Queen v. Co. Council of the West Riding of Yorkshire* [1896] 2 QB 386.

been regarded as sound law in Ireland as well, though governing a condition in an Irish theatre patent.

The English case came before the courts when the county council in the West Riding of Yorkshire imposed just such a condition on a theatre licence granted to the Princess Theatre in Hoyland Nether, a town north of Sheffield. (Councils in England had recently had transferred to them the licensing power previously exercisable by justices.)[21] The protest of the owners availed them not at all, even though it was arguable that the prohibition on seeking a drinks licence trenched on the discretionary powers of the commissioners of Customs and Excise to grant one. For the Queen's Bench Division, a ruling eight years before, in *Ex parte Harrington*,[22] was critical. Harrington, acting on behalf of the Cardiff Philharmonic Music Hall Co., had protested against the failure of local justices to renew a theatre licence that had previously been granted. Such a licence had been granted instead to another theatre in Cardiff. On the grounds that the justices possessed a complete discretion to refuse a theatre licence that had been sought under both a local Act for Cardiff in 1862 and the Acts of 1788 and 1843, without giving any reasons at all, the Queen's Bench Division and the Court of Appeal, successively, refused to grant an order of *mandamus*. The lower court took express exception to the contention of counsel for Harrington that whatever the building, the management or the nature of any planned performance, the justices were obliged to grant a licence even though the 'theatre' lacked enough exits and sufficient provision to guard against the risk of fire.[23] By the time the Hoyland Nether case came before the Queen's Bench Division the licensing power in question, as we have seen, had been transferred from the local justices to the appropriate local authority[24] – in this case the West Riding County Council. The Harrington adjudication meant, it was then held, that if the licensing authority possessed total discretion and did not even have to furnish reasons, that authority could most certainly grant a licence and make it subject to conditions.[25] Mr Justice Wills, for his part, also chose to call in aid something of the local circumstances in Hoyland Nether. 'There is already', he argued,[26]

> a public-house within twenty yards of this theatre. If, then, an unconditional licence were granted to the theatre, the effect would be to multiply facilities for drinking, and it is a neighbourhood in which it is not desirable to do so. If that is not a good ground for the exercise of their discretion by the committee in the way they have done, I cannot conceive what is.

Around this time in Ireland too grave exception, it would appear, could be taken to the suggestion that any provincial theatre was entitled to establish a bar. In 1900,

---

21 Local Government Act 1888 (51 & 52 Vict., c. 41), s. 7.
22 (1887–8) 4 Times L R 435.   23 The preoccupation discussed above in ch. 10.
24 Local Government Act 1888, s. 7.
25 *The Queen v. Co. Council of the West Riding of Yorkshire* [1896] 2 QB 386.   26 At 389.

the then recorder of Londonderry, acting under powers quite distinct from those granted the commissioners of Customs and Excise by the Excise Act of 1835, declined *tout court* to grant a retail drinks licence to the Londonderry Opera House (we have already noticed that in the 1920s the same venue would again be struggling to open a bar, though on this later occasion the proprietors were to meet with greater success).[27] The recorder in 1900 did not mince his words.[28] To open a bar in the opera house would injure the theatre and reduce it to the level of a music-hall; 'the sale of liquor was not a necessary part of a theatrical manager's business'; 'a bar was not essential for the comfort of theatrical audiences'. On the other hand, it is clear from the evidence given to the royal commission on liquor licensing in 1898 by the then Irish solicitor-general, Dunbar Barton, that a number of theatres outside Dublin had applied for, and had secured, an ordinary publican's licence[29] – presumably the state of affairs that induced Mr W. Wilkinson, the then secretary of the Irish Temperance League, to press the same royal commission to accept the need for all Irish theatres, and not just those in Dublin, to be brought within the terms of the Excise Act of 1835 and thus made subject to further restrictions.[30]

In the Republic, for the decade and more prior to abolition of theatre patents for Dublin in 1997, some confusion attended the arrangements for licensing theatres for the sale of alcohol. Outside Dublin, and with the exception of Cork,[31] no clear legislative authority appeared to exist for licensing any theatre on the basis of which the Revenue commissioners, availing of the provisions of the Excise Act of 1835, were at liberty to furnish an excise licence for the sale of intoxicating liquor. The legislation gap (if such it was and remains) began to be filled when the district court responded favourably to applications before it presented under a section of the Public Health Acts Amendment Act 1890, to grant 'music and singing licences' to theatres, leading the Revenue commissioners to treat such premises as 'other place[s] of public entertainment' under the scheme of the 1835 Act. Woods cites the instance of such a licence being granted to Sean O'Doherty in respect of the Theatre Royal in Limerick in 1991.[32] Woods adds the detail that, so far as the actions of the Revenue commissioners have been concerned, they would as a preliminary matter consult the Arts Council as to the *bona fides* of the theatre in question.[33] Excise duty in respect of the sale of alcohol in any theatre was fixed at £200 per annum by legislation in 1992.[34]

---

27 Above, ch. 7.
28 *New Irish Jurist and Local Government Review*, 1 (1900), 26.
29 *Royal commission on liquor licensing laws: minutes of evidence with appendices and index*, C. 9880, HC 1898, xxxviii, 527 at 547 (13).
30 Ibid., at 834 (300).
31 But problems in Cork were to surface in 2004 and later years: see below, p. 148.
32 J.V. Woods, *Liquor licensing laws of Ireland* (Castletroy, Limerick, J.V. Woods, 1992), p. 344.
33 Ibid. In the *Point Depot* case (see below) Mr Justice Geoghegan indicated that other excise licences on such a basis had been issued ([1993] 2 IR 551 at 554).
34 Finance Act 1992 (1992 no. 9), sch. 6.

For the duration of the regime of Dublin theatre patents, the Revenue commissioners would appear to have refused to issue excise licences in circumstances where any previously patented theatre had not had its patent renewed or any new theatre applying for a patent had failed to obtain one. So far as one can tell, there would seem to have been no great rush shown by Dublin theatre managements to travel the path pursued by their counterparts in the provinces – to seek a music and singing licence from the district court and thus hopefully qualify for an excise licence as some 'other place of public entertainment'.

There was one critical exception.[35] The owner of premises known at the time – 1992 – as the Point Depot, which premises were used for a range of indoor entertainments – concerts of popular and classical music, operas and dances – and also for the mounting of exhibitions, applied successfully to the district court for a music and singing licence under the Public Health Acts Amendment Act 1890.[36] (The owner also applied successfully for a dancing licence under the Public Dance Halls Act 1935.)[37] The next move on the part of the owner was to apply to the Revenue commissioners for the excise licence under section 7 of the 1835 Excise Act.[38] When the commissioners prevaricated, the owner of the Point Depot commenced proceedings for the order of *mandamus* against them, obliging them to grant such a licence.

The commissioners defended their stance by arguing that section 7 of the 1835 Act had been partially repealed by legislation in 1872,[39] which had the effect that non-theatres as 'other places of public entertainment' no longer enjoyed an automatic entitlement to an excise licence to dispense alcohol – an interpretation, as it happens, that was buttressed by a decision of the English Queen's Bench Division in 1882.[40] This contention was rejected by Mr Justice Geoghegan in the High Court who, however, went on to hold, dealing with another limb to the argument presented on behalf of the Point Depot, that the Point did not qualify as a 'theatre' under the 1835 Act. A theatre, in the judge's view, was a place where plays, operas, pantomimes and the like were performed on a reasonably continuous basis, but the Point did not qualify, having regard to the diverse entertainments put on there and the mounting of exhibitions.[41] This, however, did not dispose of the matter, for Mr Justice Geoghegan was convinced that the Point constituted an 'other place of entertainment' within the contemplation of the 1835 Act.[42] A further buttress for the judge's key ruling was the express language in a licensing act of 1874[43] acknowledging the validity of the grant of an excise licence to so-called 'other places of public entertainment'.

35 *Point Exhibition Co. v. Revenue Commissioners* [1993] 2 IR 551.
36 53 & 54 Vict., c. 59: see s. 51.   37 1935 no. 2.   38 5 & 6 Will. IV, c. 39.
39 Licensing Act 1872: 35 & 36 Vict., c. 94.
40 *The Queen v. Commissioners of Inland Revenue* (1882) 21 QBD 569.
41 [1993] 2 IR at 555–6.   42 Ibid., at 557–8.
43 Licensing Act (Ireland), 1874 (37 & 38 Vict., c. 69), s. 7.

Venues qualifying as some 'other place of entertainment' for purposes of the grant of a so-called 'theatre licence' under the 1835 Act have continued to pose a problem for the courts. The hurdle was successfully mounted, after a review in the High Court, in a case involving, appropriately enough, the Royal Dublin Society and its showgrounds at Ballsbridge in Dublin.[44] The Simmonscourt Pavilion at the RDS had been constructed in the mid-1970s. An upgrading of the facility took place in 1993, the object of which was to permit concerts, ice shows and operas to take place there. It had previously been designed to host exhibitions for its Spring Show, the Horse Show, and blood stock sales, in addition to furnishing a venue for indoor show jumping, other sports events, ice-skating and 'community amenity requirements.' In 1995 the Society sought a licence under the 1835 Act, arguing that the pavilion now constituted an 'other place of entertainment' for purposes of section 7. The Revenue commissioners refused the licence, and this refusal was endorsed by Mr Justice Barr in judicial review proceedings. For the judge, the preponderance of events did not have characteristics associated with the pavilion being a theatre, 'namely a static audience seated for a performance of a defined time-span limited to a period of a few hours'.

This, however, was not the end of the matter, for the Supreme Court (Chief Justice Hamilton, Mrs Justice Denham, Mr Justice Barrington, Mr Justice Keane and Mr Justice Lynch) unanimously overturned Mr Justice Barr's decision. Mr Justice Keane, in his judgment for the court, took exception to the approach the High Court judge had adopted towards the interpretation of section 7 in the 1835 Act.[45] Mr Justice Barr, in Mr Justice Keane's opinion, had wrongly regarded an 'other place of entertainment' as somehow clothed with the characteristics of a theatre – hence the reference, for example, in the High Court judge's opinion to the requirement of 'a static audience, etc.' He had in fact wrongly applied the so-called *ejusdem generis* rule of statutory interpretation. A genus, argued Mr Justice Keane, relying heavily on an English case of 1944,[46] could not be constituted by mention of a single class ('theatre') followed by words 'and other', but was constituted by the enumeration of a number of classes. Dealing with a subsidiary point, Mr Justice Keane went on to hold that exhibitions could qualify as 'entertainments' given that many people attended without any intention of buying the items displayed.[47] He added that it was not a proper approach for the Revenue commissioners or, for that matter, any trial judge to examine lists of events previously held at the venue or booked in for the future. On one point alone, Mr Justice Keane accepted the views of the Revenue commissioners. The mere fact that the district court had granted the venue – in this instance the Simmonscourt Pavilion – a music and singing licence as a place of public entertainment under the 1890 Public Health Acts Amendment Act, as in fact had occurred, did not entail

---

44 *Royal Dublin Society v. Revenue Commissioners* [2000] I IR 270.
45 [2000] I IR at 281–3. 46 *Allen v. Emmerson* [1944] KB 362.
47 *Royal Dublin Society v. Revenue Commissioners* [2000] I IR at 284.

that the Revenue commissioners were obliged to grant the 'theatre licence' under the 1835 Act.[48] It is of interest to note that, as regards this application to the district court, the RDS had listed the following events which it had hosted – ballet, opera, circus, the Eurovision Song Contest and several solo performances by singers.[49] Its treatment at the hands of the Revenue commissioners, the Society plaintively added, had placed it at a disadvantage financially by comparison with its competitor for major attractions – the Point Depot, now what is known as the 3Arena.

Mr Justice Keane's observation in the *RDS* case that the Revenue commissioners were by no means obliged to be forthcoming with a licence even after the district court had granted a music and singing licence to the venue as a place of public entertainment was plainly to the fore in the considerations of the commissioners when they declined to do just that in proceedings involving two fresh venues – the Old Harcourt Street Railway Station, otherwise known as the Odeon Bar and Nightclub and the premises at 4 Dame Lane, both in Dublin.[50] Both premises also possessed a dancing licence under the Public Dance Halls Act 1935.[51] Intriguingly, the two premises also possessed an ordinary publican's on-licence. Since these premises were in fact public houses, or pubs in the vernacular, the commissioners were not prepared to treat them as places of entertainment for purposes of the 1835 Act. In overturning that refusal when the case reached the High Court, Mr Justice Quirke argued that neither in theory nor in practice was there any objection to premises being licensed under two separate limbs of the licensing code.[52] It had not assisted the commissioners either that having requested information regarding the proprietors' claim that the premises both constituted an 'other place of entertainment' under the 1835 Act, they turned round before the proprietors had time to reply by peremptorily refusing to grant the licence sought.

An entirely different point regarding the application of the 1835 Act came before Mr Justice Hedigan in the High Court in 2007. The applicants in this case for a theatre licence under the 1835 legislation, the Cork Opera House, were to be rebuffed, but it is noteworthy that the judge recommended that the opera house should make use of the alternative method of procuring a licence by first securing a music and singing licence under the 1890 Act. In this case[53] the opera house had been licensed as a theatre by Cork City Council, acting under the relevant section, section 172, of the Cork Improvement Act of 1868.[54] Such licence had been treated over many years as enabling the grant of an on-licence warranted by section 7 of the Excise Act 1835[55] to be made by the Revenue commissioners. In 2004 the commissioners adopted a different stance, arguing that the Excise Act only

---

48 Ibid., at 284–5.   49 Ibid., at 273.
50 *Kivaway Ltd. v. Revenue Commissioners* [2005] 2 ILRM 274.   51 No. 2 of 1935.
52 [2005] 2 ILRM at 284–7.
53 *Cork Opera House plc v. Revenue Commissioners*, 21 Nov. 2007.
54 31 & 32 Vict., c. xxxiii; see above, p. 78.   55 5 & 6 Will. IV, c. 39.

authorised the grant of such a licence where the theatre in question had first been licensed by justices of the peace. Cork City Council did not come within that designation, and therefore the commissioners were not at liberty to activate the section in the 1835 Excise Act, even though down the years they had elected to do exactly that. The Revenue commissioners anticipated the opera house's further objection, based on the supposed doctrine of legitimate expectation, that the commissioners were not at liberty to alter tack in such a fashion, by contending that, as a statutory authority, they could only act pursuant to statutory powers vested in them, and that, to that limited extent, any doctrine of legitimate expectation could not, and did not, apply. As to the first point, Cork Opera House travelled back into legal history by arguing that the supposed defect in Cork City Council was cured by charters providing that the mayor and aldermen were *ex officio* justices of the peace as per charters of Elizabeth I of 1574, of James I of 1608, of Charles I of 1631 and of George III of 1785.[56] But it proved a forlorn endeavour, Mr Justice Hedigan ruling conclusively that the modern city council could not be equiparated with justices of the peace. He also upheld the contention of the Revenue commissioners on the applicability of the doctrine of legitimate expectation.[57]

In the result, the only way forward for the opera house was to apply to the district court for a music and singing licence under the Public Health Acts Amendment Act 1890.[58] That would enable the opera house to be treated as an 'other place of entertainment' for purposes of section 7 of the Excise Act of 1835. Mr Justice Hedigan's solution to the licensing problem that arose in the case was preceded by an observation falling from the judge very different in nature from one expressed by the recorder of Londonderry at the start of the twentieth century.[59] 'It is worth noting at the outset', Mr Justice Hedigan remarked,[60]

if for no other reason than to assuage the concerns of the music loving patrons of Cork Opera House, that there is little doubt that wines and spirits will continue to be served at its functions for the foreseeable future.

It remains the case, of course, that Mr Justice Keane's warning, expressed in the *RDS* case, still applies: the Revenue commissioners are not obliged to follow suit even after the district court has dubbed some venue an 'other place of public entertainment'.

To return to Northern Ireland: there the sale of intoxicating liquor in licensed theatres is now regulated by the Licensing (N.I.) Order of 1996.[61] Sales are legal if made to employees or patrons attending the theatre. Other beverages and food have also to be made available for purchase. Any additional conditions prescribed have

56 See at p. 2 of Hedigan J.'s judgment. In the judge's review, the identity of the last monarch is wrongly given as George II.
57 See at pp 6–7.   58   53 & 54 Vict., c. 59: see s. 51.   59   Above, p. 145.
60 At p. 5 of Mr Justice Hedigan's judgement.   61   S.I. no. 3158 (N.I. no. 22).

to be observed.[62] These rules apply to all places of public entertainment of any description which are licensed for the sale of intoxicating liquor.

In the Republic the reverse suffered by the Tivoli when in the summer of 1991 it failed to secure an ordinary seven-day publican's licence[63] inspired an article by a Mark O'Shea in *Irish Stage and Screen*, which drew attention to the extent to which theatres in the modern era were dependant on the income from theatre bars merely to survive.[64] 'For a commercial theatre', O'Shea argued,

> relying purely on box office receipts a bar can mean the difference between viability and closure. During the Tivoli's court case, Phyllis Ryan cited the existence of the CIÉ bar on the first floor of Busarus as an important factor helping to entice patrons to the Eblana Theatre.

There were, O'Shea insisted, other precedents besides:

> In 1970–1, Belfast's Lyric survived seven months without Arts Council subsidy on the strength of bar proceeds. Today, the Olympia stages late night shows, a major attraction being the bar. The Abbey's new portico seems to have less to do with architecture than with improving access to the bar counter.

It will not be found amiss at this point to discuss other challenges from whatever quarter that have threatened the viability of commercial theatre in Ireland. At one juncture, paying mortgagees, landlords and holders of annuities posed a heavy burden, and, as we have seen, managers and impresarios were not unknown among residents of debtors' prisons. In the twentieth century, a different sort of transient hurdle had to be surmounted: the obligation to account for what was termed 'entertainment tax'.

During the first World War entertainment duty had been added to the then United Kingdom's tax code by the appropriately entitled Finance (New Duties) Act 1916.[65] The duty was to be exacted from patrons attending 'entertainment' which was defined as 'any exhibition, performance, amusement, game or sport to which persons are admitted for payment'.[66] The rates for the duty were set down as follows.[67] For admission charging less than 2*d.* the duty was ½*d.*; between 2*d.* and 6*d.*, 1*d.*; between 6*d.* and 2*s.* 6*d.*, 2*d.*; between 2*s.* 6*d.* and 5*s.*, 3*d.*; between 5*s.* and 7*s.* 6*d.*, 6*d.*; between 7*s.* 6*d.* and 12*s.* 6*d.*, 1*s.*; for admissions charging over 12*s.* 6*d.*, the duty was 1*s.* for the first 12*s.* 6*d.* and 1*s.* for every 10*s.* or part 10*s.* over that. In later years, whilst the duty remained leviable, these rates would be regularly revised.

62 See art. 52(i).
63 *In re Tivoli Cinema Ltd.* [1992] I IR 412.
64 'Morals of the people: the 1786 Dublin Theatres Act', *Irish Stage and Screen*, Aug./Sept. 1998, p. 12.
65 6 Geo. V, c. 11.   66 S. 1 (6).   67 S. 1 (1).

1 John Ogilby (1600–76). First Master of the Revels for Ireland appointed in the late 1630s. Re-established in the post on the Restoration of Charles II. © National Portrait Gallery, London.

2 Henry Brooke (c. 1703–83). Irish playwright, first victim of British pre-censorship over his drama, *Gustavus Vasa*. Photograph © National Gallery of Ireland.

3 David Garrick (1717–79). Most celebrated eighteenth-century actor, had a successful season in Dublin in 1745–6. A collection of his correspondence has been published. © National Portrait Gallery, London.

4 Spranger Barry (1717–77). An acknowledged rival to Garrick in the playing of key roles in the theatre in the middle of the eighteenth century. Was to unveil the new Crow Street theatre in Dublin in 1758. Photograph © National Library of Ireland.

5 Robert Walpole, 1st earl of Orford (1676–1745). Responsible for the introduction of pre-censorship into Britain in 1737. © National Portrait Gallery, London.

6 Philip Dormer Stanhope, 4th earl of Chesterfield (1694–1773). Opposed unsuccessfully introduction of pre-censorship into Britain, an opposition frequently recalled. Served as Irish lord lieutenant. © National Portrait Gallery, London.

7 Thomas Sheridan (?1719–88). Historians differ vehemently on the career and achievements of this controversial eighteenth-century actor-manager, the father of Richard Brinsley. Photograph © National Gallery of Ireland.

8 Charles Macklin (c. 1695–1797). Was to sue over summary dismissals from the stage in both London and Dublin. Photograph © National Gallery of Ireland.

9 ?Nell Gwynn (?1651–87). Unknown woman, thought formerly to be Eleanor or Nell Gwynn. The most celebrated orange-seller of all time, if indeed this is Nell. © National Portrait Gallery, London.

10 Thomas Ryder (1735–91). Became lessee of Smock Alley in 1773, but on securing lease of Crow Street as well, shut Smock Alley down. Photograph © National Gallery of Ireland.

11 Michael Atkins. Prominent in theatre affairs in Belfast in the late eighteenth century. Successfully thwarted Richard Daly's attempt to exercise jurisdiction over him in 1792. Atkins is shown seated second from left, in blue, in this ensemble painting of the Adelphi Club, Belfast (1783).

13 Print illustrating Astley's circus extravaganza at his royal amphitheatre in London. Astley put on such shows on the Continent as well as in Dublin and London. © Victoria and Albert Museum, London.

12 Philip Astley (1742–1814). Prominent circus impresario. Secured in 1788 the second Dublin theatre patent under the Regulation Act of 1786. © National Portrait Gallery, London.

14 The new Theatre Royal, Dublin (1820). George IV attended a performance of Richard Brinsley Sheridan's *La Duenna* here in 1821. Three separate *Theatres Royal* occupied this site before the last of the three was demolished in 1952. Courtesy of the National Library of Ireland.

15 The Lying-in Hospital (Rotunda), Dublin. Entertainments in support of the hospital were exempted from the provisions mandating possession of a theatre patent (s. 3 of the Dublin Stage Regulation Act, 1786). Courtesy of University College Dublin (UCD) Library.

A

DEFENCE OF THE STAGE,

OR AN

INQUIRY INTO THE REAL QUALITIES

OF

THEATRICAL ENTERTAINMENTS,

THEIR SCOPE AND TENDENCY.

BEING A REPLY TO A SERMON ENTITLED

"THE EVIL OF THEATRICAL AMUSEMENTS STATED AND ILLUSTRATED,"

LATELY PUBLISHED IN DUBLIN, AND PREACHED IN THE WESLEYAN
METHODIST CHAPEL IN LOWER ABBEY-STREET, ON
SUNDAY, NOVEMBER, 4TH, 1838,

BY THE REV. DR. JOHN B. BENNETT.

INCLUDING AN EXAMINATION OF THE AUTHORITIES ON WHICH
THAT SERMON IS FOUNDED.

By JOHN WILLIAM CALCRAFT,

LESSEE AND MANAGER OF THE THEATRE ROYAL, DUBLIN.

" To every thing there is a season, and a time to every purpose under the heaven.—
A time to weep, and a time to laugh : a time to mourn and a time to dance."—*Ecclesiastes*,
iii. 1, 4.

" Be not righteous over much ; neither make thyself over wise: why shouldest thou
destroy thyself."—*Ecclesiastes*, vii. 16.

" Speak evil of no man."—*Titus*, iii. 2.

" Be not too hasty to erect general theories from a few particular observations."—
Dr. Isaac Watts, D. D.

DUBLIN :

MILLIKEN AND SON GRAFTON-STREET,

BOOKSELLERS TO THE UNIVERSITY.

M.DCCC.XXXIX.

16 Title page of *A defence of the stage* (1839) by J.W. Calcraft. Courtesy of the Board of Trinity College Dublin.

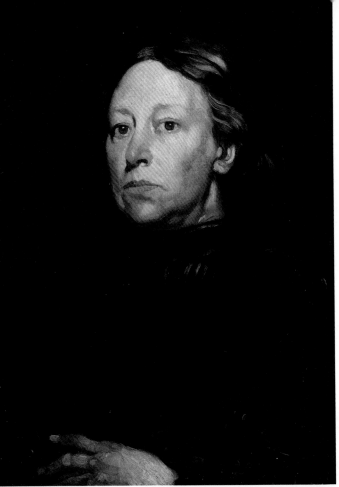

17 Augusta Lady Gregory (1852–1932). Named the recipient of the Abbey Theatre's first patent in 1904 – in preference to Miss Horniman. © National Gallery of Ireland.

18 Programme for the 1909 Abbey Theatre's production of George Bernard Shaw's *The shewing-up of Blanco Posnet*. This play was at the centre of a further dispute between Dublin Castle and the Abbey Theatre management. Courtesy of UCD Digital Library, from an original in UCD Special Collections.

THE SHEWING-UP OF BLANCO POSNET.

A Sermon in Crude Melodrama, by

BERNARD SHAW.

THE PEOPLE IN THE PLAY IN THE ORDER OF THEIR APPEARANCE.

BABSY	EILEEN O'DOHERTY
LOTTIE	DAISY REDDY
HANNAH	SHEILA O'SULLIVAN
JESSIE	MARY NAIRN
EMMA	EITHNE MAGEE
ELDER DANIELS	ARTHUR SINCLAIR
BLANCO POSNET	FRED O'DONOVAN
STRAPPER KEMP	J. M. KERRIGAN
FEEMY EVANS	SARA ALLGOOD
SHERIFF KEMP	SYDNEY J. MORGAN
FOREMAN OF JURY	J. A. O'ROURKE
NESTOR, a Juryman	JOHN CARRICK
WAGGONER JOE	ERIC GORMAN
THE WOMAN	MAIRE O'NEILL
JURYMEN, BOYS, ETC.	U. WRIGHT, J. FITZGERALD, FRED HARFORD, J. DOWNES, HUGH BARDEN, P. MURPHY, J. O'BRIEN, etc.

SCENE—A Town Hall in a Territory of the United States of America.

This Play was produced for the first time by the National Theatre Society, at the Abbey Theatre, Dublin, on 25th August, 1909, with the above cast.

19 The burning of the Ring Theatre in Vienna, Dec. 1881. Over 500 people died in this tragedy. Very different was the small-scale theatre fire alluded to by Charlotte Brontë in *Villette* (ch. 23): 'it was but some loose drapery on which a spark had fallen, and which had blazed up and been quenched in a moment'. There were no fatalities, and Lucy Snowe escaped unharmed. Courtesy of the Board of Trinity College Dublin.

23 (*left*) James Sheridan Knowles (1784–1862). Of this prolific Cork-born dramatist – 20 of his plays were to be published – it is claimed that in his 'mixture of Roman grandiloquence and English domesticity' there was recognized 'a new and distinctive voice'. In his sixtieth year Knowles commenced a new career as a Baptist preacher. © National Portrait Gallery, London

24 (*bottom left*) Edward George Bulwer-Lytton, 1st Baron Lytton (1802–73). Gave his name to the legislation of 1833, recognizing the dramatic author's performing right. Courtesy of the Board of Trinity College Dublin.

25 (*bottom right*) Bejamin Lumley (1811/12–75). Prominent opera impresario and litigant in London, a career under both heads recalled in his *Reminiscences* of 1864. © National Portrait Gallery, London.

B. Lumley.

26 Dion Boucicault (1820–90). Author of *The Colleen Bawn* and *The Shaughraun*. Notorious victim of undeveloped state of international copyright protection. Courtesy of the Board of Trinity College Dublin.

27 Eugène Delacroix. The execution of the Doge Marino Faliero. Lord Byron's play, based on Faliero's remarkable career and equally remarkable downfall, spawned a production provoking litigation that foreshadowed the inauguration of the dramatic author's performing right: *Murray v. Elliston* (1822). Courtesy of the Wallace Collection, Hertford House, London.

Exceptions from payment were sanctioned[68] where

(a) the whole of the takings were devoted to philanthropic or charitable causes;
(b) wholly educational;
(c) for the amusement of children and the admission charge was not more than 1*d.* per person;
(d) partly educational or partly scientific or provided by any society founded with the object of reviving national pastimes.

The tax was inherited by the new Irish Free State. Its fortunes under successive Irish administrations wrote a curious chapter in modern Irish history. Its existence did not, unsurprisingly, command universal acceptance. The tax itself, for instance, was blamed for the abandonment in the year 1932 of the Sandycove Swimming Gala.[69] The controversy engendered by this draconian measure led members of the Sandycove Swimming Club to chastise the Irish Amateur Swimming Association for failing to press government to secure an exemption from the tax. As we are about to discover, one lobby in Ireland was not to forego the opportunity to press for such a change to be made in its own interests: this happened ten years after the cancellation of the gala at the Forty Foot and the adjacent bathing area.

In 1943 the section in the UK Act of 1916 listing exemptions from the duty was repealed,[70] and replaced by a new provision which confirmed the exemption for entertainments covered by clause a), where 'the whole of the takings were devoted to philanthropic or charitable causes', and clause b), where 'the entertainment was wholly educational', but decidedly not for entertainments falling within the scope of clauses c) and d). In addition, however, in the case of entertainments that continued to be exempted from the duty, all expenses incurred were not to exceed a declared percentage (30 per cent) of the total takings.[71] Again, also in addition, an entirely novel category of entertainment exempted from paying the duty was added,[72] namely, an entertainment

> either ... promoted by the Gaelic League or ... promoted by some other society or organisation in respect of which it is shown to the satisfaction of the Revenue Commissioners that its primary object is the extension of the use of the Irish language, and ... in either case the whole of the net proceeds of the entertainment are devoted and will be supplied to the extension of the use of the Irish language.

Post-independence, there were to be further concessions introduced by legislation between 1948 and 1958. It is possible that some of these may have been

68 S. 1 (5).
69 Frank Power and Peter Pearson, *The Forty Foot: a monument to sea bathing* (Dublin, Environmental Publications, n.d.), pp 99–100.
70 Finance Act 1943 (no. 16 of 1943), s. 10 (7).   71 Ibid., s. 10 (4).   72 S. 10 (2) *(c)*.

inspired, in part at least, by an increasingly acrimonious debate over the tax itself in Britain. There legislation of 1946 added to the exemptions laid down in 1916 and later, where all profits generated by the stage performance or other 'entertainments' were ploughed back into the theatre itself.[73] That this was not enough to satisfy critics of the tax, who were particularly concerned by the parlous financial position of theatres in London, was demonstrated the following year when a group of MPs launched a major assault on the Finance Bill of 1947, not to abolish the tax, but to reduce the level of it. What was at stake was the level of the duty fixed in 1943; the reform group of MPs wished this to be reduced to the level fixed in 1939. In supporting the call for this change, E.P. Smith, the MP for Ashford, argued that under the then current arrangements, the average rate of entertainment duty consumed 28 per cent of gross takings in all theatres.[74] In the West End of London, in the case of a number of the theatres there, the percentage rose to 34 per cent. Smith added a somewhat cruder political afterthought. 'We ought to remember', he urged,[75]

> that in this matter of Entertainment Duty this Government are really the worst type of *rentier de luxe*. They do absolutely nothing of any value for the commercial theatre. They toil not, neither do they spin. Yet Solomon in all his glory never enjoyed such a rake-off.

The proposal to add a fresh clause to the 1947 Finance Bill to reduce the level of Entertainment Duty was moved in the House of Commons by A.P. Herbert, MP for Oxford University. Like E.P. Smith, Herbert was to offer some financial data in support of the cause. A theatre manager he knew, 'not a playboy who bounces in to make money, but a good man of the theatre', Herbert recalled,[76] had in the year 1946–7 spent £89,000 on salaries, paid £68,000 in Entertainment Duty, and incurred losses overall of £17,000. Herbert, indeed, was to lay stress on all the risks associated with managing a theatre, which, in his view, more than justified adoption of the proposal he had brought forward. 'The production of plays, concerts, recitations, variety shows', he argued,[77]

> is not like selling a packet of matches or a bottle of whisky, something for which the demand is certain, and about which there is very little difficulty today.

He continued in the same vein:[78]

> Nothing is good for the theatre. Bad weather is bad for the theatre, and very good weather is bad for the theatre. When the sun is shining, people want to

73 Finance Act 1946 (9 & 10 Geo. VI, c. 64), s. 8 (1).
74 *Hansard*, 5, ccccxxxviii, col. 1624: 16 June 1947.   75 Ibid.
76 *Hansard*, 5, ccccxxxviii, col. 1618.   77 Ibid., col. 1613.   78 Cols. 1613–14.

play tennis, and, when it is wet and cold, they would rather stay at home and read a book.

This last remark reminds me of two observations Jane Austen has John Knightley impart to Emma Woodhouse, in objecting to a decision to venture forth in deteriorating winter weather conditions to accept hospitality at the vicarage. 'It is the greatest absurdity', the complaint begins,[79]

> Actually snowing at the moment! – The folly of not allowing people to be comfortable at home – and the folly of people's not staying comfortably at home when they can!

Herbert, in his contribution to the discussion on Entertainment Duty, alluded to additional factors that required to be fed into the equation:[80]

> The tenor may develop laryngitis, or the baritone may fall under a bus, or an actress may go off and have a baby. In my last show it happened that both leading ladies after three months, went off – bless them – to increase the population.

Should a reduction prove possible, the benefits, Herbert contended, would speak for themselves:[81]

> We should have a better theatre. We should have managers who were more ready to take risks and produce British shows, and less prone to scour the by-ways of New York where they obtain plays that are not always good.

In short, the financial boost would be productive of lasting benefit to British art.

Benn Levy, a dramatist as well as a Labour MP, for Eton and Slough – and a relentless campaigner for the abolition of stage censorship – took a markedly different line.[82] He stressed the existence of the new rule whereby Entertainment Duty was not payable where all profits generated were ploughed back into the theatre.[83] Touching generally on the financial problems faced by theatre managements in the later 1940s, Levy seized the occasion to dwell rather on the level of rents.[84] That the level of rents was clearly part of the problem was by no means denied by those seeking a reduction in Entertainment Duty: these had been rising 'indefensibly'. 'The profit rentalist', E.P. Smith, for instance, remarked,[85] 'is round the neck of the production management like the old man of the sea round the neck of Sinbad the Sailor'. The observation served as the cue to Smith to sound off on other increases in the outlays forced on managers. 'The salaries of players, stage-hands and the front of the house staff', he insisted,[86]

79 Jane Austen, *Emma*, ch. 13. 80 *Hansard, 5*, ccccxxxviii, col. 1614. 81 Cols. 1640–1.
82 *Hansard, 5*, ccccxxxviii, cols. 1628–30. 83 Cols. 1629–30. 84 Cols. 1628–9.
85 Ibid., col. 1625. 86 Ibid.

have all increased … The cost of dresses, costumes, the making and painting
of scenery, furnishings and hangings, required for every production, however
simple, have all mounted.

Hugh Dalton, the Chancellor of the Exchequer, in his response to these moves,
attempted, as he put it, 'to puzzle out some of the arithmetic of the economics of
the theatre',[87] without addressing himself to all the complaints brought up by the
likes of A.P. Herbert and E.P. Smith.[88] When the House of Commons divided on
the motion to introduce the new clause, reducing the level of Entertainment Duty,
the government had a comfortable victory, the House voting 206–99 to reject it.[89]

In Ireland, some further movement was recorded after what had been approved
in 1943. In 1948 patent theatres were exempted from the duty where the entertainment consisted partly of film and partly of personal performance, provided the
latter constituted 75 per cent of the 'show'[90] – and early recognition of the
challenge live theatre faced from the cinema (which worried one MP in London
during the previous year's Commons debate on the Finance Bill 1947).[91] Lay-offs
in theatres and cinema allegedly caused by the level of Entertainment Duty were
raised by Alfie Byrne, TD, in Dáil Éireann in the autumn of 1953.[92] Mr MacEntee,
the Minister for Finance, in his response, asserted that there were no grounds for
Byrne to have drawn the connection he had.[93] The exchange may, however, have
had some effect even so, for in legislation of 1955 the critical threshold for personal
performances – under the 1948 rule – was reduced to 65 per cent.[94] Three years
later a further reduction to 50 per cent was sanctioned.[95] In other respects, a little
unusually, however, the 1958 Finance Act represented a hardening of position as
regards the collection of Entertainment Duty.[96]

Another change, dating from 1948, was no less significant. From that year on,
no duty at all was declared payable where the entertainment consisted exclusively
of a personal performance.[97] The latter, instructively, for all these purposes, was
defined[98] as

> an entertainment, the performers in which are personally present and
> performing and which consists of one or more of the following matters, that
> is to say
> (a) a dramatic performance,
> (b) a musical concert, whether vocal or instrumental, or both vocal and
>   instrumental;
> (c) a number of variety items or turns such as are ordinarily given in a
>   music-hall.

---

87 Col. 1636.   88 Cols. 1635–40.   89 Col. 1646.
90 Finance Act 1948 (no. 12 of 1948), s. 10.
91 *Hansard, 5*, ccccxxxviii, col. 1646: A.R. Blackburn, MP for King's Norton.
92 *Dáil Debates*, cxlii, col. 16: 20 Oct. 1953.   93 Ibid.
94 Finance Act 1955 (no. 13 of 1955), s. 7.   95 Finance Act 1958 (no. 25 of 1958), s. 16.
96 See s. 17.   97 Finance Act 1948, s. 10 (5).   98 See s. 10 (1).

In 1962 Entertainment Duty was abolished altogether, it ceasing to be leviable after 1 October of that year.[99]

In an earlier era it was not the state as tax-gatherer but the utterly unscrupulous and even delinquent patron that posed the greatest threat to the theatre's financial well-being. In the eighteenth century, as we have seen, management did indeed struggle to make ends meet. It did not help at all that admission practices could facilitate an amount of low-level delinquency. Counterfeit coins naturally had to be guarded against, not always successfully, as this item culled from the *Dublin Gazette* in June 1771 would seem to imply:[100]

> On Tuesday, Thursday, and Saturday last several pieces of this base coin [whole and half guineas] were imposed on the publick by sharpers dressed in laced cloaths, toupees and bag wigs, on the different door keepers of the playhouse, etc.

Silver tokens issued for various theatres – for Aungier Street in 1735; for Smock Alley and Crow Street[101] for 1758; and for Crow Street in 1803, for example – served as an alternative to current coin of the realm. As Stockwell pointed out,[102] these

> were a considerable liability upon the theatres for which they were issued, for they were not only issued for a long term of years, but also were transferable both by benefit of law and by sleight of hand.

More to the point perhaps, they could be forged and surreptitiously passed back to other intending patrons – a practice that led to managements insisting that tokens, once presented to the doorkeeper, should be retained by the latter overnight. They then had of course to be collected the next day – an irritant as well as an inconvenience.

Printed, dated tickets operated by a system of prepayment only seem to have come into circulation towards the end of the eighteenth century. The practice of issuing numbered tickets for numbered seats appears to have commenced in London in the late 1860s. It was swiftly copied in Dublin, much to the distaste of one theatre-goer, who was damning in his criticism, 'Having paid for admission to the dress circle', this patron wrote,[103]

> we were presented with a slip of paper bearing a number, which we were directed to hand to the 'attendant' within. We were met on entering the boxes

99 Finance Act 1962 (no. 15 of 1962), s. 6.
100 *Dublin Gazette*, 27 June 1771, quoted Stockwell, *Dublin theatres*, p. 235.
101 Jonah Barrington recalled such an arrangement for Crow Street, cited Stockwell, *Dublin theatres*, p. 320, n. 37.
102 Stockwell, *Dublin theatres*, p. 237.
103 *The history of the Theatre Royal, Dublin* (Dublin, Edward Ponsonby, 1870), p. 192.

by a female of grim and stony aspect, attired in a stuff dress, and whose hard, expressionless face furnished no clue to the ascertainment of her age. Receiving from us our printed slip, she glanced at the number, and taking us into immediate custody led us to a seat affixed to it a number corresponding to that upon the slip. Finding ourselves conducted to a place, of all others in the circle, the very last we would have selected had we been permitted to choose, we meekly remonstrated, and expressed our desire to sit elsewhere; but were at once silenced by a look in which surprise at our audacity and pity for our ignorance were judiciously blended, and by an intimation that the place referred to was already 'booked'.

Embezzlement on the part of boxkeepers and doorkeepers could constitute another drain on revenue. Gilbert related an episode when Daly was manager of the Crow Street theatre.[104] Apparently, a ticket-taker when on his death bed in the Marshalsea – the particular one is not identified – sent for Daly, and confessed that he, together with his confederates, had embezzled £600 of the receipts the theatre earned during Mrs Siddons' engagement there in 1793–4.

Stockwell's verdict on the situation can scarcely be faulted, 'With', she wrote,[105]

so little check upon the 'takings' of the box keepers and doorkeepers, and with the difficulties of making change in a hurry, augmented by 'odd money', 'half price' and questionable varieties of currency, the receipts of a night's performance were very largely dependent upon the integrity of those officials. Few of them, it would seem, could resist the temptation to juggle their accounts but rather maintained with dexterity the traditional dishonesty of their Elizabethan forbears.

104 Gilbert, *History of Dublin*, ii, 213.
105 Stockwell, *Dublin theatres*, p. 254. See, too, a further comment from her, at p. 371, n. 104.

CHAPTER TWELVE

Performers and managers

PROPRIETORS AND MANAGERS of Dublin's theatres were no strangers to disputes and lawsuits, even if few of these controversies have been exhaustively recorded for posterity. Those touching the issue of the employment of performers – actors and actresses in the main, but also singers, musicians and dancers – constitute a distinct group that merits special attention. A convenient place to begin is with an affair that came to the boil in 1662.

Though the battle between Davenant and Ogilby for control of Dublin's nascent theatre at the Restoration resulted in victory for Ogilby,[1] the latter did not always manage to control matters as he might have wished. In the summer of 1662 Davenant complained to the king, Charles II, that Ogilby had induced John Richards and other members of Davenant's company of actors to break their 'obligations and articles to act' in that company and join Ogilby's company in Dublin. Writing to the Irish lord lieutenant, the duke of Ormond, in August, the King plainly took a very dim view of what had occurred. Having repeated Davenant's complaint, Charles II continued:[2]

> Our Will and Pleasure therefore is & Wee doe hereby Command ye said John Ogilby to cause ye said Richards to returne with all Expidition to his former employment, and forbeare to draw away, or entertayne any of ye said Company of Players, belonging to ye said Sr William Davenant.

Irish theatre managers regularly choosing to recruit their actors in London,[3] disputes of the kind that saw Davenant challenge Ogilby are unlikely to have been a rarity. Much, naturally, depended on the precise terms of any contract – the articles – that the actor or actress had entered into. In the absence of such critical information, it is difficult to know whether to side with David Garrick or with James Lacy, the manager at London's Drury Lane at the time, over Garrick's planned winter season at Dublin's Smock Alley, 1745–6 – a season destined to stand high in the annals of Smock Alley, Sheldon observing that Garrick's presence in Dublin that winter gave 'the season an unprecedented brilliance, a

---

1 Above, p. 5.
2 Charles II to Irish lord lieutenant, 17 Aug. 1662, quoted La Tourette Stockwell, *Dublin theatres and theatre customs* (Kingsport, TX, Kingsport Press, 1938), p. 92; and see, too, K. Van Eerde, *John Ogilby and the taste of his times* (Folkestone, Kent, Wm. Dawson & Son, 1976), p. 67.
3 Stockwell, *Dublin theatres*, p. 312 n.51.

brilliance not to be surpassed in Dublin until the twentieth century'.[4] (Garrick was never to return, employing his wife's aversion to a sea crossing when pressed some thirty years later to undertake a return trip by Sir John Caldwell of Castle Caldwell, Co. Fermanagh – his wife being 'so sick and distressed by the sea that I have not had the resolution to follow my inclinations on account of her fears'.)[5] Back in 1745 the complaint voiced at the time by Lacy was to the effect that Garrick was 'making interest in Ireland' when under articles to him.[6]

At the root of this quarrel of 1745 was Garrick's contention that Lacy had not been prepared to pay him more[7] – not an uncommon complaint by London-based actors both before and after. Where, of course, there was no firm contractual commitment to perform in London, no obstacle would seem to have been placed in the way of the artiste, lured to Dublin by the prospect of higher earnings. It tells us something about the relationship between Garrick and Lacy that they were soon reconciled, Garrick eventually joining Lacy as a co-patentee at Drury Lane.[8]

The case of an actress lured to Dublin by the prospect of higher earnings there, and settling permanently, rather than whiling away a single winter season, like Garrick, was to be recalled by Colley Cibber. The actress in question was a Mrs Butler, and the episode dated from the time of Joseph Ashbury's management at Smock Alley in the 1690s.

'I cannot help observing when there was but one theatre in London', Cibber wrote in his memoirs of 1740,[9]

> at what unequal salaries, compar'd to those of later days, the hired actors were then held, by the absolute authority of their frugal masters.

Cibber then proceeded 'to quote chapter and verse'. 'Mrs Butler', he continued,[10]

> had then but forty shillings a week, and could she have obtain'd an addition of ten shillings more (which was refus'd her) would never have left their service; but being offer'd her own conditions to go with Mr Ashbury to Dublin (who was then raising a company of actors for that theatre, where there had been none since the Revolution) her discontent here, prevail'd with her to accept of his offer, and he found his account in her value.

---

4 E.K. Sheldon, *Thomas Sheridan of Smock Alley, recording his life as actor and theatre manager in both Dublin and London; and including a Smock Alley calendar for the years of his management* (Princeton NJ, Princeton UP, 1967), p. 61.

5 Garrick to Caldwell, 14 May 1776: *The private correspondence of David Garrick with the most celebrated persons of his time*, 2 vols (London, Henry Colburn and Richard Bentley, 1831–2), ii, 150.

6 Sheldon, *Sheridan of Smock Alley*, p. 60.   7 *Garrick Corr.*, ii, 150.

8 See *Garrick Corr.*, i, 50–3.

9 Colley Cibber, *An apology for the life of Mr Colley Cibber, comedian, and late patentee of the Theatre-Royal, with an historical view of the stage during his own time* (Dublin, George Faulkner, 1740), p. 97.

10 Ibid.

Cibber was in no doubt that Dublin's gain in this case necessarily fell to be contrasted with London's loss. 'Were not', he ruminated,[11]

> those patentees most sagacious oeconomists, that could lay hold on so notable an expedient, to lessen their charge? How gladly, in my time of being a sharer, would we have given four times her increase, to an actress of equal merit?

In the summer of 1775 a continuing differential between wages for actors in Dublin and those for actors in London provoked a quarrel between an actor in Dublin called Brereton and Garrick, the then manager and now co-patentee at Drury Lane in London. Brereton was an old acquaintance and the row that developed would lead to the sundering of that relationship.

The year before, in June 1774, Brereton, then based in Dublin, told Garrick he had been offered a two-year season at Crow Street at 7 and 8 guineas a week. His 'heart', however, as he put it, was in Drury Lane whilst Garrick presided there, and he would much prefer to strut his stuff on that stage. The snag was the wage on offer in London: he could not, he said, live on £3 a week in the metropolis.[12] Brereton's letter this June thus amounted to an appeal to Garrick to increase what he would have been prepared to offer. 'I am sure', Brereton wrote,[13]

> you cannot blame me for embracing so very capital a difference. If a situation could be made, and business allotted to me, that would entitle me to six pounds weekly, I should be happy in returning.

No change was made for the 1774–5 winter season, but when Brereton took up his pen again, in July 1775, reiterating his desire to go back to London, it is clear that Garrick had moved some way to increase a possible offer to Brereton. In a letter of 10 July,[14] Brereton told Garrick he was 'amply content with your very generous conduct to me as to my salary'. Could he not, however, go a little bit further? 'The pound a week might be added to the second year of my article instead of making me up four pounds for last year'. This would give him 'a kind of rank in the theatre'.

Less than a fortnight after despatching this epistle, Brereton wrote to Garrick again,[15] indicating he was obliged to abandon any idea at all of returning to London for another year. This was because he had already entered into articles with Spranger Barry, the manager at Crow Street, and risked being mulcted in a penal sum if he broke the arrangement. The tone of this second letter Garrick regarded as discourteous in the extreme and he was to endorse it 'Brereton's second letter: how unlike the first'.

11 Ibid., p. 98.   12 W. Brereton to David Garrick, 24 June 1774: *Garrick Corr.*, i, 538.
13 Ibid.   14 Brereton to Garrick, 10 July 1775: *Garrick Corr.*, ii, 67.
15 Ibid., 30 July 1775: *Garrick Corr.*, ii, 70.

What infuriated Garrick was that while he was laying plans to make Brereton a more attractive offer, the latter had already committed himself to Barry. This was scarcely a trivial matter. Responding in August, Garrick adopted a more menacing approach. 'The spirit of your last letter', he began,[16]

> is so very different from your former one, that I am obliged to say a few words to you, which shall be the last you shall ever be troubled with from me.

The sting was in the tail:[17]

> It is impossible that you can ever be engaged with me again. I wish you no harm, but hope when you meet with a better friend of a manager, that you will treat him more kindly.

In a letter which does not apparently survive, Brereton clearly attempted at this late hour to save his relationship with Garrick, by promising to travel over to London and beg forgiveness. In a final letter in this extraordinary correspondence, written by Garrick in September,[18] it was clear a) Garrick was immovable, and b) Brereton need not put himself to the bother of crossing the Irish Sea. The put-down might be thought by some to border on the cruel. 'Though', Garrick began,[19]

> I had resolved never to write to you again, yet lest you should add error to error, and plunge yourself deeper into mistakes, which may become a very serious consideration, I shall once more say a word or two, in answer to yours. By your own account, your circumstances are none of the best, and your taking such an expensive journey and voyage to England, to convince me that you have not behaved unkindly and unjustly to me, will be as ineffectual as expensive, unless you could give me a new head to conceive differently, and a new heart not to feel. Your proposition of breaking your article to come to me, at all events, is adding worse to bad, and what I would never consent to, had you all the talents of all the great actors put together. That you may not be misled again by a false light, or deceive yourself with an expectation of what cannot happen, I once more assure you that it will not be in my power to give you the situation you might have had, while I continue manager of the theatre. You may depend upon it that this is the resolution of your once very sincere friend, and not your ill-wisher even now.

Brereton seems to have had no option but to stay in Ireland, where he is recorded as having acted regularly in Cork in the late 1770s and down to 1783; he died aged 36 in 1787.[20]

---

16 Garrick to Brereton, 9 Aug. 1775: *Garrick Corr.*, ii, 73.   17 Ibid.
18 Ibid., 9 Sept. 1775: *Garrick Corr.*, ii, 93.   19 Ibid.
20 W.S. Clark, *The Irish stage in the county towns, 1720–1800* (Oxford, Clarendon Press, 1965), appendix B.

The more blatant 'poaching' of performers from some rival impresario – the delinquent act charged against Ogilby in 1662 – we are about to discover was to generate some celebrated litigation in England, litigation of which their Irish counterparts can scarcely claim to have been unaware.

But before turning to these cases, a curious affair linked to employment practices on the Dublin stage, and dating from the 1710s, merits a brief mention. This was a dispute – of a very different kind, but certainly illuminating – regarding the re-engagement of an erstwhile member of the Smock Alley company. It took place in the days of Joseph Ashbury's regime, and features the reverse of the career trajectory of Mrs Butler – who, it will be recalled, came to Dublin because it paid more. Here a Mr John Thurmond had left for London in the belief that he would do better there. The story can be pieced together principally from three petitions of 1713 which were to be transcribed by Lawrence.[21] John Thurmond left Ashbury's company around 1707 to try to better himself in London. Returning to Ireland six years later and seeking to be re-employed at Smock Alley, he faced opposition both from Ashbury and a number of actors in the company, technically known as the sharers,[22] over the terms of any conceivable re-engagement. The level of the salary at which he might be re-engaged was the bone of contention, and the opposition grounded itself largely on the argument that, when based in Dublin, Thurmond had invariably sought to advance himself financially at the expense of the interests of the other actors.[23] Donations received from 'ladies of quality' and from military men that were intended to be spread around, it was claimed, he had appropriated for his own use. Two benefit plays – John Dryden's *All for Love* (1678) and Thomas Otway's *Venice Preserv'd* – had been specially put on for him on the eve of his departure for London in 1707. What he had done, by way of return, it was alleged, was to pawn theatrical costumes that he had no right to treat of in such a manner. Thurmond denied this last charge, claiming that these costumes had either been made at his own expense or given 'by some of the Quality', and had, in any event, been seized by his creditors.[24] Ashbury and the 'sharers' retorted that this was a falsehood,[25] maintaining, in opposition to Thurmond,

---

21 W.J. Lawrence, 'New light on the old Dublin stage', *New Ireland Review*, 26 (1906–7), 156. See, too, Stockwell, *Dublin theatres*, p. 47, and Desmond Slowey, *The radicalization of the Irish stage, 1600–1900* (Dublin and Portland OR, Irish Academic Press, 2008), p. 74.

22 A sharer was a member of a company of players, who paid the expenses, and received the profits, and employed the 'journeymen' members of the company.

23 'The case of the patentee and sharers of the Theatre Royall, humbly offer'd to their Excies the Lords Justices of Ireland': Lawrence, 'New light', 159.

24 'The most humble answer of John Thurmond to a paper laid before your Excies intituled the Case of the patentees and sharers of the Theatre Royal in Dublin': Lawrence, 'New light', 160.

25 'The Sharers' reply to Mr Thurmond's answer to the Patentee and Sharers' Case': Lawrence, 'New light', 163.

That the Dresses in Thurmond's Possession were not seized but pawned, particularly His Grace the Duke of Ormond's Birthday Suit,[26] which his Grace did him the Honour to Order for his Wearing and never was heard of since. His Excie the Lord Cutts' Suit[27] was released for the sum of five Pounds at the Sharers' Expence from Mrs Smyth, a Roman Shape, Two Spanish shapes[28] and a Modern Coat trim'd with Silver, all made at the Sharers' Expence all pawn'd, the Roman shape redeemed from Mr Bradshaw by the Sharers, the rest of the Dresses never heard of since.

The original petition, Thurmond's answer, and the sharers' retort were all addressed to the Irish lords justices of the day. As Lawrence explained,[29] that they were seised of a somewhat petty dispute 'clearly indicates that the Dublin theatre still remained, as it began, a semi-government institution.'

What happened at the end of the day is revealed by Lawrence, thanks to the chance survival of two pieces of correspondence.[30] The lords justices wrote to the lord lieutenant, the second duke of Ormond, and he replied, via his secretary Edward Southwell, both to Joshua Dawson and to the lords justices on 28 May 1713. Ormond simply advised the authorities in Dublin to leave it to Ashbury to arrange an appropriate salary for Thurmond, given all the circumstances. Thurmond was certainly back in harness the following year, and it is probably from then that Chetwood, who served at the time as Ashbury's assistant manager, was able to relate another detail apropos this actor:[31] how his wife resorted to guile to retrieve from the pawnbroker a theatrical costume Thurmond desperately required for a particular performance – Ingoldsby's 'birthday suit'[32].

Summary dismissals too – always likely to cause trouble – are not absent from the record at this period.

It was in one of the earlier years of Thomas Sheridan's management at Smock Alley that he, unsurprisingly, found himself sued by the actor Charles Macklin. Macklin, in Sheridan's eyes, had perpetrated a gross breach of protocol by announcing from the stage of Smock Alley, without any advance warning to Sheridan, the date and details of a benefit performance for his wife. Macklin and his wife were then both summarily dismissed from the troupe. Macklin procured a bill in Chancery, maintaining he had been dismissed in mid-season without notice and in the absence of any cause. Earnings of £800 had not been made over. Sheridan was induced by this turn of events to lodge £300 in court, which Macklin elected to take, having decided, together with his wife, to move *instanter* to

26 Persons of the first rank would customarily present suits of apparel to their favourite actors to be worn by them at performances put on on their birthdays.
27 Lord Cutts was an Irish Lord Justice who died in 1707.
28 A shape was a theatrical dress or suit of clothes.   29 Lawrence, 'New light', 156.
30 Ibid., 168.
31 W.R. Chetwood, *A general history of the stage; (more particularly the Irish theatre) from its origin in Greece down to the present time* ... (Dublin, E. Rider, 1749), p. 226.
32 Richard Ingoldsby also served as another Irish Lord Justice; he died in 1712.

England, and, it would seem, to drop the legal proceedings in Dublin.[33] This was by no means an unexpected turn of events, relations between the two actors having perceptibly soured over the previous months: Macklin apparently had taken to measuring the names of Sheridan and himself in Smock Alley's playbills to ensure his equal billing.[34]

Many years later, Macklin was back in court – in London this time – protesting against his summary 'discharge' and consequent loss of earnings. The circumstances could not have been more different. Orchestrated disruption at Covent Garden during performances of *Macbeth* and *The Merchant of Venice* designed to drive Macklin off the stage succeeded to an extent when, out of fright, the management caved in and 'discharged' Macklin. The criminal proceedings resulting from this sequence of events are related elsewhere.[35] Macklin's civil action against Colman the manager of the theatre, finally came on for hearing in the King's Bench in 1781. Lord Mansfield suggested that the matter might be compromised with an award of £500, although Macklin had originally sought £1,000. Mansfield's suggestion was adopted by both sides.[36]

It is from the 1750s that we have the first authentic Irish record of a different kind of dispute between performers and management: the actor – in this case, an actress – who, having been contracted to appear, declined to do so – an instance of no-show.[37] In England, from the reign of William III, there had occurred a case with certain similarities that had a quite extraordinary sequel.[38] The actor Thomas Doggett (*c*.1670–1721) was under articles to Drury Lane. Sensing himself mistreated by the management – unfortunately over a matter the details of which do not appear – Doggett in 1697 declined to turn up for his scheduled performance, preferring instead to move to Norwich to perform under the aegis of the duke of Norfolk. The Drury Lane's patentee then secured orders for Doggett's apprehension, so as to induce him to perform back in London: this development precipitated an application for habeas corpus and for Doggett's release. Lord Holt, the lord chief justice, obliged, and granted the remedy. Cibber, who tells the story, says 'Doggett had money in his pocket and the cause of liberty at his heart'.[39] In 1716, two decades later, Doggett was again to be involved in litigation.[40] Now a patentee himself at Drury Lane, but obliged, his co-patentees contended, to cooperate both in the acting and in the management, which Doggett had declined to do, a battle developed over Doggett's claimed share of the profits. In the resultant Chancery suit Doggett was awarded a sum rather less than what he had originally been offered: £600 plus interest at a rate of 15 per cent from a specified date. Thomas Doggett, it would seem, may not, therefore, have been at all 'easy to

33 Sheldon, *Sheridan of Smock Alley*, p. 150; W.W. Appleton, *Charles Macklin: an actor's life* (Cambridge MA, Harvard UP, 1961), p. 91.
34 Appleton, *Macklin*, p. 90. 35 See below, pp 183–5. 36 Appleton, *Macklin*, p. 268.
37 Victor, *History of theatres of London and Dublin*, 2 vols (London, T. Davies, 1761), ii, 226–9.
38 Cibber, *Apology*, pp 204–5. 39 Ibid., p. 205.
40 Ibid., pp 281–8; see, too, *Oxford DNB*, xvi, 451 at 452.

handle' – as Personnel in some large organisation or institution today might care to express it. That there was another side to Doggett is, however, plain from one other detail regarding an actor so regularly embroiled in controversy. Seemingly incongruously, Doggett was to set aside a sum for the Waterman's Hall in London, to buy a coat and a silver badge to be rowed for on the Thames each 1 August by apprentices who had completed their indentures.[41]

The background to the Irish case, alluded to above, was as follows.[42]

In the spring of 1758 Benjamin Victor, on the instructions of Sheridan, was in London to engage two actresses, Mrs Gregory and Mrs Hamilton, for the upcoming winter season at Smock Alley. 'After a Negotiation of seven weeks', Victor records,[43] it lasting so long,

> as the Demands of those Ladies so far exceeded what we had settled, and indeed all Imagination … the Articles were signed for Mrs Gregory at the moderate Price of five hundred, and Mrs Hamilton at four hundred Pounds.

There was to be no difficulty over the bargain with Mrs Gregory. It was to be otherwise in the case of Mrs Hamilton. 'Mrs Hamilton had a Husband', Victor writes,[44]

> a Gentleman I was a stranger to; and therefore, the Attorney was necessary to draw an Article in Form; such as would bind the Parties by Law, in a Penalty of five hundred Pounds.

'A remarkable Circumstance followed', as Victor described it, 'which showed the Necessity of these Exact Proceedings'.

'Long before the Time necessary for Mrs Hamilton to set out on her Journey' to Dublin, Mr Hamilton wrote to Victor,[45] conveying

> an Apology for his wife's not coming to Dublin to perform her Article, and hoped her not coming would be of no Disadvantage to the Manager.

Victor and Sheridan, non-plussed by such a setback in the midst of their concern about the future of Smock Alley in face of the impending opening of Spranger Barry's new Crow Street theatre, dug in their heels, intent, as they both plainly were, to insist on their pound of flesh. 'I consulted Mr Sheridan' on Mr Hamilton's letter, Victor goes on,[46]

41 Ibid.; Chetwood, *General history of the stage*, p. 170; T.J. Walsh, *Opera in Dublin, 1705–1797: the social scene* (Dublin, Allen Figgis, 1973), pp 6–7; *Oxford DNB*, xvi, at 452.
42 Victor, *History of theatres of London and Dublin*, ii, 226–8.
43 Ibid., ii, 226.   44 Ibid., ii, 227.   45 Ibid., ii, 228.   46 Ibid.

and wrote an Answer back directly, observing, that we, on that side [of] the Water, were drove to the utmost Distress by these Disappointments; and as all the Comedies must suffer, which Mrs Hamilton was engaged to support, he might depend on it, if she did not come, he would be prosecuted on the Article.

Hamilton's response to this mingled bravado and the law. He was sorry if his wife's not showing up was 'of any real Disadvantage', going on to advise his Dublin correspondent 'that he was easy about any Prosecution, as he was indemnified from any Danger at Law'. Resort to the law courts followed, as Victor explains. 'Accordingly', he writes,

> the Article [i.e., the key clause in the contract with Mrs Hamilton] was put into the Hands of Mr Palmer, (who was then in Dublin) an attorney of great Worth and Agility, of the Temple, who prosecuted the Affair through two or three of the Courts, and after the Delay of three Years, recovered the five hundred Pounds Penalty, with Costs.[47]

In 2008, it is worth recalling, Prince, the pop superstar, cancelled at a late hour a concert he was scheduled to give that summer in Dublin's Croke Park. He had been guaranteed a fee of $3 million for his appearance. No reason was ever given for the cancellation, though it was to be argued, in court proceedings in February 2010 launched by the Dublin promoters of the event who were now out of pocket, on the part of Prince, orse Price Rogers Nelson, that his supposed agents had had no authority to bind him to the concert.[48] After a couple of days of a hearing in the High Court in Dublin before Mr Justice Kelly, the case brought by the Dublin promoters was settled. The terms of the settlement were not made public.

In fiction, it might also be recalled, the fall-out from the no-show of the singer-songwriter, Anya King, in Denver, Colorado, and at other venues on the projected tour in the United States, is exhaustively and engagingly examined in one of Sebastian Faulks' character studies. It is enough to know here that Anya's litigation adversaries did not escape unscathed from the inevitable ensuing confrontation.[49]

From the eighteenth century Victor recalls what in England at the time counted as another *cause célèbre*, albeit with an unusual twist.[50] William Powell, a promising young actor, was under contract to the Drury Lane theatre for a period of three years, 'in a penalty of £1,000'. Powell, however, was to contribute £15,000 as his quarter share to a four-man consortium that purchased in 1766 the patent for Covent Garden, Drury Lane's rival. Powell was to die unexpectedly in 1769, and

47 Ibid., ii, 228–9.
48 See *Irish Times*, 24 and 25 Feb. 2010.
49 Sebastian Faulks, *A possible life* (London, Vintage Books, 2013), 'Part V – You next time'.
50 Victor, *History of theatres of London from 1760 to the present time* (London, T. Davies, 1771), pp 149–52.

Victor comments that the law would unquestionably have compelled him to pay the £1,000 penalty for breach of his contract had he lived, 'as the damages sustained by his defection were apparent'.

The difficulties managers at the various theatres faced of a financial nature – paying rent, paying tradesmen, paying annuities – entailed that on several occasions the performers themselves were left unrewarded – a state of affairs which in the mid-eighteenth century particularly irked Thomas Sheridan. The latter, unusually perhaps, sought to establish a principle of punctual payment; he was also to earn a reputation for not being averse to raising salaries either.[51] This, of course, could make his own personal financial situation precarious enough, and it is significant that several years later after his abandonment of his position as manager at Smock Alley, he so much dreaded incarceration at the hands of his creditors in Ireland that he sought and obtained protection from them when the 1765 Act for the relief of insolvent debtors was passed by the Irish parliament.[52] This measure applied both to individuals already incarcerated in some debtors' prison – including the Dublin Marshalsea – and to individuals like Sheridan who risked being so incarcerated.[53] A scheme protecting such individuals from prison, setting out the composition to be made with creditors and endorsed either by the court of King's Bench or that of Common Pleas, was given legislative sanction. Individuals had to prepare details of all their assets, minus clothes, bedding and tools of trade under £10 in value. Under the 1765 Act, 'Thomas Sheridan comedian', was specifically listed alongside 116 others – mostly merchants of one sort or another, but including a brass and ivory turner, a lapper, a stoneblue maker and a chocolate maker – in the second schedule as entitled to avail of the relief enshrined in the measure. It might here be remarked that being in the business of manufacturing chocolate, of contriving a compound of indigo with starch or whiting for use in laundries, of folding linen in a big way, or of turning brass and ivory could prove to be equally precarious to the profession of actor and theatre manager. A creditor by the name of Whyte, Sheldon tells us, was responsible for making Sheridan beneficiary no. 117.[54]

Walsh's verdict on the actor-managers who dominated Dublin theatre from the time of Sheridan down to the end of Richard Daly's holding of the reins in 1797 indicates very well the price exacted in financial and in other terms. 'Thomas Sheridan', he wrote,[55]

> left Dublin a disillusioned man. Henry Woodward had returned to London, having lost most of his savings. Spranger Barry, 'ruined and harassed in mind and body', had yielded Crow Street Theatre to Henry Mossop, and Mossop, in turn, had died of pulmonary tuberculosis, literally almost penniless. His successor, Thomas Ryder, had squandered a fortune though,

51 Sheldon, *Sheridan of Smock Alley*, p. 77.   52 5 Geo. III, c. 73.   53 See s. 12.
54 Sheldon, *Sheridan of Smock Alley*, p. 269, n. 65.
55 Walsh, *Opera in Dublin, 1705–1797*, p. 310.

let it be said, more in extravagant living than on his theatre, and then had changed places in his company with one of his actors – Richard Daly. Of all the managers, Daly was the only one with sufficient judgment to know that, like the wise gambler who leaves the green baize table while he is winning, the time had come for him to leave the green baize of the eighteenth-century theatre.[56]

The remuneration earned by actors and actresses was rarely enough, and, in consequence, several performers sought other sources of income by taking on a huge variety of different employments, mindful all the time, one presumes, to do nothing contrary to the articles they might have signed.[57] Spranger Barry's widow behaved differently, and, in so doing, carved a unique niche for herself in the history of the Irish stage: she would positively refuse to go on stage unless she had been paid in advance.[58] Details of the wages actually paid in the Dublin theatre in the 1770s are supplied by Stockwell.[59] Further information on this key question for the eighteenth century is in short supply, though Victor also manages to shed some light on it.

So-called benefit performances – such as those that had been put on for John Thurmond in 1707 on the eve of his departure for London[60] – naturally constituted an additional source of income, and, for that reason, were very welcome indeed. Greene and Clark explain how they operated.[61] The actor, for whose benefit a particular performance was earmarked, was entitled to keep the profits generated by the evening in question, subject to the deduction of running expenses. These could be not inconsiderable, for they encompassed (i) the salaries of performers and sundry stage-hands, (ii) the cost of general wear and tear to the theatre's fabric, costumes and scenery, (iii) charges for the candles and oil to light the theatre, and (iv) the cost of advertising. On the night of a benefit performance the cost of seats for patrons was slightly increased. We have the salient details for Aungier Street in 1735. Then the price of a seat in the boxes, on the stage or in the lattices was 5s. 5d.; in the pit 3s. 3d.; and in the 1st gallery 2s. 2d. On a benefit night prices were 1s. 1d. dearer in each category.[62] These prices show little difference from those recorded for performances of *The Beggar's Wedding* at Smock Alley in 1728–9:[63] a seat in boxes: 5s.; in the pit 3s.; in the middle gallery 2s.; and in a box in the upper gallery: 1s.

Greene furnishes further details on benefit performances at the provincial theatre in Belfast, probably in the latter half of the eighteenth century.[64] Actors and

56 In addition to this splendid summation, Walsh prints Daly's farewell to the Dublin public that appeared in the *Hibernian Journal* of 18 Aug. 1797: *Opera in Dublin, 1705–1797*, p. 309.

57 Stockwell, *Dublin theatres*, p. 317, n. 11.   58 Ibid., p. 371, n. 104.   59 Ibid., p. 332, n. 26.

60 Above, p. 161.

61 J.C. Greene and G.L.H. Clark, *The Dublin stage, 1720–1745: a calendar of plays, entertainments and after-pieces* (Bethlehem, PA, Lehigh UP; London and Toronto, Associated UP, 1993), p. 39.

62 Ibid.   63 Walsh, *Opera in Dublin, 1705–1797*, p. 36.

64 J.C. Greene, *Theatre in Belfast, 1736–1800* (Bethlehem, PA, Lehigh UP; London, Associated UP, 2000), p. 34.

actresses of primary rank or degree were entitled to two benefit performances each season; in addition, they had the right to pick the play to be performed. Those of secondary rank were entitled to one benefit per season, and those of tertiary rank one benefit also, to be shared with other performers in the same category.

The arrangements that Thomas Sheridan made with David Garrick for the winter season of 1745–6 included Garrick's right to claim two benefit performances. Rejecting Sheridan's first proposals for extra remuneration, Garrick successfully negotiated an additional deal under which profits for the season at Smock Alley would be divided equally between the proprietors, Sheridan and himself.

Thirty years later Garrick, as manager at Drury Lane, found himself involved in an unseemly quarrel with two of his actresses, a Mrs Abington and a Miss Younge, over the scheduling of the benefit performances to which each was entitled.[65] In the spring of 1776 two dates were made available: Saturday 16 March and Monday 18 March. As the senior actress, the fourth degree of eminence, Mrs Abington had first choice, but the difficulty was created when she could not make up her mind. Saturday was an opera night, and that at first disinclined her to choose the 16th. She then had second thoughts and pronounced for the Saturday. Miss Younge then picked the Monday. Mrs Abington, clearly someone whom it was difficult to handle or at least pin down – not, perhaps, unlike Thomas Doggett – then sought to change her mind yet again, expressing a distinct preference for the Monday. She was then told the Monday was no longer free, whereupon, according to Garrick, Mrs Abington started to broadcast the story that she was being denied her 'benefit' altogether, a serious blow indeed as she was now set in her mind to quit the theatre. What appears in Garrick's correspondence at this juncture is the opinion of James Wallace as counsel on the options now left to Garrick.[66] Wallace, quite understandably in the circumstances, makes it plain that further obtuseness on Mrs Abington's part would lead to her being very properly deprived of any right to a benefit at all. In the end, a compromise appears to have been reached, under which the benefit for Mrs Abington was switched to a date in May.[67] Her appearances on the stage in 1776 did not after all represent Mrs Abington's swan song, for she was to be recorded as acting still at Cork in 1786 and at Limerick in 1793.[68]

The actor Edmund Kean (1787–1833) was the principal protagonist in the first in a series of English cases dealing with breaches of contract by performers, breaches seemingly connived at or even procured by rival theatre managements. We thus return to the problem rehearsed at the outset of this chapter which had set Ogilby and Davenant at loggerheads. Kean was no habitué of the courts, but he was familiar with them. His career, it is generally accepted, went into decline after his defeat in the criminal conversation case of *Cox v. Kean*.[69] A break in America

65 *Garrick Corr.*, ii, 140.   66 Counsel's opinion of March 1776: *Garrick Corr.*, ii, 141.
67 Ibid.   68 Clark, *Irish stage in county towns*, appendix B.
69 *Oxford DNB*, xxx, 947 at 952 (entry by Peter Thomson).

was followed by his return to the stage in London where a little later, in February 1828, he entered into an agreement with Charles Kemble, the proprietor at Covent Garden, that he would do twenty-four performances at a rate of £50 per night, and for the duration not to perform elsewhere. The agreement was readjusted when the gasworks failed at Covent Garden but Kean remained under the obligation, still not completely discharged, when in November 1830 he acted at Drury Lane. Kean was living at the time with Ophelia Benjamin, described as 'the formidable Irish prostitute'.[70] Whether she had anything to do with Kean's conduct towards Kemble at this juncture is not clear. Kemble sought an injunction to prevent Kean from continuing to appear at Drury Lane. The then British lord chancellor, Lord Lyndhurst, on an *ex parte* application, granted it, but the vice-chancellor, Sir Lancelot Shadwell, overturned that decision.[71] This was in a judgment that was later to be re-examined by a different lord chancellor, Lord St Leonards, in what, to law students at least, is the much better-known litigation over a similar breach of contract by a German opera singer, Johanna Wagner.[72]

Benjamin Lumley, the manager of His Majesty's Theatre in London, entered into an agreement with Ms Wagner that she would sing opera over a three-month period starting from 1 April 1852. The agreement detailed the six operas in which Ms Wagner agreed to appear and the roles she would take. There were three operas by Mayerbeer (1791–1864): *Le Prophète*, in which she would sing Fides; *Les Huguenots*, Valantine; *Robert le Diable*, Alice; one by Bellini (1801–35): *Montecchi e Capuletti*, in which she would sing Romeo; one by Gluck (1714–87): *Don Juan*, Anna; and a sixth opera to be chosen by mutual consent. The original agreement specified the earnings Ms Wagner might expect. At a later stage, Lumley realised he had not required of Ms Wagner an undertaking that during her London tour she would not sing elsewhere, an undertaking that was given in an addendum to the agreement written in French which in translation read:

> Mademoiselle Wagner engages herself not to use her talents, at any other theatre, nor in any concert or reunion, public or private, without the written authorization of Mr Lumley.

Lumley, in his memoirs, proffered this description of Ms Wagner: 'a magnificent voice, a broad and grand school of vocalization, and a marvellous dramatic power, joined to a comely person'.[73]

Lumley's plan for the 1852 opera season at His Majesty's came unstuck, when Ms Wagner never appeared there, she in league with her father having been

---

70 Ibid., at 953.

71 *Kemble v. Kean* (1829) 6 Sim 333, 58 Eng Rep 619; W.N.M. Geary, *The law of theatres and music-halls* (London, Stevens & Sons, 1895), p. 97.

72 See generally the excellent survey by Stephen Waddams, 'Johanna Wagner and the rival opera houses', *Law Quarterly Review*, 117 (2001), 431.

73 Benjamin Lumley, *Reminiscences of the opera* (London, Hurst & Blackett, 1864), p. 328.

tempted by the prospect of larger earnings to perform instead at Covent Garden, at what at the time was known as the Royal Italian Opera. Frederick Gye was the manager at Covent Garden and was viewed by Lumley as the villain of the piece. The Wagners, father and daughter, were not excused either. 'What was good faith, in their minds', Lumley ruminates in his memoirs,[74] 'when weighed in the balance with a somewhat bigger heap of gold?' Reflecting after the events that were about to unfold, events that were far from being as agreeable as Lumley would have preferred, the manager of His Majesty's did not modify his attack. 'I had suffered before', he wrote,[75]

> it is true, from the vacillations, the overstrained susceptibilities and unsteadiness of purpose inherent in the Teutonic nature; but I had not been placed face to face with mean chicanery and disingenuous evasion of obvious truth. But now I was about to reap a harvest of sad experience.

Lumley first proceeded against the Wagners, seeking an injunction against Johanna continuing to perform at Covent Garden. On 9 May 1852 the vice-chancellor, Sir James Parker, granted the relief sought, and this decision was affirmed by the lord chancellor, Lord St Leonards, on 26 May.[76] Neither judge was prepared to order specific performance of the agreement to appear at His Majesty's. Lord St Leonards, for his part, did go out of his way to berate the refusal of Sir Lancelot Shadwell, the vice-chancellor at the time,[77] to injunct Kean in the case of 1830 where the actor had reneged on his understanding with Kemble.[78] The upshot was that Ms Wagner ceased to perform at Covent Garden and never appeared at His Majesty's.

Lumley then turned his attention to Gye, alleging against the latter that he was tortiously liable for inducing Ms Wagner to breach her contract. On the hearing of the demurrer – a challenge to the law as set down in Lumley's original declaration – a majority of the court of Queens' Bench (Wightman, Erle and Compton JJ) all held that the demurrer was to be overruled.[79] In other words, that Lumley's interpretation of the law was correct. In an unusually long dissenting judgment, Mr Justice Coleridge disagreed.[80]

The issue now required to be tried by a jury who were invited to award £30,000 damages. First, procedural difficulties arose in connection with the securing of

---

74 Ibid., p. 331.   75 Ibid., pp 330–1.

76 *Lumley v. Wagner* (1852) 1 De G, M & G 604, 42 Eng Rep 687.

77 Shadwell, we are told by the entry for him in the *Oxford DNB* (xlix, 921), was in the habit, as President of the Society of Psychrolutes, of bathing every day of the year, whatever the weather, in one of the creeks of the Thames near Barn Elms, and was said, while thus engaged, once to have granted an injunction.

78 1 De G, M & G, at 623, 42 Eng Rep at 695.

79 *Lumley v. Gye* (1853) 2 El & Bl 215, 118 Eng Rep 749; Geary, *Law of theatres*, p. 128.

80 2 El & Bl at 244–69, 118 Eng Rep at 759–69.

evidence from Ms Wagner by commission in Prussia. Once these were resolved,[81] the jury reached its conclusion, finding in favour of Lumley but declining to award the damages sought, on the grounds, as Lumley later expressed it, that Gye was unaware of the existing contract.[82]

There is a patent contradiction here that it is difficult to explain. The author of the entry on Lumley in the new *Oxford DNB* accuses his memoirs of being self-serving and disingenuous, a word, as we have seen, that Lumley threw at the Wagners.[83] That Lumley himself was no paragon of virtue is abundantly illustrated by the circumstance that some five or so years earlier Lumley had paid the Swedish opera diva Jenny Lind (1820–87) to breach her contract with another theatre.[84]

The affair of Johanna Wagner had its counterpart in Ireland in the year 1819, in a case linked to another opera singer, one Mary Byrne.[85] Ms Byrne was a member of the Crow Street troupe, having been engaged to sing in opera there while based in England, late in 1818. The engagement she then made with the agent, a Mr Taylor, acting on behalf of Crow Street's patent-holder, F.J. Jones, made no mention of her being prevented while resident in Dublin from assisting at concerts. However, on her arrival in Dublin, she was presented with a document that required her to agree not to assist at any other musical entertainment without Jones' permission. She objected, but having been reassured by Taylor that this was merely a matter of form, she relented and signed. On a night when there would be no opera performance, Ms Byrne, judging that she was in fact free to act, agreed to perform at a concert given for the benefit of one Percival Panormo. This, in retrospect, was a mistake, for the upshot was a letter, written on behalf of Jones,[86] in which he said that if Ms Byrne had sung at the Panormo concert, as he had been informed she had, he was

> in justice to the preservation of his own property, obliged to consider your engagement violated, and to look on you as no longer a member of the company.

There was uproar a few days later when no opera was put on and no Ms Byrne appeared, and Crow Street was the scene of a serious riot. There was uproar at the theatre too for the four ensuing nights until a planned arbitration of the dispute provoked a reconciliation between artiste and management and Ms Byrne was reinstated.

Management's failure to produce on stage an artiste that the auditorium very much wanted to see and hear in the flesh – a failure, which, as we have just appreciated, was capable of precipitating riot or boycott – was not invariably related

81 See *Lumley v. Gye* (1854) 3 El & Bl 114, 118 Eng Rep 1083.
82 Lumley, *Reminiscences*, p. 333.   83 *Oxford DNB*, xxxiv, 745 at 746.   84 Ibid.
85 T.J. Walsh, *Opera in Dublin, 1798–1800: Frederick Jones and the Crow Street theatre* (Oxford, Oxford UP, 1993), pp 208–11. See, too, below, p. 196.
86 Quoted, Walsh, *Opera in Dublin, 1798–1820*, p. 208.

causally to the individual artiste like Mary Byrne having broken the terms of her contract. Other factors could enter the picture, producing a state of affairs unlikely to have been welcomed by management. The so-called Tamburini row at Her Majesty's Theatre in London in 1840 offers us an excellent example.[87] Antonio Tamburini, a celebrated baritone of the period, was a member of a group of Italian opera singers that included Giovanni Matteo Mario, Giulia Frisi and Fanny Persiani, known at the time as *La Vielle Garde*, who jointly declared that none of these would accept an engagement in London unless the rest of their number was also engaged. When, for whatever reason, the management of Her Majesty's declined to engage Tamburini for the forthcoming season, the group put its programme into action. Nightly demonstrations by the public in Her Majesty's ensued until in the end the management capitulated, and the baritone was re-engaged.

The particular difficulties that F.J. Jones had had with Mary Byrne did not constitute the first occasion in Ireland when this species of problem had arisen.

As long ago as 1749 Thomas Sheridan, the manager at Smock Alley, had had comparable difficulties with his musicians.[88] A convention had established itself that no performances took place on Tuesdays and band members were accordingly free to perform elsewhere on that day, if minded to do so. Bartholomew Mosse at this time was into the business of raising funds for a new lying-in hospital, and announcements were made to the effect that regular nightly concerts to raise such funds would be held in the New Garden. Sheridan's musicians had been engaged for this series of nightly performances, which were not restricted to Tuesdays. He was horrified when advised that band members were planning to exempt themselves from attendance at Smock Alley; and he retaliated by putting into force the articles in the band members' contracts against their performing elsewhere in the evenings.

Visiting the episode, Sheldon concluded that Sheridan 'had the literal right of it', but his judgment at the crucial moment was hasty and ill-advised. Mosse had established Dublin's first lying-in hospital in George's Lane in 1745, taking over the building where Madame Violante had established her second 'theatrical booth'.[89] The site proving unsatisfactory, plans were soon hatched to move to where the Rotunda Hospital (which is still extant) stands today. Charity theatrical performances as well as charity concerts constituted essential elements in the nine-year fund-raising programme, the precursor to the eventual opening of the Rotunda in 1757. Lottery funds were made available as were sums voted by parliament. Overall, it was an anxious period for Mosse, who in 1753 avoided imprisonment for debt, following an arrest in Holyhead, on Anglesey, by escaping and hiding in the Welsh mountains before managing to return to Ireland. He had

87 Harold Rosenthal, 'Opera and music at Covent Garden' in *A history of the Royal Opera House Covent Garden, 1732–1982* (London, Royal Opera House, 1982), p. 96.
88 Sheldon, *Sheridan of Smock Alley*, pp 144–9.
89 Chetwood, *General history of the stage*, p. 61n.

also contrived to rebut allegations regarding the supposed misappropriation of funds. Charity concerts in support of the Rotunda, doubtless to pay off the original debt as well as to support ongoing expenses, were to continue for some forty years.

Sheridan was not the only manager who had problems with his musicians. Later in the century, in 1787, Richard Daly at Smock Alley had occasion to discharge most of the orchestra in advance of the performance of Arnold's opera, *Inkle and Yarico*. Daly then brought in in their stead band members from London. The ploy was not appreciated, and opposition was expressed in the form of disturbances particularly in the Upper Gallery.[90] Foreign singers taking leading roles in operas were not always welcome either.[91]

A group of cases litigated in England in the 1870s tackled the legal aspects of every impresario's nightmare – the performer who cries off because of illness. Understudies and stand-ins who fill the breach, sometimes at less than a moment's notice, have in a few instances gone on to achieve fame and glory, but not all presenters of stage entertainments have laid contingency plans that enable understudies or stand-ins to be rapidly engaged, even if, in the particular circumstances of the entertainment, plans along such lines are appropriate or even called for. Management can pay a substantial price as a consequence. In 1791, when the leading tenor for Thomas Arne's opera *Artaxerxes*, Charles Incledon, fell ill, the cancellation and the substitution of a different opera caused tumult at Crow Street for Richard Daly.[92]

The first of the cases involved a pianist known professionally as Arabella Goddard who was engaged to perform along with an accompanying vocalist at a concert to be given at Brigg in Lincolnshire on 14 January 1871.[93] The engagement had been concluded the previous December.

On the morning of 14 January, the impresario, a Mr Robinson, described as 'a professor of music and giver of musical entertainments' from Gainsborough in Lincolnshire, received a letter from Ms Goddard telling him she was too ill to perform and enclosing a medical certificate. Robinson took steps to advise those who had bought tickets that the concert was cancelled, but he still lost £70. He was to complain that his loss would have been considerably less, if he had received news of the illness on the 13th by telegraph. The trial judge instructed the jury that a condition could be implied into the contract that the performer, in this case Ms Goddard, could be excused if she fell ill. A new trial was sought on the grounds that this ruling was wrong, but in the Exchequer Chief Baron Kelly, while he agreed it would have been better if news of Ms Goddard's disability had been forwarded earlier, refused to dissent from the views of the trial judge. In the process,[94] he endorsed the stance adopted by Chief Baron Pollock, in the

---

90 Walsh, *Opera in Dublin, 1705–1797*, p. 274.   91 Ibid., p. 123.

92 Walsh, *Opera in Dublin 1705–1797*, p. 285.

93 *Robinson v. Davison* (1871) LR 6 Ex 269. Davison was Ms Goddard's married name, and it was her husband who was sued. See further Geary, *The law of theatres*, p. 84.

94 LR 6 Ex at 274.

remarkable case of *Hall v. Wright* in 1859.[95] There, in a dissenting judgment in the Exchequer Chamber Pollock had accepted, unlike the majority of the court, that a serious illness could constitute a good defence to an action for breach of promise to marry. 'All contracts for personal services', Pollock had argued,[96]

> which can be performed only during the lifetime of the party contracting, are subject to the implied condition that he shall be alive to perform them: and should he die, his executor is not liable to an action for the breach of contract occasioned by his death. So a contract by an author to write a book, or by a painter to paint a picture within a reasonable time, would, in my judgment, be deemed subject to the condition that, if the author became insane, or the painter paralytic, and so incapable of performing the contract by the act of God, he would not be liable personally in damages any more than his executors would be if he had been prevented by death.

The second case reintroduces us to Mr Gye,[97] still the manager at the Royal Italian Opera, and the victor in *Lumley v. Gye*, the battle that evolved over Johanna Wagner. In this entirely unrelated case, Gye had made a contract with Mr Bettini in Milan in December 1874 that the latter would sing at the Royal Italian Opera in London as the primo tenor assoluto for a fee of £150 a month from March to July 1875. Bettini undertook not to perform anywhere else in the United Kingdom during this period without Gye's written permission (though there were two exceptions made). More important, though, in this instance, was the requirement that Bellini should attend for rehearsals six days before the opera season opened. This was scheduled for 30 March 1875. Sometime previous to this, Gye was advised that illness would prevent Bettini from being in London before 28 March. Gye treated this as something that entitled him to rescind and have nothing further to do with Bettini. In the Queen's Bench Division, Mr Justice Blackburn, addressing himself to the question of Bettini's right to sue for damages, said that depended on whether his arriving in London six days before 30 March was

> a condition precedent to the defendant's liability, or only an independent agreement, a breach of which will not justify a repudiation of the contract, but will only be a cause of action for a compensation in damages.[98]

He concluded that, taking into account the length of the planned engagement – three-and-a-half months – the delay in arrival at the initial rehearsals could not amount to a breach of a condition precedent to the defendant Gye's liability to employ Bettini. In short, to make use of language later in vogue in the courts, Bettini's promise to turn up six days early fell to be regarded as a warranty, not a

95 El, Bl and El 746, 765, 120 Eng Rep 688, 695.
96 El, Bl & El at 793, 120 Eng Rep at 706.
97 *Bettini v. Gye* (1876) 1 QBD 183; Geary, *Law of theatres*, p. 86.   98 1 QBD at 187.

vital condition of the contract.[99] In all such cases, there could not thus arise any right to repudiate the contract entirely.

A rather different approach was taken by the same judge in the Queen's Bench Division later in 1876 in another case where a performer – in this case a singer – fell ill.[100] Spiers was the owner of the Criterion Theatre in London and his manager, a Mr Hingston, made a contract with the artist's husband on 16 October 1874 that she would play a part in an opera by Lecocq. The opera was *Les Prés Saint Gervais* and the part Mme Poussard was to play was that of Friquette. The opera was to open on 28 November and Mme Poussard was to be paid £11 a week. A 'run' of three months was projected. Mme Poussard attended a number of rehearsals, but fell ill before these were concluded, and she remained ill on the opening night – 28 November – as a consequence of which the stand-in, a Ms Lewis, played the part in her stead, and continued for several nights to do so. By 4 December Mme Poussard was restored to health, and she sought to resume her role, but this was refused. Litigation followed, but here the artist lost. In Mr Justice Blackburn's view, Mme Poussard's inability to perform for the period in question went to the root of the matter, and Spiers had been entitled to rescind the contract. This conclusion was in line with what the trial judge in the case, Mr Justice Field, had earlier decided at the Middlesex Michaelmas sittings the previous year: Mme Poussard's failure to be ready to perform, under all the circumstances of the case, 'went so much to the root of the consideration as to discharge the defendants [Spiers and Pond]'.[101] Mr Justice Blackburn went into the particular circumstances in a little more detail, by way of justifying the decision of the full Queen's Bench Division (Quain and Field JJ, in addition to Blackburn J. himself). 'We think', he began,[102]

> that, from the nature of the engagement to take a leading, and, indeed, the principal female part (for the prima donna sang her part in male costume as the Prince de Conti) in a new opera which (as appears from the terms of the engagement) it was known might run for a longer or shorter time, and so be a profitable or losing concern to the defendants, we can, without the aid of the jury, see that it must have been of great importance to the defendants that the piece should start well, and consequently that the failure of the plaintiff's wife [Madame Poussard] to be able to perform on the opening and early performances was a very serious detriment to them.

In the eighteenth century, as Stockwell relates,[103] contracted artistes could be prevented from putting in an appearance on the Dublin stage or elsewhere in the country on the date specified for the most telling of reasons – gales and other adverse conditions on the Irish Sea. Madame Violante's experience in the autumn

---

99 See further D.W. Greig, 'Condition – or warranty?' *Law Quarterly Review*, 89 (1973), 93.
100 *Poussard v. Spiers and Pond* (1876) 1 QBD 410; Geary, *Law of theatres*, p. 90.
101 See 1 QBD at 413.   102 1 QBD at 414.   103 Stockwell, *Dublin theatres*, p. 372, n. 111.

of 1729 is proof enough of what conditions could be like. She finally arrived in Dublin from England 'after a tedious and dangerous passage of six weeks'.[104] Much later in the century, the celebrated tenor, Charles Incledon, had a lucky escape when returning across the Irish Sea after an engagement in Dublin. The ship he was travelling on was wrecked, and several passengers were drowned. 'He saved himself', we are told,[105]

> by climbing to the roundtop with his wife lashed to him, in which perilous condition he was several hours, till at length delivered by some fishermen who saw their distress from shore.

Incledon was fortunate in comparison with all those – actors included – who perished in the loss of *The Dublin* off south-west Scotland in October 1758.[106]

Jonathan Swift wrote savagely on his experience of being held up for days at Holyhead:[107]

> Holyhead Sept. 25 1727[108]
> Lo! Here I sit at Holyhead
> With muddy ale and mouldy bread:
> All Christian victuals stink of fish,
> I'm where my enemies would wish
> Convict of lies is every sign
> The inn has not one drop of wine.
> I'm fastened both by wind and tide
> I see the ship at anchor tide.
> The captain swears the sea's too rough
> He has not passengers enough
> And thus the Dean is forced to stay
> Till others come to help to pay.

Fifty years later Arthur Young was among a host of others who were also inconvenienced by such endless delays.[109] How many actors and actresses, even singers, musicians and dancers, were similarly obliged on occasion to twiddle their thumbs and patiently wait for storms to abate – at the risk of failing to make some deadline for an appearance in Dublin – is impossible to ascertain. It is known, though, that performances were put off at Smock Alley in both September 1748 and October 1760 and at Crow Street in December 1800 for this most understandable of

104 Ibid., p. 66.   105 Quoted, Walsh, *Opera in Dublin, 1705–1797*, p. 285.
106 Above, p. 25.
107 Irvin Ehrenpreis, *Swift, the man, his work, and the age*, 3 vols (Cambridge MA, Harvard UP, 1983), iii, 540–3.
108 Jonathan Swift, *The complete poems*, ed. Pat Rogers (London, Penguin Books, 1983), p. 329.
109 Arthur Young, *A tour in Ireland, 1776–1779*, ed. A. W. Hutton, 2 vols (London, Bohn's Library, 1892), i, 417–18.

reasons.[110] Earlier in the eighteenth century, performances of Handel's oratorio *Joshua*, announced for January 1730, only took place two months later, 'Part of the Musick for the above Oratorio being delayed in England by contrary winds'.[111] No legal issues are thought to have been presented by these assorted delays: none at least are trumpeted.

Given the hazards associated with crossing the Irish Sea by boat, even in more modern and substantial craft, the decision of Henry Irving early in the twentieth century, when travel by air was still precluded as a option, to slot in a command performance at Sandringham during a 'run' of *Faust* in Belfast is to be reckoned courageous, though some may have preferred to call it foolhardy. Irving's biographer explains what was involved.[112] Edward VII was host to the Kaiser at the time, and hence the idea of a command performance and the invitation to Irving:

> After the performance of *Faust* on 13 November, the troupe caught the late boat for Liverpool. The next morning they took a train journey which ended at King's Lynn in Norfolk, having passed through Crewe, Rugby and Peterborough. A special train was then laid on for them that took them to Wolferton, the station nearest to Sandringham. The command performance was scheduled for 10 p.m. Immediately it was over, Irving and his troupe entrained at 1 a.m. for the return journey. They appear to have made it back to Belfast by 5 p.m. on the 15th for the next performance of *Faust*.

By the end of the nineteenth century the more celebrated performers in theatre and in opera had, through their own efforts or through those of their agents, brought about changes in the wording of their contracts as performers which rebounded very much to their advantage. Whether management viewed this development in quite the same way may be doubted. The actress Helen Faucit (1817–98) benefited from a clause in her contract at the Haymarket giving her an absolute choice of plays in which to appear.[113] Opera stars were destined to achieve very much more. Adelina Patti (1843–1919), for instance, secured a clause in her contract excusing her from attending rehearsals; a second clause stipulated the size in which her name was to appear on posters.[114] As for Dame Nellie Melba (1861–1931), she was given the final word on the engagement of singers and on the castings in operas in which she would be appearing.[115] Such arrangements had a knock-on effect in another quarter:[116]

110 Stockwell, *Dublin theatres*, p. 372, n. 111.   111 Walsh, *Opera in Dublin, 1705–1797*, p. 77.

112 Jeffrey Richards, *Sir Henry Irving: a Victorian actor and his world* (London, Hambledon Continuum, 2005), p. 75.

113 B.A. Young, 'From play house to opera house' in *A history of the Royal Opera House* (London, Royal Opera House, 1982), p. 53.

114 Harold Rosenthal, 'Opera and music at Covent Garden' in *A history of the Royal Opera House*, p. 99.   115 Ibid., p. 100.

116 *History of opera*, ed. Stanley Sadie (Houndsmills, Basingstoke, Hampshire, Macmillan, 1989), p. 399.

The need to meet a prima donna's demands shaped many librettos and opera scores particularly because her status was reflected in the number and character of the arias allotted to her.

In the reign of Edward VII, a case brought by a young actress in the Irish courts introduces us to a world very far removed for one enjoyed by those at the pinnacle of their careers. The case, claiming wrongful dismissal, and heard by the Irish lord chief justice, Lord O'Brien of Kilfenora, was brought by the young and charming actress, Minnie Cunningham. Ms Cunningham had refused to wear a certain dress, on the ground that it was so short as to be indecent. The management of the Theatre Royal thought otherwise, and when Minnie remained obdurate, they terminated her engagement. Maurice Healy who was to recall the episode – without indicating the outcome – does not quite leave matters up in the air, for he reports the rumour that Lord O'Brien had attributed to him the suggestion that Ms Cunningham should put on the offending garment in his room so that the jury might judge for themselves.[117]

The question of providing financial security for actors and actresses can scarcely be dismissed as irrelevant in the context of this chapter. The expedient itself was to be linked to the establishment of the General Theatrical Fund in 1839 – four years before the major legal change affecting London's theatres – and the associated royal charter of 1853. And also, naturally, with the founding of the Actors' Association in 1891 and the British Actors' Equity Association in 1929, linked as they were to be with Sir Frank Benson.[118]

These initiatives have attracted little legal attention; and the same can be said of the process and progress of unionisation with each separate theatrical company. Conor O'Malley, however, in his cameo of the Lyric Theatre in Belfast, has, however, touched on this latter question, and what he has to say is instructive. For a start, in 1967 the Lyric's management agreed to pay Union rates to its actors.[119] While management thus facilitated its actors joining the British Actors' Equity Association (Equity), this did not entail any prohibition on the part of management to engage non-Equity actors. A view that O'Malley expressed in 1988 concerned two aspects of the new dispensation: the inconvenience that could result from the strict separation of the work of actor and of stage hand and the level of earnings on the Equity scales for young actors (too high).[120]

Somewhat earlier – in 1960 – when the Lyric Theatre was still based in Derryvolgie Avenue – it moved to Ridgeway Street in 1968 – management had adopted a new rule of thumb in regard to its troupe of actors.[121] Members of the permanent company, the Lyric Players, were to make themselves available for at least two productions in the season. The arrangement plainly anticipated that all

117 Maurice Healy, *The old Munster Circuit* (London, Michael Joseph, 1948), p. 269.
118 Richards, *Sir Henry Irving*, pp 68–9.
119 Conor O'Malley, *A poets' theatre* (Dublin, Elo Press, 1988), p. 33.   120 Ibid., pp 33–4.
121 Ibid., p. 30.

its actors would be available to perform elsewhere, possibly even for most of the time. Under the agreement concluded at the same period, it was accepted that 50 per cent of any profit made by individual productions would be divided among members of the cast.[122]

Labour Law problems affecting management as much as performers are by no means things of the past. Confirmation is to hand in a case that went to the Employment Appeals Tribunal in Dublin in the spring of 2013. A stage adaptation of *Dracula* opened at the Tivoli Theatre in late September 2010. It was hoped it would run to the end of November, but the box office takings were so dismal that the run ended in early October. Actors from the production then brought a claim under the Payment of Wages Act 1991.[123] The phrase 'run of the show' that featured in the actors' contracts was interpreted by management to mean just that – so long as the show did actually run.[124] The Rights Commissioner upheld that contention and thus dismissed the claim lodged under the terms of the Payment of Wages Act by eight of the actors and the one stage manager. Seven of the actors and the stage manager appealed unsuccessfully to the Employment Appeals Tribunal, the tribunal dismissing the appeal in the spring of 2013: *Nolan v. Tivoli Theatre*: Case no. PW 460/2011.

The details of what actually transpired are instructive and contain warnings for actors tempted to harbour similar aspirations. The performance of *Dracula* opened on 28 September 2010, but ticket sales were sluggish, and management induced members of the cast and others involved to accept reduced pay – a 25 per cent cut – with the possibility of restoration or even bonuses if certain attendance levels were attained. The moneys thus saved by management, it was planned, would be utilised to boost advertising. This agreement was made on 2 October, but later that day, the actors' union representative, having become involved, remonstrated with the theatre's management that the new bargain was unfair, repugnant and totally unacceptable. The agreement of 2 October was thus repudiated and this repudiation was confirmed two days later. In the circumstances, the Employment Appeals Tribunal was satisfied there was no breach of section 5 of the Payment of Wages Act and dismissed all the appeals.

122 Ibid.   123 No. 25 of 1991.   124 *Irish Times*, 21 Mar. 2013.

CHAPTER THIRTEEN

Disruption and riot

IT IS BY NO MEANS TO DOWNGRADE the significance of the many riots that have taken place in Dublin theatres – or in those of London either – to highlight comparable occurrences that form part of the theatrical heritage of continental Europe. In territories of northern Italy still under Austrian control Verdi's operas not infrequently served as a flashpoint during the years of the Risorgimento that led to Italian unification. Shouts of 'Viva Verdi', seemingly innocuous enough, were by no means so regarded by Austrian administrations and their sympathisers. V.E.R.D.I. was soon transformed into a shout of political support for Vittorio Emmanuale Re Di Italia, the king of Piedmont, whom liberals in Italy hoped to designate king of a united country, which did in fact come to pass in 1861. Nor could the cry be voiced openly in Bourbon-controlled Naples. The identification of Giuseppe Verdi with liberal ideals, as has been pointed out,[1] 'was not just an acrostic. He was sympathetic to the liberal cause' – a pronouncement that is confirmed from even the most cursory examination of his operas and their libretti.

Much further north several years later angry scenes erupted in the Norwegian capital Oslo, then known as Christiania, over the refusal of the management of the official theatre to accept for performance Henrik Ibsen's play *Ghosts*. On 17 October 1883, the Swedish producer August Lindberg put on the first perfor- mance of *Ghosts* in Norway itself at the Moellergaten Theatre in Christiania, availing of the talents of his own touring company. William Archer, in the audience that night, was to leave a record of something of the surrounding circumstances. 'It happened', Archer was later to recall,[2]

> that on the same evening a trivial French farce, *Tête de Linotte* (known in England as *Miss Featherbrain*) was being played at the Christiania Theatre; and the contrast could not but strike people. They saw a masterpiece of Norwegian literature acted by a foreign (Swedish) company at a minor playhouse, while the official theatre of the capital was given over to a piece of Parisian frivolity. The result was that on the following evening, and for some time afterwards, demonstrations were held at the Christiania Theatre against the policy of the management in rejecting Ibsen's play.

1 Arthur Jacobs and Stanley Sadie, *Opera: a modern guide* (Newton Abbot, David & Charles, 1973), p. 131.
2 Quoted in the introduction to Henrik Ibsen, *Ghosts*, transl. and introd. by Michael Meyer (London, Eyre Methuen, 1973), pp 16–17.

As this episode demonstrates, only too graphically, not all the troubles for the stage that chance to be on record are ostensibly political at all. And this is certainly not the explanation for the extraordinary scenes that took place in Paris at the Théâtre de Champs Elysées on the night of 29 May 1913. This was the first night of the performance of Igor Stravinsky's new work *Le Sacre du Printemps, The Rite of Spring*, produced by Sergey Diaghilev and danced by the Ballets russes, with choreography by Vaslav Nijinsky; Pierre Monteux was the conductor. Accounts of what transpired complement each other. Stranvinsky recalled that mild protests could be heard from the very beginning. Then when the curtain opened with a group of knock-kneeded and long-braided Lolitas jumping up and down, the storm had broken. Cries of *la gueule* (shut up) came from behind the composer, who left the theatre in a rage:

> The music was so familiar to me; I loved it, and could not understand why people who had not heard it wanted to protest in advance.

Another source tells us that pandemonium broke out when the audience very plainly was not in agreement as to how it should respond. One faction resorted to catcalls, arguments flared, and fist fights broke out. It was a 'revolt of snobs', Diaghilev's most recent biographer, Sjeng Scheijen, was to maintain:[3]

> In previous years audiences had tolerated Diaghilev's musical and choreographic experiments because doing so meant being treated to exoticism, eroticism and glamour. Now, however, theatre-goers were being served up a work with serious pretensions, which made no attempts to ingratiate itself with the public. Nijinsky's movements were devoid of any eroticism as were Roerich's prehistoric tent dresses, which completely covered the dancers' bodies, showing no skin and obscuring bodily forms. There were no plunging necklines or sheer fabrics to ogle.

Sixteen years later, in July 1929, after *Le Sacre Du Printemps* had finally been generally accepted and performances in London in particular had won over the critics, the dying Diaghilev reflected on the original controversy in a note to his new 16-year-old admirer, Igor Markevich:[4]

> Yesterday *Le Sacre* was a real triumph. The imbeciles finally grasped it. *The Times* says that *Le Sacre* is for the twentieth century what Beethoven's Ninth Symphony was for the nineteenth. At last! In life one must have patience and be somewhat philosophical, so as to look down from on high at the obstacles

3 Sjeng Scheijen, *Diaghilev: a life*, transl. Jane Hearey-Prôle and S.J. Leinbach (London, Profile Books, 2009), p. 270. In a strategy of limited success, Diaghilev on the night in question, to combat the noise in the auditorium, apparently instructed the electrician to keep turning the lights on and off: ibid., p. 272.
4 Diaghilev to Markevich, 23 July 1929, quoted Scheijen, *Diaghilev*, p. 438.

which small and limited people put up against any attempt to overcome mediocrity. My God, it's all so vulgar, like good weather, but it can't be helped – one can't live without the hope of seeing again at dawn the rays of the rising sun.

Diaghilev travelled from London to Venice, and within a month he was dead.

Disturbances in the theatre have had a long history – certainly from long before 1913 – as have judicial attempts to explain the exact legal position. Such disturbances have had different targets – the management, the choice of play, individual actors and actresses, even, as events at Dublin's Abbey Theatre that unfolded at the première of Lady Gregory's *Gaol Gate* on 20 October 1906 were to demonstrate, some controversial celebrity in the audience.[5] The performance at this first night had been delayed until W.B. Yeats himself arrived. He was accompanied by a tall woman dressed in black – Maud Gonne – and the occasion was her first public appearance in Ireland since her separation from John MacBride, a hero of the advanced nationalist cause, almost two years earlier. At once, having recognised who it was who had entered the auditorium, an element in the pit began to hiss and shout 'Up, John MacBride!' Soon a counter-hissing was set up. Many years previously, as we will shortly learn, it was the presence of a viceroy in an Irish theatre that precipitated somewhat more violent scenes.[6]

To return to France, the well-known play by Edmond Rostand, *Cyrano de Bergerac*, first performed in Paris in 1897, incorporates an element of theatrical disruption into an early scene when Cyrano interrupts proceedings to drive the bad actor Montfleury off the stage.[7] Asked to explain his antipathy towards Montfleury, Cyrano claimed – [8]

> C'est un acteur déplorable qui gueule,
> Et qui soulève, avec des han! de porteur d'eau,
> Le vers qu'il faut laisser s'envoler!
>
> (An actor villainous! who mouths,
> And heaves up like a bucket from a well
> The verses that should, bird-like, fly!)

He was, in short, a poor performer. Montfleury in real life, it might be noted, was the stage name of the actor Zacharie Jacob, who died in 1667 and is said to have done so as a result of his histrionics in the part of Oreste in Jean Racine's *Andromaque*.

---

5 See Caoimhe Nic Dháibhéid, "'This is a case in which national considerations must be taken into account": the breakdown of the MacBride-Gonne marriage, 1908–9', *Irish Historical Studies*, 37 (2010), 241.   6 Below, p. 197.

7 Edmond Rostand, *Cyrano de Bergerac*, act 1, scene 4. See, conveniently, the edition by Geoff Woollen (London, Bristol Classical Press, 1994), p. 28.

8 Act 1, scene 4, lines 244–6. English translation: Project Gutenberg's Etext at www.gutenberg.ord/dirs/etext98/cdben 10.txt.

Chetwood, the first of the historians of the Irish stage, published his *General view of the stage* in 1749, a mere two years after major rioting at Smock Alley in Dublin. He had acted as assistant manager there in the 1714 winter season, before returning to London where he functioned as prompter at Drury Lane for some twenty years.[9] It is unlikely that Chetwood would not thus have been *au fait* with the 1747 riot in Dublin, but his discussion of the menace, as he would have viewed it, of disruptive tactics in the theatre, was most probably inspired by personal knowledge of what had occurred in recent years in London. Chetwood dwells in particular on the case of an actor called Peter Bardin.[10] The latter became embroiled in a private quarrel with some individual who resorted to the extraordinary tactic of recruiting a gang of musicians to burst forth with sound from the gallery every time Bardin appeared on stage. There is no excuse whatever, Chetwood opined, 'for doing an injury to a multitude' – the obvious interpretation to place upon such disruptive conduct. An analogy furnished the remedy:

> It is the same right that a man has in a ferry-boat that is (if he behaves himself properly) to be safely and pleasantly landed on the opposite shore; but if he disturbs the passage and endangers the boat, the ferry-man and passengers will certainly join and throw him overboard.

An actual English prosecution resulting from disrupting the performance of an individual actor took place in 1775. The actor targeted on the occasion in question was Charles Macklin, and best known, perhaps, for his interpretation of the part of Shylock in *The Merchant of Venice* (he even performed the role at the age of 89). Shylock, we are told, in the eighteenth century, 'was always played as a clown, but Macklin dressed him as a Venetian Jew, with black gabardine and red hat, and played him with the emotions proper to the part'.[11] It was Macklin's performances at Covent Garden in the autumn of 1773 in the roles both of Shylock and of Macbeth that attracted a faction determined, through constant hissing whenever he appeared on stage, to drive Macklin off it.[12]

The background to what undoubtedly constituted a conspiracy has been ascribed to 'theatrical politics', individuals supportive of the claims to excellence in the roles Macklin also sought to perform, individuals such as William Smith,[13] who had previously acted these parts at Covent Garden, and even David Garrick himself, and their assorted acolytes. 'Over a bowl of turtle soup at the Bedford', we

9 *Oxford DNB*, xi, 360.
10 Chetwood, *General history of the stage*, pp 108–10.
11 B.A. Young, 'From playhouse to opera house' in *A history of the Royal Opera House, Covent Garden, 1732–1982* (London, Royal Opera House, 1982), p. 46.
12 Appleton, *Macklin*, p. 177.
13 Macklin having been engaged for the season, the management to keep Smith sweet had offered a programme in which the two actors could perform certain roles turn and turn about. Smith was not won over: 'to compete with a lumbering Irish septuagenarian was not to his taste' (Appleton, *Macklin*, p. 170).

are told,[14] 'or a tumbler of ale at the Cocoa Tree, the partisans of Garrick and Smith initiated their campaign'. A letter was published in the *Morning Chronicle* – a journal clearly sympathetic to the plotters – in support of any campaign; here Macklin was described as an 'old toothless dotard with the voice of a tired boatswain'.[15] The conspiracy against Macklin hotted up after Macklin himself, before one performance began, charged particular individuals with orchestrating the hissing to which he had been subjected. The performance at Covent Garden scheduled for 18 November signified the final showdown. The conspirators took the precaution of recruiting 'all idle journeymen tailors' to swell the audience for that night's performance. Macklin had only to appear when the hissing started. The theatre became a bear garden, and the management, having considered their options, decided to cave in and summarily discharged Macklin. He, of course, was now out of work. The affair generated a civil action brought by Macklin against Colman the manager. But criminal proceedings alleging both riot and conspiracy were instituted as well, and these came to a hearing first.[16] In May 1774, the King's Bench granted informations against six named individuals. Reviewing the matter the following month, Lord Mansfield, the chief justice, agreed that five of those named should face trial – Clarke, Aldus, Leigh, James and Miles; Sparks was discharged. At a trial held before Mr Justice Aston in February 1775, Clarke was found guilty of riot, all the others of both riot and conspiracy.

When the question of sentence arose, Mansfield purported to assist the process of calculating the fine to be imposed by putting a monetary value on the two years' unemployment Macklin had suffered following his 'discharge' by Colman.[17] This worked out at £400 a year, plus two 'benefits' worth £230 each. At this point, it appears that Macklin interrupted with his own suggestion to the effect that the defendants should undertake to recoup him for the costs he had incurred in launching the prosecutions. In addition, the five should purchase £100 worth of tickets for his daughter's 'benefit'; £100 worth of tickets for his own 'benefit', £100 worth of tickets from the management too. Mansfield, it is recorded, applauded this initiative, which received his blessing, and is immortalised in a note in the law report some seventy years later setting down the outcome in these Macklin-inspired prosecutions.[18] Addressing the actor himself in the court, Mansfield went out of his way to praise Macklin for the attitude he had chosen to adopt. 'I think', the chief justice began,[19]

> you have done yourself great credit and great honor by what you have said; and I think your conduct is wise, too; and I think it will support you, with the public, against any man that will attack you. You will do more good by this in the eyes of the public than if you had received all the money you had a right to receive.

---

14 Ibid., p. 177.   15 Ibid., p. 180.   16 Ibid., pp 189 ff.   17 Ibid., p. 192.
18 Note to *Gregory v. Duke of Brunswick* (1843) 1 Car & K 24, 174 Eng Rep 696, at 698.
19 Quoted, Appleton, *Macklin*, p. 194.

...

You have met with great applause today. You never acted better.

If the business received any kind of publicity at the time, it would not seem to have magically put an end to the practice of hissing. Drury Lane the following February of 1776 was witness to four successive nights of hissing and booing during the first act of Henry Bates' drama, *The Blackamoor*. Woodfall, Garrick's informant, described the theatre as representing another 'beargarden' for the nights in question.[20]

Long regarded as a leading judicial pronouncement on disruption in a theatre was the opinion of Sir James Mansfield, chief justice of the Common Pleas, delivered by him in 1809. This was in a case in which a leading barrister, who appears to have masterminded disruption at Covent Garden, sought damages for assault and false imprisonment when forcibly removed and brought before the magistrate.[21] Clifford and others had launched a campaign of protest over increases in admission charges to the pit and to the boxes and, as it might be expressed today, an increase in the number of boxes that were 'privatised'. The background needs to be explained: Covent Garden had been burnt down in 1808, and these changes were introduced by Charles Kemble to help defray the cost of the capital expenditure involved in the construction of the larger replacement theatre.[22]

Disturbances linked to unwelcome increases in prices of admission were, of course, nothing new. Victor, for instance, tells of such disturbances that broke out at Drury Lane in the middle of the eighteenth century over just such a grievance.[23] There had been riots too at Covent Garden when Fleetwood raised prices there in 1744.[24] And towards the end of the nineteenth century, in 1880, there were to be protests at the Haymarket over abolition of the pit.[25]

The disruption that took place at Covent Garden on 31 October 1809 is described in detail in the law report. Different groups occupying different parts of the theatre would interfere with the proceedings at intermittent intervals by bursting out in song, singing 'God Save the King' and 'Rule Britannia'. Horns were blown, bells rung and rattles sprung. Placards were exhibited exhorting the audience to resist the oppression of management. Men wore hats with certain combinations of capital letters – 'OP' standing for 'Old prices' and 'NPB' for 'No private boxes'. No violence was displayed. There was thus no pulling up of the benches. And a nice touch this, that may appeal to aficionados familiar with *The*

20 W. Woodfall to David Garrick, 13 Feb. 1776: *The private correspondence of David Garrick with the most celebrated persons of his time*, 2 vols (London, Henry Colborn and Richard Bentley, 1831–2), ii, 136.   21 *Clifford v. Brandon* (1809) 2 Camp 258, 170 Eng Rep 1183.
22 Thomas, Carlton & Etienne, *Theatre censorship*, p. 51.
23 Victor, *History of theatres of London and Dublin*, i, 43–6.
24 Sheldon, *Thomas Sheridan of Smock Alley*, p. 52.
25 J.R. Stephens, *The profession of the playwright, British theatre, 1800–1900* (Cambridge, Cambridge UP, 1992), p. 143.

Phantom of the Opera 'no breaking of chandeliers'. Even so, in Chief Justice Mansfield's estimation,[26] the scenes were 'a disgrace to the country, and which tend to bring us back to a state of barbarism'.

Turning to what he understood the law to be, this is what the chief justice declared:[27]

> The audience have certainly a right to express by applauses or hisses the sensations which naturally present themselves at the moment; and nobody has ever hindered or would ever question, the exercise of that right. But if any body of men were to go to the theatre with the settled intention of hissing an actor, or even of damning a piece, there can be no doubt that such a deliberate and pre-concerted scheme would amount to a conspiracy, and that the persons concerned in it might be brought to punishment.

The scenes described, Mansfield added, clearly constituted a riot.

The articulation of these views was designed to advise the jury whose task it became to adjudicate on the allegations of assault and false imprisonment preferred by Clifford. The jury had to decide two principal questions: Had Clifford instigated a riot? And had the riot terminated prior to Clifford's arrest?

The jury, perhaps a little surprisingly, returned a verdict in Clifford's favour, awarding him £5 damages.

Concurrently, the King's Bench had given leave for the filing of a criminal information against Clifford, based on the same set of facts, for conspiracy. But early in 1810, the management at Covent Garden signalled an about-turn. The higher price for admission to the boxes would be retained, but the old price for admission to the pit was restored and the increase in the number of privatised boxes cancelled. At the same time, the pending prosecutions were all dropped.[28]

The forcible removal of three patrons from the English Opera House in London some twenty years later also precipitated suits for assault and false imprisonment, but on this occasion the verdict returned exonerated theatre management. The three in question had bought tickets for the pit at the advertised half-price. They had been advised there was still room there. When it emerged that this was not the case, the three – in an episode that must have threatened an amount of disruption – forced their way into a private box. Here management relented to the extent of telling the three patrons that they could stay there, but would have to pay a supplement of two guineas. This they refused to do, whereupon management arranged for their forcible removal, action which provoked the resultant law suits: see *Lewis v. Arnold*.[29]

The judge in the case, Chief Justice Tindal, expressed the opinion that the proper course of action for the three to have followed once they discovered the pit

26 *Clifford v. Brandon*, 2 Camp at 369.   27 Ibid.
28 2 Camp at 372n. On the OP riots, see Saint et al., *A history of the Royal Opera House, Covent Garden, 1732–1982* (London, Royal Opera House, 1982), pp 20, 50–1.
29 (1830) 4 Ca & P 354, 172 Eng Rep 737.

was full to overflowing, was to leave the theatre and seek the return of their money. The reporters Carrington and Payne, in a curious footnote, defended this counsel of perfection, even if the naive patron might have been disinclined to do so, from the legend commonly to be found at the bottom of the play bills – 'No money to be returned'. These words, they argue, would not have applied. Such a legend, they helpfully explain,[30]

> applies to a practice that prevailed at the theatres some time ago. If a person entered a theatre and could not get so good a place as he liked,[31] he might, before the curtain drew up, have his money returned to him and leave the house. This practice discontinued, on the ground that it gave a great facility to pickpockets to enter the theatre with the crowd, for the purpose of picking pockets, and then to have their money returned and go away.

It is not without interest to note that a matter of concern to the Commons select committee of 1866 was the presence in a typical London auditorium of the period of a large number of 'ladies of the night'.[32]

Dublin was to be no stranger to such scenes as well. The first recorded major incident occurred on 4 November 1712 when, in direct contravention of a government ban, one Dudley Moore, the younger brother of an Irish MP, delivered what was deemed an incendiary harangue before the curtain rose on a Smock Alley production of Nicholas Rowe's drama, *Tamerlane*. The harangue in question was Garth's prologue to the play, the recital of which had been forbidden the previous year as well.[33] The prologue invoked the memory of William III in the interest of renewing war with France and their Jacobite allies. Two stanzas furnish the flavour of Garth's entire approach:[34]

> Today, a mighty Hero comes to warm
> Your curdl'd blood and bids you Britons arm,
> To Valour much he owes, to Virtue more;
> He fights to save and conquers to restore.
> ...
>
> His generous Soul for Freedom was Design'd,
> To pull down Tyrants, and unslave mankind;
> He broke the Chains of Europe; and when we
> Were doom'd for Slaves, he came and set us free.

---

30 Ibid.
31 This was before the practice had been established of selling tickets for specific number seats – row J11 and 12, for example.
32 *Report from the select committee on theatrical licences and regulations; together with the proceedings of the committee, minutes of evidence and appendix*, HC 1866, xvi, 1: passim.
33 Helen M. Burke, *Riotous performances: the struggle for hegemony in the Irish theatre, 1712–1784* (Notre Dame, IN, Univ. of Notre Dame Press, 2003), p. 45.
34 Ibid., p. 46; W.S. Clark, *The early Irish stage* (Oxford, Clarendon Press, 1955), p. 130.

Chaos, we are told, ensued:[35]

> Ladies wearing orange ribbons cheered, and ladies wearing red roses hissed;
> seats were torn up. And the performance was postponed amidst servants
> brawling in the upper gallery, brandished swords in the pit and an indecorous
> exodus of silk and taffeta from the boxes.

Moore, predictably, was proceeded against, but when the Dublin grand jury,
dominated by Whigs and presumed, therefore, to be sympathetic to Moore and to
what he had done, mistakenly returned a true bill, rather than *ignoramus* on the
indictment, legal confusion ensued. An *ex officio* information was then obtained,
the jury in consequence empanelled to try the issue was then struck according to
English rather than Irish practice.[36] In the end, come the ensuing February, the
charge against Moore was simply abandoned. Needless to say, as Morash points
out, there had occurred 'the obligatory post-riot fusillade of pamphlets and
satirical poems'.

Just a few years later, there was to be another minor upset. In May 1715, an
Alexander Hall, hissed the prologue of the same play, *Tamerlane*. A Major Dunbar
and others, 'resenting it', we are told,[37] then drew their swords, made Mr Hall
prisoner, 'and committed him to the Guard all night'.

In 1746, the year before major riots were to interfere with performances at
Smock Alley, Thomas Sheridan – a year into his management of the theatre – was
sufficiently perturbed by outbreaks of disorder particularly among the patrons of
the theatre's gallery to introduce remedial measures.[38] What had occurred was that
a rowdy clientele ensconced in the gallery would hurl apples and even stones at the
band. This, in Sheridan's estimation, could no longer be tolerated, so he
announced as follows in notices posted up, that

> Proper Men will be placed to mark the Offenders, who will certainly be
> prosecuted the next Day to the utmost Rigour of the Law; and a Reward of
> three Guineas will be paid by the Manager, upon the Conviction of any
> Offender.

In the early months of 1747 riotous scenes at Smock Alley, however, became so
regular a feature that at last the lords justices ordered the Master of the Revels to
close the theatre – a decision hailed by Victor as 'a wise and prudent step', the
theatre having been made 'the Seat of War'.[39] Trouble had flared up when a young
man from Connacht, Edmund Kelly, much the worse for drink, during the staging

---

35 Morash, *History of Irish theatre*, p. 30.
36 Stockwell, *Dublin theatres*, pp 48–9; Burke, *Riotous performances*, p. 48.
37 Stockwell, *Dublin theatres*, p. 55.
38 Sheldon, *Thomas Sheridan of Smock Alley*, p. 80; Walsh, *Opera in Dublin, 1705–1797*, p. 73; Burke,
    Riotous performances, p. 163.
39 Victor, *History of theatres of London and Dublin*, i, 123.

of Vanburgh's *Aesop*, forced his way on stage and then continued to the greenroom. Sheridan, as we have seen, ran Smock Alley at the time, but it is his assistant manager, Benjamin Victor, to whom we are principally indebted for knowledge of what then transpired.[40] In the greenroom Kelly 'addressed one of the actresses in such indecent terms aloud, as made them all fly to their dressing-rooms'.[41] This was a Mrs Dyer. Kelly also pursued a Miss Bellamy thither, 'but being repulsed by the door, he made such a noise there as disturbed the business of the scenes'. Miss Bellamy was then needed on stage, but could not or would not come out, 'for fear of this dragon'. A Miss Banford, one of the dressers, was also to be attacked.[42] Sheridan, at this juncture, ordered Kelly's forcible removal from back stage which then occurred. By way of riposte, Kelly then armed himself with a basket of oranges commandeered from one of the orange-women at the theatre and employed the oranges as missiles to target Sheridan when the latter emerged on stage. Subsequently, there took place a fight between Kelly and Sheridan in the latter's dressing-room. Things then settled down, but the peace was deceptive, for in Kelly's eyes, that a player should beat a gentleman, and that a player should consider himself a gentleman, was totally unacceptable.

The status of actors *vis-à-vis* members of the audience was indeed a central issue. Contemporaneously in England the identical issue had come to the fore, and could be dealt with in different ways. After an actor by the name of Powell struck a gentleman in a coffee house, the Vice Chamberlain imposed a ban on performances of the theatre company to which Powell belonged. That ban lasted three days.[43] Around the same time, however, when an actor by the name of Smith was assaulted by a patron, the King, James II, forbade the patron presence at court.[44] Like Kelly in Dublin half a century and more later, this patron could not forgive the perceived insult, formed a protest group, and the next time Smith appeared on stage greeted him with a chorus of cat-calls which forced the dropping of the curtain.[45] Smith sadly was then obliged to quit the stage, but, as Cibber remarked, the original royal intervention in favour of an actor and against a 'gentlemen' was regarded at the time as unprecedented.

The altercations between Sheridan and Kelly occurred on Monday, 19 January 1746/7. The next night, the Tuesday, things remained quiet – again a deceptive peace. On the Wednesday, the 21st, Smock Alley put on a performance of *The Fair Penitent* for the benefit of the insolvent debtors in the Marshalsea Prison. In the

---

40 The episode has been regularly revisited. See, e.g., Gilbert, *History of Dublin*, ii, 81; Stockwell, *Dublin theatres*, pp 93–100; Victor Power, 'The Kelly theatre riot', *Eire-Ireland*, 7 (1972) no. 1, 53; Morash, *History of Irish theatre*, pp 47–9; Michael Brown, 'The location of learning in mid-18th century Ireland' in Muriel McCarthy and Ann Simmons (eds), *Marsh's Library: a mirror on the world: law, learning and libraries, 1650–1750* (Dublin, Four Courts Press, 2009), p. 104; Burke, *Riotous performances*, ch. 4.

41 Gilbert, *History of Dublin*, ii, 81.

42 Fintan O'Toole, *A traitor's kiss: the life of Richard Brinsley Sheridan* (London, Granta Books, 1998), p. 65.

43 Cibber, *An apology*, p. 204.   44 Ibid., p. 49.   45 Ibid.

course of the evening, a group of Kelly's supporters – some fifty of them – ensconced in the pit, rose up, disrupted proceedings, and, in fact, orchestrated a riot. The upshot was that Sheridan then shut Smock Alley for two-and-a-half weeks to effect repairs.[46] Meanwhile, seven men including Kelly had been indicted for riot (but Sheridan, as we are about to discover, was not to be immune from legal proceedings himself).

Things were still tense, an 'apology' from Sheridan still on the list of demands from the protesters when Smock Alley opened again for a performance of Shakespeare's *Richard III* on 9 February. More disruption occurred, but a majority of the auditorium having voted for the play to continue, the Kelly faction admitted defeat and retired, but vowed revenge. Two days later, on Wednesday 11 February, during a benefit performance on behalf of the Hospital for Incurables, a full-scale riot was unleashed when thirty armed men rose from the pit, ordered Sheridan off the stage and demanded an apology. Trinity College students became involved, and rioting moved outside to the public street. Shopkeepers shut up their shops, and students were confined to their quarters.[47] The lords justices sensed they had no option other than to close both of Dublin's theatres – Smock Alley, naturally, but also the so-called City Theatre in Capel Street.[48]

At the Dublin city and county commission on 19 February Sheridan, who had been indicted on the initiative of Kelly, was acquitted. Though it had originally been planned to try seven of Kelly's gang, the decision was taken to charge only three, and to charge these with the lesser offence of assault.[49] Kelly and one associate, by the name of Brown, were found guilty. Kelly was fined £500, given one month in gaol, and was bound over for seven years, and Brown was fined £100 and bound over for twelve months. It was to be claimed that after the first week Kelly had spent in gaol, Sheridan arranged to have his fine cancelled and undertook to be his bailsman.[50]

Kelly's trial before Lord Chief Justice Marlay and Mr Justice Ward evoked from Marlay the pronouncement that any person who forced his way behind the scenes should feel the utmost severity of the law.[51] Hitchcock, in his coverage of the affair, sensed that the attitude adopted by the two judges probably owed something to the strong statement attributed to Lord Chief Justice Lee in London after the 1743 riot at the Drury Lane theatre, to the effect that a critical hissing was a manifest breach of the peace as it was the beginning of a riot.[52] Applauding the outcome, Hitchcock concluded,[53]

> Thus was the long usurped tyranny of a set of wanton dissolute gentlemen (the greatest nuisance that any city ever groaned under) effectually subdued, and the liberties of the people recovered <u>by a spirited public, aided</u> by a worthy lord chief justice and an honest jury.

46 Sheldon, *Thomas Sheridan of Smock Alley*, p. 89.   47 Ibid., pp 92–3.
48 Gilbert, *History of Dublin*, ii, 85; Hitchcock, *Historical view of Irish stage*, i, 171.
49 Sheldon, *Thomas Sheridan of Smock Alley*, p. 94.   50 Ibid.
51 Hitchcock *Historical view of Irish stage*, i, 190.   52 Ibid., i, 171.   53 Ibid., i, 191.

Victor, in his account of the aftermath of the Kelly-inspired disruptions, prints this paragraph too, but with the omission of the phrase that has been underlined.[54] Hitchcock, whose account post-dates that of Victor by some twenty odd years, obviously decided to insert this evocative phrase in Victor's stridently expressed paragraph.

The closure insisted upon by the lords justices lasted three weeks. Smock Alley itself reopened on 3 March. Three petitions inviting the lords justices to countermand their closure order were forwarded to the lords justices, and were to be transcribed by Lawrence.[55] One was from Sheridan; the second from 51 of the employees at Smock Alley. The third was from the City Theatre on Capel Street. They certainly were entitled to gripe. And gripe they did, complaining that 'after performing peaceably since 1 November, they have been shut up through no fault of their own, but through disturbance at a rival theatre'.

For Benjamin Victor, the Kelly-inspired riots and disruption, Sheridan's handling of them and the judicial outcome appear to have constituted a high point in his years associated with Smock Alley. The entire business was to find him in philosophic mood as he penned his reminiscences. 'In a great and populous City', he wrote,[56]

> the gay and wanton young men are, indeed, the constant visitors to a theatre, and they are also the constant pests; they had rather see an irregular performance, it best suits their genius; they can hiss, and laugh, and talk loud, and become, by that means, actors themselves. This was the unhappy situation of the theatre in Dublin for many years; the audience part was a bear-garden, and the other a brothel. The grave and decent of both sexes absented themselves, of course, from a place of such irregularity.

'But when decency was restored and established', Victor continued, 'regular and good entertainments followed; then the sensible and virtuous again frequented the theatre'.

Praise needed to be handed out where it was due. 'Be it here with truth recorded', he continued,

> that this reformation and improvement was entirely owing to Mr Sheridan, whose spirit and good character carried him through, and supported him in this arduous undertaking.

Chetwood, writing a little earlier, penned his own encomium. 'To Sheridan', he wrote,[57]

54 Victor, *History of theatres of London and Dublin*, i, 129–30.
55 *Irish Times*, 2 Sept. 1922, summarised in Sheldon, *Thomas Sheridan of Smock Alley*, p. 104.
56 Victor, *History of theatres of London and Dublin*, ii, 87–9.
57 Chetwood, *General history of the stage*, p. 220.

we owe the decency that has been long wanting on the Hibernian stage; a difficulty no one person could have surmounted but himself: and tho' merit does not always meet its proper reward, yet the seeds of flowers and roots he had planted and sown in this theatrical garden, flourish sweet and amiable.

If it is to Victor that we are originally endebted for details of the confrontation between Kelly and Sheridan,[58] it is not to be forgotten that Sheridan himself discussed the episode in a pamphlet brought out later in 1747 when tempers had cooled, and the two men had apparently become reconciled. Peace may have broken out, but Sheridan was to stand his ground when stating at some length the proper procedure to be followed by a manager when faced with disruption by a sizeable element in the auditorium. In *A full vindication of the conduct of the manager of the Theatre Royal*,[59] Sheridan contended that a manager should take the audience into his confidence, and consult them as to whether they would wish the performance to continue and to continue in the absence of disruption of any kind. It was his equal conviction that the majority view when then expressed was necessarily to prevail and be fully respected. If, Sheridan wrote,[60] the doctrine

> that any dispute which should arise ought to be determin'd by a Majority of the Audience, be not establish'd, it follows, that if any two or three Persons shall take it into their Heads, either thro' Spleen to any particular Actor, or thro' mere Wantonness, it will be in their Power to disturb the entertainment of six or seven hundred.

'And would not that be extreamly unreasonable?' he demanded to know.

The risk of proceeding in any different fashion was then highlighted. 'Once a Point is determin'd by a Majority', Sheridan went on,[61]

> they who attempt to controvert it afterwards are sowing the Seeds of perpetual Discord. For they may depend upon it, that Majority will always think themselves bound in Honour to support their determination. And this has been the very Cause of all the Tumults, Disorders and Heart-burnings which for some Time past have reigned in this city.

Sheridan had previously referred to an incident that had occurred to his certain knowledge a few years before that served to illustrate the point.[62] An attempt had then been made to drive out an actor because of distaste for his private behaviour. A majority of the audience, when consulted, refused to align themselves with this attempt, being guided by the principle that the excellence of the actor's performance on stage was the audience's sole proper concern. (This sort of problem, we shall see from later litigation in England, was not, of course, unknown

58 Victor, *History of theatres of London and Dublin*, i, 93–123.   59 Dublin, G. Faulkner, 1747.
60 *A full vindication*, p. 14.   61 Ibid., p. 16.   62 Ibid., p. 13.

there either.) This view of the majority appears to have been accepted, and the performance was permitted to continue on the night in question. A few nights later, a member of the dissenting minority stood up, and repeated the objections against the actor in question. What happened next is then described by Sheridan. Another member of the audience, one John Trot, then got up and hit the protester. And so

> the gentleman had the comfort, besides having his Head broke, to be hiss'd and hooted out of the theatre by both Parties.[63]

Thomas Sheridan, despite the stance he had adopted over the Kelly-inspired rioting, was to continue to encounter difficulties in implementing his mission to reform practices in the Dublin theatres. At the representation of Voltaire's *Mahomet*, put on at Smock Alley on 2 February 1754, the pit, Gilbert tells us,[64]

> was filled with the leaders of the country party, who, with much violence, insisted that the actor [West] Digges, who performed Alcanor, should repeat the following lines of his speech in the first act, which they considered applicable to the venality of their opponents:

> If, ye Powers Divine!
> Ye mark'd the Movements of this nether World,
> And bring them to account, Crush, crush those Vipers
> Who, singled out by a Community
> To guard their Rights, shall, for a Grasp of Ore,
> Or paltry Office, sell 'em to the Foe!

The play was due to be repeated on 2 March, but the night before Sheridan told his assembled actors in the greenroom 'that it was derogatory to the dignity of the stage for any performer to Pander to the humours of an audience by repeating what they regarded as a party speech'. He declined, however, to give Digges explicit instructions.[65]

The following night news of Sheridan's stance leaked out when West Digges was again urged to repeat the salient lines from the first act, but declined. The rabble in the audience demanded to hear from Sheridan himself, and when it became clear that Sheridan would not oblige, and had in fact retired for the night, hell was to break loose. This was after the curtain had been brought down and the prompter had come forward to announce that if the audience were quiet, the play

63 Ibid., p. 14.
64 Gilbert, *History of Dublin*, ii, 88. See, too, Victor, *History of theatres of London and Dublin*, i, 160–79; Stockwell, *Dublin theatres*, pp 111–44; O'Toole, *A traitor's kiss*, pp 17–21; Morash, *History of Irish theatre*, pp 48 and 58–66.
65 Gilbert, *History of Dublin*, ii, 88.

would continue; otherwise, they could seek to have their money back. At a given signal, however, the discontented element in the audience sought to ransack the theatre in a riot which lasted from 8p.m. to 2a.m.[66] Benches were torn down, the wainscoting destroyed, the curtain set on fire and then cut to shreds. After the rioters had withdrawn, a mob entered, seeking to plunder whatever they could carry away. Officers whose task it was to restore law and order were nowhere to be found, having been advised, so it was rumoured, to ensure they would not be available.[67] Curiously, this second riot does not feature in Hitchcock's coverage of the period. One immediate outcome needs to be recorded – it precipitated Sheridan's decision to retire from the management of the Dublin stage, to which, however, he was to return in two years' time in 1756.[68] It was at this juncture, too, according to James Boswell, that Sheridan was to be awarded his £200 annual pension – an act of governmental munificence that startled Samuel Johnson when a pension of £300 in 1762 was granted to him. An author, Johnson protested to Boswell, was worth more than a mere actor. Whether a mortified Johnson was in any way mollified when Boswell sought to explain that Sheridan's pension

> was granted to him not as a player, but as a sufferer in the cause of government, when he was a manager of the Theatre Royal in Ireland, when parties ran high in 1753 [*sic*][69]

is not immediately clear.

Sheridan, in his efforts to reform Dublin theatre customs, had an ally in Charles Lucas. That both men followed an agenda that was fundamentally unsound is the thesis propounded by Helen Burke in her impressive reinterpretation of the events described above, set out at length in her *Riotous performances*.[70] Aspects of the struggle for hegemony in the Irish theatre of the period – where different shades of 'nationalism' did battle with each other – are dealt with at different stages in the argument in *Riotous performances*, the focus being tightest in the chapter with the evocative title 'Attacking the Lucasian Stage: Edmund Burke, Paul Hiffernan and the Paper War of 1748' (chapter 5).

A proportion of rioting in theatres seems to have had causes quite separate from any dissatisfaction with management, the choice of play or the standard of the performers. A riot recorded for Smock Alley in April 1778 falls into this category. A row flared up between gentlemen's servants and certain soldiers. The latter were armed, shots were fired and one James Martin was killed. Of three others who were wounded, one also died.[71]

66   Ibid., ii, 89.
67   Ibid., ii, 91.
68   The entire episode is dealt with in most detail in Sheldon, *Sheridan of Smock Alley*, pp 199–209.
69   James Boswell, *The life of Samuel Johnson*, abridged ed. (London, Hutchinson & Co., 1906), pp 90–1.
70   *Riotous performances*, ch. 5 (pp 147–82).   71   Walsh, *Opera in Dublin, 1705–1797*, p. 198.

Objections to the identity of fellow patrons as the cause of disturbances are recorded around this time, if a little earlier, in England. At Covent Garden in 1762, elements in the audience objected to the presence of two Highland officers at a play. 'No Scots! No Scots!', they proclaimed, demanding their forcible eviction. Apples were later thrown at them. James Boswell was at Covent Garden that night. He was suitably enraged, and jumped up, berating the protesters with the cry 'Damn you Rascals'. We have Boswell's reflections on the episode. 'I hated the English', he began:[72]

> I wished from my soul that the Union was broke, and that we might give them another battle of Bannockburn.

Disturbances in the Upper Gallery at Dublin's Smock Alley in 1789[73] represented a return to form. Richard Daly as manager had offended an element in the auditorium for discharging most of the orchestra on the occasion of his production of Arnold's opera *Inkle and Yarico*; Daly brought in a band from London instead. Daly managed finally to restore order and, as it was put, the audience were suffered to enjoy their evening's entertainment without further molestation, or having their ears wounded by indelicacies more savage than the war-hoops [*sic*] of the Indians which the piece presented.

Richard Daly's management of the Crow Street theatre, to which he transferred a year or so later, in 1790, was not without incident either. The unpopularity that descended on him as a result of his lawsuits against John Magee – and the extraordinary judicial action against Magee that followed (the abusive employment of so-called judicial *fiats*) – had a predictable enough outcome. Magee's supporters, of whom there were legion – for he edited the patriotic newspaper, the *Evening Post* – would regularly stage disturbances, even riots, in Crow Street.[74]

Daly, in conjunction with an ally, Francis Higgins, resorted to counter-measures which, in Higgins' opinion, were not unsuccessful.[75] To combat disturbances in the upper gallery, compliant magistrates were attached to the theatre, who were on hand to commit all rioters, utterers of seditious expressions and violators of the public peace. In addition, 50 security men had been dispersed throughout the theatre. As a consequence, Higgins was later to confide to his contacts in Dublin Castle, 'in a very few nights all reasonable language and outrage was suppressed'. Assuming all this to have been the case, it would appear that lessons had been

---

72 Quoted, Janet A. Smith, 'Some eighteenth century ideas of Scotland' in N.T. Phillipson and Rosalind Mitchison (eds), *Scotland in the age of improvement* (Edinburgh, Edinburgh UP, 1970), p. 109.

73 Walsh, *Opera in Dublin, 1705–1797*, p. 274.   74 Morash, *History of Irish theatre*, p. 75.

75 Higgins' letter to his Dublin Castle contacts, 17 Dec. 1797, quoted in Thomas Bartlett, *Revolutionary Dublin, 1795–1801; the letters of Francis Higgins to Dublin Castle* (Dublin, Four Courts Press, 2004), at p. 204, and interpreted by Bartlett to refer to an earlier period which would have been 1789–90, the period of disruption occasioned by the Daly-Magee quarrel.

learnt from previous episodes of disruption, when assistance from the magistracy
or the embryo police force was simply not there to be had.[76]

Much earlier on in Daly's management at Crow Street, in 1791, he had faced
tumult when a performance of Arne's opera *Artaxerxes* was cancelled on account
of the illness of his leading tenor, Charles Incledon. Daly announced a change to
Charles Dibdin's opera, *Lionel and Clauson*, and a thousand handbills advertising
the change were printed. However, on 3 August, the scheduled performance of the
substitute opera was 'through the clamour of a few individuals, and contrary to the
general sense of the audience, not suffered to proceed'.[77] In the issue of 4/6 August
1791 the *Freeman's Journal* criticised the turn of events:

> The late disturbances at the Theatre ... reflect great discredit on the
> metropolis. Better to have no places of public amusements than to have them
> thus disgraced by indecency and tumult. We cannot help thinking that the
> more respectable part of the audience are much to blame for their passiveness
> on these occasions. If they were more forward to interpose their authority,
> the galleries, but particularly the second one, could not presume to disturb
> the Theatre as they have lately done, with their noise and impertinence ...
> Welcome, therefore, must be the intelligence to every friend to public
> decorum and amusement, that the most determined and legal steps will be
> taken against the instigators of so scandalous a riot.

Morash, in his account of the Irish stage in the eighteenth century, sought a
context in which to explain some of the disruption that had been associated with
particular performances. 'Many people', he was to conclude,[78]

> still thought of the Irish stage as a sort of alternative parliament, both an
> embodiment of Irish rights and the place in which rights denied could be
> debated – or, if necessary, demanded.

It is a fair enough interpretation. Arguably, the ensuing century only brought
modest relief.

The *casus belli* in the case of rioting at the Crow Street theatre in the spring of
1819 was linked to a dispute between F.J. Jones (in his last months of holding the
patent for the theatre) and one of his artistes, the singer Mary Byrne.[79] Byrne had
been peremptorily dismissed from the theatre company, for being in breach of
contract – something Ms Byrne denied. The auditorium plainly sided with Ms
Byrne. Following the news that she would not be appearing, an alternative

---

76 Higgins' letter refers to these precautionary measures being taken both at Crow Street and at
    Smock Alley.
77 Walsh, *Opera in Dublin, 1705–1797*, p. 286.
78 Morash, *History of Irish theatre*, p. 57.
79 T.J. Walsh, *Opera in Dublin, 1798–1820: Frederick Jones and the Crow Street theatre* (Oxford,
    Oxford UP, 1993), pp 208–11. See, too, above, p. 171.

performance of *The West Indian* was announced, but straightaway 'strong marks of dissatisfaction were apparent' when the curtain went up. There were to be frequent cries of 'Miss Byrne and an Opera'. An explanation not having satisfied that element in the auditorium, seats in the galleries were torn up and flung into the pit. Velvet-covered hand-rails of several of the upper boxes and lattices were also torn off and hurled in the same direction. The Dublin sheriff, Sheriff Wood, made an appearance and, having failed to produce calm, saw instead to a reasonably orderly evacuation of the theatre. There was to be uproar for a further four nights, and peace was only restored when an accommodation was reached between Ms Byrne and the management, and she was permitted to rejoin the Crow Street company.

In the middle of the eighteenth century a not-dissimilar species of riot had engulfed the Drury Lane theatre in London, when an artiste advertised to appear did not do so on account of illness, of which, however, the management had elected to give no notice.[80] The occasion was the production of a new pantomime, which ended with a grand dance, generally, aficionados claimed, the best part of the entire show. The dancer all wanted to see was a Madam Chateauneuf, reckoned the best French dancer in London at the time. She fell ill, the dance was cancelled, and yet, as Victor puts it, 'the Manager published her name [as appearing] three Nights running, without the least Apology'. On the third night, when again Madam Chateauneuf did not appear, a peer of the realm no less, in Victor's account of what occurred, sought the sanction of the audience to set fire to the building. 'That being carried in the Negative', the audience had other ideas:

> They began with the Orchestra, broke the Harpsichord and Base Viols, broke all the Looking-Glasses, pulled up the Benches in the Pit, broke down the Boxes, even the King's-Arms in the Front (a Sort of petty Treason) fell a Victim to their Rage!

Another peer of the realm, an earl (who was said to have been in 'a state of drunkenness for six years'), fomented a riot at Lincoln's Inns Fields in 1721, when he and his entourage, armed with swords, hacked at the sconces and the hangings (which were gilt leather finely painted) in the boxes in the theatre.[81]

On 14 December 1822, in the interval between performances of a dual bill at the Theatre Royal in Hawkins Street – *She Stoops to Conquer* by Oliver Goldsmith and *Tom Thumb* – disruption, engineered by an Orange faction and aimed at the new lord lieutenant, Marquis Wellesley, made theatrical history.[82] This was the so-called 'Bottle Riot'. A bottle was indeed thrown, but it was thrown from the gallery and landed finally on the stage before rolling into the orchestra. Splinters from a watchman's rattle, in a separate incident, were hurled down from the gallery and

80   Victor, *History of theatres of London and Dublin*, i, 42–3.
81   Victor, *History of theatres of London and Dublin*, ii, 148–50.
82   This account follows Morash's reconstruction of events: *History of Irish theatre*, pp 94–102.

one of these, stated to be eight inches long, hit the cushion of the box beside Wellesley. Once order was eventually restored, a number of arrests were made, including that of one of the principal protagonists, James Forbes. By Christmas Day no less than twelve rioters had been arrested and these, to the amazement of a number of individuals, were first charged with conspiracy to murder the lord lieutenant. That was the decision of the attorney-general of the day, William Conyngham Plunket, who took a serious view of what had transpired, not least perhaps because he had been seated beside Wellesley when the riot broke out.

Doubtless despite Plunket's best efforts, the grand jury refused to return a true bill against the assorted rioters, and Plunket, to save face, then resorted to the unusual, controversial, but still valid stratagem of proceeding against all the accused by means of an *ex officio* information. From Ireland's theatre history there happened to be one precedent for this: exactly the same tactic, as we have seen, had been employed in the case of Dudley Moore, arrested after the scenes at Smock Alley in November 1712. But it availed Plunket not at all, for the petty jury, now instructed to deal with the reduced charges of conspiracy to riot and to insult and assault the lord lieutenant, after 24 hours deliberation, could not agree, except to acquit one of the charged rioters, one William Brownlow. In the circumstances, the court of King's Bench, which had conducted this trial at bar, ordered the discharge of all the remaining accused, including Forbes.

The affair had an important sequel – the appointment of an inquiry focusing on supposed Orange influence in the Irish legal system. But the case was noteworthy for another reason – the opportunity it afforded the then chief justice of King's Bench, Charles Kendal Bushe, in his summing-up for the benefit of the jury, to detail the rights of an audience in a theatre. The views Bushe expressed were plainly influenced by precedent laid down in England. Nor were these destined to be forgotten, being made use of again in Ireland in 1907. The audience, Bushe declared, in his observations of 7 February 1823,[83]

> may cry down a play or other performance, which they dislike, or they may hiss or hoot the actors who depend upon their approbation, or their caprice. Even that privilege, however, is confined within its limits. They must not break the peace, or act in such a manner as has a tendency to excite terror or disturbance. Their censure or approbation, although it may be noisy, must not be riotous. That censure or approbation must be the expression of the feelings of the moment; for if it be premeditated by a number of persons confederated beforehand to cry down even a performance of an actor, it becomes criminal. Such are the limits of the privileges of an audience, even as to actors and author.

In *Great Expectations*, published in 1861, Charles Dickens furnishes us with instances of conduct on the part of the auditorium at a London production of

---

83   *Rex v. Forbes* (1823) 1 Crawford & Dix 157 at 158.

Hamlet which constituted a form of disruption assuredly, but which nevertheless might well have escaped judicial sanction, tested by the legal precedents, *Rex v. Forbes* included.[84] Pip had learned that Mr Wopsle, the clerk at church in Pip's ancestral village, had forsaken his employment for a career on the stage – a totally unexpected turn of events that decided Pip, in the company of Herbert Pocket, to patronise the theatre where the new Roscius handled the eponymous role of Hamlet himself. The production of the play, to judge from Dickens' account of it, was nothing short of disastrous. Wopsle's portrayal of Hamlet did little to save the play, and the audience was merciless. 'Whenever that undecided Prince', we read,[85]

> had to ask a question or state a doubt, the public helped him out with it. As, for example; on the question whether 'twas nobler in the mind to suffer, some roared yes, and some no, and some inclining to both questions said 'toss up for it'; and quite a Debating Society arose. When he asked what should such fellows as he do crawling between earth and heaven, he was encouraged with loud cries of 'Hear, hear!'

And so it went on. Pip averred that Herbert and himself 'made some pale efforts in the beginning to applaud Mr Wopsle; but they were too hopeless to be persisted in'. Dickens himself goes to considerable lengths to supply us with intelligence of the depressingly steady downward trajectory of Wopsle's subsequent theatrical career.[86]

There was to be one English case after Ireland's 'Bottle Riot' case that merits a mention. This is *Gregory v. Duke of Brunswick and Vallance*, litigated in 1843.[87] At a performance of *Hamlet* given at the Covent Garden theatre on 13 February 1843, Gregory, who played the title role, was repeatedly hissed. The suit alleging conspiracy against the duke and others followed. The evidence presented showed that the auditorium had been deliberately packed with 200 supporters, who hooted, hissed, groaned or yelled every time Gregory (Hamlet) appeared. It emerged that the plan had been conceived by way of retaliating against Gregory personally for views he had expressed on Queen Victoria in a sheet known as 'Satirist'. Chief Justice Tindal of the Common Pleas, who in 1830 had heard the case of *Lewis v. Arnold*,[88] in directing the jury, advised them that the public enjoyed the right to express their views of an actor, but that they enjoyed no right by a pre-concerted plan to drive an actor from the stage. The jury were plainly not sympathetic towards Gregory, for their verdict went in favour of the defendants. Gregory was granted a new trial on the grounds that the verdict was against the weight of the evidence, but the final outcome represented no change.

Political objections lay at the back of protests directed in recent times from the stalls at a ballet-dancer performing with the English National Ballet at the London

---

84 *Great expectations*, ch. 31.   85 Ibid.   86 *Great expectations*, ch. 47.
87 1 Car & K 24, 174 Eng Rep 696.   88 4 Car & P 354, 172 Eng Rep 737. Above, p. 186.

Coliseum.[89] This was the dancer Simone Clarke who had disclosed that since 2005 she had been a member of the British National Party. Ms Clarke was to leave the ballet company in January 2008 'for personal reasons'. Many years before this – back in 1793 – a different legal angle linked to the prospect of a performer being hissed at or booed was explored by the English King's Bench. This was in the case of *Ashley v. Harrison*.[90] The plaintiff had engaged a Madame Gertrude Mara to sing in oratorios. Madame Mara had incurred the wrath of members of the oratorio-attending public for her 'insolence, contempt of the audience, and want of respect to His Majesty'. These objections had been publicized in the media, the upshot being that Madame Mara, from fear of being hissed at and otherwise ill-treated, declined to perform. Ashley sued for the loss of his profits, but in the King's Bench, the chief justice, Lord Kenyon, held that the action was not maintainable.

Fast forward 109 years and change the country. At Dublin's Theatre Royal, now re-established a decade or more in Hawkins Street, on 14 April 1902, disturbances occurred during a performance of *The Dandy Fifth*, a musical play by the prolific popular playwright, George Sims. The play focused on a British Army regiment – not an institution over-favoured in the imaginations of those with Irish nationalist predilections – and on the night in question, a group of young men in the audience interrupted the artistes by singing 'Who fears to speak of '98', stamping with their feet, and yelling and screaming. The men in question were forcibly removed by the police, and the next day before Thomas Wall, the chief Dublin metropolitan magistrate, one James Bradley and several others were convicted of disorderly conduct, and each fined 40s. or a month in gaol in default.[91]

Five years later, in January 1907, the disruption caused by audiences who came to see J.M. Synge's *The Playboy of the Western World* at the new Abbey Theatre became instantly celebrated, and the episode itself has been regularly revisited.[92] Morash, in his analysis of these events, contended that the play

> had offended against an imaginative geography, which idealised the western seaboard (the part of the country most remote from English influence) … and of equally sentimentalised notion of Irish femininity.[93]

C.P. Curran, for his part, stressed the discomfiture within the audience at the arrival on stage of a parricide, at Pegeen's earlier expressions of belief and at the heightened language.[94] But he placed particular emphasis on the shock occasioned by the hitching of the rope around Christy's neck as the prelude to roasting him on the fire, and the sight of Pegeen blowing the turf, by way of preparing to light

89 *Daily Telegraph*, 20 Nov. 2008.   90 (1793) 1 Esp 48, 170 Eng Rep 276.
91 *Irish Times*, 16 Apr. 1902.
92 Most recently, and exhaustively, by Morash: *History of Irish theatre*, pp 130–8. And see, too, Dean, *Riot and great anger*, pp 77–85.
93 Morash, *History of Irish theatre*, pp 136–7.
94 C.P. Curran, *Under the receding wave* (Dublin, Gill and Macmillan, 1970), p. 107.

the sod to scorch Christy's shins. The whole scene, he protested,[95] was 'more revolting than even Shakespeare's gouging out of Gloucester's eyes in *King Lear*'.

Morash's more philosophical explanation and Curran's down-to-earth *post mortem* both deserve to be set beside the conclusion offered by Thomas Le Fanu, chief clerk in the Irish Office, in the evidence he tendered to the 1909 parliamentary committee on stage censorship. 'It was thought by some', Le Fanu averred,[96] 'to be a caricature of the Irish people which a part of the audience resented'. Conor O'Malley's stance was to be markedly different. 'The hostile reception', he wrote,[97] 'afforded to the first performance of Synge's masterpiece *The Playboy of the Western World*, showed just how low was the general level of artistic appreciation'.

As in the case of *The Dandy Fifth*, criminal prosecutions of the protesters against Synge's play were also set in train. Daniel Mahony, one of the Dublin metropolitan magistrates, fined two of the rioters, Patrick Columb and Piáras Beaslai, following convictions for disorderly behaviour, forty shillings each, binding both over on sureties of £10 to be of good behaviour.[98] A few days later, other protesters, James Delaney, Patrick Hughes and John Duane, came before a different magistrate, Thomas Wall, who had dealt with the Theatre Royal disturbances of April 1902. Wall adopted a somewhat different attitude. In the first place, he reckoned it not inappropriate to quote from Chief Justice Bushe's instructions to the jury in *R. v. Forbes*, the 'Bottle Riot' case of 1822.[99] The passage Wall repeated was where Bushe laid it down that the sole condition limiting the right to cry down a play was that the action had to be spontaneous:

> If it be premeditated by a number of persons confederated beforehand to cry down even a performance of an actor, it becomes criminal.[100]

Wall went on to ask of the crown prosecutor why a charge of riot had not been preferred.[101] Receiving no clear answer, Wall continued by mounting an attack on the management of the Abbey Theatre for putting on *The Playboy* in the first place. 'It might be well to consider on the part of the Crown', he began,[102]

> whether those who persisted in bringing forward theatrical procedure of such a character as to excite popular odium and opposition, and which could not be tolerated, at all events, in Ireland, where, practically, there were two worlds, one wishing to be at the throat of the other, and one wishing to avoid what the other wished to intrude – whether those who were responsible for that should not themselves be brought forward.

95 Ibid., p. 108.   96 *1909 joint select committee report*, at p. 187.
97 *A poet's theatre* (Dublin, Elo Press, 1988), p. 14.
98 Robert Hogan and James Kilroy, *The Abbey Theatre: the years of Synge, 1905–1909* (Dublin, Dolmen Press, 1978), pp 132–3.
99 *Rex v. Forbes* (1823) 1 Crawford & Dix 157.   100 At 158.
101 See Hogan & Kilroy, *Abbey Theatre*, p. 138.   102 Ibid.

Possibly mischievously – though, doubtless, Wall would not have so considered it – the chief Dublin metropolitan magistrate went on to demand to be told why persons in the audience who had enthusiastically applauded the play, together with the actors, had not also been prosecuted.[103]

A contemporary editorial in the *Irish Independent* sang from the same hymn sheet as that brandished by Wall. 'The staging of the piece [i.e., *The Playboy*]', the editorial ran,[104] 'was an act of inexplicable stupidity on the part of the management on whom the heaviest censure should fall.' Nor did the Abbey's managing director personally escape unscathed. Synge, 'as a dramatist', the same editorial insisted,[105] 'is a discovery for which that rather tiresome chatterer and poseur, Mr William Butler Yeats, takes credit'.

Arthur Clery, writing under the pseudonym 'Chanel', in his 1907 collection of essays,[106] struck a very similar note – evidence yet again that the birth of the Abbey did not enjoy widespread approval. Far from it. The Irish people, the future University College Dublin law professor wrote,[107] had 'a right to protest if they find their National theatre tending towards immoral, anti-Christian or anti-human propaganda'. Clery went on to deride modernist features in fiction and in drama. 'In much of contemporary French literature', the mind of the author, Clery wrote,[108]

> dwells with a morose satisfaction on the diseases of life. Such an attitude of mind was in great measure exhibited in *In the Shadow of the Glen*, and it was this rather than any moral it taught that made one turn away from it. And *The Playboy of the Western World* merely showed the same tendencies in a more exaggerated form.[109]

If such expressions of opinion represented a change in the public mood as regards the staging of *The Playboy of the Western World*, it was a change of which Wall was prepared to take note. The three protesters hauled before him, Delaney, Hughes and Duane, were each fined the scarcely astronomical amount of ten shillings.[110]

That this was to be Wall's approach would have been clear to any who had taken the trouble to study accounts of his handling of the prosecutions mounted over disturbances at the performance of *The Dandy Fifth* in April 1902. Before convicting those in the audience in the Theatre Royal on that occasion, Wall specifically inquired of the principal police witness, Constable 199B, whether there had been anything objectionable in the performance itself, to which the witness had

---

103 Ibid., p. 139.   104 Quoted, Hogan & Kilroy, *Abbey Theatre*, p. 141.   105 Ibid.
106 *The idea of a nation* (Dublin, James Duffy & Co. Ltd, 1907).   107 Ibid., at p. 49.
108 At p. 50.
109 On Clery, see Patrick Maume, 'Nationalism and partition: the political thought of Arthur Clery', *Irish Historical Studies*, 31 (1998), 222.
110 Hogan & Kilroy, *Abbey Theatre*, p. 140.

replied in the negative.[111] If there had been 'anything objectionable' – whatever that might have conveyed – the inference that is there to be drawn is that the outcome very likely would have been rather different.

Morash concludes his account of the 1907 *Playboy* riot by furnishing the intriguing detail that when Synge's play was produced in New York in the winter of 1911–12, it met with organised disruption far more violent than anything experienced in Dublin: the throwing of stink bombs and a barrage of rotten vegetables.[112]

A few years later, the Theatre Royal – the scene of the disturbances over *The Dandy Fifth* – witnessed a minor kefuffle during a run of the play *Sir Walter Raleigh* by William Devereaux.[113] On 11 October 1910 a character in the play made some critical remarks regarding the Holy Office, better known as the Inquisition. 'Immediately', so we are told by the *Freeman's Journal*, 'a large number of the audience stood up and sang "Faith of our fathers".'

Following the decision of the Free State government in 1925 to give the Abbey an annual subsidy, a government appointee, George O'Brien, was added to the Abbey board. His arrival posed a problem for Yeats and the other directors when the board met to decide whether to accept for performance Sean O'Casey's *The Plough and the Stars*. The play deals with the 1916 Rising introducing a set of characters by no means, to judge from their actions and words, supportive of this critical episode in the history of modern Ireland. In a letter to Yeats, O'Brien took exception to all manner of things.[114] He found especially offensive, for example, the prostitute Rosie Redmond's song scheduled for act 2:

I once had a lover, a tailor, but he could do nothin' for me
An' then I fell in with a sailor as strong an' as wild as th' sea.
We cuddled an' kissed with devotion, till th' night from th' morning had fled!
An' there, to our joy; a bright bouncin' boy
Was dancin' a jig in th' bed!

Yeats sprang to O'Casey's defence, but, following a heated directors' meeting in September 1925, agreed to ask O'Casey to cut Rosie Redmond's song, in which O'Casey himself ultimately acquiesced.[115]

The play opened on Monday 8 February 1926, when there were no problems. Trouble was brewing on the Tuesday when Sighle Humphreys, vice-president of Cumann na mBan, started hissing from the back of the pit.[116] But it was only on the Thursday, the 11th, that matters threatened to get completely out of control. There is no need here to rehearse Morash's masterly evocation of the disturbances that were to ensue.[117] 'Anyone looking around the auditorium before the play began', Morash writes, 'would have missed neither the large Cumann na mBan

111 *Irish Times*, 16 Apr. 1902. 112 Morash, *History of Irish theatre*, p. 146. 113 Ibid., p. 156. 114 Ibid., p. 164. 115 Ibid., p. 165. 116 Ibid., p. 166. 117 Ibid., pp 167–8.

presence, nor the prominent members of Sinn Féin'. The appearance of Ria Mooney, acting the part of Rosie Redmond in act 2, was followed by a yell from someone in the auditorium, 'Put that woman off the stage'. At that 'pennies and lumps of coal began to rain down on the actors'. Protesters later started to rush the stage, and at the start of act 3 there were to be fights with the actors. 'You have no right to earn your bread by insulting Ireland', one voice yelled from the pit. Yeats was summoned and, after calling for the police, addressed the auditorium in a speech that contained the well-known sentence, 'You have disgraced yourselves again'.[118] As Morash tells it, someone threw a shoe at him: a comparable episode involving George Bush, junior, in the Green Zone in Baghdad in 2008 was not the first of its kind.

Christopher Murray, in his evocation of events on the night of 11 February 1926, argues that matters first threatened to go beyond the point of no return when in act 2 of *The Plough and the Stars* the tricolour was brought into the pub.[119] A contemporary editorial in the *Evening Herald* may be confirmation, with its emphasis on this particular detail. 'There is an effort abroad to destroy Nationalism', it argued,[120]

> and supplant it by internationalism, and the desecration of the National flag of a country. I should imagine the play would come under the Treason Act.

This was heady stuff, and it goes a good deal of the way to explain why, unlike in the case of *The Dandy Fifth* in 1902 and the *Playboy* riot in 1907, there was to be no prosecution of those who participated in the disruption of 11 February 1926. As it has been expressed to me, 'it would have been the height of foolishness to prosecute the rioters, mainly members of Cumann na mBan, and O'Casey's name would have been ruined'.[121] The fact that we were now in an independent Ireland, with the creation of the Irish Free State, may have had a lot to do with it. But there were other factors besides – a changing attitude on the part of the representatives of officialdom towards disruption at theatrical performances. Metropolitan Police Magistrate Thomas Wall's reservations over the prosecutions resulting from the *Playboy* riot[122] are suggestive of the way the wind was blowing. That was in 1907. In 1914 another Dublin magistrate, Mr Drury, in the Southern Police Court, went a step further. At a performance in the Gaiety of the French farce, *Who's the Lady?* one William J. Larkin sparked a minor riot when he rose from his seat and objected to the play. At Larkin's subsequent court appearance, Mr Drury dismissed the charge and actually praised Larkin for his 'public service'.[123]

Earlier in 1914, in February, a riot that attended a performance of George A. Birmingham's satirical comedy, *General John Regan*, in Westport, Co. Mayo, was

---

118   Ibid., p. 168.
119   Christoher Murray, *Sean O'Casey: writer at work – a biography* (Dublin, Gill & Macmillan, 2004), p. 172.
120   See Murray, *Sean O'Casey*, p. 178.   121   Christopher Murray to the writer, 13 Mar. 2009.
122   Above, pp 201–2.   123   Dean, *Riot and great anger*, p. 110.

followed by court proceedings in Castlebar, where a jury took but twenty minutes completely to exonerate the accused. At the trial, the defence argued strenuously for the upholding of the principle that a member of the audience had the right to express offence at any play or scene in it. *General John Regan* is the story of the plan to raise funds for a statue to be erected in honour of a local born hero of some South American liberation movement. It is thought that the depiction of the parish priest, Father McCormack, slyly slipping into Doyle's Hotel for a drink, may have unsettled the auditorium;[124] this rather than the pageant in which the character Mary Ellen, who was impersonating General Regan's niece, was attended by a troupe of fairies – in a parody of 'the *tableaux vivants* that were regular features of the Gaelic League's feisanna and nationalistic theatre groups'.[125]

The last episode of disruption in any Irish theatre recorded by Morash occurred at the Peacock Theatre – part of the new Abbey complex – on 16 September 1970.[126] A production of *A State of Chassis*, a satirical revue, penned by Tomas MacAnna and John D. Stewart was under way on the opening night, when, shortly before the intermission, Eamonn McCann, chairman of the Derry Labour Party, interrupted proceedings to object to the characterization of Bernadette Devlin on the stage. Morash tells us what happened next:[127]

> Some of McCann's supporters in the audience cheered him, but there were also calls from the audience: 'Go to hell', and 'Throw him out'. A couple of men attacked McCann when he began handing out leaflets, before he was finally escorted from the hall by MacAnna.

The troubles in Northern Ireland, when represented on the stage, threatened much more than a few cross words in a comfortable auditorium in Dublin. And so it turned out on 4 September 1973 when a group, to indicate their displeasure at the production of Patrick Galvin's *Nightfall to Belfast* at the Lyric Theatre on Belfast's Ridgeway Street, left a car bomb to explode outside the theatre.[128] The bomb, in fact, was to be defused.

Around this time too the supporters of the Revd Ian Paisley objected to the Lyric Theatre's production of the musical *Jesus Christ Superstar*, a picket being mounted outside the theatre in Ridgeway Street on the occasion of its opening.[129] A letter was also forwarded to the Lyric's management, purporting to be based on the language in verses 22 and 23 of chapter 2 of the 1st Epistle of John. 'We solemnly warn you', it thundered,

> that all who partake in this diabolically inspired and iniquitously blasphemous production come under the consideration of God Whose Word declares them to be liars and antichrists.

---

124 Ibid., p. 101.   125 Ibid., p. 106.   126 Morash, *History of Irish theatre*, p. 230.
127 Ibid.   128 Ibid., p. 244.   129 O'Malley, *A poet's theatre*, p. 65.

The entitlement of theatre management to take action to thwart the likelihood of disruption in the theatre whether during a performance or otherwise received oblique endorsement from Mr Justice McCardie when charging the jury in the unusual English case of *Said v. Butt* back in 1920.[130] The defendant was Sir Alfred Butt (1876–1962), the proprietor of the Palace Theatre, of whom it was to be said that he made this theatre 'into one of the most prestigious and financially successful variety theatres in London'.[131] The plaintiff was a Mr Said, described as a Russian gentleman. Said, despite his possessing a ticket, was denied admission to the première of *The Whirligig* at the Palace on 23 December 1919. Said had on a previous occasion made verbal attacks on the theatre's staff and he knew, accordingly, that if he sought to buy a ticket for the première on 23 December by himself, this would be refused; so he arranged for a friend, a Mr Pollock, to do so on his behalf. At the entrance to the theatre, bearing the ticket Pollock had procured, Said was identified, and on instructions from Butt was refused admission. Said failed to convince Mr Justice McCardie and the trial jury that he could justly claim that Butt had wrongfully procured the theatre company to break the contract constituted by his ticket of admission. It was McCardie's view that the non-disclosure by Pollock at the time of the purchase by him of the critical ticket that it was intended for Said was a fatal flaw, so much so in fact that there was no valid contract.

In the text of McCardie's ruling in the law applicable to the case, there is to be found a description of the significance of a play's first night, which is not without a certain sociological value (if, perhaps, a trifle dated). 'A first night at the Palace Theatre', the judge was to observe,[132]

> is, as with other theatres, an event of great importance. The result of a first night may make or mar a play. If the play be good, then words of its success may be spread, not only by the critics, but by members of the audience. The nature and social position and influence of the audience are of obvious importance. First nights have become to a large extent a species of private entertainment given by the theatrical proprietors and management to their friends and acquaintances, and to influential persons, whether critics or otherwise. The boxes, stalls and dress circle are regarded as parts of the theatre which are subject to special allocation by the management. Many tickets for those parts may be given away. The remaining tickets are usually sold by favour only. A first night, therefore, is a special event, with special characteristics.

Descending from the general to the particular, Mr Justice McCardie continued:[133]

---

130 [1920] 3 KB 407.   131 *Oxford DNB*, ix, 246 (Andrew Crowhurst).
132 [1920] 3 KB at 501.   133 Ibid.

As the plaintiff himself stated in evidence, the management only disposes of first night tickets for the stalls and dress circle to those whom it selects. I may add that it is scarcely likely to choose those who are antagonistic to the management; or who have attacked the character of the theatre officials.

Sir Alfred Butt was thus held to be well within his rights in seeking to prevent orchestrated opposition on the first night of *The Whirligig*. Around forty years earlier the management at the Vaudeville found themselves with a problem on their hands at the first night of James Albery's *Jacks and Jills*. The disruption was so pronounced that eventually the author himself was produced and there made a speech at the footlights – a mixture of menace and defiance – but in effect an appeal for calm.[134] At St James' in 1892, at the first night of Oscar Wilde's *Lady Windermere's Fan*, something very different transpired when the ecstatic reception given the comedy afforded Wilde the opportunity to ingratiate himself with his audience in a manner very much his own.[135] Wearing a green carnation and languidly smoking a cigarette, he congratulated the actors on their 'charming rendering of a delightful play', before moving on to applaud the audience for its intelligent and enthusiastic reception of his comedy, 'which persuades me that you think almost as highly of the play as I do myself'.

Not everyone was prepared to relish the conventions associated with premières in the theatre – James Agate, the drama critic, for instance. In his diary entry for 19 January 1939, Agate, following his experience at one first night that very day, mounted a criticism in full-flowing prose.[136] 'Can nothing be done', Agate ventured to inquire,

> about these ridiculous first-night scenes after the fall of the curtain? At the Shaftesbury to-night, after a tepid thriller, there appeared from nowhere a tall, thin gentleman, followed by a short, round gentleman, followed by a large, beaming gentleman who proceeded to kiss everybody's hand. None of these had been called for by the audience, which had not the vaguest notion who any of them was. The result of all this fuss is the elaborate destruction of whatever has been achieved.

Continuing in the same vein, Agate pens a conclusion to his entry tailor-made to ensure his readers wake up and take notice. 'How tolerate', he is bold enough to ask,

> a stammering mooncalf whose trousers are as much too short as his acts have been too long: why must Joan descend from her pyre to tell us that our reception has made her feel hot all over?

134   J.R. Stephens, *The profession of the playwright: British theatre, 1800–1900* (Cambridge, Cambridge UP, 1992), p. 143.
135   Richard Ellmann, *Oscar Wilde* (London, Penguin ed., 1988), p. 346.
136   James Agate, *A shorter ego: second selection* (London, George G. Harrap & Co. Ltd, 1945), pp 23–4.

CHAPTER FOURTEEN

Censorship

AMBIGUITY HELPS TO DEFINE the attitude to the theatre adopted by the state and its organs. Suspicion of the actor has had a lot to do with it. Take portion of James I's advice on kingship imparted to his eldest son, Prince Henry, in *Basilikon Doron* brought out in 1603.[1] 'Delight not', James advises,[2]

> to keep ordinarily in your company Commoedians or Balladines: for the Tyrants delighted most in the[m], glorying to be both aut[h]ors and actors of Comoedies and Tragoedies themselves!

Predictable references to the tyrant of Syracuse in Sicily and to the Roman emperor Nero follow.

There was nothing ambiguous about the stance adopted in England less than thirty years later in relation to the theatre. This argued not for censorship but for total abolition – pressure that was to succeed in its aim. This remarkable outcome owed a great deal to an extraordinary tract brought out in 1631 by the lawyer and leading Puritan, William Pyrnne (1600–69). The tract in question was his *Histrio-Mastix*, all 1006 pages of it, supplemented by two Epistles Dedicatory, one to the Masters of the Bench at Lincoln's Inn (6 pages), and one to the students of the Inns of Court (12 pages), and an additional preface dedicated 'To the Christian Reader' (11 pages).[3] The full title of this remarkable tract merits being set down:

> Histrio-Mastix. The Players Scourge, or Actors Tragaedie, Divided into Two Parts, Wherein it is largely evidenced, by divers Arguments, by the concurring Authorities and Resolutions of sundry texts of Scripture; of the whole Primitive Church, both under the Law and Gospell; of 55 Synodes and Councels; of 71 Fathers and Christian Writers, before the yeare of our Lord 1200; of above 150 foraigne and domestique Protestant and Popish Authors, since; of 40 Heathen Philosophers, Historians, Poets, of many Heathen, many Christian Nations, Repubiques, Emperors, Princes, Magistrates; of sundry Apostolicall, Canonicall, Imperiall Constitutions; and of our owne English Statutes, Magistrates, Universities, Writers, Preachers. That popular Stage-playes (the very Pompes of the Divell which we

---

1 *ΒΑΣΙΛΙΚΟΝ ΔΩΡΟΝ, or His Majesties Instructions to his Dearest Sonne, Henry the Prince* (London, E. Allde for E.W. and others of the company of Stationers, 1603).
2 Ibid., p. 99.   3 London, E.A. & W.I. for Michael Sparke, 1631.

208

renounce in Baptisme, if we believe the Fathers) are sinfull, heathenish, lewde, ungodly Spectacles, and most pernicious Corruptions; condemned in all ages, as intolerable Mischiefes to Churches, to Republickes, to the manners, mindes, and soules of men. And that the Profession of Play-poets, of Stage players; together with the penning, acting and frequenting of Stage-playes, are unlawfull, infamous and misbeseeming Christians. All pretences to the contrary are here likewise fully answered; and the unlawfulness of acting, of beholding Academicall Enterludes, briefly discussed; besides sundry other particulars concerning Dancing, Dicing, Health-drinking etc. of which the Table will informe you.

The title page in this massive production is embellished by appropriate quotations from Cyprian, Chrysostom and Augustine.

The content of *Histrio-Mastix* led to Prynne being prosecuted in Star Chamber, as a result of which the following year he was sentenced to be fined, to be placed in the pillory and to have his ears cropped. That Prynne's attack helped to occasion Parliament's first order for the closure of London's theatres in 1642, during 'Times of Humiliation' ('the distressed Estate of Ireland, steeped in her own Blood, and the distressed Estate of England, threatened with a Cloud of Blood by a Civil War'), appears undeniable. On 2 September 1642 Parliament ordered that 'Public Stage Plays' were to cease and be forborn,

> instead of which are recommended to the People of this Land the profitable and seasonable considerations of Repentance, Reconciliation, and Peace with God, which probably may produce outward Peace and Prosperity, and bring again Times of Joy and Gladness to these Nations.[4]

Further enforcement measures were taken by Parliament in 1647[5] and 1648[6]. The preamble to the measure of 11 February 1647/8 rehearsed something of the religious thinking that again lay behind these draconian interventions. 'Whereas', that measure recited,

> the Acts of Stage-Playes, Interludes, and common Playes, condemned by ancient Heathens, and much less to be tolerated amongst Professors of the Christian Religion is the occasion of many and sundry great vices and disorders, tending to the high provocation of Gods wrath and displeasure, which lies heavy upon this Kingdom to the disturbance of the peace thereof
> ...

This ordinance went on to deem all stage players rogues; authorised the pulling down of all stage galleries, seats and boxes; sanctioned the whipping of actors;

---

4 C.H. Firth and R.S. Rait (ed.), *Acts and ordinances of the Interregnum, 1642–1600*, vol. 1: 1642–9 (London, HMSO, 1911), pp 26–7.
5 Ibid., p. 1027 (22 Oct. 1647).   6 Ibid., pp 1070–2 (11 Feb. 1647/48).

made moneys gathered for performances forfeit to the poor of the parish; and exposed spectators at plays to a fine of 5 shillings.[7]

The environment in which Ogilby sought to launch his Irish initiative[8] could hardly have been less encouraging, and, as we have seen, his enterprise languished, and the Interregnum wrote finis to the theatre in Ireland for the moment, only for it to be revived on the occasion of the Restoration of Charles II in 1660.

Prynne's hostility to the theatre is worth revisiting. A few personal details that he furnishes are illuminating. As a young student, he had attended four plays in London, to which he says, 'the pressing importunity of some ill acquaintance drew me while I was yet a novice'; he had then witnessed 'such wickedness and such lewdness as then made my penitent heart to loath'. Rake's progresses abounded, too, he sought to persuade his readers. 'Some young Gentlemen of my acquaintance', Prynne explains,

> who though civill and chast out first, became so vitious, prodigall, incontinent, deboist [debauched], (yea so farre past hopes of all amendment) in halfe a yeares space or lesse, by their resort to Playes, where whores and lewd companions had inveigled them, that after many vaine assaies of their much desired reformation, two of them were cast off, and utterly disinherited by their loving Parents.

The Epistle Dedicatory from which these details have been extracted continues the tirade. 40,000 play books, Prynne was assured, had been printed in the last two years; they were 'more vendible than the choysest Sermons'. The plays of Shakespeare were printed on better paper than the Bibles. In recent days in London, two theatres had been re-edified – The Fortune and The Red Bull. And a new one had been erected – the White Friers Playhouse. This brought the number of theatres in London to six; compare that, Prynne injuncts his readers, with Nero's Rome where there were but three.

In the Preface To the Christian Reader Prynne refuses to accept as 'laudable, good and Christian' his choice list of abominations –

> effeminate mixt Dancing, Dicing, Stage-playes, lascivious Pictures, wanton Fashions, Face-painting, Health-drinking, Long haire, Love-lockes, Periwigs, women's curling, pouldring, and cutting of their haire, Bone-fires, New-yeares-gifts, May games, amorous Pastoralles, lascivious effeminate Musicke, excessive laughter, luxurious disorderly Christmas-keeping, Mummeries, with sundry such like varieties which the world now dotes on.

Prynne also attaches an apology for the length of his treatise, which might be thought part-justification for the reader not actually to read every page in this lump of a book. He thus craves indulgence for

7   All expressed to apply to London, Westminster, and the counties of Middlesex and Surrey.
8   Above, p. 2.

its tedious prolixities, which as it far exceeds its primitive intended Brevity, so it may somewhat derogate from its welcome acceptation, as being too large for so slight a subject.

Turning to censorship rather than outright prohibition – the experience of the Puritan-dominated English Interregnum – the story here is longer, and a good deal more complex. The story is one of control, with a lengthy pedigree. We encounter it even in the early days of the theatre in Athens, invariably identified as the birthplace of the drama itself. In the course of the prolonged struggle between the Greeks and the Persians, the Greeks at one point suffered a major reverse with the loss in BC494 of Miletus, the city in Asia Minor that had been at the centre of the Ionian revolt. The defeat was a terrible blow, and when the Athenian playwright Phrynichus put on a play called *The Fall of Miletus*, the audience burst into tears. As recently recalled by Kapuściński,[9] the authorities in Athens

> imposed a draconian fine of a thousand drachmas on the play's author and banned any future productions of it in their city.

Kapuściński's source is of course Herodotus who furnishes these details in book six of his *Histories:*[10]

> Ἀθηναῖοι μὲν γὰρ δῆλον ἐττοίησαν ὑττεραχθεσθέντες τῇ Μιλήτου ἁλώσι τῇ τε ἄλλη ττολλαχῇ, καὶ δὴ καὶ ττοιήσαντι Φρυνίχῳ δρᾶμα Μιλήτου ἅλωσιν καὶ διδάξαντι ἐς δάκρυά τε ἔττεσε τὸ θέητρον, καὶ ἐζημίωσάν μιν ὡς ἀναμνήσαντα οἰκήια κακὰ χιλίῃσι δραχμῇσι, καὶ ἐττέταξαν μηδένα χρᾶσθαι τουτῳ τῷ δράματι.

As the author of *Travels with Herodotus* judiciously goes on to point out, 'A play was meant to raise one's spirits, not reopen wounds'. This episode was to become well-known to historians of the theatre. It is recalled, for example, in J.W. Calcraft's defence of the stage, the tract he published in Dublin in 1839.[11]

In Britain, it is important to note, censorship was not unknown before 1737. Colley Cibber, writing three years later in 1740, mounted a strong defence of the changes introduced in 1737 and at the same time provided details of instances of censorship of the English stage before that date.[12] In the reign of Charles II, Nathaniel Lee's *Lucius Junius Brutus* was banned after three performances in 1680: its republican sentiments were too boldly vindicated. In the same reign, the Lord Chamberlain (clearly already flexing his muscles) laid a ban on Francis Beaumont

9 Ryszard Kapuściński, *Travels with Herodotus* (London, Penguin Books, 2008), 'Honors for the head of Histiaeus', p. 161.
10 Herodotus, *Histories*, 6. 21.
11 J.W. Calcraft, *A defence of the stage, etc.* (Dublin, Milliken & Son, 1839), p. 135; above, p. 100.
12 Colley Cibber, *An apology for the life of Mr Colley Cibber, etc.* (Dublin, George Faulkner, 1740), pp 199–200.

and John Fletcher's *The Maid's Tragedy*: it featured the killing of a king. In May 1689, in the early months of the reign of William III, and while the king was actually fighting for his crown in Ireland, Lord Dorset, the Lord Chamberlain, who served in that office from 1689 to 1697, vetoed the recitation of Dryden's prologue to another of Beaumont and Fletcher's plays, *The Prophetess*, after just one performance. The prologue, Cibber explained,[13]

> had familiar metaphorical sneers at the revolution itself; and as the poetry of it was good, the offence of it was less pardonable.

The lines to which exception was taken were, apparently, these:[14]

> Go unkind Hero's, leave our Stage to mourn;
> Till rich from vanquish'd Rebels you return;
> And the fat spoyls of Teague in Tryumph draws
> His Firkin-Butter and his Usquebaugh.

Dorset's action in the spring of 1689 can be regarded very much as the deed of a poacher turned gamekeeper. He had scarcely an unblemished record, having been associated, when styled Lord Buckhurst, in both 1663 and 1668 with the perpetration of notorious acts of gross indecency in the company of Sir Charles Sedley. In the 1668 'frolic', the two friends had run 'up and down all the night with their arses bare through the streets'; they had then gone on to fight with, and being beaten up by the watch, as a consequence of which they were 'clapped up all night'.[15] At the trial before Lord Chief Justice Foster for the act of gross indecency of 1663, the judge, having had it confirmed to him that Buckhurst was the same man who had been tried and acquitted for a robbery and murder at Stoke Newington a few months earlier,[16] remonstrated with Buckhurst, upbraiding him for having, in Samuel Pepys' words, 'so soon forgot his deliverance', and admonishing him 'that it would have more become him to have been at his prayers, begging God's forgiveness, than now running into such courses again'.[17]

Cibber concluded his short inventory of instances of censorship, not otherwise easily known, by recalling that for twenty years, in view of 'the suspicions' of the English Master of the Revels, *The Tragedy of Mary Queen of Scots* was not acted. On the accession of Queen Anne the new monarch was in 1705 approached to

13 Ibid., p. 201.
14 See Walsh, *Opera in Dublin, 1705–1797*, p. 56: *The works of John Dryden, vol. 3: poems 1685–1692* (Berkeley and Los Angeles, Univ. of California Press, 1969), p. 255 at p. 256.
15 *The diary of Samuel Pepys*, ed. Robert Latham and William Matthews, 11 vols (London, G. Bell, 1970–83), ix, 335–6.
16 See *Pepys diary*, iii, 34: 22 Feb. 1662; HMC, *Var. coll.*, viii, 66.
17 *Pepys diary*, iv, 209–10: 1 July 1663. For the prosecution of Sedley for acts of gross indecency (in deeds and words) see *Le Roy v. Sir Charles Sidley* (1663) 1 Sid 118; 82 Eng Rep 1036.

secure her views. She apparently raised no objection, and after this extraordinarily lengthy delay, the play was finally put on.[18]

Returning to the reign of Elizabeth I, it is well known, of course, that excisions were made in performances of Shakespeare's *Richard II* during the queen's lifetime. *Richard II* was first published in quarto, in 1597, a year that also saw a second edition with Shakespeare's name on the title-page. Neither of these editions contains the text of the deposition scene – act 4, scene 1, lines 154–318 – that comes down to us from the third quarto published in 1608. In the presence of Bolingbroke, the future Henry IV, Richard yields up his kingly office; the third quarto has these lines:[19]

> Now mark me, how I will undo myself:
> I give this heavy weight from off my head
> And this unwieldy sceptre from my hand,
> The pride of kingly sway from out my heart;
> With mine own tears I wash away my balm,
> With mine own hands I give away my crown,
> With mine own tongue deny my sacred state,
> With mine own breath release all duty's rites:
> All pomp and majesty I do forswear;
> My manors, rents, revenues I forgo;
> My acts, decrees, and statutes I deny:
> God pardon all oaths that are broke to me!

We owe our knowledge of Elizabeth's sensitivity over the play to a conversational exchange set down by William Lambarde, the keeper of records in the Tower of London. Appointed to this post early in 1601, Lambarde, at an audience of the queen at her palace of Greenwich the following August, produced for her majesty's inspection a synopsis of the royal records he held – his *Pandecta rotulorum* – and some of the actual records themselves. The memorandum of the conversation that then apparently ensued was in the late eighteenth century handed over by a descendent of Lambarde's to John Nicholls, then engaged in collecting material for his major collection of memorabilia respecting the queen, and included in that compilation.[20]

Lambarde showed the queen 'rolls, bundells, membranes, and parcells', which she 'chearfullie received ... into her hands'. The scrutiny covered the eleven reigns from John to Richard III, 286 years in all. On the first page of the synopsis the queen demanded the meaning of the words 'oblata, cartae, litterae clausae and

18 Cibber, *An apology*, p. 200.
19 *Richard II*, act 4, scene 1, lines 203–14.
20 *The progresses and public processions of Queen Elizabeth. Among which are interspersed other solemnities, public expenditures, and remarkable events during the reign of that illustrious Princess*, ed. John Nichols, 3 vols (London, J. Nichols, 1788–1805), ii, B–H, pp 41–2.

literae patentes.' Lambarde, no mean lawyer as well as an antiquary, obliged. Elizabeth expressed her satisfaction and continued:

> She would be a scholar in her age, and thought it no scorn to learn during her life, being of the mind of that philosopher, who in his last years began with the Greek alphabet.

More words defeated her, and again she asked for clarification: 'ordinationes, parliamenta, rotulus cambii, rediseisnes'. Lambarde again obliged, the queen taking the explanation 'in gratious and full satisfaction'.

The queen then came upon records from the reign of King Richard II. Elizabeth then blurted out: 'I am Richard II. Know ye not that?' To which Lambarde diplomatically responded, with an oblique reference to Essex's rebellion which had only so recently been put down: 'Such a wicked imagination was determined and attempted by a most unkind gent., the most adorned creature that ever your Majestie made'. The queen plainly concurred: 'He that will forget God, will also forget his benefactors'. What irked her still was not thus to be lost sight of. 'This tragedy', she tells Lambarde, 'was played 40tie times in open streets and houses'.

The subject is changed momentarily, when Elizabeth asks the meaning of another Latin word – praestita. Lambarde responds that these were moneys 'lent by her progenitors to her subjects ... but with assurance of good bond for repayment'.

The question of Richard II having been aired, it was difficult to let it be. There was now to be a different tack. The queen then asked Lambarde, as he recalled, 'whether I had seen any true picture, or lively representation of his countenance and person'. After Lambarde responded, 'None but such as be in common hands', Elizabeth intimated she could go much further than that. 'The Lord Lumley', she revealed,

> a lover of antiquities, discovered it fastened on the backside of a door of a base room, which he presented unto me, praying, with my good leave, that I might put it in order with the ancestors and successors.

Nor was there to be any getting away from recent political events after Lambarde had shown, and the queen had examined, lists of fines imposed on wrongdoers. 'In those [earlier] days', the queen ruminated, 'force and arms did prevail; but now the wit of the fox is every where a foot, so as hardly a faithful or vertuouse man may be found'.

A fortnight later, on 19 August, Lambarde, who had recorded the events of this audience at Greenwich, was to die.

Returning to the theme of productions of Shakespeare's *Richard II*, it is far from irrelevant that in 1599, two years before, Sir John Hayward had been imprisoned in the Tower for publishing his *History of the life and raigne of Henry the Fourth*, with its account of the deposition of Richard II, and was to remain incarcerated there until the queen's death in 1603.

Discretion, having already been heralded as the better part of valour, it must have made prudent sense in the London of these anxious months to suppress the drama of the actual deposition scene in all pre-1603 productions of the play. As was to prove to be the case as well with Beaumont and Fletcher's *The Maid's Tragedy*, where the killing of a monarch featured, there are dangers very clearly in the theatre and theatre management sailing too close to the wind.

France knew censorship too. Perhaps the most notorious instance of the exercise of the power was the ban imposed on Molière's *Tartuffe*, first performed in 1664, but instantly banned for its criticism of ecclesiastics, and only finally licensed for public performance in 1669. The conditions imposed were a mite unusual – the play was re-entitled *The Imposter* and Tartuffe was now to be called Panulphe. Attacks on Molière accompanied this surge of complaint. One anonymous author labelled him 'a demon clothed in flesh and dressed as a man, the most outstandingly impious libertine that has ever lived'.[21]

So far as the theatre in Britain and Ireland in more recent times is concerned, the most commented-upon instrument of censorship was to be the introduction in Britain in 1737 of the regime of pre-censorship linked to the office of Lord Chamberlain. This regime continued for well over two centuries before it was abandoned on the enactment of the Theatres Act in 1968.

This naturally constituted a major difference in the regulatory regimes for theatre as between Britain and Ireland. In theory it entailed, for example, that managers of Irish theatres could arrange for the performance of plays prohibited in London. In charting the fortunes of the theatre in Ireland it is not, however, possible to ignore the import of the more draconian regime in the larger island. There are a number of reasons for this. First, but perhaps of the least importance, occasions would arise, and did arise, when the absence of pre-censorship in Ireland was regarded as an anomaly, so much so in fact that it was argued that the Lord Chamberlain's writ should run in Ireland as well. Second, visits by travelling theatre companies from Ireland are on record from the late seventeenth century, and these of course were to continue after the British legal change of 1737. Performances of plays by theatre companies irrespective of their place of origin were all encompassed by the rules introduced in 1737. Irish companies, no less and no more than their English or Scottish counterparts, had to obey the British rules when performing in Britain. But, thirdly, and unsurprisingly, when British companies toured in Ireland the flavour of the performances put on by them was dictated by Britain's indigenous rules. If there is a single case of any such touring company performing before an Irish audience a script that had been turned down

21 J.B.P. Molière, *The Misanthrope, Tartuffe and other plays*, trans. and intro. Maya Slater (Oxford, Oxford UP, 2001), p. xix.

by the Lord Chamberlain, none such has been highlighted by those historians of theatre in the British Isles who have focused on censorship. As it was, in the eighteenth century at least the repertoires of the London and Dublin theatres 'were clearly inextricably linked'.[22] A fourth reason is that Irish authors had a vested interest, like their British counterparts, in the actual state of affairs in Britain – an interest illustrated not least by the circumstance that both J.M. Synge and W.B. Yeats were among the 71 signatories of a celebrated letter sent to *The Times* in 1909 which led to the setting up of a parliamentary committee to examine the question of stage censorship in Britain yet again.

Lacking a regime of pre-censorship, Ireland was yet subject to other forms of censorship, and, in relation to this, Dean in her wide-ranging survey made a point scarcely requiring undue emphasis. 'Whereas', Dean wrote,[23]

> Britain's Lord Chamberlain evaluated a fixed script, Irish censors, would-be censors, protesters and picketers often were less than familiar with the plays they condemned.

Whether this was the case so far as the episode with which Dean commences her survey – a ban pronounced in 1819 – is impossible to establish. The episode itself constitutes a marker, the significance of which ought not to be lost sight of in what follows here. 'On 24 September 1819', Dean recalls for us,[24]

> Reverend W.C. Armstrong, then Provost of Sligo, suspended performances of *The Hypocrite*, Isaac Bickerstaffe's 1768 adaptation of Molière's *Tartuffe*.

Armstrong apparently believed the play represented an unacceptable calumny on certain of the denizens of Sligo. Armstrong had form: the previous month he had objected to a performance of John Gay's *The Beggar's Opera*,[25] not the first person, of course, to have been disturbed by that celebrated offering from Gay.[26]

Managers, citing matters of public taste, could equally decline to authorise productions of individual plays. In Dublin city and county, they needed to be especially careful in view of the language contained in the patents issued both before the 1786 Dublin Stage Regulation Act and afterwards. Such patents would prescribe the sort of entertainment that was not to be tolerated and which, if persisted in, could lead to the withdrawal of the patent itself. Prohibitions could be couched in general language forbidding profanity, for instance, but sometimes too with a much narrower focus – forbidding attacks on religion. That the authority to put on plays could indeed be cancelled from the revocation of any patent was well understood: it hardly needed Michael Gunn, the then manager of Dublin's Gaiety

22 Greene & Clark, *The Dublin stage, 1720–1745*, p. 81.
23 Joan Fitzpatrick Dean, *Riot and great anger: stage censorship in twentieth-century Ireland* (Madison, WN, Univ. of Wisconsin Press, 2004), p. 4.
24 Ibid., p. 3.   25 Ibid., p. 4.   26 See above, p. 32.

Theatre, to recall that this was the position in remarks addressed to certain critics in 1900.[27] Other factors naturally were to come into play once the State agreed to subsidise the Irish stage.

The history of theatre in Ireland is replete with instances of controversy, usually involving questions of political sensitivity. This has perhaps always been so – and not just in Ireland. The *Lysistrata* of Aristophanes, composed and first performed in Athens in 411BC, a mere two years after the disastrous failure of the Sicilian adventure at Syracuse, so grippingly evoked by Thucydides, attacked, as Dean has recalled,[28] the core values of Aristophanes' society. The appeals to feminism and panhellenism relegated, in a remarkable piece of satirical writing, to a very bleak lumber-room indeed much-vaunted ideologies of patriarchy, militarism and nationalism. To confine ourselves for the moment to the targeting of unwelcome and thus controversial drama in Ireland, we are brought face to face with action ranging from the government or management seeking to prohibit individual plays, to performances on stage or conduct in the auditorium exceeding what was adjudged allowable. At this point, the suggestion is advanced that the present chapter might profitably be read in tandem with that devoted to riots and disruption in the theatre. At a later stage in the history of Irish theatre, the focus of attention was to shift rather on to sexual matters, the high point here being the prosecution, ultimately unsuccessful, launched against a production of Tennessee Williams' play, *The Rose Tattoo*, in 1957.

The reform of 1737 in Britain, by no means uncontroversial at the time, was to be regularly revisited over the two centuries and more when it remained in place. Such re-examination of it that was undertaken in Victorian England, however, found nothing to complain about. There were to be two major parliamentary inquiries by select committee, in 1866 and 1892 respectively.[29]

The select committee of 1866 heard evidence from the Hon. S.C.B. Ponsonby to the effect that the approach adopted in his day was to refuse stage entertainment a licence when it dealt with a scriptural subject, exalted highwaymen or immorality, or tackled 'personal or personally political questions'.[30] In the period between 1852 and 1865, 2,816 plays had been forwarded to the Lord Chamberlain's office for scrutiny. Of these 2,816, 19 had been rejected – 2 for the exploration of some scriptural theme; 7 'of the swell mob and burglary school'; and the rest being French plays of an immoral tendency or English versions of them.[31] The Lord Chamberlain had put his foot down over licences for spectacular shows as well; as it was pithily expressed to the select committee of 1866, there were 'no wild beasts'; 'no Blondin'.[32] The committee itself found no fault with any of this at all. Indeed,

---

27 (1900) 1 *NIJ & LGR* 17.   28 Dean, *Riot and great anger*, p. 5.
29 David Thomas, David Carlton and Anne Etienne, *Theatre censorship: from Walpole to Wilson* (Oxford, Oxford UP, 2007), pp 65–8, 69–107.
30 *Report from the select committee to inquire into the working of Acts of Parliament for licensing theatres*, HC 1866, xvi, 1, p. 6.
31 Ibid., p. 282. The details are furnished in appendix K.   32 Ibid.

quite the reverse, actually urging that the Lord Chamberlain's remit should be extended. 'The censorship of plays', they reported, 'has worked satisfactorily'. It was not desirable that it should be discontinued. Rather, they added, 'it should be extended as far as practicable to the performance in music-halls and other places of public entertainment'.[33] The select committee of 1892 agreed, whilst supporting at the same time, as we have seen, the loosening of the regulatory regime so far as ballets and sketches in music-halls were concerned.[34] There was one early dissenting voice – that of Dion Boucicault. Though he elected not to press the point, Boucicault told the 1866 select committee that he regarded the Lord Chamberlain as 'a very improper person' to exercise censorship, the gravamen of his complaint being that lords chamberlain were notoriously inconsistent in their approach.[35] Boucicault told the constitutional truth, too, when he added that 'The office of licenser of plays is very foreign to the remainder of [the Lord Chamberlain's] functions'.

Two years before, as it happens, Boucicault had himself climbed down when the Irish government pressed an objection to a detail in his production of *Arrah-na-Pogue* in Dublin.[36] When the play, based on the events of 1798, arrived for performance at Hawkins Street late in 1864, it originally contained the rebel ballad, 'The wearing of the green'. Boucicault caved in once Dublin Castle had made its views known, and Boucicault replaced the ballad with a long speech in which an Irish landlord leaps to the defence of the wrongly accused peasant hero, Shaun the Post. This is what the audience of 1864, were debarred from hearing:

> O Paddy dear and did you hear the news that's going round?
> The Shamrock is by law forbid to grow on Irish ground;
> St Patrick's Day no more we'll keep, his colours can't be seen,
> For there's a bloody law against the wearin' of the green.

By the time of the revival of *Arrah-na-Pogue* in Dublin a few years later, two things had occurred. In the first place, 'The wearing of the green', an old Dublin street ballad with updated words to produce a distinctive anti-English lyric, had become 'the unofficial anthem of the Irish freedom movement', and, second, there had taken place the Fenian-contrived explosion at Clerkenwell Prison in London which killed 12 and injured 120.[37] On grounds of expediency, Boucicault was again asked to drop the song, which he agreed to do. Boucicault's most recent biographer adds the claim that the play itself was ordered to be banned throughout the British Empire.[38]

33 *1866 select committee report*, p. iv.
34 *Report of the select committee on theatres and places of entertainment*, HC 1892, xviii, 1 at p. vii.
35 *1866 select committee report*, p. 142.
36 Morash, *History of Irish theatre* (Cambridge, Cambridge UP, 2002), pp 91–2.
37 Richard Fawkes, *Dion Boucicault: a biography* (London, Melbourne and New York, Quartet Books, 1979), p. 158.
38 Ibid. Intriguingly, in 1865, Boucicault had been party to a suit in which John Berger, the editor of

Charles Reade, the contemporary dramatisation of whose novel, *Never too late to mend*, became the focus of a curious digression for the 1866 select committee,[39] might be reckoned a partial dissenter, for Reade strongly advocated the right of appeal against any adverse decision of the Lord Chamberlain[40] – a point of view equally strenuously opposed by the then holder of the office, Viscount Sidney (1859–66, 1868–74).[41] Boucicault and Reade were plainly in the minority. A majority viewpoint was probably expressed by a third witness who appeared before the 1866 select committee, Horace Wigan, the manager of London's Olympic Theatre. Wigan ridiculed the notion that 'public taste' could be relied on to control the stage.[42] He adopted the stance that the Lord Chamberlain's office was not censorious enough. He drew particular attention to exchanges between Don Pedro, Claudio and Benedick that occur in act 5 of *Much Ado About Nothing*, which Wigan was horrified to reveal were spoken every night at then current performances in St James' Theatre. The lines are not omitted from the parliamentary paper's verbatim account of Wigan's evidence, but I note that they were marked for deletion in a production in which my great grand-aunt Dorothy (Dolly) Tedlie would have participated. The passage is as follows:[43]

Don Pedro	Good morrow, Benedick. Why, what's the matter,
	That you have such a February face,
	So full of frost, of storm, and cloudiness?
Claudio	I think he thinks upon the savage bull.
	Tush, fear not, man; we'll tip thy horns with gold,
	And all Europa shall rejoice at thee;
	As once Europa did at lusty Jove,
	When he would lay the noble beast in love.
Benedick	Bull Jove, sir, had an amiable law;
	And some such strange bull leap'd your father's cow,
	And got a calf in that same noble feat
	Much like to you, for you have just his bleat.

Theatre censorship by the Lord Chamberlain's office was the specific focus of yet another parliamentary committee – the joint select committee of the House of Lords and House of Commons – that heard evidence and reported in 1909.[44] It had one Irish member – Hugh Law. This new inquiry was precipitated by a letter signed by seventy-one authors, which had appeared in *The Times* on 28 October

the *London Herald*, was faulted for having serialised the plot line of *Arrah-na-Pogue*, without permission: Fawkes, *Boucicault*, pp 157–8.

39 As to why the crank in the early prison scene was dropped: was the cause the censor, public distaste or a strike by stage carpenters?

40 *1866 select committee report*, p. 236.   41 Ibid., p. 267.   42 Ibid., p. 165.

43 *Much Ado About Nothing*, act 5, scene 4, ll. 40–51.

44 *Report from the joint select committee of the House of Lords and House of Commons on the stage plays (censorship)*, HC 1909, viii, 451. See, too, Dean, *Riot and great anger*, pp 88–90, 96–7.

1907. Synge and Yeats, as we have noted, were among the signatories, as were J.M. Barrie, Joseph Conrad, John Galsworthy, W.S. Gilbert, Thomas Hardy, Henry James, John Masefield, W.S. Maugham, George Meredith, Gilbert Murray, A.W. Pinero, G.B. Shaw, A.C. Swinburne, and H.G. Wells. The letter read as follows:[45]

> Dear Sir,
> The Prime Minister has consented to receive during next month a deputation from the following dramatic authors on the subject of the censorship of plays. In the meantime may these authors, through your columns, enter a formal protest against this office, which was instituted for political, and not for the so called moral ends to which it is perverted – an office autocratic in procedure, opposed to the spirit of the Constitution, contrary to common justice and to common sense?
> They protest against the power lodged in the hands of a single official – who judges without a public hearing and against which dictum there is no appeal – to cast a slur on the good name and destroy the means of livelihood of any member of an honourable calling.
> They assert that the censorship has not been exercised in the interests of morality, but has tended to lower the dramatic tone by appearing to relieve the public of the duty of moral judgment.
> They ask to be free from the menace hanging over every dramatist of having his work and the proceeds of his work destroyed at a pen's stroke by the arbitrary action of a single official neither responsible to Parliament nor amenable to law.
> They ask that their art be placed on the same footing as every other art.
> They ask that they themselves be placed in the position enjoyed under the law by every other citizen.
> To these ends they claim that the licensing of plays shall be abolished. The public is already sufficiently assured against managerial misconduct by the present yearly licensing of theatres, which remains untouched by the measure of justice here demanded.

The next month Shaw, one of the seventy-one signatories, who had also given evidence to the joint select committee on 30 July,[46] and whose play *The Shewing-Up of Blanco Posnet* was to attract adverse criticism on both sides of the Irish Sea, returned to the fray by launching a withering attack on the then Examiner of Plays, Alexander Redford, in the letters page of *The Nation*. Discussing the office, Shaw wrote as follows:[47]

> You want a man who will undertake to know, better than Tolstoy or Ibsen or George Meredith or Dickens or Carlyle or Ruskin or Shakespeare or Shelley,

45 Reproduced in *1909 joint select committee report*, at p. 351.
46 *1909 joint select committee report*, p. 46.
47 Quoted, Thomas, Carlton & Etienne, *Theatre censorship*, p. 79.

what moral truths the world needs to be reminded of – how far pity and horror and tragedy dare be carried – on what institutions the antiseptic derision of comedy may be allowed to play without destroying anything really vital in them. Now it is clear without argument that no man who was not a born fool would pretend for a moment to be capable of such a task; and the reason that some censors have been born fools.

This joint select committee represented a break with the past, for in its recommendations[48] it proposed making an application for a licence optional and leaving it to the courts (in cases of alleged indecency) or a mixed committee of the privy council ultimately to decide on future performances of unlicensed plays. More detailed guidelines for the Lord Chamberlain to follow were also drawn up. These proposals were both unexpected and would almost certainly have been difficult to implement. If the entire exercise was ultimately shown to be abortive, two achievements deserve to be recorded. In the first place, the committee produced in an appendix to its report data on the state of stage licensing in sundry continental jurisdictions – Baden, Bavaria, Belgium, Denmark, France, Hesse, Holland, Italy, Portugal, Saxony, Spain and Sweden.[49]

Second, it brought the debate on censorship right up to date by setting forth unemotionally and fairly the contesting points of view in the Britain of 1909. 'With rare exceptions', the committee were to pronounce,[50]

> all the dramatists of the day ask either for the abolition of the Censorship or for an appeal from its decisions to some other authority.... They urge that to suppress a play without trial or possibility of appeal is an excessive use of the executive power; that official control conventionalises the stage; that in practice the possible growth of a great drama, critical of contemporary life and of contemporary ideas is hampered.

The committee at this juncture would seem to have been influenced by the bishop of Southwark who in his evidence had indicated he favoured censorship, adding, however, that it could prove injurious if it hindered 'the treatment, quite free and bold, of what may be called moral questions'.[51]

On the other hand, as the committee were swift to point out, all the managers of the several theatres were enthusiastic supporters of censorship[52] – an attitude their predecessors had taken as well and which their successors later in the twentieth century were to assume too. Bram Stoker, the author of *Dracula*, and, from 1878, Henry Irving's manager at the Lyceum Theatre in London, for instance, emerged as a strident supporter of censorship.[53] At a hearing of the

---

48 See at p. xi of the *1909 report*. These recommendations are briefly set out by Dean: *Riot and great anger*, pp 96–7.
49 *1909 joint select committee report*, pp 374–5.   50 Ibid., p. vii.   51 Ibid.
52 *1909 joint select committee report*, pp vii–viii.   53 Ibid., p. 160.

committee on 13 August, he told of stage performances he had attended at St Louis in the United States. He did not soften his words.[54] These were 'unspeakably vile … shameful in every form of human lubricity and wrongness of every sort and kind, in gesture, in word, in looks, in action'.

Predictably enough, Sir William Gilbert, one of the seventy-one signatories, condemned the prohibition, out of regard for the country's Japanese allies, of performances of *The Mikado*, labelling it 'an unwarrantable and illegal act'. It constituted, he averred in his evidence,[55]

> an act of depredation to take my play, which was worth £10,000 to me, and without any communication with me, to prohibit its performance.

On the other hand, giving credit where credit was due, Gilbert, on mature reflection, felt that the Lord Chamberlain had been correct in the attitude he had adopted towards *The Happy Land*.[56]

In the end, the government shied away from backing any reform at all,[57] and pre-censorship accordingly was fated to remain *in situ* until abandonment in 1968. The outcome of the campaign of 1907 to 1909 to introduce change was to be admirably summarised in the following fashion by the authors of *Theatre censorship: from Walpole to Wilson*. 'The dramatists and their supporters in Parliament', Thomas, Carlton and Etienne write,[58]

> were all seen off by a combination of unfortunate political 'events' (all associated with the constitutional crisis of 1909–11); the obdurate attitude of a reactionary monarch; the refusal of the Prime Minister to challenge the monarch on a second constitutional matter when he was already locked in a constitutional battle for reform of the House of Lords; the implacable opposition of theatre managers to any suggestion that the censorship should be abolished; and finally the well-rehearsed arguments in favour of inertia that characterized Home Office policy.

In this passage, the reference to Asquith's reluctance to disabuse Edward VII that the matter had any connection at all to do with the royal prerogative alone stands in need of a modicum of elaboration.

Evidence given to the 1909 parliamentary committee shed light on a number of forgotten censorship controversies. Late on in the nineteenth century the manager of the Theatre Royal in Dublin, though under no compulsion to do so, asked the lord lieutenant if the theatre's plan to put on a production of Frank Marshall's *Robert Emmett* would be objectionable. The reply was to the effect that it would be, on the grounds that it could lead to a breach of the peace. The management thereupon drew in its horns and decided at that juncture not to produce the play.[59]

---

54 Ibid., p. 163.   55 Ibid., pp 190–1.   56 Ibid., p. 193.
57 Thomas, Carlton & Etienne, *Theatre censorship*, pp 101–7.   58 Ibid., pp 106–7.
59 *1909 joint select committee report*, p. 187 (evidence of Thomas Le Fanu, chief clerk at the Irish Office).

Stoker, in his evidence to the 1909 committee, recalled that somewhat earlier in England, in around 1879, the Lord Chamberlain had similarly given the thumbs down. His interference, Stoker explained, had had its origin in 'the recrudescence of the Fenian trouble in Ireland'.[60] Irving had wanted to put on the play. Stoker revealed that the then Lord Chamberlain had instructed his emissary, Sir Spencer Ponsonby Fanu, to apprise Irving of the Lord Chamberlain's views:

> It might be provocative of a good deal of public feeling and that it would be antagonistic to the public good.

The Lord Chamberlain in his message 'ventured to suggest that he [Irving] should not put the play forward'. According to Stoker, in his evidence, by way of reply to Robert Harcourt, the chairman at this meeting of the joint select committee on 13 August 1909, 'Mr Irving said that he was only too willing to do anything that was right in the matter; and accordingly he shelved the play entirely'. As Irving's manager at the Lyceum Theatre, Stoker, of course, was in a position to know all of this. He had earlier added, for good measure, the detail that Irving had actually commissioned the play itself from Marshall, promising an advance of £450.[61]

Stoker in his evidence went on to detail another episode:[62] the decision of the Lord Chamberlain to veto a production of Count de Bornier's play, *Mahomet*, not to be confused with Voltaire's drama with the identical title, which had caused difficulties for Thomas Sheridan at Smock Alley in Dublin in the middle of the eighteenth century.[63] The Lord Chamberlain's office told the salient theatre management why. 'Inasmuch', the joint select committee was enlightened as to the considerations that had weighed with the Lord Chamberlain,[64]

> as there were in Her Majesty's dominions so many millions of Mahometans, who would have been gravely offended by any representation of the Prophet put on the stage (it being part, we understood, of the Mahometan idea that any representation of the Prophet would not be proper; they considered it sacrilege even to paint it), the play could not be performed.

Stoker expanded on this a little himself. There was, he contended,[65]

> absolutely nothing in the play at all to give offence; it was a romantic play and a very fine play; but the representation of Mahomet at all on the stage under any form would have been offensive to Mahometans, and as there were so many millions of them it might have been a very grave public evil.

---

60 Ibid., p. 162.
61 £250 by July 1880, and the final £200 by July 1883. See further J.R. Stephens, *The profession of the playwright: British theatre, 1800–1900* (Cambridge, Cambridge UP, 1992), p. 68.
62 *1909 joint select committee report*, p. 163.   63 Above, p. 193.
64 *1909 joint select committee report*, p. 163.   65 Ibid.

That Irish theatre managements had throughout more than a passing interest in the decisions of the English Lord Chamberlain is well established, and for the reasons set out above.[66] There were linked issues too that would likewise have attracted their attention – problems thrown up by individual managers and performers who, for whatever reason, chose to disobey the rules.

The temptation put before producers of plays to depart from the text and accompanying stage directions as approved in Britain by the Lord Chamberlain (exercising the power that had its origins in the Act of 1737) was always there, and it is probable that such departures were more numerous than any that chanced to be recorded. A price naturally was to be exacted whenever individual departures were brought to light and prosecutions resulted.

Two such prosecutions made their way into the law reports, both in England, one from 1941, the other from 1953. The first concerned the performance of a play *To See Such Fun – An Act: Movies in the Making*, as performed in Northampton on 6 May 1941.[67] The complaint here averred that on three occasions the actors had incorporated in the production additions that had not been seen or approved by the Lord Chamberlain. Certain words and passages in the play had been accompanied by gestures of a suggestive character. The local magistrates had convicted, a decision that the King's Bench Division (Viscount Caldecote, LCJ and Humphreys and Asquith JJ) endorsed. The defendant, one Grade, had been called up into the forces a fortnight before the offending performance had taken place, but it was held that though he had given instructions for 'the script to be adhered to', he was answerable as the controlling partner in a partnership devoted to the production and presentation of theatrical and variety shows. In the King's Bench Division the judges made it clear that not all departures from a script approved by the Lord Chamberlain would require to be deemed 'unauthorised'.[68] A word or a 'gag' extraneous to the proceedings would not attract that label, nor would an actor's inventiveness where he forgot his lines.

The case from 1953 dealt with a production of Jean-Paul Sartre's *The Respectable Prostitute*, put on at the Pavilion Theatre in Liverpool.[69] The performance that took place on 2 November 1953, it was contended, ended in a manner that had not been approved by the Lord Chamberlain. The play should have concluded with an actress relaxing into the arms of a male actor. Instead, the actor carried the actress to a bed on the stage, laid her on it and then went through certain movements simulating sexual intercourse. Both Lovelace, the licensee of the theatre, and Patrick Lawrence, the principal actor who was also the producer, were prosecuted, and both were convicted. Lawrence did not appeal, a decision that Lord Goddard LCJ in the Queen's Bench Division insisted was clearly right.[70] Lovelace did appeal, relying largely, it would appear, on the same argument that had been employed by Grade in the Northampton case: the producer had been

66 Above, pp 215–17.   67 *Grade v. DPP* [1942] 2 All ER 118.   68 At 120.
69 *James Lovelace v. DPP* [1954] 1 WLR 1468.   70 At 1471–2.

told to stick to the script. It availed him not at all, the remaining members of the Queen's Bench Division, Lynskey and Ormerod JJ, agreeing with Lord Goddard that the conviction had to stand.

A number of other instances of departures from approved scripts, not considered of sufficient significance to be recorded in any law report, have been tracked down by the authors of *Theatre censorship: from Walpole to Wilson*.[71] All such cases, whether in the law reports of otherwise, could not fail to draw attention to a very obvious weakness in the system of regulation: the lack of staff in the Lord Chamberlain's office to check on the compliance of actual performances with what had been approved.

In Britain, the Lord Chamberlain's role as a censor of plays came under increasing scrutiny after the Second World War. There were difficulties with Frank Marcus' *The Killing of Sister George*, on account of its lesbian content, and with John Osborne's *A Patriot for me* – suicide by a blackmailed homosexual. In 1951, the then Lord Chamberlain, Lord Clarendon (1938–52), wrote to Lord Olivier at the National Theatre, reminding him of the precedents that forbade references to homosexuality and lesbianism. There was one notorious English prosecution, of a private club production of Edward Bond's *Saved* (1966) – not altogether a surprise, given the quantum of foul language and the scene in which a gang of youths torment a baby in its pram, roll it in its excrement and finally stone it to death.[72] In this case the defendants were found guilty and given a 12-month conditional discharge; there were costs of 50 guineas. And one rather less well-known prosecution, that of a strip-tease show, *Folies Strip-Tease*, put on at the Royal Pavilion, Blackpool in 1965. Here fines of £40 were imposed together with £35 costs.[73]

In 1956 the critic Kenneth Tynan ridiculed the banning by the Lord Chamberlain's office of three plays: Arthur Miller's *A View from the Bridge*, Robert Anderson's *Tea and Sympathy*, and Tennessee Williams' *Cat on a Hot Tin Roof*. Also criticised was the licence given to the performance of John Osborne's early play *Personal Enemy*, subject to the deletion of any reference to Walt Whitman's *Leaves of grass*.

Parliamentary questions kept the censorship issue firmly in the public eye, and there was to be a five-hour debate in the House of Lords in February 1966. Lord Birkett made, perhaps, the most original of the contributions to that debate.[74] He started with a quotation from Henry James which made it very clear the stance he, Birkett, proposed to take. 'The Censor's arbitrary rights', James had declared,[75]

> must be a deterrent to men of any intellectual independence and self-respect. We rub our eyes, we writers accustomed to freedom in other walks, to think that this cause has still to be argued in England.

71 Thomas, Carlton & Etienne, *Theatre censorship*, pp 120–1.
72 John Johnston, *The Lord Chamberlain's blue pencil* (London, Hodder & Stoughton, 1990), p. 214.
73 Ibid., p. 185.   74 *Hansard, 5 (lords)*, cclxxii, col. 1202.   75 Ibid.

An amount of anecdotal and other evidence is then introduced. Having asserted that during the madness of George III Shakespeare's *King Lear* had been deliberately forbidden the stage,[76] Birkett goes on to recall the circumstances of the first legal performance given in London in the inter-war years of Richard Strauss' opera *Salome*, with a German libretto based on Oscar Wilde, and conducted by Sir Thomas Beecham. The Lord Chamberlain's office insisted on a number of cuts and new lines for the singers. Birkett's account continues:[77]

> Under stress and excitement of every first night – and no doubt under the sway of the music – very early on in the performance the singers forgot all the alterations they had been forced to learn, and reverted immediately to the original text and continued so until the end of the opera.

An official from the Lord Chamberlain's office had been in attendance, had spotted nothing amiss, and told Birkett how enjoyable the evening had been. And Birkett concluded by reiterating the views expressed by Lord Chesterfield in opposition to the licensing provision in the original Act of 1737.[78] 'Do not let us', Chesterfield had averred,[79]

> subject them [authors] to the arbitrary will and pleasure of any one man. A power lodged in the hands of one single man, to judge and determine, without any limitation, without any control or appeal, is a sort of power unknown to our laws, inconsistent with our constitution. It is a higher, a more absolute power than we trust to the King himself; and, therefore, I must think, we ought not to vest any such power in His Majesty's Lord Chamberlain.

The outcome of this debate in 1966 was the establishment of a Joint Committee on Censorship of the Theatre which, in a report of 1967 of some 200 pages,[80] among the various options they considered, including continuation of the work of the Lord Chamberlain, finally plumped for total abolition. A bill to implement the Joint Committee's recommendation was introduced early in 1968, and received the royal assent on 26 July. The Theatres Act 1968 is described as an Act to abolish censorship of the theatre and to amend the law in respect of theatres and theatrical performances.[81] It repeals the Act of 1843 (which had continued the regime introduced in 1737), and ends the powers of the Lord Chamberlain by, or on behalf of, the sovereign by virtue of the royal prerogative. The licensing of all theatres is

76 Ibid.   77 *Hansard, 5 (lords)*, cclxxii, col. 1203.   78 Ibid., at col. 1208.
79 *A collection of the parliamentary debates England from the year MCDLXVII to the present time* (s. l., 1740), vol. 15, p. 302 at pp 311–12; *Cobbett's Parliamentary history of England from the earliest period to the year 1803*, x (London, 1737–9), col. 328 at col. 335.
80 *Report of the Joint Committee on Censorship of the Theatre with Proceedings, Evidence, Appendices and Index*, HC 1966–7, x, 191.
81 1968, c. 54.

transferred to the respective local authority. Plays deemed obscene remain liable to be prosecuted, and it is also confirmed as a criminal offence the presentation of any play with intent to – or that was likely to – stir up racial hatred or to provoke a breach of the peace.

Of the many books published in Britain dealing with its experience of theatre censorship, one of the most recent to appear – a joint effort by Thomas, Carlton and Etienne – focuses very largely on the changing fortunes of the debate on censorship itself.[82] It explores in considerable detail the work of the various inquiries and the role of parliament itself up to and including the movement that brought about the Theatres Act of 1968. It can be read with great profit.

It would be disingenuous to claim that controversy over sexual themes introduced on stage, such as those alleged to have been to the fore in *The Rose Tattoo* prosecution of 1957, is exclusively modern. The shared views of the Revd Bennett and J.W. Calcraft from the early nineteenth century have already been set down.[83] Hitchcock, the author of an absorbing account of the Irish stage published late in the eighteenth century, records an incident that took place on St Stephen's Day 1701, when, during a production of a play by Thomas Shadwell (1640–92), *The Libertine* (1675), the galleries in the Smock Alley theatre collapsed.[84] No one was killed, but several members of the audience were injured. Hitchcock described the play itself as 'extremely loose and improper for representation', and repeats what could well have been the folklore that enveloped the accident, that the injuries sustained in the audience were a proper penalty for going to see that particular play. The rumour-mongers of the period enjoyed something of a field-day, as Hitchcock hastened to explain. 'Nay, so far did their extravagance carry them', he writes, apropos of this accident in Smock Alley,[85]

> that it was even asserted by some, that the candles burnt blue, and went out, that two or three times a dancer extraordinary, when nobody knew, was seen, that he had a cloven foot, etc. etc., with many other ridiculous stories.

A sequel of sorts was played out when a monument to Shadwell was erected in Poet's Corner in Westminster Abbey. The inscription had to be replaced when objection was successfully registered to the encomium of Shadwell's dramatic works that appeared in the original inscription.[86]

A further incident at Smock Alley in 1712 introduces us to what for most of the time was the focus of concern for would-be-censors – what was deemed politically objectionable. This incident, as things turned out, sparked off one major row. It came at a time of heightened tension between whigs and tories in the politics of

82 David Thomas, David Carlton and Anne Etienne, *Theatre censorship: from Walpole to Wilson* (Oxford, Oxford UP, 2007).
83 Above ch. 8.
84 Robert Hitchcock, *An historical view of the Irish stage*, 2 vols (Dublin, 1768–94), i, 33–4.
85 Ibid., i, 34.   86 See entry on Shadwell in the *Oxford DNB* (xlix, 922).

Ireland no less than in those of England. In 1711 Joseph Ashbury planned to put on a production of the *Tamerlane* (1701) of Nicholas Rowe, the future poet laureate (1674–1718).[87] Approaches were made to him to allow the performance to be preceded by the recitation of a politically lively prologue by the well-known English whig, Dr Samuel Garth. Anticipating trouble, Ashbury approached the two lords justices at the time, Sir Constantine Phipps, the unpopular tory lord chancellor and Lieutenant-general Richard Ingoldsby, the commander-in-chief in Ireland, for their views. Together, they said the prologue was not to be delivered, a message Ashbury then relayed to those who had made the original request.

The approach to the lords justices was renewed the following year, but they again said 'no'. On this occasion, however, as a performance of *Tamerlane* was about to start on 4 November 1712, one Dudley Moore marched on to the stage and delivered Garth's supposedly incendiary harangue. This speech, trumpeting the virtues of King William, included the following lines (as previously recalled – see p. 187):

> His generous Soul for Freedom was Design'd.
> To pull down Tyrants, and unslave mankind;
> He broke the Chains of Europe; and when we
> Were doom'd for Slaves, he came and set us free.

'The effect was, quite literally, to bring the house down'.[88] Moore and his allies were arrested and charged with riotous and seditious practices. A whig majority on the grand jury refused to return a true bill, but Ralph Gore, the lord mayor, who was the foreman, wrote the opposite on the indictment – 'billa vera' – and despite the protests, the court held the return valid and sanctioned a trial. When the case eventually came to trial in February 1712/3, the court did, however, quash the indictment. Ashbury, as a witness to what had transpired, gave evidence that was hostile to what in fact had become a riot in the theatre. Phipps used the occasion to harangue the mayor, aldermen and magistrates that their duty as office-holders was 'to exert themselves in defence of Her Majesty's authority'. Turning to the prologue itself, the lord chancellor pointed out, as if this needed to be done, that it had been spoken in defiance of the government's edict, had sounded 'an alarm', and invited 'Her Majesty's subjects to make war against those [the French], with which Her Majesty thinks fit to make peace.'

Another (for Ireland) early instance of political pressure being applied to abort the projected run of a new play occurred in 1747, and was recalled by Benjamin Victor.[89] Smock Alley accepted for production 'an allegorical piece' by Henry

---

87 The account follows that given by Clark, *Early Irish stage*, pp 128–33. See, too, La Tourette Stockwell, *Dublin theatres and theatre customs* (Kingsport, TX, Kingsport Press, 1938), p. 49; John T. Gilbert, *A history of the city of Dublin*, 3 vols (Dublin, Gill & Macmillan, 1978), ii, 71–2; Morash, *History of Irish theatre*, p. 30.

88 Morash, *History of Irish stage*, p. 30.

89 Victor, *The history of theatres of London and Dublin from the year 1730 to the present time*, 2 vols (London, T. Davies, 1761), i, 138–40.

Brooke (*c*.1703–83), the author of *Gustavus Vasa: The Deliverer of His Country* (1739). *Gustavus Vasa* had earned the distinction of the first play to be prohibited in England after the introduction of prior censorship in 1737.[90] This had not stopped it being put on at Smock Alley in Dublin by Thomas Sheridan in December 1744, though this was a revised version and retitled *The Patriot*.[91] There had been one earlier performance in Dublin of a play vetoed in London – Mallet's *Mustapha* which had been performed in May 1739.[92]

The new play offered to Sheridan by Henry Brooke was entitled *Jack the Giant Queller*. The decision to press ahead with this latest offering from Brooke did not meet with Victor's approval, but Sheridan was enthusiastic and Victor said nothing. 'This strange Piece', Victor recalled later,[93]

> was got up with no little Trouble, was well performed, and with great Applause; but as there were two or three satirical Songs, against bad Governors, Lord-Mayors, and Aldermen, some weak Person belonging to the Government, happening to be present the first Night, went off to the Lords Justices with his Complaints against it.

'The next morning', we are told, 'the Master of the Revels sent his Prohibition to the Manager', and so it ended, at one performance. W.H. Grattan Flood, in his rather different interpretation of events, simply records that, in his view, certain of the songs featured in *Jack the Giant Queller* were deemed to be Jacobite in sentiment.[94] Whatever the explanation for the ban, the lords justices – Archbishop Stone, Lord Newport and Henry Boyle – had plainly been busy.

This, however, was not the end of the story, for a few years later, with a new lord lieutenant installed at the Castle, the duke of Devonshire,[95] someone had the bright idea that *Jack the Giant Queller* could profitably be revived. Smock Alley decided to secure the government's approval, and Brooke was thus advised to employ his contacts at Dublin Castle to see what might be done. Devonshire adopted a markedly different stance, indicating that he had no manner of objection at all to *Jack the Giant Queller* being performed.[96] Devonshire, according to Victor, 'had judgment to distinguish universal from personal satire, and was above mean

---

90 Victor, *Annual register of all the tragedies, etc.* (London, T. Davies, 1771), pp 116–17, Thomas, Carlton & Etienne, *Theatre censorship*, p. 45.

91 Greene & Clark, *The Dublin stage, 1720–1745*, p. 83; Christopher Morash, 'Theatre and print, 1550–1800' in Raymond Gillespie and Andrew Hadfield (eds), *The Irish book in English* (The Oxford History of the Irish Book, iii) (Oxford, Oxford UP, 2006), 319 at 331.

92 Greene & Clark, *The Dublin stage, 1720–1745*, p. 83.

93 Victor, *History of theatres of London and Dublin*, i, 140.

94 *A history of Irish music* (Dublin, Browne & Nolan, 1905), p. 256. For further discussion see Burke, *Riotous performances*, p. 196.

95 Devonshire was appointed lord lieutenant in 1755. The earl of Harrington held the post from 1746 to 1750.

96 Victor, *History of theatres of London and Dublin*, i, 200–1.

suspicions'.[97] And so the play was resurrected. W.J. Lawrence, in a newspaper article on theatre censorship in Ireland, written in 1909, did not overlook the significance of the earlier ban of 1747 on the play.[98] *Jack the Giant Queller* was 'the only new piece whose performance has been prohibited on the Irish stage' before the twentieth century. Sadly, as K.J. Donovan has pointed out, in revisiting the entire episode,[99] we cannot be entirely certain, despite the clues that Victor left for us, as to what exactly about the play had given offence. While the text of the lyrics of the songs in the play was soon published, the full text of the play, giving, for example, stage directions, only saw the light of day very much later, in 1778, and can scarcely be regarded as reliable.[100] These controversies, now all but forgotten, have been recently revisited by Michael Brown, who goes on to examine more generally Brooke's aspirations as a playwright.[101]

James Joyce's unfinished novel, *Stephen Hero*, with its focus on Stephen Daedalus' experience of college life – in the Jesuit-run University College in Dublin around 1900 – has things to say about censorship in the arts. Stephen is shown preparing a paper on aesthetics for delivery at a meeting of the Literary and Historical Society. Convention – if not something more formal – provided for the vetting of all papers about to be read before the Society by the College President, Revd Dr Dillon, a portrayal based on the Revd Dr William Delany, the actual rector of University College at the time.[102] Stephen was flabbergasted to discover that Dr Dillon proposed to veto the paper's delivery. The scene is thereby prepared for a key episode in *Stephen Hero* where the President and the student set out their respective stalls. Dillon does not diminish the tone of his words when he finds Stephen planning to discuss the contribution to art of Ibsen and Maeterlinck. 'I am surprised', he tells Stephen,[103]

> that any student of this College could find anything to admire in such writers, writers who usurp the name of poet, who openly profess their atheistic doctrines and fill the minds of their readers with all the garbage of modern society. That is not art.

Stephen naturally disagrees, and the upshot is that, without Dillon altering his general stance, the prohibition on the delivery of the papers is in fact withdrawn.

The real-life threat of the censorship of Joyce's actual paper on 'Drama and life', on which the episode in *Stephen Hero* had been based, was to be recalled in a

97 Ibid., i, 201.   98 'Irish censorhip: an account of its history', *Freeman's Journal*, 24 Aug. 1909.
99 '*Jack the Giant Queller*: political theatre in Ascendancy Dublin', *Eire/Ireland*, 30:2 (Summer 1995), 70.   100 Ibid., 79–80.
101 Michael Brown, 'Farmer and fool: Henry Brooke and the late Irish Enlightenment' in idem and S.P. Donlan (eds), *The laws and other legalities of Ireland, 1689–1850* (Farnham, Surrey, Ashgate, 2011), 301 at 307–11.
102 T.J. Morrissey, *Towards a National University: William Delany SJ (1835–1924) – an era of initiative in Irish education* (Dublin, Wolfhound Press, 1983), p. 163.
103 James Joyce, *Stephen Hero* (London, Paladin ed., 1991), p. 95.

volume devoted to the history of University College Dublin's Literary and Historical Society.[104] The paper, Hackett there records,[105] was eventually delivered on 20 January 1900, just a few months before Joyce was defeated (15–9) by Hugh Kennedy, the future chief justice of the Irish Free State, in the election for the post of auditor of the Literary and Historical Society.[106] Hackett's treatment of the affair is not without interest. 'The account', he was to write,[107]

> given in *Stephen Hero* of the interview with the President, when walking in the handball alley, may be as biased as the reports of Dr Johnson of the debates in the House of Commons which ensured that the Whig dogs had not the best of the argument, yet it reads as a reasonable presentation of what took place.

The previous May, as it happens, Joyce had conspicuously declined to add his signature to the protest of 'Dublin Catholic students of the Royal University' against W.B. Yeats' *The Countess Cathleen* for its 'dispassionate art', which critics claimed had offered 'as a type of our people a loathsome brood of apostates'.[108]

The skirmish over *The Countess Cathleen* in the spring of 1899 is worth revisiting, for the controversy served as a curtain-raiser for the much more serious affair of the riots a few years later over *The Playboy of the Western World*, John Millington Synge's major contribution to European drama. Yeats stated that his play was 'an attempt to mingle personal thought and feeling with the beliefs and customs of Christian Ireland'. An earlier version entitled *The Countess Kathleen* had been licensed for public performance in England by the Lord Chamberlain there in May 1892, when nothing was found objectionable, though later, the Irish would say of the reworked text that it was blasphemous. A short run of *The Countess Cathleen*, under the aegis of the new Irish Literary Theatre, commenced in the Antient Concert Rooms on today's Pearse Street on 8 May 1899. Two days later, relying on extracts from a version of the play furnished by one of Yeats' adversaries, Cardinal Michael Logue, in a letter to the press, cautioned Catholics against the play as being 'morally and theologically dangerous'. The same day, by coincidence, a second letter again criticising the play appeared in a different newspaper over the signatures of Catholic students of the Royal University in attendance at the old UCD.[109] This was the letter Joyce declined to sign; another conspicuous absence was the signature of Arthur Clery, later in the 1910s to become one of the law professors at the new UCD. Patrick Pearse joined the fray

104 Jones Meenan (ed.), *Centenary history of the Literary and Historical Society of University College Dublin, 1855–1955* (Dublin, A. & A. Farmer, 2005).
105 Felix Hackett in Meenan, ed., *Centenary history of the L. & H.*, p. 50.
106 Meenan (ed.), *Centenary history of the L. & H.*, p. 264.   107 Ibid., p. 50.
108 Meenan (ed.), *Centenary history of L. & H.*, pp 47–8.
109 C.P. Curran, *Under the receding wave* (Dublin, Gill & Macmillan, 1970), ch. 6: 'University College and the Countess Cathleen'; Dean, *Riot and great anger*, pp 48–59.

in the pages of *An Claidheamh Soluis* ten days later, on 20 May.[110] Pearse argued that the play was not really Irish at all, and he castigated the Irish Literary Theatre as 'more dangerous than Trinity College: let us strangle it at birth'. What caused offence was the preparedness of the peasants featured in the drama to sell their souls, and a stage direction, seemingly countermanded by Yeats in the end, sanctioning the kicking on stage of the shrine of Our Lady. Accompanying comment in *An Claidheamh Soluis*[111] heaped praise on 'the manful protest of Catholic University students … clean, sane, cultured young Irish men'.

To return to the fictional dialogue in *Stephen Hero* between Stephen and Dr Dillon, the mention in that exchange of Henrik Ibsen is not without interest, very obviously from the standpoint of today. Ibsen's concern as a dramatist in exploring the phenomenon of the dysfunctional family – something that today is accepted as an eminently legitimate focus of the would-be artist (consider, for instance, the aplomb with which the German cineáste, Michael Haneke, brought the problem to the screen in 2009 in his *Das Weisse Band* (*The White Ribbon*)) – won him few enough plaudits at the time. *A Doll's House* (1879) and *Ghosts* (1881) were to be savaged by those critics who belonged to the Revd President Dillon's school of thought. The *Daily Telegraph*, in its review of *Ghosts* that appeared in the spring of 1891, could not have made plainer its distaste. The play, its review ran,[112] was 'an open drain, … a loathsome sore unbandaged, … a dirty act done publicly, … a lazar-house with all its doors and windows open'. Dion Boucicault, too, it deserves to be noted, refused to join the bandwagon that spoke highly of Ibsen, the dramatist. 'Constance's speeches in *King John*', Boucicault was to declare,[113]

> have no rival in drama for passionate rhetoric. Yet we are told this is all wrong, false, unnatural, and we should go to Mr Ibsen to learn in his domestic drama *The Doll's House* how an ill-used woman feels, behaves and expresses herself, according to the ethics of the modern apostle by whom the drama is to be led to salvation.

This last sounds like a veiled allusion to George Bernard Shaw.[114]

Remarks of the German Kaiser, Wilhelm II, around the time in which Joyce set his *Stephen Hero*, made it plain as to the side he would have supported in the exchange between Stephen and the Revd President Dillon. Speaking in 1901, the Kaiser told his painters in no uncertain terms what he expected from them. 'When art … as often happens today', he began,[115]

110 *An Claidheamh Soluis*, 20 May 1899, p. 55.
111 Ibid., p. 153.   112 14 March 1891. Quoted, Thomas, Carlton & Etienne, *Theatre censorship*, p. 70.   113 Quoted, Fawkes, *Boucicault*, pp 233–4.
114 For an overview of theatre censorship as actually exercised in Britain between 1800 and 1900, see conveniently J.R. Stephens, *The profession of the playwright: British theatre 1800–1900* (Cambridge, Cambridge UP, 1992), pp 181–3.
115 Quoted, Giles MacDonogh, *Berlin: a portrait of its history, politics, architecture, and society* (New York, St Martin's Press, 1997), p. 375.

shows us only misery, and shows it to us even uglier then misery is anyway, then art commits a sin against the German people. The supreme task of our cultural effort is to foster our ideals. If we are and want to remain a model for other nations, our entire people must share in this effort, and if culture is to fulfil its task completely it must reach down to the lowest levels of the population. That can be done only if art holds out its hand to raise the people up, instead of descending into the gutter.

The fate of theatrical productions under the Third Reich introduces us to another distinct chapter in the story of censorship, and this we will briefly consider in the proper chronological sequence.

It is possibly no coincidence that, in the very year of 1900, in a sign of the times or possibly prophetic of anxieties destined to be expressed more forcefully in the future, the Roman Catholic archbishop of Dublin, the Most Revd William Walsh, following in the wake of Cardinal Logue from the year before,[116] protested against the sort of play then being put on in Dublin.[117] The author of an unsigned article in the *New Irish Jurist and Local Government Review* sprang to the archbishop's defence. In the light of 'irresponsibility as to the character of the plays produced', our author proclaimed,

> and the chaos of the authorities, it must be conceded that reform is demanded. In Ireland there is no examiner of plays and practically no check upon the matter produced.

'In such a state of affairs', he went on,

> it is a little surprising we have not been experimented upon more than we have been, with first productions, but possibly that is due to the ignorance of managers and playwrights.

'But it is more than surprising', he concluded,

> – it is amazing – that with all these facts before the Select Committee of 1892, they should have put this sentence in their report: 'We have no reason to think that the public or the managers of places of amusement in Ireland are dissatisfied with the present state of the law upon the subject'.

One Irish witness appeared before the select committee in 1892 – Michael Gunn. Gunn at the time held two patents, one for the Gaiety and one for the Leinster Hall, the large concert hall occupying the site of the Theatre Royal in Hawkins Street which had been burnt down in 1880.[118] Gunn's views, expressed at

116 Above, p. 231. 117 (1900) 1 *NIJ & LGR* 17.
118 *Report of the select committee on theatres and places of entertainment, 1892*, HC xvii, i, at 232.

a later date, on the prospect of the revocation of a theatre patent as a weapon in the censor's armoury, we have already encountered.[119] The 1892 select committee seems to have been particularly preoccupied by the growth of music-halls and by the fire hazards too often presented by the actual state of existing theatres, especially in London. On 11 May 1892, the day Mr Gunn gave his evidence, members of the select committee pressed him on the circumstance that the Lord Chamberlain's writ did not extend to Ireland. Gunn, in his response, indicated that he did not believe theatre managers in Ireland such as himself would raise any objection to a plan to extend the Lord Chamberlain's jurisdiction. But it was his conviction that the matter was hardly urgent. 'Conditions of a stringent character', he argued,[120]

> are inserted in the patents as to no plays being produced which shall be contrary to good morals or manners, indecent, subversive of law and order, or inimical to religion or the good of the country.

He concluded:[121]

> The fact of there being no obligation to have plays licensed in Ireland has never, in my experience, given rise to any difficulty, no plays having ever been produced which have offended public taste.

Gunn's response to a further question undoubtedly furnished the grounds for the tone adopted by the select committee in denying the need for remedial legal action,[122] in the statement attacked by the author of the article in the *New Irish Jurist* in 1900.[123] 'The managers of places of public amusement in Dublin, as well as the public', Gunn assured the members of the select committee,[124]

> are quite satisfied with the existing state of the law and power of the authority (Lord Lieutenant and Privy Council) to enforce every requirement for the public safety and comfort, and the propriety of the performances.

Gunn's expenses for his three day absence from Dublin (which he was allowed) came to £8 3s. 6d., of which his travel costs were £5 0s. 6d.[125] There were to be critics in Dublin who would later fulminate that this was not money that had been well spent.

The decision by the new Abbey Theatre to put on Shaw's play, *The Shewing-Up of Blanco Posnet*, during Dublin's Horse Show week in August 1909 created an actual problem both for the powers that be and for the Abbey management. It constituted the first major problem over theatre censorship to be agitated in

---

119 Above, pp 216–17.   120 *1892 select committee report on theatres*, p. 233.   121 Ibid.
122 Ibid., p. iv.   123 Above, p. 233.   124 *1892 select committee report on theatres*, p. 234.
125 Ibid., p. xviii.

twentieth-century Ireland. The controversy itself has been regularly revisited.[126] The plot – such as it was – need not concern us overmuch. It is enough to know that Blanco was a horse-thief who in confessing mood reveals that he had given up the horse he had stolen to save a sick child. The tale of a sinner wrongfooted as it were by Christian charity was one long known. The difficulty was that Shaw had Blanco call God 'a sly one', and in England at any rate that could not pass muster. In England the Lord Chamberlain banned *The Shewing-Up of Blanco Posnet* on the ground of blasphemy. Dublin Castle was distinctly unhappy when the Abbey announced its intention of putting on the play. There was a threat to withdraw the Abbey's patent of 1904. 'A game of bluff and brinkmanship followed'. Yeats and Lady Gregory, in a public statement issued on 22 August, declared that 'if our patent is in danger, it is because the decisions of the English Censor are being brought into Ireland'. They both stood firm. Writing later, Lady Gregory explained that they had given their word; and that if they did not keep it, they would never be trusted again.[127] The stance paid off, as Morash was to report:[128]

> In the end, the Castle blinked, hoping for objections from the churches once the play was staged; none were forthcoming, and *Blanco Posnet* played to large (and well-heeled) audiences, most of whom enjoyed it, but left a bit mystified as to the source of the controversy. In the end, it was an almost perfect public relations victory for the Abbey.

In the short term, relations with Dublin Castle would not seem to have suffered; in 1911, as we have seen,[129] the Abbey's patent was renewed for the more customary twenty-one-year period.

There might well have been another major tussle between Dublin Castle and the Abbey Theatre over another play by Shaw seven or so years after *Blanco Posnet*. Late in 1916 management of the Abbey was taken over by J. Augustus Keogh, who, as a long-time admirer of Shaw's work, decided to put on a succession of his plays. Faced with the intelligence that among Keogh's plans was a production of *O'Flaherty V.C.*, the Castle sensed enough was enough, and protested. The play, as Morash explains it,[130] is 'a ... parable about an Irish soldier, home on leave, who finds his beloved mother more frightening than shellfire in the trenches.' In short, it was 'subversive of ideals of family and home – dear to both Irish republicans and supporters of the British war effort', so much so in fact, Morash contends, that the Abbey would have found few friends to support any decision to put on the play. In the end, the Abbey caved in, and *O'Flaherty V.C.* was not performed.[131] Along with the furore over *Blanco Posnet*, *O'Flaherty V.C.* constituted another chapter in

126 See, e.g., Morash, *History of Irish theatre*, pp 143–4.
127 Augusta Gregory, *Our Irish theatre: a chapter of autobiography* (London and New York, G.P. Putnam's sons, 1913).
128 Morash, *History of Irish theatre*, p. 145.   129 Above, p. 119.
130 Morash, *History of Irish theatre*, p. 158.   131 Ibid.

Shaw's exhaustive and exhausting battle with the censor. In England Shaw first sought a licence from the Lord Chamberlain for *Mrs Warren's Profession* in 1898. After six further unsuccessful applications, a licence was finally granted in 1924 by the then Lord Chamberlain, the earl of Cromer.[132] In 1933 Shaw was also to fall foul of the Irish book censors – the Censorship Board – over his novel, *The Adventures of the Black Girl in her Search for God*.[133] Shaw was still to the fore in campaigns against theatre censorship in Britain in the late 1940s.[134]

When the Gate Theatre, under Edwards and MacLíammóir, announced their intention to mount a production of Oscar Wilde's *Salome* in December 1928, a possible repeat of the furore over *Blanco Posnet* was certainly in prospect. *Salome* had been refused a licence by the Lord Chamberlain in 1892 in view of the ban on representation of biblical subjects. And controversy surrounding Wilde's play had continued: a private performance given in 1918 had occasioned a parliamentary question addressed to the Home Secretary, Sir George Cave, exception having been taken not only to the character of the play, but also to 'the scanty costumes of the actresses'.[135] Any Irish production would emphasise once more the independence of the Irish theatre.[136] Though there were certainly enough critics and writers to express opposition to the plan – and Father Devane, whose article on censorship in *Studies* in 1927[137] indicates he would have had to be counted among their number – in the end there were no difficulties placed in the way of the production.

The year before – 1926 – the rioting that greeted O'Casey's *The Plough and the Stars* had been preceded by controversy among the directors of the Abbey over whether the play should be put on at all, or at least without major changes.[138] The opposition was led by George O'Brien who became the first government-appointed director in the wake of the decision by the government to assist the Abbey financially. As is now quite clear, the Abbey was obliged to pay a price for its resolve to seek, and to accept, a State subsidy: it lost control over decisions on the choice of plays to be accepted for performance. Transporting ourselves a little into the future, for the Abbey to fly in the face of objections relayed by the new post-1932 government-appointed director, Richard Hayes, could conceivably lead to a failure to secure renewal of the theatre's patent. Critically, with talk of a substantial injection of government money to effect reconstruction of the theatre itself in the late 1930s, keeping the government 'on side' as regards the Abbey's schedule of

132 Johnston, *The Lord Chamberlain's blue pencil*, pp 77–8, 90.
133 Brad Kent, 'The banning of George Bernard Shaw's *The Adventures of the Black Girl in her Search for God* and the decline of the Irish Academy of Letters', *Irish University Review*, 38 (2008), 274.
134 Thomas, Carlton & Etienne, *Theatre censorship*, p. 142.
135 *Hansard, 5 (commons)*, cviii, cols. 879–80 (16 July 1918); Thomas, Carlton & Etienne, *Theatre censorship*, p. 117. For the London premiere of Strauss' opera based on Wilde's play, see above, p. 226.
136 Morash, *History of Irish theatre*, pp 183–6.
137 R.S. Devane, 'Suggested tariff on imported newspapers and magazines', *Studies*, 16 (1927), 552.
138 Above, ch. 13.

new plays became, understandably perhaps, a regular obsession. Arrington, unlike certain other critics who also identified the problem and the risks,[139] is in no doubt that censorship at the Abbey did in fact occur, such instances of censorship being 'inextricably tied to the financial relationship between the theatre and the state'.[140] Arrington's inventory lists changes made to Cormac O'Daly's *The Silver Jubilee* in 1936; the suppression of W.B. Yeats' own *The Herne's Egg* also in 1936; and the cancellation of the plan to put on Paul Vincent Carroll's *The White Steed* in 1938. The major source consulted by Arrington for purposes of her critique was to be the Abbey Theatre Minute Book, and her conclusions accordingly can scarcely be faulted.

The Gate Theatre, if it escaped the dread hand of government over *Salome*, fell foul of the authorities with their production of Lennox Robinson's *Roly Poly*, put on during the Second World War in November 1941.[141] Robinson's adaptation of Maupassant's *Boule de Suif* offended the German and Vichy French legations in Dublin, and brought protests to the Department of External Affairs that the portrayal of French and German nationals in the drama was unacceptable and violated Ireland's official stance of neutrality. Edwards and MacLíammóir were advised of the government's thinking, and the threat of the cancellation of the Gate's patent and the arrival of the police at the theatre forced the two men to abort the performance planned for a second night, not long before the lights were due to dim and the performance to commence.[142]

We earlier quoted remarks of the Kaiser on the creative artist uttered by him in 1901.[143] Turning to the plight of the theatre in Germany under the Third Reich we can, I believe, usefully compare the Kaiser's words with the actions and remarks of Joseph Goebbels, the Nazi Propaganda and Public Information Minister in the spring of 1933. These were recounted at the time by Leo McCauley, the Irish Chargé d'affaires in Berlin.[144] The Propaganda Ministry, McCauley reported, had arranged for a play called *Schlageter* (dealing with the execution by the French of a German patriot of that name in the Saar territory) to be performed not only at the State Theatre in Berlin, but in theatres all over Germany, so that an enormous number of persons would be subjected to the influence of this particular piece. Nor was this all, apropos matters theatrical. In a speech on 8 May, McCauley continued,[145]

139 Peter Martin, *Censorship in the two Irelands, 1922–1939* (Dublin, Irish Academic Press, 2006); Dean, *Riot and great anger*.
140 Lauren Arrington, '"I sing what was lost and dread what was won": W.B. Yeats and the legacy of censorship', *Irish University Review*, 38 (2008), 222.
141 Dean, *Riot and great anger*, pp 138–45.
142 See, too, Michael J. O'Neill, *Lennox Robinson* (New York, Twayne Publishers, Inc., 1964).
143 Above, pp 232–3.
144 McCauley to Joseph Walshe, 11 May 1933: *Documents on Irish foreign policy, vol. 4, 1932–1936*, ed. Catriona Crowe, Ronan Fanning, Michael Kennedy, Dermot Keogh and Eunan O'Halpin (Dublin, Royal Irish Academy, 2002), pp 248–9.
145 Ibid.

at a gathering of persons interested in the theatre, Herr Goebbels said that the whole theatre system must be re-organised, so as to breathe the spirit of nationality and be brought closer to the life of the people. He denied the proposition that art was international.

How things had changed following the rise to power of the Nazis is also made pellucidly clear in Klaus Mann's novel *Mephisto*.[146] Hendrik Höfgen is advised thus in no uncertain terms by Caesar von Muck, the director of the State Theatre in Berlin, following Höfgen's return from Paris. 'I don't know', von Muck begins,[147]

> whether you will manage to settle down among us again, Herr Höfgen. You will find that a very different spirit now reigns in this house from the one to which you have been accustomed. The days of cultural Bolshevism are over … You will no longer have an opportunity of appearing in the works of your friend Marder or in the French farces you like so much. We now produce neither Semitic nor Gallic works, but German art.

Höfgen, a thinly veiled portrayal of the real-life Gustaf Gründgens (Mann's brother-in-law), is to benefit from the patronage of Field Marshal Hermann Göring and succeeds von Muck as director of the State Theatre in Berlin. There was no question, Höfgen swiftly learns, of putting on plays that could be suspected of tendencies the regime would find objectionable.[148] Classics such as Schiller's *Don Carlos* or *The Brigands* were 'out', a development which, when allied to the additional disapproval of 'the most demoralizing products of cultural Bolshevism', made things for him as director very difficult.[149] Not that our once flamboyant champion of Communism, who had made his own 'pact' with the new regime, showed himself unduly troubled.

Opera, too, could present problems. It is very likely indeed that the Gestapo were none too pleased when prolonged applause greeted Franz Völker in the role of Florestan in Beethoven's *Fidelio* for his singing of the lines

> Wahrheit wagt ich kühn zo sagen, und die ketten sind mein Lohn.
>
> (I bravely dared to tell the truth and was rewarded with chains.)[150]

On another occasion, equal suspicions were aroused during a performance of Umberto Giordano's *Andrea Chenier*, when another baritone, Willi Domgraf-Fassbaender, sang the lines:

---

146 Klaus Mann, *Mephisto*, transl. Robin Smyth (Harmondsworth, Middlesex, Penguin Books, 1995).
147 At p. 167, in ch. 7, 'The pact with the Devil'.
148 At p. 227, in ch. 10, 'The threat'.   149 Ibid.
150 Giles MacDonogh, *Berlin*, p. 130.

Nicht hier ist das Vaterland, wo man die Dichter mordet.

(This isn't my country, where writers are murdered.)[151]

Domgraf-Fassbaender was apparently interrogated by the Gestapo for seven hours.

The liberal sentiments expressed in the libretti of a good many operas continue to present a challenge of sorts to any would-be authoritarian regime.

The notorious prosecution of Alan Simpson over the presentation of Tennessee Williams' play, *The Rose Tattoo*, during the Dublin Theatre Festival in 1959 was set to produce as much drama off stage as on it. That the play had been thought in certain quarters as offensive[152] – came as something of a shock. A review in the *Irish Press* had been enthusiastic. 'Once again', its reviewer wrote, 'the Pike must be highly recommended for giving Dublin a remarkable piece of theatre'.[153] Despite this, Simpson was arrested and faced prosecution 'for showing for gain an indecent and profane performance'. The charge related to performances of the play put on at the Pike Theatre in Herbert Lane in Dublin on three nights in May 1957 – the 13th, the 14th and the 21st. From Simpson's own account of the sequence of events, it would appear that, the threat of prosecution having been conveyed to him, if he undertook to cease performances of the play for the few remaining nights of the projected 'run', no prosecution would in fact ensue.[154] Simpson thus was faced with a dilemma. If he said 'yes', this involved a loss of face. If he had said 'no', as he later ruminated, the prospect of a trial and conviction was equally unattractive; as a serving officer in the Defence Forces, he risked dismissal and the loss of his pension rights.[155] The plan to transfer the play to the Gate was in any event shortly to be aborted when the earl of Longford cited his concern that the fuss that had already been made could imperil the renewal of the Gate's patent.[156]

Discretion in this case was shown decidedly not to be the greater part of valour. Simpson said 'no', whereupon, to use his own words, he was 'plunged into a nightmare of melodrama which was to continue for over a year.'[157]

Following his arrest, Simpson spent one night in custody in the Bridewell before being admitted to bail. Bail was set at £100, £50 from Simpson himself and £50 from an independent surety. Simpson's night behind bars was not without incident.[158] A warder in the Bridewell, Simpson tells us, 'inquired with sincere sympathy "if it were naked women I was in for"'. When Simpson said 'no', the same man went on: 'They' were 'very funny in this country about them things'. A little later, the warder surreptitiously slipped Simpson a miniature bottle of Irish whiskey.[159]

---

151 Ibid.   152 See, e.g., Desmond Reid, 'Tennessee Williams', *Studies*, 46 (1957), 431.
153 13 May 1957.
154 Alan Simpson, *Beckett, Behan and a theatre in Dublin* (London, Routledge Kegan & Paul, 1962),
    p. 140.   155 Ibid., p. 150.   156 Ibid., pp 140, 145.   157 Ibid., p. 141.
158 Ibid., pp 148–50.   159 Ibid., p. 149.

Fears that the cast of *The Rose Tattoo* would themselves be arrested following the decision not to end the 'run' having proved groundless, the matter of their immediate re-employment, once the prospect of the transfer to the Gate had fallen through, was one of considerable concern. The Grand Opera House in Belfast came to the rescue.[160] George Lodge, the manager there, offered to stage the play, and that offer was accepted. As an old Campbell College boy and knowing too well the psyche of some at least of Belfast's theatre-goers, Simpson naturally harboured a few reservations over the circumstances in which his troupe of actors would be welcomed north of the border with open arms.

Committal proceedings commenced before District Justice Cathal Flynn on 4 July 1957; the proceedings, however, were not destined to conclude until 9 June 1958, for reasons about to be explained. On this last date, the district justice refused informations and the case was accordingly dismissed.[161] Flynn argued that to justify the committal of Simpson for trial on indictment there had to be furnished evidence of the intent on the part of the accused to deprave and corrupt those viewing the performance whose minds were open to such immoral influences. He did not consider that standard had been met. A linked concern was the prospect of any jury convicting on such a charge or charges in all the circumstances. In the report of Flynn's decision to dismiss the case, the district justice expatiates on his understanding of the sort of jury he had in mind. A jury, he wrote,[162]

> does not connote twelve self-righteous bigots, or twelve hypocrites, or twelve humbugs or twelve hysterics, or twelve amorists, or twelve debauched roués, or twelve dedicated thespians, or twelve lubricists, or twelve ritualistic liberals who have made up a martyrdom of authors or playwrights who have suffered from enforcement of the laws of obscenity.

A jury, Flynn concluded, 'represents a cross-section of the community and has a special aptitude for reflecting the view of the average person'.

A succession of police officers gave evidence at the preliminary investigation that began on 4 July. It emerged that these officers, 'all of high standing', as Flynn was later to remark,[163] had been given instructions by a senior member of the Garda Síochána. Simpson's lawyers sought clarification as to what those instructions had been. The officers claimed privilege and declined to answer. Flynn disallowed the claim, and ordered the matter to be dealt with. The lawyers for the prosecution challenged this decision of Flynn's and asked the district justice to state a case on the validity of the claim of privilege for consideration by the High Court. Reluctantly, as Flynn was later to express it, he agreed to do so, and the preliminary examination – the committal proceedings – came to an abrupt halt. This was on 18 July.

---

160 Ibid., pp 159–60.   161 *AG v. Simpson* (1959) 93 ILTR 33.   162 93 ILTR at 36.
163 Ibid., at 41.

In October 1957 the High Court heard the case stated, and in December the court ruled that the police officers' claim to privilege was valid and should have been upheld.[164] The lawyers for Simpson then appealed to the Supreme Court, where the High Court's decision of December 1957 was questioned in proceedings that commenced in April 1958. There matters took a very curious twist indeed, the majority ruling that the proceedings in the High Court had been entirely misconceived, a district justice conducting a preliminary examination not possessing, whilst exercising this jurisdiction, any authority to state a case.[165] The Supreme Court's decision was handed down in May. Mr Justice O'Daly, later the chief justice, dissented.[166] This majority decision Simpson himself described as 'a cunning judgment worthy of King Solomon and the Baby'.[167]

Flynn's preliminary examination resumed on 3 June 1958 and he handed down his decision on the 9th. In a historical review, he traced the origins of the law on obscenity, touching on leading English authority and the Model Penal Code in the United States. Flynn mentioned that the book of Williams' play had not been banned under the Censorship of Publications Acts, 1929 to 1946.[168] For him, the key question was, was the play 'a filthy play'?

> That is the question. Not is it a great work of art in the tradition of Euripedes, Aeschylus, Sophocles, Shakespeare.[169]

Flynn thought it not irrelevant that the play had been produced 'during An Tostal, our National Festival. The play was part of a National Theatre Festival during An Tostal'. A synopsis of Williams' play itself then follows. 'It appears', wrote Flynn,[170]

> that while there is a theme relating to sexual behaviour between men and women in the play, there are also many other themes in it. The mother is very concerned with the preservation of the virginity of her daughter; she despises modern women who at the age of thirty discontinue the use of the conjugal double bed and have recourse to a single bed; she glories in what might be regarded by some as excessive conjugal relations; she despises the use of contraceptives;[171] finding after his death that her deceased husband had not been faithful to her, she is crushed; she despairs once in her religious faith, and she has one lapse from the path of virtue. The secret of the Sacred Tribunal of Penance is portrayed as being utterly and absolutely inviolable.

164 *AG v. Simpson* [1959] IR 105.   165 *AG v. Simpson* (no. 2) [1959] IR 335.
166 [1959] IR 343–6.
167 Simpson, *Beckett, Behan and a theatre in Dublin*, p. 163; 1 Kings, ch. 3, vv. 16–26.
168 *AG v. Simpson* (1959) 93 ILTR 33 at 41.   169 93 ILTR at 43.   170 Ibid., at 44.
171 A view based on the widow Sarafina's rejection of the advances of Alvaro and the accompanying circumstances: the dropping of a small packet (condoms?) from his pocket. See Simpson, *Beckett, Behan and a theatre in Dublin*, p. 142.

Flynn's synopsis of the play, unprecedented for any Irish law report, ends with his asking the question, 'What is the over-all effect of the play?' It is a question to which he gives this answer:[172]

> I think that it is one of sadness, that this humble woman, a woman of great sexual appetite who is widowed by sudden disaster to her husband, lapses once from the path of virtue.

More rhetorical questions follow. 'Does the play as described in the evidence?', he asks,

> tend to corrupt and deprave? Does it lead to certain lascivious thoughts and lustful desires which will affect character and action? Is the play a cloak for something sinister, and to repeat the words of Mr Justice Stable,[173] 'is it camouflage to render the crudity, the sex of the book sufficiently wrapped up to pass the critical standards of the Director of Public Prosecutions?'

Language of this ilk anticipates District Justice Flynn's conclusion more than a year after the commencement of this extraordinarily protracted saga. 'In applying what I consider to be the correct legal test of obscenity to the charges', he begins, in finally wrapping things up,

> in carefully reviewing the evidence adduced by the prosecution in support of those charges and in exercising my discretion judicially, and taking into consideration the evidence tendered on behalf of the Attorney General, I am of the opinion that no jury weighing the probabilities of this case might reasonably convict. I am of the opinion that no jury would or ought to convict.

Informations were accordingly refused and Alan Simpson was discharged.[174] Funds had been raised to help meet Simpson's legal costs; even so, he remained in considerable debt to his legal team.[175] The fact that shortly afterwards the Pike was to close and that this closure was to be permanent tells its own story. Dean, in *Riot and great anger*, was to write of the benefits that can accrue to the artist from controversy and censorship. 'Protests', she wrote,[176]

> especially organized protests, against plays by those who sought a play's withdrawal by management or its boycott by potential audiences almost invariably had exactly the opposite effect: throngs of often unlikely ticket buyers besieged the box office. Performances sold out. Runs were extended.

172   93 ILTR at 44.   173   As enunciated in *R. v. Secker and Warburg* [1954] 2 All ER 683.
174   93 ILTR at 44–5.   175   Simpson, *Beckett, Behan and a theatre in Dublin*, p. 165.
176   *Riot and great anger*, p. 199.

Plainly and sadly, Simpson's actual experience was to be at odds with all of this.

It was to be a consolation of sorts for Simpson, however, that so many in the world of theatre had been supportive. Samuel Beckett, for instance, had written in August 1957. 'Sorry about all your trouble over *The Rose Tattoo*. Bastards, bastards'.[177] The Pike never recovered from the affair. The debts he had incurred crippled Simpson and, after a while, as we have already recalled, the theatre closed, never to open again. Simpson continued a career in drama in England, but never in charge of his own theatre. He died in 1980.

In his judgment in *The Rose Tattoo* case refusing informations, that is, that Simpson was no longer to face a full-blown trial on indictment, District Justice Flynn saw fit to castigate the part played by the authorities in the affair. 'I can only infer',[178] he commented,

> that by arresting the accused, the object would be achieved of closing down the play. But, surely, if that was the object, nothing could be more devastating than to restrain the production before even a hearing is held. It smacks to me of the frontier principle – 'shoot first, and talk over'.

Having been told at the outset of his long-drawn-out ordeal that Tennessee Williams' play was reckoned to contain 'objectionable passages', Simpson remained at a complete loss to discover what were the passages involved and why the decision to prosecute had ever been reached. Rumours of course abounded,[179] but neither in his own memoir of 1962 nor in that of his wife, Carolyn Swift's of 1985,[180] are any of these mysteries penetrated.

Swift herself in collaboration with Gerald Whelan revisited the controversy in another book brought out in 2002, the principal object of which was to examine the relevant archival sources in order to get to the bottom of the affair, and thus, hopefully, bring closure to the entire business.[181] Gaps in the record made it impossible for Whelan and Swift to do other than to offer what they term 'a plausible scenario'.[182] Their thesis is that the decision to prosecute was taken by the Department of Justice, with the advice of the Office of the Attorney-General, to forestall possible criticism from church and other quarters that the Department was soft on censorship. Anxieties over the kinds of play sometimes being put on in Dublin coincided on this occasion with a major controversy over the composition of the membership on the Censorship of Publications Board. To force the Pike's closure by availing of the provisions of the Dublin Theatre Act of 1786 was treated

177 Quoted, Simpson, *Beckett, Behan, and a theatre in Dublin*, p. 168.
178 93 ILTR at 43; *Beckett, Behan, and a theatre in Dublin*, p. 164.
179 As Simpson noted: *Beckett, Behan, and a theatre in Dublin*, p. 141.
180 Carolyn Swift, *Stage by stage* (Swords, Co. Dublin, Poolbeg Press, 1985).
181 Gerald Whelan with Carolyn Swift, *Spiked: Church-State intrigue and The Rose Tattoo* (Dublin, New Island, 2002).
182 Ibid., p. 307.

by the Attorney-General's Office as an alternative course of action, but unattractive for a number of reasons including problems of procedure. To indict for putting on an indecent play was the only feasible option.[183] The prospect of a transfer to the larger venue of the Gate Theatre, immediately after the conclusion of the short run at the Pike, meant that no time was to be lost if action was to be taken:[184] a consideration that dictated when exactly Simpson was to receive his ultimatum. The mid-1950s was a period when Ireland's so-called experts on censorship indulged in what Whelan and Swift term 'one form or another of casuistry, zealotry, crawthumping, humbug or even all four'.[185] Having finally advanced their thesis, they leave for the reader to ponder two key rhetorical questions:[186]

> But would any Irish Government, however cynical, put innocent people through all that Simpson and Swift endured on such grounds? Would it legally persecute them – or <u>need</u> to persecute them – for over a year, and destroy their theatre, just for the sake of neutralising a perceived threat from an opponent in a political fight in which the Pike was completely uninvolved?

Two years later, in what threatened to be a re-run of *The Rose Tattoo* affair – but which did not, in fact materialise – a play, based on J.P. Donleavy's *The Ginger Man*, survived three performances in October 1959 at the Gaiety before it was prematurely closed. Whether the Roman Catholic archbishop of Dublin, Archbishop McQuaid, was involved is a question raised by Dean, but is not answered.[187]

In Northern Ireland the Council for the Encouragement of Music and the Arts (CEMA), succeeded in 1962 by the Arts Council for Northern Ireland, had commenced the practice of subsidising live theatre.[188] The price of this support was an insistence that representatives of the public serve on the boards of management of the theatres concerned. Episodes occurring in 1958 presaged a re-run of difficulties that the Abbey in Dublin had experienced when it too received financial support from the State.[189] The first problem concerned a recommendation presented to the board of the Group Theatre (now afforced by four representatives of Belfast Corporation) that the theatre accept for performance Gerard McLarnon's play *The Bonefire*. There was to be no criticism of this play's sectarian theme by Belfast's lord mayor, but changes to the text were demanded; and after some discussion, these were made; McLarnon himself does not appear to have objected; and the play was performed as scheduled.[190]

It was very different in the case of Sam Thompson's play, *Over the Bridge*, which dealt with sectarianism in the Belfast shipyards. Provisionally accepted by the

---

183 See memorandum from the Office of the Attorney-General, quoted, *Spiked*, pp 147 and 313.
184 Quoted, *Spiked*, pp 149–50.   185 *Spiked*, p. 226.   186 Ibid., p. 305.
187 Dean, *Riot and great anger*, p. 165.
188 Conor O'Malley, *A poet's theatre* (Dublin, Elo Press, 1988), p. 33 ff.
189 Above, p. 236.   190 O'Malley, *A poet's theatre*, p. 73.

Group Theatre, it was in the end to be turned down, on a 6–2 vote, when Thompson refused to make the deletions requested, in an announcement made by the theatre's chairman, J. Ritchie McKee.[191] The Ulster people, McKee argued in support of this decision, were fed up with religious and political controversy. The management, accordingly, was

> determined not to mount any play which would offend or affront the religious or political beliefs or sensibilities of the man in the street of any denomination or class in the community and which would give rise to sectarian or political controversy of an extreme nature.

Thompson sued for breach of contract, a suit which was apparently settled in his favour out of court.[192] An alternative venue for a production of *Over the Bridge* was eventually found in January 1960, when a run of the play opened at the Empire Theatre in Victoria Square,[193] a venue that was to be demolished in 1961.[194] *Over the Bridge* went on to enjoy successful runs in Dublin, Scotland and England. Sam Hanna Bell greeted the eventual outcome by observing[195] that there had occurred

> a quite extraordinary feeling of relief that at least the unclean spirit of sectarianism had been dragged before the footlights and examined with passion, pity and corrosive laughter.

The Ulster Hall, where the Group Theatre usually put on its productions, thus never had the opportunity to stage *Over the Bridge*. At least the Abbey had been in a position to reverse Yeats' error in refusing to accept for production Sean O'Casey's *The Silver Tassie*. This unfortunate decision of 1928 was partly rectified when a short run of *The Silver Tassie* was put on there in 1935.[196]

It would be quite wrong, even so, to seek to maintain that Dublin was necessarily more liberal when it came to matters of stage censorship. A curious affair from 1951 six years before the saga of *The Rose Tattoo* gained any kind of traction clearly merits a mention. That year the Belfast Arts Theatre Company travelled to Dublin to put on a performance of Jean-Paul Sartre's *Huis Clos* in the premises of the Royal Irish Academy of Music in Westland Row. The company was asked to remove posters outside the building which advertised the show. The protesters, rebuffed on this score, then lowered their demands by asking instead that Sartre's name should be removed. And this, the company, whether willingly or unwillingly, were prepared to do. And did.[197]

---

191 Ibid., p. 73; Sam Hanna Bell, *The theatre in Ulster* (Dublin, Gill and MacMillan, 1972), p. 92; Dean, *Riot and great anger*, p. 171.
192 Bell, *Theatre in Ulster*, p. 92.   193 Ibid.
194 The Empire was the venue where the present writer first trod the boards as a child in the 1940s acting the part of the spider in his harassment, plainly indictable, of Little Miss Muffett.
195 Bell, *Theatre in Ulster*, p. 93.   196 Morash, *History of Irish theatre*, pp 189–90.
197 Bell, *Theatre in Ulster*, p. 109.

It is difficult to leave off discussion in particular of the sorry business that was the prosecution of Simpson over *The Rose Tattoo* without some mention, however fleeting, of a short story by Sean Ó Faolain, appearing as long ago as 1937, that touches, albeit obliquely, on the issues that have been involved here. In 'The Old Master'[198] we are introduced to a lawyer in Cork rejoicing in the name of John Aloysius Gonzaga O'Sullivan. Dismayed at the news that the first night of a performance by a Russian ballet company had been poorly supported, O'Sullivan resolves, as a matter of principle and by way of showing solidarity, personally to swell the audience on the second night. Matters do not turn out as he would have preferred. Approaching the theatre's entrance, he is shocked to discover that the names of all those actually entering the theatre were being taken down, a practice, as it chanced, *The Leader* had advocated back in 1914.[199] Via the stage-door O'Sullivan learns from a member of the touring ballet company the hostility that they had earlier encountered on their tour. Returning to the front of the building, which he does not enter, O'Sullivan is coerced into joining a protest demonstration led by a Canon Paul. Participants start to sing hymns and hold aloft a placard bearing this legend:

> MEN OF SAINT MARK
> WE HAVE YOU MARKED!
> DOWN WITH IMMORAL PLAYS!

O'Sullivan finally makes a break for it, and escapes into – of all things – a public convenience (a little green, iron building down a side street). He does not deliver on his undertaking, communicated to Rachmanoff, one of the dancers, that he would use a public forum to denounce the protesters and expose all these shenanigans. His views nonetheless had been made crystal-clear. 'St. Petersburg comes to Cork', he ruminated,[200]

> And Cork ignored her.
> The Nevsky Prospect … ; the sleighs on the Voznesensky; the Gorokhovaga Ulitsa, lit from end to end by the rising sun …. The Neva frozen and glittering! All that! And Cork ignores it.

But then, if Rachmanoff was to be credited, so had Sheffield and Cardiff.

The experience did John Aloysius Gonzaga O'Sullivan no good at all. He never denounced the protest. Rather, he developed a cold, which led in a short space of time to pneumonia, of which our elderly lawyer promptly expired.

198 Reprinted in *The collected stories of Sean Ó Faolain*, vol. 1 (London, Constable, 1980), p. 174.
199 *The Leader*, 7 Mar. 1914, cited, Dean, *Riot and great anger*, p. 110.
200 *Collected stories of Ó Faolain*, i, 176.

CHAPTER FIFTEEN

The dramatic author's performing right

THE STARTING-POINT FOR ANY examination of the dramatic author's performing right has to be the year 1709 when copyright law, of which our performing right was to become a constituent part, was first placed on a statutory footing. The preamble to what is described as 'As Act for the Encouragement of Learning, by vesting the Copies of Printed Books in the Authors or Purchasers of such Copies, during the Times therein mentioned'[1] usefully described the background or the motive behind adoption of the measure. 'Whereas', it began,

> Printers, Booksellers and other Persons have of late frequently taken the liberty of printing, reprinting and publishing or causing to be printed, reprinted and published Books and other Writings without the Consent of the Authors or Proprietors of such Books and Writings to their very great Detriment and too often to the Ruin of them and their Families.

And the preamble continued, significantly: 'For preventing therefore such Practices for the future and for the Encouragement of learned Men to compose and write useful books ...'

The legislation went on to acknowledge the existence of a property right in books, limiting claims for breach of copyright, however, solely in respect of books that had been registered in Stationer's Hall,[2] and adding provision for a remedy where the price of copyrighted works was adjudged too high.[3]

As the eighteenth century wore on, attention in Britain was concentrated on difficulties to which this Act of 1709 was thought to give rise, difficulties examined in such leading cases as *Millar v. Taylor* in 1769[4] and *Donaldsons v. Becket* in 1774.[5] Little of this was of any concern in Ireland where the Act of 1709 did not apply and where authors, accordingly, were hard-pressed to vindicate their proprietary interests in any of their published work. It was a lacuna in legal protection in the smaller jurisdiction that incensed Jonathan Swift, as he told Alexander Pope in a letter in the spring of 1733.[6] 'There is', Swift wrote, 'no property among Printers here, neither will it be one farthing in my pocket. For among us, mony for Copys is a thing unheard of.' It had been the Dublin publisher George Faulkner's plan at

1 8 Anne, c. 19.   2 S. 2.   3 S. 3.   4 4 Burr 2303, 98 Eng Rep 201.
5 4 Burr 2408, 98 Eng Rep 257.
6 Jonathan Swift, *The Correspondence of Jonathan Swift*, ed. Harold Williams (Oxford, Clarendon Press, 1963–5), vol. iv, 154 (1 May 1733).

this time to bring out a collection of Swift's published writings that had caused the
dean of St Patrick's to broach the question with Pope. And Swift was to return to
the theme in a succession of letters to other correspondents – Charles Ford, the
earl of Oxford, William Pulteney (who was to become the earl of Bath in 1742), and
Charles Wogan.[7]

As it happens, the law on the entire subject became the target of a sustained
attack when thirty years later Faulkner brought out another edition of Swift's
writings. Faulkner did not mince his words in the accompanying preface. 'In
England', he explained,

> the Property in Copies of Books is as fully secured by Law and Custom, as
> any Lands, Houses, Tenements, or Funds, etc. to the very great Advantage of
> Learning and Authors, and to the Production of many fine printed Editions
> of Books and Prints ...[8]

He continued:

> The parliament of Great Britain, being truly sensible of the great Advantages
> of Learning, Wit and Humour to that Nation, have made many Acts of
> Parliament to secure the Property of Writing, not only to Authors and
> Booksellers, but even for Inventors of Painting and Engraving.

In an informed digression, Faulkner went on to draw attention to the circumstance that in England, under its more beneficent regime, 'Many Gentlemen of
Genius, Learning and Fortune' had set up printing-houses in their own residences,
citing the cases of Viner, author of his twenty-five-volume *Abridgment* (at his house
near Aldershot in Hampshire), and of Horace Walpole, who produced *A catalogue
of the royal and noble authors of England* and several editions of 'the Classicks' (at
his house, Strawberry Hill, at Richmond in Surrey).

The legal position in Ireland was then denounced. 'But, alas!' Faulkner
continued in his preface,

> it is not so in Ireland, where many, without any Cause whatever, immediately
> pyrate on their innocent Brethren, who never once offended them in their
> Property, either by Word, Thought, or Deed, which is a Reason that few
> Books have been well printed here, nor will be for the future, the Demand
> here being so small.

7   *The correspondence of Jonathan Swift*, vol. iv, 197 (Ford, 9 Oct. 1733); vol. iv, 222 (Oxford, 16 Feb.
    1733/4), 248 (Oxford, 30 Aug. 1734); vol. iv, 304 (Pulteney, 8 Mar. 1734/5), 338 (Pulteney, 12 May
    1735); vol. iv, 469 (Wogan, Mar. 1735/6).
8   'To the Reader: Faulkner's Preface to his Edition of Swift's Works, Dublin 1763' in Jonathan
    Swift, *Directions to servants and miscellaneous pieces*, ed. Herbert Davis (Oxford, Basil Blackwell,
    1959), p. 201, at pp 206–7.

Returning to the theme a little later, Faulkner expressed the hope that the Irish parliament would act, 'otherwise the State of Learning must daily decline, which is now at a low ebb in Ireland.'

One consequence of this striking difference between the laws of the two kingdoms has been highlighted by Morash,[9] and will serve as an introduction to the topic of the relationship of copyright law to the claims, legal, financial and otherwise of the dramatic author. Morash was to assert that Dublin publishers were not slow themselves to capitalise upon this very obvious legal variation, alluding to 'the dizzying rate at which the publishing of plays [in Ireland] expanded over the course of the eighteenth century.'[10]

Eighteenth-century Ireland has thus to be reckoned a copyright wasteland. Even so, particularly, it would appear, so far as the productions of opera were concerned, theatre managements both in London and Dublin itself were known to fight battles to seek reversal of that dismal classification. In the spring of 1777, for instance, the management of Covent Garden in London sought an injunction from the English Court of Chancery to prevent a performance of Richard Brinsley Sheridan's *La Duenna* being put on at Dublin's Fishamble Street theatre.[11] The management defended this remarkable resort to an unprecedented extra-territorial remedy on the grounds that it had purchased the rights to *La Duenna* from Sheridan. The English lord chancellor refused the injunction – a decision warmly welcomed by the *Freeman's Journal* in Dublin: 'By this decision, an arbitrary restraint by English despots can no longer prevent this oppressed country from being a little entertained, as a consolation in times when they are greatly taxed.'[12]

Five years later, in 1782, the two leading Dublin theatres, Smock Alley and Crow Street, contended for the right to put on the first Dublin production of the opera *The Castle of Andalusia* with a score by Samuel Arnold and libretti by John O'Keeffe. In the end, Smock Alley prevailed, and the opera was presented in that venue on 13 January 1783.[13] It emerged that the theatre had bought from Covent Garden, for the sum of 200 guineas, the words and music, together with accompaniments, models of scenes and costumes. Bested in the competition to secure the rights to put on the opera, Crow Street yet determined to mount their own production of *The Castle of Andalusia*, which they did the following April, though well aware that Richard Daly, the actor-manager at Smock Alley, had acquired what we would now term the Irish 'sole right'. The *Freeman's Journal*, in its comment on the affair,[14] chose to castigate Crow Street. 'With complete disdain for the

9 Christopher Morash, 'Theatre and print, 1550–1800' in Gillespie and Hadfield (eds), *The Irish book in English*, The Oxford History of the Irish Book: Volume 3 (Oxford, Oxford UP, 2006), at p. 319.
10 Ibid., p. 325. 11 T.J. Walsh, *Opera in Dublin, 1705–1797* (Dublin, Allen Figgis, 1973), p. 179.
12 24/26 April 1777, quoted by Walsh, *Opera in Dublin, 1705–1797*, p. 180.
13 Walsh, *Opera in Dublin, 1705–1797*, p. 221.
14 11/14 Jan. 1783, quoted Walsh, *Opera in Dublin, 1705–1797*, pp 223–4.

author's right to his property', it thundered, the proprietors of Crow Street had had the effrontery to announce in an advertisement that, although, they 'have not purchased their copy from the manager of Covent Garden, yet they beg leave to assure the public, that theirs is a genuine one, as they hope the representation will testify.' We will hear more in a moment of this underhand traffic in copies of plays and operas, to which this advertisement from Crow Street in 1783 made reference.

Ireland ceased to be a copyright wasteland when British copyright was extended to it in 1801.[15] A second lacuna, common to both Britain and Ireland in the years following and down to 1833, was the failure of the law to extend recognition to the dramatic author's performing right. A comparable deficiency in France was rectified by a law of 13 January 1791, article 3 of which laid down that works of living dramatists were not to be represented in any public theatre in the country without the formal consent in writing of the dramatist.[16] It is now time to turn to the sequence of events that led the parliament of the United Kingdom to follow France's lead forty-two years later in 1833.

Litigation in 1822 over a version of Lord Byron's play *Marino Faliero* held the promise of a major reworking of the law in a direction favourable to dramatists, but it was not to be.[17] *Marino Faliero*, a full-length five-act play completed in 1820,[18] rehearsed the extraordinary story of a fourteenth-century Doge of Venice who plotted a *coup d'état*, was betrayed, put on trial, sentenced to death, and beheaded – a remarkable sequence of events in the case of a septuagenarian. Faliero considered himself insulted when his noble confrères in the administration of La Serenissima, sitting as a court of trial, La Quarantia, refused to take seriously, and punish accordingly, a doggerel inscription placed on the ducal throne in the Council Chamber that cast aspersions on the Doge's wife, Angiolina. The inscription read: 'Marin Falier de la bella mujer, lu la mantien e altri la galde.' (Marin Falier has a wife that is fair, he has to keep her while other men lay'er.).

The revenge that Faliero planned was nothing less than the massacre of all the city's young nobles summoned on to the Piazza by a contrived emergency summons. Faliero would then be proclaimed Prince of Venice, and his title ratified by popular acclamation. The dramatic potential of this extraordinary turn of events is captured very well by Norwich in his history of Venice. 'History', he writes, 'provides innumerable instances of aristocrats who have turned against their own class to put themselves at the head of a popular movement: few, however, have

---

15 41 Geo III, c. 107.
16 See the evidence of Monsieur C. Gavard, Chargé d'Affaires at the French embassy in London, to the royal commission on copyright law in 1878: *Report of the commissioners to make inquiry with regard to the laws and regulations relating to home, colonial and international copyright: minutes of evidence*, HC 1878, xxiv, p. 95.
17 See further on this Gavin McFarland, *Copyright: the development and exercise of the performing right* (Eastbourne, John Offord, 1980), pp 37–8.
18 Byron, *The poetical works of Lord Byron*, ed. E.H. Coleridge (London, John Murray, 1905), p. 464; Richard Lansdown, *Byron's historical drama* (Oxford, Clarendon Press, 1992), ch. 4.

done so in their late seventies, or from a position of a least theoretical supremacy.'[19] Norwich continues:

> In such circumstances, the usual motives of ambition and self-interest can be ruled out; Faliero seems to have been impelled, quite simply by hatred and rancour, by a desire for revenge magnified and distorted by advancing senility into a single overpowering obsession.[20]

The story appealed to Byron, who includes these lines in his play. They are spoken by Israel Bertuccio, the chief of the Arsenal, and a key conspirator: 'Until this hour, what Prince has plotted for his people's freedom? Or risked a life to liberate his subjects?'[21] Delacroix too, who was to furnish a splendid portrayal of Faliero's actual beheading.

The year after Byron finished writing his play, on 14 April 1821, he assigned to one Murray for the sum of £1,050 his copyright in it: 'for printing, and publishing and all the benefit and advantage thereof.'[22] A week later, on 21 April, copies of the text of *Marino Faliero* had been printed and were for sale. Three days after this, on the 24th, Elliston, the manager of the Theatre Royal, Drury Lane, advertised the intention of the theatre to mount a performance of a version of the play the very next night, that is, on the 25th. The posters up on the 24th made it clear to potential patrons that the *Marino Faliero* they would be experiencing would diverge in a number of respects from the play as written by Byron. An explanation was appended:

> Those who have perused *Marino Faliero* will have anticipated the necessity of considerable curtailments; aware that conversations or soliloquies, however beautiful or interesting in the closet, will frequently tire in public recital. This intimation is due to the ardent admirers of Lord Byron's eminent talents, and will, it is presumed, be a sufficient apology for the great freedom used in the representation of this tragedy on the stage of the Drury-Lane Theatre.

Elliston's approach would be hard to fault. In the original, Byron gives Faliero very long speeches indeed. Drury Lane had approached neither Byron nor Murray, the owner of the copyright, for permission to stage its version, whereupon on 25 April Murray filed a bill in Chancery to restrain Elliston from putting on his version of *Marino Faliero*. Whether an action could be maintained by Murray against Elliston 'for publicly acting and representing for profit the tragedy' became the principal question requiring to be answered.

---

19 John Julius Norwich, *A history of Venice* (London, Penguin Books, 1983), p. 226. 20 Ibid.
21 *Marino Faliero*, act 2, scene 2, lines 437–9.
22 *Murray v. Elliston* (1822) 5 B & Ald 657, 106 Eng Rep 1331.

James Scarlett, the future Baron Abinger, appeared for Murray and argued for an affirmative answer to that key question. The moment, Scarlett contended, a right of property in this work is established, 'the consequences must follow that any injury done to the property is the subject of legal redress.' This, of course, was to come very close to asserting the existence of a performing right, the breach of which would attract an award of damages. Unsurprisingly, Adolphus, the counsel who appeared for Elliston, would have none of it. It is instructive to note, however, that the arguments adduced by Adolphus are given at much greater length by the law reporter, and that these focus, not so much on the possibility of an infringement of a performing right, but on the circumstance that the play put on at the Drury Lane Theatre was not Byron's original, but an abridgment.

Adolphus' contentions merit being set out at length. 'The plaintiff', he begins, 'contends for a far more comprehensive security, and one coexisting with the statute (8 Anne, c. 21), and restraining the public in points of which the statute takes no notice.'[23] If, he goes on, the play is a *bona fide* abridgment, the plaintiff can have no remedy.

There then follows a final observation which if it truly captures the accepted wisdom of the times as regards the difficulty of slotting 'performance' into the straitjacket of a breach of copyright, clearly presaged the necessity for a statute-law readjustment. 'As regards the present theatrical exhibition,' Adolphus concludes,

> We say:
> Persons go thither, not to read the work, or to hear it read, but to see the combined effect of poetry, scenery and acting. Now of these three things, two are not produced by the author of the work; and the combined effect is just as much a new production, and even more so than the printed abridgment of a work. There are many instances in which works published have thus, without permission of their authors, been brought upon the stage.[24]

Lord Eldon, the lord chancellor, sent the case to the court of King's Bench, for a decision by that court as to whether Murray's action was maintainable. A brief entry by the reporter tells us that that court (Lord Chief Justice Abbott, Mr Justice Bayley and Mr Justice Holroyd) found that it was not maintainable, the single ground cited being that the Drury Lane Theatre's *Marino Faliero* was an abridgment.[25] *Murray v. Elliston* was to be cited as authority for the proposition that abridgments did not breach copyright, when the problem of a version for the stage of Charles Reade's novel *It is Never too Late to Mend* came before the courts later in the century.[26] The next stage in the battle being fought to establish a dramatist's performing right came ten years later.

On 31 May 1832 Edward Bulwer Lytton, the MP at the time for St Ives, moved a motion in the House of Commons for the setting up of a select committee to

23   5 B & Ald at 658, 106 Eng Rep at 1331.   24   Ibid.   25   Ibid., p. 1332.
26   *Reade v. Conquest* (1861) 9 CB (ns) 755, 142 Eng Rep 297.

inquire into the state of the laws affecting dramatic literature, and the performance of the drama.[27] Lytton had a personal interest in the question: he was also a playwright. He was, however, better-known as a novelist. His *Eugene Aram* was published in 1832 and he followed this up two years later with another of his better known works, *The Last Days of Pompeii*. Lytton enjoyed a not undistinguished later political career even if the verdict expressed by Tennyson in 1848 demonstrated that not everyone agreed. Lytton Tennyson unkindly described as 'a padded thing that wears the stays.' This scarcely detracts from the circumstance that the year after Lytton sought his select committee, he successfully brought forward the measure that introduced the dramatic author's performing right.

Lytton's speech in May 1832, like the speeches of the others MPs on the occasion, focused on two key issues, aside altogether from the lack of a performing right for playwrights: the future of the patent theatres in London, principally Covent Garden and Drury Lane, and the law on the licensing of theatres. Our concern here is with the plight of the dramatic author, deprived as he was at this time, in contrast to his counterpart in France, of any performing right. Lytton insisted that parliament had been indifferent to 'the property that is derived from intellectual exertions.'[28] 'The instant', he went on, 'an author published a play, any manager might seize it – mangle it – act it – without the consent of the author – and without giving him one sixpence of remuneration.'[29] Writing a play, he continued, constituted 'a labour often more intense and exhausting than the severest mechanical toil.'[30] No one should doubt the proof of this:

> The commonest invention in a calico – a new pattern in the most trumpery article of dress – a new bit to our bridles – a new wheel to our carriages – might make the fortune of the inventor; but the intellectual invention of the finest drama in the world, might not relieve by a groat the poverty of the inventor.

A predictable enough allusion followed. 'If', Lytton continued,

> Shakespeare himself were now living – if Shakespeare himself were to publish a volume of plays, they might be acted every night all over the Kingdom – they might bring thousands to actors, and ten thousands to managers – and Shakespeare himself, the producer of all, might be starving in a garret.[31]

The present laws, he ended, were 'glaringly unjust in themselves, and so pernicious to one of the loftiest branches of intellectual labour.'

Daniel O'Connell seconded the motion,[32] but it was opposed by Sir Charles Wetherell, the MP for Boroughbridge.[33] (He later relented, and served on the

27 *Hansard, 3*, xiii, col. 239; McFarlane, *Copyright: the performing right*, pp 40–1.
28 *Hansard, 3*, xiii, col. 246.   29 Ibid.   30 Ibid., 247.   31 Ibid.
32 *Hansard, 3*, xiii, col. 248.   33 Ibid.

resultant select committee.) Interpreting the motion, insofar as it targeted the patent theatres in London, as trenching on the rights of the Crown, Sir Edward Sugden, the future Lord St Leonards and lord chancellor in both Ireland and Britain, also spoke against;[34] but all the other speakers were in favour.

George Lamb, the brother of Viscount Melbourne, and who was to join Lytton in seeing the bill of 1833 successfully brought through the Commons, recalled his authorship of an abortive bill on performing rights that he had been persuaded to withdraw on the grounds that it 'would be useless and nugatory unless breach of the right was made an offence'[35] Richard Lalor Sheil, MP at the time for Milbourne Port in Dorset, and like Lytton, a playwright too, addressed himself first to the role of the Lord Chamberlain as censor.[36] Turning to the problem of emoluments for dramatists, Sheil confirmed the existence, in certain theatres at least, and in certain circumstances, of the convention, under which during the 'run' of a play the author might receive sums generated by performances on the third night, on the ninth and on the twentieth.[37] But, asked Sheil, why should the author's emoluments end there? He then introduced the case of the writer Sheridan Knowles. His *Virginius*, he went on, as performed by Macready was the best proof yet that the tragic muse was far from dead. 'Was it not most unjust', however, 'that from the performance of his tragedies in the theatres of Dublin, Liverpool and Edinburgh he could derive no sort of emolument?'[38] At the end of the debate the Commons agreed a select committee to inquire into the matters that Lytton had brought before the House. The committee's published report with its attached minutes of evidence[39] constitutes a prime source of information on the state of the theatre immediately prior to the adoption of what became known as Bulwer Lytton's Act of 1833.

The picture that witnesses appearing before the select committee gave of the earnings of playwrights in the last decades of the eighteenth century and the first decades of the nineteenth indicates that it would be a mistake to offer broad conclusions. Practices pursued by theatre managers varied enormously. One theatre engaged its own resident author. This was one William Thomas Moncrieff who claimed in his evidence to have written 200 plays, on one occasion being told he had a deadline of 24 hours.[40] Thomas Morton, a playwright himself who also served as a reader vetting plays submitted for performance at Drury Lane, would not have been impressed, quoting, as he did, in his evidence the opinion of Voltaire that nothing in literature was so difficult as the writing of plays.[41] A hack author

34 *Hansard, 3*, xiii, col. 258.   35 Ibid., col. 252.   36 Ibid., col. 256.   37 Ibid., col. 257.
38 Ibid.
39 *Report from the select committee on dramatic literature 1832*, HC 1831–2, iii, 1. See, also, John Russell Stephens, *The profession of the playwright: British theatre, 1800–1900* (Cambridge, Cambridge University Press, 1992), p. 31.
40 *Select committee report on dramatic literature*, p. 175; McFarlane, *Copyright: the performing right*, p. 46.
41 *Select committee report on dramatic literature*, p. 143.

like Moncrieff scarcely advanced the case for the introduction of a performing right, and William Wilkins, a builder of provincial theatres and with a continuing proprietorial interest in them – in Norwich, Bury St Edwards, Cambridge, Ipswich, Great Yarmouth and Colchester – did not fail to speak his mind:[42] he was utterly opposed to conferring performing rights on 'authors of a certain stamp.' These were 'not original writers, such as furnish plot and character, and so on, by their own ingenuity.' Much of what in his day was presented on stage was a disappointment. How many contemporary dramatists in Wilkins' book would have been entitled to claim any projected performing right could well have been very small indeed. The works of 'original writers', Wilkins argued, 'are not the sort of plays which go down in the present day; the public taste is altered, and melo-drama and translations from the French, and old plays modernised and adapted to our customs, and sometimes to particular performers, are the only things that are successful.'[43] Wilkins drew the inevitable conclusion: 'I look upon such writers as not entitled to the same degree of reward.'[44] They were 'mere workers-up of dramas ... hardly ... literati.'

A resident playwright such as Moncrieff was engaged on a retainer basis. Others with a somewhat higher reputation could well benefit from the sale of copyright in their plays to particular theatres or, in a case like Byron's interest in *Marino Faliero*, to some book publisher. David Edward Morris, the proprietor of the Haymarket Theatre in London, furnished for the benefit of the select committee details on the purchase by the Haymarket of copyright in the plays of the Irish actor and author John O'Keeffe,[45] who, as may be recalled, had also produced the libretti for *The Castle of Andalusia*. The theatre had paid 40 guineas for *The Son-in-Law* in 1779, another 40 guineas for *Dead Alive* in 1781, a further 40 guineas for *The Agreeable Surprise* in 1782, £50 for *Peeping Tom* a little later and £30 for *Beggar on Horseback* in 1785. O'Keeffe had also received £102 12s. for the copyright of a five-act regular comedy, *The Young Quaker*. Today's authors, Morris claimed, fared somewhat better,[46] alluding to the sum of £1,000 paid to Colman for *The Africans* and another £1,000 for his *John Bull*.[47] Another witness, Douglas Jerrold, averred that Sheridan Knowles had also benefited from an increase in the going rate: he had earned £400 for the copyright of *The Hunchback*.[48] Jerrold, however, declined to draw the conclusion that the level of remuneration was sufficient to attract first-rate talent into writing for the stage. 'Certainly not', he expostulated when this proposition was put to him, 'when periodical writing and novels are so highly paid for. A gentleman will get £1,000 for a novel, and Mr Sheridan Knowles only £400 for *The Hunchback*.'[49]

42 Ibid., p. 210.   43 Ibid.   44 Ibid.
45 *Select committee report on dramatic literature*, pp 150–1.   46 Ibid., p. 150.
47 Ibid., p. 151.   48 Ibid., p. 157.
49 Ibid. For further details on these financial matters, see Stephens, *Profession of the playwright*, pp 31–50.

A convention that had established itself at certain theatres, but had since languished, was to arrange for the author of a play to be given the profits on certain nights of the play's performance during its scheduled run – an arrangement to which Richard Lalor Sheil had chosen to allude in his speech in the Commons on 31 May 1832.[50] Nights 3, 6, 9 and 20 had represented the convention at one theatre.[51] Doubtless there were variations, and in some venues the convention was not followed at all. Profits, of course, could be negligible if the play did not 'sell', and it needs to be remembered that payments to actors and the theatre's overheads remained mandatory deductions from the takings on the designated author's nights.[52]

The belief long lingered that an author could control what happened to his play up until at least the point of publication. That was the view expressed by the actor William Charles Macready in his evidence to the select committee;[53] support for it was certainly supplied by a decision of the English Chancery in 1770.[54] Charles Macklin was the author of the two-act *Love à la Mode*, which he saw to it was never printed or published. Once any performance of the farce was concluded, Macklin would take away his manuscript copy of it from the prompter. He had charged 20 guineas to one actor who chose the farce for his benefit night, and 30 guineas to a second actor for the same purpose. Macklin, however, had not been privy to what the proprietors of the *Court-Miscellany, or Gentleman and Lady's Magazine*, Messrs Richardson and Urquhart, then planned. They engaged a short-hand writer, one Gurney, for a flat fee of one guinea, to attend a performance of *Love à la Mode*, and take down *verbatim* the actual words of the actors. The text of act 1 of the farce, having been obtained in this way, was then published in the April 1776 edition of the *Court-Miscellany*; the text of act 2 was promised for a future number. Counsel for the defendants, who resisted the motion for a perpetual injunction and an account of the profits made by the publication, mounted a charm offensive. 'The Magazines', counsel asserted, 'are useful, and are an article of trade, and often of service to authors, by giving a specimen of their works, and by that means serve as a recommendation of them, where they are deserving of it.'[55] Macklin was to waive his claim for an account, but insisted on his injunction, which Chancery granted him.[56]

In 1832, the practice of surreptitiously obtaining the text of a play in the manner practised by Richardson and Urquhart's Mr Gurney was far from unknown.

---

50 See above, p. 254.

51 *Select committee report on dramatic literature*, p. 143: evidence of Thomas Morton (Drury Lane.)

52 For more on the system of remuneration for dramatists at the time, see the synopsis in McFarlane, *Copyright: the performing right*, pp 42–8.

53 *Select committee report on dramatic literature*, p. 136.

54 *Macklin v. Richardson* (1770) Amb 694, 27 Eng Rep 451. See, too, McFarlane, *Copyright: the performing right*, pp 36–7.

55 Amb at 696, 27 Eng Rep at 452.

56 Lord Commissioner Smythe and Lord Commissioner Bathurst.

Managers, according to Jerrold in his evidence to the select committee,[57] would pay as little as £2 for copies of the text of a play secured in this underhand way from Mr Kenneth's agency 'at the corner of Bow-Street'. Charles Matthews, the joint proprietor of the Adelphi Theatre, echoed Jerrold's concerns over such practices.[58] The short-hand writers in the pits were engaging in theft 'without any ceremony', the texts secured in this fashion having 'become a kind of property among booksellers and adventurers'. Matthews evoked sympathy too for prompters who had lost one of their perquisites, an allusion to some form of in-house traffic in the manuscript text of plays.

Matthews' evidence is remarkable for another reason. That the more unscrupulous manager was well aware of the green light accorded abridgments by the King's Bench in *Murray v. Elliston* in 1822 seems to be confirmed by one incident he related.[59] A play *Wreck Ashore*, of which he part-owned the copyright, was due to be performed without his consent at the Queen's Theatre. A lawyer was sent round, and the planned performance was aborted. The Queen's then put on what Matthews describes as 'our *Bold Dragoons*' with minor modifications and under the title *The Dragoons of Normandy*.

Wilkins, as we have seen, entered a note of caution in the case of any plan to concede a general performing right. Most of the witnesses who touched on the question attached no caveats at all. Authors, they argued, had undoubtedly been hard done by: John Poole, for instance, the author of *Paul Pry*, had got £400 for the copyright. He calculated that if he had in addition been accorded a performing right, he would have earned £4,000,[60] perhaps something of an over-estimate.

Enthusiastic support for the necessary legal change was scarcely in short supply. For W.C. Macready, 'it would be only justice to [the author], and a benefit to dramatic literature.'[61] He thought 'it very hard that the author should not derive benefit from the acting of [his play] even after it is published.' For Matthews, bestowing a performing right constituted 'one of the best sources of reviving a taste for the drama.'[62] For Captain John Forbes, the proprietor of Covent Garden, it was a scandal authors were not paid: 'It is hardship we should have remedied if we had had it in our power.'[63]

One difficulty arose: extending the suggested performing right to performances in provincial theatres. D.E. Morris was not clear about this at all. 'I should think', he began,

> the scanty and uncertain audiences of provincial theatres would enable them to pay scarcely anything; if anything, it would be a very inconsiderable sum, and when it was offered, it would be hardly worth a gentleman's

---

57 *Select committee report on dramatic literature*, p. 157. See, too, McFarlane, *Copyright: the performing right*, pp 44–5.

58 *Select committee report on dramatic literature*, p. 170.   59 Ibid.

60 *Select committee report on dramatic literature*, p. 190.   61 Ibid., p. 136.

62 Ibid., p. 170.   63 Ibid., p. 115.

consideration. I should conceive also they would have the greatest difficulty in getting the money from a provincial manager, and from the uncertainty and thinness of their audiences, they could not afford it.[64]

Provincial managers would now only be likely to be in a position to pay £10 or £20 for permission to put on a play if they came from one of the five leading provincial venues – Bath, Norwich, Edinburgh, Liverpool and Dublin.[65] Richard Malone Raymond, the joint manager at one of these venues – Liverpool – broadly agreed.[66] He would be prepared to put down £20 as the performing right fee if the play was likely to be productive in proportion to that kind of outlay. Macready, too, urged caution. Any change to introduce a performing right 'should be done very carefully, inasmuch as sometimes the receipts of the provincial theatres may be very small.'[67]

Two witnesses, Morton and Macready, mentioned in their evidence that Lord Kenyon, a former chief justice of King's Bench, in an unreported decision regarding a claim in respect of a play by O'Keeffe had apparently held, remarkably, that 'acting' could amount to 'publication' and thus, in itself, might constitute breach of copyright.[68] Scarlett, in his argument on Murray's behalf in the latter's suit against Elliston, would seem to have come close to maintaining a similar position.[69] It is wiser to assume that Adolphus' rejection of that contention in the same case[70] represented what had become received opinion, and that Kenyon's pronouncement, even if it could be proved that he had uttered it, was now regarded with disfavour: 'acting' could not be so regarded. It is equally significant that in its report of July 1832 the select committee made no mention at all of this possible legal solution to the impasse, which thus headed straightaway for the limbo that pays host to legal developments destined never to prosper. A united committee, consisting of Bulwer Lytton, Lamb, Sheil, William Braugham and Sir Charles Wetherell, made a strong plea for the introduction of what was to become the dramatist's performing right. 'In regard to dramatic literature', the committee reported,

> it appears manifest that an author at present is subject to indefensible hardship and injustice; and the disparity of protection afforded to the labours of the dramatic writer, when compared even with that granted to authors in any other branch of letters, seems alone sufficient to divert the ambition of eminent and successful writers from that department of intellectual exertion.[71]

64 Ibid., p. 152.   65 Ibid.   66 *Select committee report on dramatic literature*, p. 209.
67 Ibid., p. 136. See further McFarlane, *Copyright: the performing right*, pp 47–8.
68 *Select committee report on dramatic literature*, p. 143 (Morton), p. 136 (Macready). But see further on this case the evidence of Morris, p. 153.
69 *Murray v. Elliston* (1822) 5 B & Ald 657 at 658, 106 Eng Rep 1331.
70 Ibid.   71 *Select committee report on dramatic literature*, p. 5.

Addressing their fellow MPs in the Commons, the committee continued:

> Your Commissioners, therefore, earnestly recommend that the author of a play should possess the same legal rights, and enjoy the same legal protection, as the author of any other literary production; and that his performance should not be legally exhibited at any Theatre, Metropolitan or Provincial, without his express and formal consent.[72]

The dust can hardly have settled on this key report of the select committee when Bulwer Lytton again seized the momentum. In March 1833, he sought the approval of the House of Commons for the introduction of a measure that would enshrine the playwright's entitlement to a performing right in statute law.[73] The arguments in favour were now well known. But, at the risk of boring his captive audience, he did not shirk from repeating them. 'Dramatic authors', he told the House, 'possessed no control over the use of their property such as was very properly given to other labourers in the field of literature by the law of copyright.' 'A play when published', he continued,

> might be acted upon any stage without the consent of the author, and without his deriving a single shilling from the profits of the performance. It might not only be acted at one theatre, but at 100 theatres, and though, perhaps, it filled the pockets of the managers, not a single penny might accrue from its performance, however successful, or however repeated, to the unfortunate author.

Bulwer Lytton's plan was that this form of copyright should last for twenty-eight years or the life of the author. And the sanction where plays were performed without the author's consent envisaged that the author could sue for damages, up to a maximum of £50, with a minimum of £10, for each unauthorized performance, against the proprietor of the theatre in question. He had high hopes for the alteration in the law he advocated:

> The evil of the existing system was pretty abundantly evinced by the striking decline of the modern drama ... The result of the proposed changes would be that greater talents and a high order of genius would be enlisted in the service of the stage, and that the dramatic literature of the country would once more regain that exalted position from which it had been degraded by the want of the necessary encouragement and protection.[74]

Bulwer Lytton's proposal was backed by George Lamb. Lamb was a good amateur actor who had also produced opera at Covent Garden. One minor criticism he voiced was that setting the minimum sum of damages at £10 was

72 Ibid.   73 *Hansard, 3*, xvi, col. 560 (12 Mar. 1833).   74 Ibid., cols. 560–1.

setting it too high. It was, he contended, too large in the case of the manager of a company of strolling players.[75] Lamb could also have taken into account the difficulties for provincial theatres which had been brought to the attention of the select committee.

The Act to amend the law relating to dramatic literary property received the royal assent on 10 June 1833. Section 1 noted the new principle in stark terms. 'The author', it provided,

> of any tragedy, comedy, play, opera, farce, or any other dramatic piece or entertainment ... not printed and published ... shall have as his own property the sole liberty of representing or causing to be represented, at any place or places of dramatic entertainment whatsoever, in any part of the United Kingdom of Great Britain and Ireland ... and shall be deemed and taken to be the proprietor thereof.

And the section continued:

> And the author of any production, printed and published within ten years before the passing of this Act by the author thereof ... or which shall hereafter be so printed and published ... shall from the time of passing this Act, or from the time of such publication respectively, until the end of twenty-eight years from the day of such publication of the same, and also if the author or authors, or the survivor of the authors shall be living at the end of that period, during the residue of his natural life, have as his own property the sole liberty of representing or causing to be represented, the same at any such dramatic entertainment as aforesaid, and shall be deemed and taken to be the proprietor thereof.

A proviso covering a limited range of transitional cases – where previous to the Act consents had been given – was then appended.

Lamb's criticism on one point of detail had been taken into account. Persons responsible for any unauthorised representation (i.e., one without the consent in writing of the author, etc.) was made liable in respect of each representation

> to the payment of an amount not less than 40 shillings [£2], or to the full amount of the benefit or advantage arising from such representation or the injury or loss sustained by the plaintiff therefrom, whichever shall be the greater damages, to the author or proprietor.

The author was also to be entitled to double the costs of any suit brought by him to enforce his rights. Any claim, however, had to be brought within twelve months of the alleged breach.

75 Col. 561.

A copyright consolidation measure of 1842[76] extended Bulwer Lytton's Act to acknowledge the existence of performing rights in respect of musical compositions, the critical enabling section in the measure simply stating that it was 'expedient' to do so. This section, section 20, announced: 'the sole right to represent or perform any dramatic piece or musical composition shall endure and be the property of the author thereof.' It went on to clarify one point of some uncertainty: 'The first public representation or performance of any dramatic piece or musical composition shall be deemed equivalent in the construction of this Act, to the first publication of any such book.' 'Acting', by statutory diktat, now equalled 'publication'.

There is little discussion of the dramatic author's performing right in the record of the proceedings of the royal commission of the 1870s or in its report of 1878. It is otherwise so far as the composer's performing right was concerned. A rector from Markshall in Essex, the Revd J.W. Bennett, gave evidence on the exactions of the owner of copyright in *Lurline*, one of the operas composed by William Vincent Wallace, better known for *Maritana*. At an entertainment to raise funds for the cricket club at Coggeshall, a village some ten miles to the west of Colchester, also in Essex,[77] Mrs Eve, from Braintree close by, had sung 'Sweet spirit, hear my prayer' from *Lurline*; and it was over this performance in particular that a Mr Bodda, now the owner of the copyright in *Lurline*, had sent in his bill, which, with some reluctance, the cricket club had paid. On the night in question, 10 February 1876, supporters of the Coggeshall Cricket Club had paid 1s. each for front seats in the hall where Mrs Eve, amongst others, was to perform, and 6d. for back seats.

In earlier evidence before the royal commission Arthur Sullivan, in response to a question from an equally distinguished figure who served on the commission, the writer Anthony Trollope, bluntly assailed the statute law provision which gave the owner of the performing right the entitlement to claim £2 per performer for each song sung in the absence of any licence to perform. 'If there was', Sullivan began,

> a performance in which 2000 took part at the Crystal Palace, and they performed something of Mr Balfe's or of Mr Wallace's, and if this common informer went down, every one of those 2000 persons in the chorus and the orchestra would be liable to a penalty of £2, making a very nice little fee of £4,000 payable, which is ridiculous on the face of it.[78]

The allusions here are to Michael William Balfe, best known for his opera *The Bohemian Girl*, and the song in it 'I dreamt that I dwelt in marble halls', and to William Vincent Wallace. What offended Sullivan even more was that the money thereby obtained would not have gone to the composer but to the two or three

---

76 An Act to Amend the Law of Copyright, 1842 (5 & 6 Vict., c. 45), s. 20. See also McFarlane, *Copyright: the performing right*, pp 52–6. The 1842 Act is known as Serjeant Talfourd's Act.

77 *Report of the royal commission on copyright: minutes of evidence*, p. 115; McFarlane, *Copyright: the performing right*, pp 81–2.

78 Ibid., p. 113.

individuals, on whose behalf the informer would have acted, who had purchased old copyrights of Balfe and of Wallace.[79] In the *Oxford dictionary of national biography* it is recorded that Wallace disposed of his copyright in *Lurline* to the Pyne-Harrison Opera Company for the princely sum of 10s.

The royal commission in its report agreed that the 40s. penalty provided for in the legislation had been much abused, and they proposed a remedy. The matter was dealt with at some length. 'Copyright in favourite songs from operas and in other works', the members of the commission say in their report,

> have been bought, and powers of attorney have been obtained to act apparently for the owners of the copyright in such works, and to claim immediate payment of £2 for the performance of each song. These songs are frequently selected by ladies and others for singing at penny readings and village charitable entertainments, and they sing them not for their own gain, but for benevolent objects. In such cases there is manifestly no intention to infringe the rights of any person; the performers are unconscious that they are infringing such rights; and no injury whatever can be inflicted on the proprietors of the copyrights. In many cases of this kind, and under a threat of legal proceedings in default of payment, the penalty has been demanded, and we have reason to believe that the money so demanded has been generally paid.[80]

The commission went on to propose to constrain the entitlement of individuals possessed of the performing right to take proceedings over the performance of single songs. The exercise of that right, when possessed by persons other than the composer, was capable of inflicting injury on composers. Public performance of their music was of course advantageous to composers since it served to advertise their works. At the same time it was necessary that copyright owners should retain sufficient control to enable them to save the music of any composer from inferior or unsuitable performances.[81]

The commission then went on to suggest that every printed musical composition should state on the title page that the right of public performance was reserved. Claims for damages for infringing the performing right would only be admissible where such statement had been made. And compensation for each transgression should be set at a level according to the actual damage sustained; the 40s. rule per each transgression was thus to be ended.[82]

Legislation along the lines the commission had proposed was to follow in the 1880s. In 1882 statute made it obligatory for anyone seeking to enforce a

79 Ibid.
80 *Report of the royal commission on copyright, 1878*, at xxviii.
81 Ibid. And see the instance recalled by Arthur Sullivan in his evidence: *Report of the royal commission on copyright – minutes of evidence*, p. 113.
82 *Report of the royal commission on copyright*, p. xxviii.

performing right as regards a musical composition to demonstrate publication of the score and the presence on the title page of that score of the prescribed statement to the effect that the right of public performance was reserved.[83] Four years later another statute altered the law on the quantum of damages exigible for violations of the performing right. The judge, it was laid down, henceforth 'may award a less sum than 40s., in respect of each and every such unauthorised representation or performance as aforesaid or a nominal penalty or nominal damages as the judgment of the case may require.'[84] The old rule of damages – the 40s. rule – the same statute was at pains to emphasise still applied in instances of interference with the performing right in the cases both of opera and of stage plays.[85] Curiously, but significantly, both these statutes were repealed by the Copyright Act of 1911.[86] Compliance with international convention – the Berlin revision of the Berne Convention of 1908 – demanded no less.[87]

Though, as we shall see, the royal commission in its report had things to say regarding the dramatic author's performing right, rather more was to be gleaned as regards the treatment of that right from a study of the salient, if scarcely over-extensive, case-law. An early case focused on proofs of assignment of the performing right.[88] Elsewhere the protagonists in two key groups of cases featured the author Charles Reade and the author and actor-manager Dion Boucicault. A curiosity from this period in the history of the dramatic author's performing right is that these two individuals were to collaborate in the writing of the novel *Foul Play* published in 1869.[89]

Reade is best known today for his fine historical novel *The Cloister and the Hearth* (1861), set in Europe on the eve of the Reformation. Markedly different had been a novel he had brought out five years before, *It is Never too Late to Mend*, where the emphasis had been on the English prison system of the times, the practice of transportation, and the life of a miner in the country to which transportees had traditionally been exported. *Foul Play*, written with Boucicault's assistance, owed something of its inspiration to *It is Never too Late to Mend* with its tale of a convicted fellow enduring the challenge of the separate system in the English prisons of the day before being sent to a penal colony. But there are scenes in exotic locations anticipating the oeuvre of a Stevenson or a Conrad; and more in point, perhaps, the identity of the convicted felon – an ordained clergyman, the

83 An Act to amend the law of copyright relating to musical compositions, 1882 (45 & 46 Vict., c. 40), s. 1.

84 An Act to amend the law relating to the recovery of penalties for the unauthorised performance of copyright musical compositions, 1888 (51 & 52 Vict., c. 17), s. 1.

85 Ibid., s. 4.

86 1 & 2 Geo V, c. 46, sch. 2.

87 McFarlane, *Copyright: the performing right*, pp 91, 115–16.

88 *Shepherd v. Conquest* (1856) 17 CB 427, 139 Eng Rep 1140: Stephens, *Profession of the playwright*, p. 95.

89 Charles Reade and Dion Boucicault, *Foul Play* (London, Bradbury Evans & Co., 1869).

victim of the foul play in the novel's title, the Revd Robert Penfold – owes not a little to the character of the Revd Josiah Crawley in Trollope's *The Last Chronicle of Barset*, published two years before *Foul Play* in 1867.

It is Never too Late to Mend started off life as Reade's play *Gold*. Scenes from this, extended and elaborated, grew into the novel. Conquest, the brother of the manager of the Grecian Theatre in London, brought out a dramatised version of the novel itself which he entitled 'Never too Late to Mend' and which the Grecian Theatre went on to perform. Reade sued for breach of copyright in the novel, only to be rebuffed by a decision on the resultant demurrer in the Court of Common Pleas that Conquest's version involved no breach,[90] the court citing the case from 1822 involving the abridgment of Byron's *Marino Faliero* in its grounds.[91] Later, however, the same court was to hold that Conquest had nonetheless breached Reade's performing right[92] – arguably, a curious outcome, but one, nonetheless, that inspired the royal commission in its report of 1878 to take pains to stress the existence of two distinct rights:

> While in books there is only one copyright, in musical compositions and dramatic works there are two, namely, the right of printed publication and the right of public performance. These rights are essentially different and distinct, and we find that many plays and musical pieces are publicly performed without being published in the form of books, and thus the acting or dramatic right is in force, which as to literary copyright such plays and pieces retain the character of unpublished manuscripts.[93]

The legal difficulties facing Dion Boucicault as he sought to have protected by the courts his claims to a performing right were of a different order altogether.

Boucicault's *The Colleen Bawn* was first performed in New York in 1860. When a production was announced for London, he sued, alleging a breach of his performing right. That the first representation had occurred abroad in a foreign country – the United States – was adjudged fatal to his claim, an outcome dictated by the undeveloped state of international copyright protection at the time.[94]

Boucicault was destined to suffer defeat again when problems arose over a planned revival of another of his plays, *The Shaughraun*, at London's Adelphi Theatre in 1876. *The Shaughraun*, like *The Colleen Bawn*, saw its first stage performance in New York, in its case in 1874. The play was put on at Drury Lane in London in 1875, with a transfer shortly afterwards to the Adelphi. Boucicault himself acted the eponymous role, and there seem to have been no difficulties.

90 *Reade v. Conquest* (1861) 9 CB (ns) 755, 142 Eng Rep 297.
91 *Murray v. Elliston* (1822) 5 B & Ald 657, 106 Eng Rep 1331.
92 *Reade v. Conquest* (1862) 11 CB (ns) 479, 142 Eng Rep 883; Stephens, *Profession of the playwright*, p. 98.
93 *Report of royal commission on copyright*, at xv.
94 *Boucicault v. Delafield* (1863) 1 Hen & Miller 597, 71 Eng Rep 261.

With Boucicault back in New York, the Adelphi in 1876 sought to mount a revival. Contact with Boucicault was made and this indicated a preference on his part for a delay, since it was his wish to reprise his own performance in the role of the Shaughraun. The Adelphi took umbrage at this, and pressed ahead with its own plans. Boucicault sued, but was again unsuccessful, on exactly the same grounds that had led to his losing in the case of *The Colleen Bawn*.[95] The decision of the vice-chancellor, Sir Richard Malins, who criticised Boucicault for what he described as the latter's unreasonable conduct during the negotiations, was to be affirmed by the Court of Appeal. The imbroglio in which Boucicault again found himself involved helps naturally to explain the amount of attention that the royal commission of a few years later devoted to the large gaps in international copyright protection.

The problems thrown up by Reade's earlier entanglement with the law had necessarily engaged the attention of the royal commission as well. 'Music printed and published becomes a book for the purpose of the literary copyright', the commissioners declared in their report,

> and so, we presume does a play, but it is a question what becomes of the performing copyright on the publication of the work as a book; and there is a further question, whether the performing copyright can be gained at all, if the piece is printed and published as a book before being publicly performed.[96]

The report of the royal commission makes compelling reading, not least for the identification by the commissioners of what they perceived as uncertainties such as this in the existing state of the law.

Within its pages the reader will also find a heterodox view of the law of copyright in general, expounded by a distinguished member of the royal commission, Sir Louis Mallet, a civil servant of long standing and an acknowledged authority on commercial policy. Mallet questioned the rationale for such a law at all. 'The right conferred by a copyright law', he wrote in a dissenting minority report, 'derives its chief value from the discovery of the art of printing; and there appears no reason for giving to authors any larger share in the value of a mechanical invention, to which they have constituted nothing, than to any other member of the community.'[97] Turning to the traditional *raison d'être* given for such a law, Mallet continued:

> I suppose that the presumption of a copyright law is that it is only by conferring a monopoly for a term of years on an author that sufficient inducement can be afforded to literary effort, and that without such form of

95 *Boucicault v. Chatterton* (1876) Ch Div 274.
96 *Report of the royal commission on copyright*, at xv.
97 *Report of the royal commission on copyright*, at xlvi.

protection the literature of a country would suffer, either from a diminished supply or a deterioration in quality.[98]

This led on to the conclusion he then drew – which preceded his call for a system of royalty payments in lieu: 'From this point of view the question becomes a purely practical one, viz., whether any special interference by law is required to ensure for a community the best possible literature at the cheapest possible price.'[99]

All of this constituted far too bitter a pill for the majority on the royal commission to swallow. The latter, nonetheless, made aware, as we have already had occasion to point out, of the anomalies and uncertainties in the then current state of the law, levelled a scathing attack on it in a passage in the commissioners' report, which has often been cited.[100] 'The law', the royal commission's report announced, 'is wholly destitute of any sort of arrangement, incomplete, often obscure, and even when it is intelligible upon long study, it is in many parts so ill-expressed that no one who does not give such study to it can expect to understand it.'[101]

One question not adverted to by the royal commission in its 1878 report related to a further legal issue markedly different from any of those raised either by Charles Reade or by Dion Boucicault; the identification of the sorts of performance of dramatic works in respect of which performing rights might appropriately and legitimately be claimed. An incident in one of Jane Austen's novels, published in 1814 some nineteen years before Bulwer Lytton's Act, may be called in aid here by way of introduction to the problem.

In 1798 Covent Garden in London put on what is thought to have been the first performance of Elizabeth Inchbald's play *Lovers' Vows*, a drama founded on August Kotzebue's *Child of Love* with its sympathetic portrait of a fallen woman and her illegitimate son. It was this play that the younger denizens of Mansfield Park decided finally to stage in their new-found enthusiasm for amateur theatricals. Edward Bertram and Fanny Price were opposed, but they were in a minority, and so the rest pressed ahead with the plan. If the Act of 1833 had been in force at the time, and Mrs Inchbald's permission had not been sought – she died in 1821 – were the circumstances of the projected staging, in the mansion's converted billiard-room, such that it could be said that performing rights had been breached? Common sense might suggest that the answer would depend on things such as the make-up of the intended audience. Jane Austen tells us that the original scheme was only to secure the attendance of the Grants and Mrs Rushworth;[102] but she adds, as the day of the performance approached, Tom Bertram, we are told,[103] 'was giving an invitation to every family who came his way.'

As aficionados of Austen's *Mansfield Park* will be aware, no performance of Mrs Inchbald's *Lovers' Vows* actually takes place, following Sir Thomas Bertram's unannounced and unexpected arrival back from Antigua.

98 Ibid., at xlix.   99 Ibid.
100 The passage, for instance, is repeated in McFarlane, *Copyright: the performing right*, p. 61.
101 *Report of the royal commission on copyright*, p. vi.
102 Jane Austen, *Mansfield Park*, chapter 16.   103 *Mansfield Park*, chapter 18.

The precise scope of the performing rights enjoyed by dramatic authors further to the Act of 1833 has been the focus of germane litigation in England; there is no record of comparable lawsuits in Ireland. Two of these English lawsuits – one from 1883 and the other from 1933 – are worth revisiting for the light they cast on the critical qualifying conditions for the dramatist claiming his performing right. In any comprehensive survey (which this is not), account would necessarily also have to be taken of the decisions in cases launched by composers or their assignees over breaches of performing rights involving musical compositions

In 1883, three performances of H.J. Byron's play, *Our Boys*,[104] were put on by an amateur drama club in Guy's Hospital in London for the benefit of nurses and other medical staff. The play was performed in the board-room at Guy's. There was no admission charge, but tickets were made available which were transferable. One reporter was present. Duck, the assignee of the copyright in the play claimed damages for breach of the salient performing right, *Our Boys* having been performed in what was argued 'any place or places of dramatic entertainment', the 'public forum' requirement laid down by the 1833 statute. The county court judge accepted that, *prima facie*, the place where the performance occurred was one of dramatic entertainment, but, since the public had not been admitted, it could not in the end be so regarded. By a majority, the Queen's Bench Division, Sir William Brett and Lord Justice Bowen, Lord Justice Fry dissenting, agreed.[105] All three judges accepted that those claiming breach of a performing right were not restricted to claims relating to productions in recognised theatres.

Counsel for Bates had argued the contrary, that that indeed was the thrust of Bulwer Lytton's Act. The Queen's Bench Division disagreed, and that disagreement was most forcefully expressed by the dissenter, Lord Justice Fry, who manages to intrude a *soupçon* of theatrical history in his reasoning. 'It has been said', he began,

> that we must have regard to the state of things in 1833 when the Act was passed; and that as plays were, for the most part, then acted in playhouses, we should conclude that the legislature referred to playhouses only. That, it appears to me, would be misinterpreting the words of the legislature. The legislature must have known that great changes had taken place in the mode of acting dramatic pieces, and that comparing the modes of such performances in the reign of Elizabeth or James I with those in the reign of William IV, very considerable alterations had occurred. It is probable that there were far more strolling players in the former reigns than in the latter. It is certain that in the Elizabethan period plays were acted in many other places than regular theatres, and that masques then prevailed which had fallen into desuetude in the reign of William IV. It seems to me, therefore, to be plain that the legislature must have contemplated the probability of

---

104 On this play's successful long run, 1874–79, at London's Vaudeville Theatre, see Stephens, *The profession of the playwright*, p. 64.   105 *Duck v. Bates* (1884) 13 QBD 843.

changes taking place also in the future. Therefore it is that such general words are used.[106]

Sir William Brett, the Master of the Rolls, had earlier expressed his concurrence. 'A dramatic piece', he averred, 'may be acted elsewhere than in a licensed theatre, and persons without the author's consent may act his drama in places not habitually devoted to dramatic entertainment.'[107]

Where the bench disagreed was over the divide between a private and domestic performance and a public one, and whether indeed a performance in the former category necessarily lay at all outside the scope of the dramatist's rights conferred by the 1833 legislation. Lord Justice Bowen accepted the conclusion of the county court judge when he argued as follows:

> The body of dramatic performers were desirous of amusing those in the service of the hospital. There was, therefore, no appropriation of the building even for the occasion to the entertainment of any portion of the public: it was to be an entertainment of a domestic character.[108]

The Master of the Rolls had raised the stakes considerably in intimating his approval. 'There must be present', Sir William Brett urged, 'a sufficient part of the public who would go also to a performance licensed by the author as a commercial transaction; otherwise the place where the drama is represented will not be a "place of dramatic entertainment".'[109] Lord Justice Fry's rejection of these approaches to the interpretation of the key clause in the 1833 Act is both stern and reasoned. 'According to my view of the usage of the English language,' he announced, 'the performance of a dramatic piece in a large drawing-room, or in the hall of a large mansion or at a castle in the country, although the public may not be invited to it, would be a dramatic entertainment.'[110]

There were policy considerations that ought not to be lost sight of, which were set down by him in a passage in his judgment that merits extended quotation. 'It has been said', Fry went on to claim,

> that it is absurd to extend the words of the Act to internal and domestic representations. It is quite true that there may be some internal and domestic representations which it would be absurd to suppose that the legislature had in its mind. It is difficult to suppose that the acting of some children before their parents in the nursery or drawing-room would be a dramatic entertainment within the meaning of the Act.[111]

But there were other cases. 'On the other hand,' Fry went to explain,

---

106 Ibid., p. 853.   107 Ibid., p. 846.   108 At 850.   109 At 847.   110 At 853.
111 At 853.

it seems to me that there may be internal and domestic representations, which are well within the purview of the statute. Suppose, for instance, that a nobleman possessed of a large mansion in the country, having his house full of distinguished guests, invites them, his servants, and such of the residents in the county as are in the habit of visiting him, to witness the representation of a dramatic piece; is not such a performance domestic and internal? But is it not at the same time a performance which would probably interfere with the proprietary rights of the owner of the piece? What would be the chance of the next company which came to the adjoining town to perform the same piece, getting together so good an audience as they would get, had the piece not been performed in the neighbouring mansion of the nobleman? It appears to me, that the rights of the proprietor of the piece would have been seriously interfered with.[112]

The astringent views expressed by Lord Justice Fry in *Duck v. Bates* were not destined to prevail, and when changes were made to Bulwer Lytton's statute on the enactment of the Copyright Act of 1911[113] matters appeared to have been put beyond all doubt when it was made plain that the dramatist's copyright meant 'the sole right to produce ... the work ... in public.'[114] But that still left unresolved as to what kind of performance of a play was to be designated a performance 'in public'. This was the question explored in a seven-day hearing before Mr Justice Crossman in the London High Court in 1934 and which eventually engaged the attention of the Court of Appeal as well.

In February 1933 the monthly meeting of the branch of the Women's Institute at Duston, a village a couple of miles west of Northampton, took the form of attendance at a drama evening laid on by the Overstone and Sywell Dramatic Society, another amateur group like the one that had performed *Our Boys* at Guy's in 1880s. Two plays were presented, Gertrude Jennings' *The Rest Cure* which had first been performed in London in 1914 and the focus of attention in the subsequent lawsuit, and *Mechanical Jane*.

The Rest Cure might be described as a light one-act comedy – an unlikely focus of performing right litigation.[115] Clarence Reed, a poet suffering from what would be described today as 'writer's block', has entered a nursing home in central London for a 'rest cure', perhaps today's 'rehab'. He need not have bothered, for the ambiance is not to his taste at all, and on day two he contrives a furtive exit. The noise was no advertisement for the home, there was the residential parrot, the sound of coal from the scuttle being thrown on his bedroom fire. And from the outside came the racket produced by the passing buses and the raucous notes of some street singer. Food when it came was scarcely *cordon bleu*: boiled mutton and suet pudding. The mutton, our poet complains, was half cold, a verdict endorsed

---

112 Ibid., pp 853–4.   113 1 & 2 Geo V, c. 46.   114 S. 1 (2).
115 Gertrude Jennings, *Four One Act plays* (London, Samuel French Ltd, Sidgwick & Jackson Ltd, 1914), p. 11.

by May Williams, one of the nurses: 'It may be a little chilly.' Another inmate found a piece of glass in their jelly. To cap it all, an outbreak of scarlet fever is recorded. Alice Palmer, the other nurse we meet, thinks nothing at all of slandering Clarence behind his back, labelling him a 'tiresome little toad'. Needless to say, none of the staff could be said to follow the guidelines laid down in the nursing home's bible, the *Nurses' Pocket Book*. If the quality of nursing home care was plainly in Gertrude Jennings' sights as she composed this drama, so, too, arguably, were the foibles of the cantankerous male – something that could well have added to the appeal of the play for the women of the Duston W.I. Gertrude Jennings died in 1958. She continued to write plays until the mid-1950s. Most were one-act dramas, but a number of full-length, three-act plays were also among her *oeuvre*.

For purposes of the lawsuit that followed, which had the hallmark of a test case, considerable care was taken to furnish data regarding the Women's Institute. Founded after the First World War, it had thrived in rural areas, providing an opportunity for women to gather together socially, hear lectures,[116] and learn handicrafts. (Having participated in a Women's Institute bookbinding course at Husborne Crawley in rural Bedfordshire in the early 1950s, I can vouch for the excellence of the instruction local committees were able to commandeer.) In Ireland, the objects of the Irish Countrywomen's Association, founded, apparently, somewhat earlier, in 1910, were not so very different: 'to bring women together in fellowship and through cooperative effort to develop and improve the standard of rural and urban life in Ireland.'[117]

In Duston itself at the time there were 1085 females in the village; 109 were members of the Institute. At the drama night on 23 February 1933, 62 of those members were present. In attendance in Duston village hall were these 62 and the 5 actors; there were no guests.

On these facts Mr Justice Crossman held that the performance of *The Rest Cure* was not in public; and he thus dismissed the claim for damages brought by Jennings against Stephens, the president of the Overstone and Sywell Dramatic Society.[118] A unanimous Court of Appeal (Lord Wright, Master of the Rolls, Lord Justice Romer and Lord Justice Greene) reversed, thus upholding Jennings' claim.[119] The key adjudication at appellate level was to the effect that the fact the audience resided in the same village in different houses was not sufficient to make it a domestic or quasi-domestic audience. There was, in addition, to be an echo of Lord Justice Fry's reliance on policy considerations in a concluding observation of Lord Wright, the Master of the Rolls:

---

116 In the film *Calendar Girls*, satire is directed at Women's Institute lectures on rugs, broccoli and the Milk Marketing Board.

117 As set down by Hardiman J in *Equality Authority v. Portmarnock Golf Club* [2010] 1 ILRM 237, at 247.

118 *Jennings v. Stephens* [1935] Ch 703.

119 *Jennings v. Stephens* [1936] Ch 469. See further McFarlane, *Copyright: the performing right*, pp 121–2.

If the performance in question is held not to be a performance in public, the rights of owners of dramatic copyright, copyright in music or copyright in lectures all over the country will be seriously prejudiced; their plays will be liable to lose novelty, and the public demand for performance will be affected: the public appetite will be exhausted. The same is true of musical compositions and of lectures. It is the duty of the Court to protect the rights of authors, composers and lecturers, according to a fair construction of the Act.[120]

In Scotland a key adjudication in this area of difficulty concerned musical compositions performed without a licence having been obtained before a football supporters club in Greenock.[121] The outcome was identical – the performing right had been breached.

Almost the last official mention of performing rights in relation to stage plays is to be found in the report of a British committee on copyright in 1952.[122] The opening words of the relevant paragraph in the report would not have displeased Bulwer Lytton. The principle of recognition for performing rights, the committee declared,[123] was not open to question. A reference to the United Kingdom Copyright Act of 1911 and to the Berne Convention followed. The committee continued:

Plays and musical works are written to be performed, and the dramatist and the composer must look to performance in public for the greater part of their earnings; they would have every reason to be dissatisfied if their receipts were restricted to those derived from the sale of sheet music or of copies of a play.[124]

The committee went on, however, to express reservations on one important aspect of the contemporary situation. 'On the other hand,' the committee pointed out,

the general public (and entertainment promoters meeting the demands of the general public) also have their interest in the conditions under which copyright works are allowed to be performed, and we have been faced with a large volume of criticism from many quarters directed at the way in which rights of public performance are exercised. The evidence leaves us little doubt that this criticism is not without its justification.[125]

120 [1936] Ch at 480.
121 *Performing Right Society v. Rangers Supporters Club, Greenock*, 1973 SLT 198, [1975] RPC 626. See further McFarlane, *Copyright: the performing right*, pp 126–8.
122 *Report of the copyright commission*, Cmd 8662.
123 At 43.   124 Ibid.   125 Ibid.

Similar anxieties were certainly to be expressed in Ireland as well.[126] As we are about to discover, one major change to be adopted in both the United Kingdom and Ireland was to delimit the meaning of 'public performance' in one specific context, but controls over restrictions on the right of public performance are also a feature of modern law.

In the Republic legislative action taken in 1963 and found in that year's Copyright Act[127] placed restrictions on the scope of performances deemed to be performances in public. The critical sub-sections of the section of the Copyright Act in question, section 53, provided as follows:

> (3) For the avoidance of doubt it is hereby declared that, where a literary, dramatic or musical work –
>> (a) is performed in class, or otherwise in the presence of an audience, and
>> (b) is so performed in the course of the activities of a school, by a person who is a teacher in, or a pupil in attendance at, the school,
> the performance shall not be taken for the purposes of this Act to be a performance in public if the audience is limited to persons who are teachers in, or pupils in attendance at, the school or are otherwise directly connected with the activities of the school.
>
> (4) For the purposes of the last preceding subsection of this section a person shall not be taken to be directly connected with the activities of a school by reason only that he is a parent or guardian of a pupil in attendance at the school.

These provisions are identical with those introduced for the United Kingdom by its Copyright Act of 1956.[128] Its section 41, like section 53 of the later Irish Act, dealt generally with the use of copyright material for educational purposes, which it validated – conspicuously removing from the taint of a breach of copyright law copyrighted matter featured in an examination question.[129]

In the Republic section 53 of the 1963 Act has been superseded by sections 53 to 55 of the consolidation copyright measure of 2000.[130] As regards performance rights, a critical change has been to extend the exemption granted in respect of performances at schools to other 'educational establishments', it being left to the relevant government minister, in 2000 the Minister for Enterprise, Trade and Employment, to specify such educational establishments other than schools.[131]

The United Kingdom's Copyright Bill of 1955, introduced in the House of Lords in the autumn of 1955, did not include any of these concessions in respect

126 Consider, e.g., the remarks of Liam Cosgrave on fees charged by the Performing Right Society in respect of events held in parochial halls: 199 *Dáil Debates*, col. 1427 (14 Feb. 1963).
127 No. 10 of 1963.   128 4 & 5 Eliz II, c. 74.
129 Copyright Act, 1956, s. 41(1)(b)(UK); Copyright Act, 1963, s. 53(1)(b) (Ireland).
130 Copyright and Related Rights Act 2000: no. 28 of 2000.   131 S. 55.

of schools. But on the occasion of the Bill's second reading on 15 November two peers, Viscount Bridgeman and Lord Burden, drew attention to what they regarded as an omission, and pressed for something to be done. Lord Burden accepted that schools could not be totally excluded from the scope of protection for copyright owners. 'When a school has a public concert,' he argued, 'or, shall we say, a youth organisation connected with the school has a public performance, then of course the rightful claims of copyright holders must be fully recognised and appropriate arrangements made to safeguard these rights.'[132] But, he went on, the fundamental position of teachers in schools had to be faced,[133] as Viscount Bridgeman, in an earlier intervention in the Lords debate, had argued as well.[134] Bridgeman was concerned at the legal implication of two situations – where a teacher turned on a gramophone record during a music lesson in class and where a school quoted in an examination paper a passage of a copyright work in order that it might be translated by students into French.

Bridgeman acknowledged that there was no evidence that bodies such as the Performing Right Society pressed strongly for royalties to be paid in any of these cases, but it was his view, even so, that the matter should be cleared up – something that was plainly also the opinion of the County Councils Association and the Association of Municipal Corporations, both with responsibilities for schools, who had lobbied on the question. Lord Mancroft, the Joint Parliamentary Under-Secretary for the Home Department, promised to take these representations on board.[135]

In due course a number of amendments were moved to the Lords to give effect to the concerns that had been expressed. One moved by Lord Burden himself at the Bill's Committee Stage on 29 November proposed as follows:

> No fair dealing with a literary, dramatic or musical work for purposes of teaching in [a school] shall constitute an infringement of the copyright in the work: Provided that this subsection shall not apply to any performance or exhibition to which members of the public are admitted, whether on payment or otherwise.[136]

Reacting for the government, the lord chancellor, Viscount Kilmuir, took exception to any ameliorative scheme which relied so heavily on a concept of 'fair dealing'.[137] But, as is plain from Kilmuir's concern over the possible plight of an art teacher who reproduced copies of a painting by Utrillo for pupils to try to copy,[138] he was totally sympathetic to the initiative taken by Bridgeman and Burden. 'If we can find a way', Kilmuir recognised, 'of helping education more widely than in the last amendment, we will certainly try to do it ... but ... it must not be at the expense of our obligations under the [Brussels] Convention.'[139]

132 *Hansard, 5 (lords)*, cxciv, col. 529.   133 Col. 531.   134 Cols. 521–2.
135 Col. 558.   136 Cols. 905–6.   137 Col. 910. And cf. the views of Earl Jowitt: col. 1050.
138 Cols. 928–9.   139 Col. 931.

At the resumed Committee Stage on 1 December this spirited debate continued. Earl Jowitt, the former lord chancellor, identified the nub of the problem – which takes us back to reflecting on *Duck v. Bates*[140] and *Jennings v. Stephens*.[141] 'I shall be entitled, if I like', Jowitt hypothesised,

> to play a copyright piece on my own piano in my own house, or even, if anybody should be rash enough to ask me, to sing a copyright song. What I cannot do is to play that piece or sing that song in public. It is difficult to see what is in public or what is not in public. There are many illustrations, but crudely and unscientifically, anything outside one's own home may be said to be in public.[142]

In the course of a debate which ranged far and wide – and which discussed, among other things, the ramifications of a performance of T.S. Eliot's *Murder in a Cathedral* in an actual cathedral[143] – it was inevitable, perhaps, that some member of the House of Lords should go very much further in seeking to restrict the scope of performances deemed to be in public. Lord Lucas of Chilworth was one such. At a further session at the Committee Stage on 6 December, he moved as follows, that

> a recording shall be deemed not to be heard in public if (1) the object of the performance of the recording is to afford social amenities to residents in hotels, boarding houses or other residential premises at which no charge is made for admission to the performance, or (2) the performance is not made for profit other than profit to be devoted to charitable or religious purposes or purposes beneficial to the community.[144]

This rather different initiative did not prosper, and was soon forgotten.

Finally, at the Report Stage on 21 February 1956 Viscount Kilmuir introduced a major amendment designed to answer the concerns raised by Bridgeman and Burden.[145] It was this amendment that became section 41 of the United Kingdom Copyright Act of 1956 and thus was the inspiration of section 53 of the Irish Act of 1963. In the light of the further change introduced in the Republic in 2000, it is instructive to note Kilmuir's opposition to extending the concession announced for schools in 1956 any further at all. Extending the exemption beyond schools, he averred, 'would be represented as contrary to Article 11 of the Brussels Convention, which explicitly gives to authors the exclusive right of authorising the public presentation and public performance of their works'.[146]

A linked change may be briefly noted. In the Republic since 1963 it has been made clear that the performing right is infringed where any person permits a place

<hr/>

140 (1884) 13 QBD 843.   141 [1936] Ch 469.   142 *Hansard, 5 (lords)*, cxciv, col. 1050.
143 Cols. 897–903 (29 Nov. 1955).   144 Col. 1098.
145 *Hansard, 5 (lords)*, cxcv, cols. 1164–65.   146 Col. 1168.

of entertainment to be used for an unauthorised performance of the dramatic work in question in public; and 'a place of public entertainment' is defined to include 'any premises occupied for other purposes but are from time to time made available for hire to such persons as may desire to hire them for purposes of public entertainment.'[147]

Another section in the Irish Act of 1963, in line with a provision in the British Act of 1956, settled a problem that had long perplexed practitioners in the field. The exercise of the performing right could now be claimed in respect of all sorts of performance occurring on stage so long as the contours of the performance had been reduced to writing. This was brought about by the attaching of a legislative imprimatur to a fresh definition of 'a dramatic work': this now included 'a choreographic work or entertainment in dumb show if reduced to writing'.[148]

Reverting to the concerns expressed by the British commission of inquiry in 1952, both jurisdictions have made fresh provision for dealing with disputes over the licensing by the copyright owner of the performing right. In Britain such disputes were referable in 1956 to a new body, the Performing Right Tribunal.[149] The comparable jurisdiction in the Republic has resided since 1963 in the Controller of Industrial and Commercial Property.[150]

Down the years, arguably the main change in the relevant law, however, has been to extend the period for which this unusual species of copyright, like copyright in general, subsists. Under Bulwer Lytton's original Act, exercise of the performing right was protected for 28 years from the date of the publication of the play or the life of the author.[151] In the Republic today – since 2000 – exercise of that right is protected for seventy years from the death of the author.[152]

Much Irish law is based on previous English statutory reform. One intriguing variant will be found in section 55 of the Irish Copyright Act of 1963. This casts on the proprietors of theatres, etc., a duty to keep a register of 'all dramatic works performed in the presence of persons who have paid for admission.' Entries in the register must give particulars of the work and of the persons presenting it. Such registers are to be made available on demand by any copyright owner. Jack Lynch, Minister for Industry and Commerce at the time, introduced what is now section 55 as an amendment to the Copyright Bill of 1962 during the latter's Committee Stage in Dáil Éireann. He explained the background in the following terms. 'The amendment was being introduced', he claimed,

147 Copyright Act 1963, s. 11(4), (6).
148 Copyright Act 1963, s. 2; Copyright Act 1956, s. 48 (UK).
149 Copyright Act, 1956, ss. 23–30. See further McFarlane, *Copyright: the performing right*, ch. 12.
150 Copyright Act, 1963, s. 30; Copyright and Related Rights Act, 2000, ss. 149–81.
151 3 Will IV, c. 15.
152 Copyright and Related Rights Act, 2000, s. 24. Voices objecting to the extensions have seemingly been few. For the criticisms of Sir Arnold Plant in 1953, and further discussion see McFarlane, *Copyright: the performing right*, p. 172.

as a result of representations made by dramatists, mainly. A register was required to be kept of dramatic works performed in halls and was inspected as long as the entertainment duty was charged in respect of performances in these halls. There was an inspection system by the Revenue Commissioners for the purpose, mainly, of entertainment duty, but when the entertainment duty was taken off, there then remained no inspection system which could also be used for the inspection of records of performances in these halls of dramatic works. Playwrights and others felt we should, nevertheless, continue to have a register maintained.[153]

It is clear that in today's world dramatic authors even so are not as well placed as owners of musical copyright to capitalise on their possession of performing rights.[154]

---

153 199 *Dáil Debates*, col. 1473 (14 Feb 1963). On Entertainment Duty, see above, ch. 11.
154 See McFarlane, *Copyright: the performing right, passim*, but especially at 65, fn. 19. For a complementary account of nineteenth-century developments as they affected dramatic authors, see Stephens, *The profession of the playwright*, ch. 4: 'Piracy and the defence of dramatic property'.

Appendix

Letters Patent (Litreacga paitinne)
for The Gate Theatre, Dublin
2 October 1959

DE BHRÍ go n-achtaítear i measc nithe eile le h'Alt 1 d'Acht áirithe ó Pharlaimint na hÉireann a bhí ann go deireanach dar teideal *"An Act for regulating the Stage in the City and County of Dublin"* a ritheadh sa bhliain 1786 (caibidil 57) mar a oiriúnaíodh agus mar atá i bhfeidhm anois gur dleathach agus go mbeadh sé dleathach don Rialtas Litir nó Litreacha Paitinne a dheonú ar feadh cibé téarma nach faide ná bliain is fiche agus faoi cibé sriantachtaí, agus coinníollacha agus teorainneacha is cuí leo ó am go ham, agus aon uair agus gach uair is oriúnach leo é, do dhuine nó do dhaoine chun amharclann nó amharclanna nó teach nó tithe aisteoireachta dea-rialaithe a bhunú agus a choimeád i gCathair Bhaile Átha Cliath agus i saorthais i mbruachbhailte agus i gcontae na Cathrach sin agas i gContae Bhaila Átha Cliath.

AGUS DE BHRÍ gur chuir an *Dublin Gate Theatre Company Limited* a bhfuil a oifig chláraithe i Rae Cavendish i gCathair Bhaile Átha Cliath i bhfios don Rialtas le Meabhrachán uaidh dar dáta an 13ú lá de Mheitheamh 1955, gur corpraíodh in Éirinn é mar Chuideachta Theoranta an 24ú lá de Nollaig 1929.

AGUS DE BHRÍ gur chuir Cuideachta an Mheabhracháin i bhfios freisin don Rialtas lena Meabhrachán go bhfuil ar theachtadh acu an t-áitreabh dá ngairtear anois *"The Gate*

WHEREAS by Section 1 of a certain Act of the late Parliament of Ireland entitled "An Act for regulating the Stage in the City and County of Dublin" passed in the year 1786 (chapter 57) as adapted and now in force it is amongst other things enacted that it shall and may be lawful to and for the Government to grant for such term not exceeding twenty-one years and under such restrictions conditions and limitations as to them shall seem meet from time to time, and when and as often as they shall think fit, one or more Letters Patent to one or more person or persons for establishing and keeping one or more well-regulated theatre or theatres, playhouse or playhouses in the City of Dublin and in the liberties suburbs and county thereof and in the County of Dublin.

AND WHEREAS by its Memorial dated the 13th day of June 1955 the Dublin Gate Theatre Company Limited whose registered office is at Cavendish Row in the City of Dublin represented to the Government that it was incorporated in Ireland as a Limited Company on the 24th day of December 1929.

AND WHEREAS by its Memorial the Memorialist Company further represented to the Government that the premises now known as "The Gate Theatre" consisting of part of

Theatre" agus arb é atá ann cid de na foirgnimh agus na háitribh atá i gceangal le hOspidéal Luí Seoil an Rotunda agus ina bhfuil an halla éisteachta, an stáitse, seomraí gléasta, oifigí agus stórais maraon leis na forsheomraí agus na hoinnaltáin a ghabhann leo sin agus na pasáistí agus na bealaí chucu agus an halla ionadachta ar chothrom na talún maraon leis na comhghabhálais agus arb é an t-áitreabh é atá ina iomláine línithe níos cruinne agus imlíne dhearg timpeall air ar an léarscáil atá greamaitha de Dhintiúr áirithe Léasa dar dáta an 6ú lá de Shamhain 1953, agus a rinneadh idir Gobharnóiri agus Caomhnóiri an Ospidéil chun Fóirithint ar Mhná Seoil Bochta i mBaile Átha Cliath de pháirt agus Cuideachta an Mheabhracháin den pháirt eile agus go bhfuil an t-áitreabh sin ar teachtadh acu go ceann téarma bliana is fiche ón 24ú lá de Dheireadh Fómhair 1952, a deonaíodh leis an Dintiúr Léasa sin.

AGUS DE BHRÍ gur impigh Cuideachta an Mheabhracháin ar an Rialtas Paitinn faoi théarmaí an Achta sin ó Pharlaimint na hÉireann a bhí ann go deireannach a ritheadh so bhliain 1786 (caibidil 57) a dheonú do Edward Arthur Henry Earl of Longford agus do Louis Jammet mar iontaobhaithe do Chuideachta an Mheabhracháin go ceann téarma bliana is fiche chun a chumasú dóibh amharclann dearialaithe a choimeád i gCathair Bhaile Átha Cliath san áitreabh sin dá ngairtear an *Gate Theatre* agus aon idirdhréacht traigéide coiméide réamhdhréacht ceoldráma burletta dráma fronsa nó geamaireacht nó aon ghníomh radharc páirt nó páirteanna díobh de chineál ar bith a aithris nó a léiriú nó a thaibhiú go poiblí gach tráth.

AGUS DE BHRÍ go ndearna an Rialtas an Meabhrachán sin a chur faoí bhráid an Ard-Aighne chun é a bhreithniú agus chun a thuairisciú don Rialtas cad ba chuí a dhéanamh ina thaobh.

AGUS DE BHRÍ go ndearna an tArd-Aighne an Meabharchán sin a bhreithniú go cuí agus fiosrúchán poiblí a chur ar siúl ag ar éist sé Abhcóide thar ceann Chuideachta an Mheabhracháin, thar ceann an Gharda

the buildings and premises annexed to the Rotunda Lying-in Hospital consisting of the auditorium, stage, dressingrooms, offices and stores together with the ante-rooms and lavatories connected therewith and the passages and approaches thereto and its entrance hall on the ground floor together with the appurtenances all of which said premises are more particularly delineated and surrounded with a red verge line on the map annexed to a certain Indenture of Lease dated the 6th day of November 1953 and made between the Governors and Guardians of The Hospital for the Relief of Poor Lying-In Women in Dublin of the one part and the Memorialist Company of the other part are held by them for a term of twenty-one years from the 24th day of October 1952 granted by the said Indenture of Lease.

AND WHEREAS the Memorialist Company prayed that the Government might be pleased to grant to Edward Arthur Henry Earl of Longford and Louis Jammet as trustees for the Memorialist Company a Patent under the terms of the said Act of the late Parliament of Ireland passed in the year 1786 (chapter 57) for a term of twenty-one years to enable them to carry on in the said premises known as the Gate Theatre a well-regulated theatre in the City of Dublin and therein at all times publicly to act represent or perform any interlude tragedy comedy prelude opera burletta play farce or pantomime or any act scene part or parts thereof of what nature and kind whatsoever.

AND WHEREAS the Government referred the said Memorial to the Attorney General to consider the same and report to the Government what might be proper to be done thereon.

AND WHEREAS the Attorney General duly considered the said Memorial and held a public enquiry at which he heard Counsel upon behalf of the Memorialist Company, upon behalf of the Garda Síochána and the

Síochána agus Choimisinéiri na nOibreacha Poiblí agus Aturnae thar ceann Bhardas Bhaile Átha Cliath agus Aturnae thar ceann Chumann no nGrósaeirí agus na bhFíoncheannaithe Ceadúnaithe.

AGUS DE BHRÍ gurbh é tuairim an Ard-Aighne, tar éis dó an Meabhrachán sin a bhreithniú go hiomlán agus ag féachaint don mhéid a dúradh ag an bhfiosrúchán sin agus do no doiciméid agus na tuairscí eile a cuireadh faoina bhráid thar ceann na bpáirtithe sin a rabhthas ag feidhmiú amhlaidh ar a son ag an bhfiosrúchán sin maidir leis an Meabhrachán sin go bhféadfaí Litreacha Paitinne a dheonú don Edward Arthur Henry Earl of Longford agus don Louis Jammet a dúradh ar iontaobhas do Chuideachta an Mheabhracháin chun amharclann nó teach aisteoireachta dea-rialaithe a choimeád san áitreabh sin i gCathair Bhaile Átha Cliath ar feadh téarma bliana is fiche ón 24ú lá de Dheireadh Fómhair 1952 faoi na coinníollacha agus na sraintachtaí agus na teorainneacha atá leagtha amach anseo.

BÍODH A FHIOS AG GACH nAON DÁ BHRÍ SIN go ndéanann an Rialtas i bhfeidmiú na gcumhachtaí a bheirtear leis an Acht sin ó Pharlaimint na hÉireann a bhí ann go deireannach dar teideal "An Act for regulating the Stage in the City and County of Dublin" a ritheadh sa bhliain 1786 (caibidil 57) mar a oiriúnaíodh agus mar atá i bhfeidhm anois agus i bhfeidhmiú gach cumhachta agus aon chumhachta eile lena gcuirtear seo ar chumas an Rialtais lán-chumhacht agus lán-údarás a dheonú leis seo don Edward Arthur Henry Earl of Longford agus don Louis Jammet a dúradh (beirt de Stiúrthóiri Chuideachta an Mheabhracháin) dá seiceadóirí dá riarthóirí agus dá sannaithe faoi na coinníollacha agus na sriantachtaí agus na teorainneacha a luaitear anseo ina dhiaidh seo chun amharclann nó teach aisteoireachta dea-rialaithe a bhunú agus a choimeád san áitreabh sin dá ngairtear an *Gate Theatre* atá suite i Rae Cavendish i gCathair Bhaile Átha Cliath agus arb é an t-áitreabh é a thuariscítear níos cruinne agus atá línithe ar thrí shraith pleanna

Commissioners of Public Works and Solicitor upon behalf of the Dublin Corporation and Solicitor upon behalf of the Licensed Grocers' and Vintners' Association.

AND WHEREAS the Attorney General having fully considered the said Memorial and having regard to what was said at such enquiry and the further documents and reports submitted to him upon behalf of the said parties so represented at the said enquiry in connection with the said Memorial was of opinion that Letters Patent might be granted to the said Edward Arthur Henry Earl of Longford and Louis Jammet in trust for the Memorialist Company for keeping a well-regulated theatre or playhouse in the said premises in the City of Dublin for a term of twenty-one years from the 24th day of October 1952 under such conditions restrictions and limitations as are herein set forth.

KNOW YE THEREFORE that the Government in the exercise of the powers conferred by the said Act of the late Parliament of Ireland entitled "An Act for regulating the Stage in the City and County of Dublin" passed in the year 1786 (chapter 57) as adapted and now in force and of every and any other power the Government in this behalf enabling do hereby grant unto the said Edward Arthur Henry Earl of Longford and Louis Jammet (two of the Directors of the Memorialist Company) their executors administrators and assigns under the conditions restrictions and limitations hereinafter mentioned full power and authority to establish and keep in the said premises known as the Gate Theatre situate at Cavendish Row in the City of Dublin which said premises are more particularly described and delineated on three sets of plans of the said premises each set whereof is duly identified and authenticated by having affixed thereto the Common Seal of the Memorialist Company one of which sets is deposited with the Secretary to the Government another whereof

den áitreabh sin a bhfuil gach sraith díobh
aitheanta agus fíordheimhnithe go cuí trí
Ghnáthshéala Chuideachta an Mheabhracháin
a bheith greamaithe di, agus a bhfuil sraith
díobh taiscthe le Rúnaí an Rialtais agus sraith
eile le hArd-Mhéara Ró-Onórach, Seanóirí
agus Buirgéisigh Bhaile Átha Cliath agus an
tríú sraith le taisceadh í bPríomh-Oifig na
hArd-Chúirte Breithiúnais agus (ach amháin
nuair a fheifear do chomhalta den Rialtas cúis
a bheith ann chun toirmeasc a chur le haithris
nó le taibhiú aon dráma nó aon chineál drámaí
taispeántas nó siamsaí amharclainne) chun
aithris nó leiriú nó taibhiú a chéanamh nó a
chur á dhéanamh ann go poiblí gach tráth ar
aon idirdhréacht nó traigéide nó coiméide nó
réamhdhréacht nó ceoldráma nó burletta nó
dráma nó fronsa nó geamaireacht nó ar aon
chuid nó codanna de shaghas nó de chineál ar
bith díobh AR CHOINNÍOLL I gCÓNAÍ go
mbeidh gach idirdhréacht traigéide coiméide
réamhdhréacht ceoldráma burletta dráma
fronsa geamaireacht agus taibhiú den sórt sin
modhúil cuíúil ar gach slí agus nach mbeidh
sé naomhaithiseach diamhaslach
mígheanasach graosta ceannairceach ná
gráiniúil ar chuma eile LEIS AN ÁITREABH
A SHEALBHÚ AGUS A THEACHTADH
chun an Edward Arthur Henry Earl of
Longford agus an Louis Jammet a dúradh
chun a seiceadóiri chun a riarthóiri agus chun
a sannaithe ar iontaobhas don *Dublin Gate
Theatre Company Limited* a dúradh dá
gcomharbaí agus dá sannaithe chun aithris nó
léiriú nó taibhiú a dhéanamh ar gach
idirdhréacht traigéide coiméide
réamhdhréacht ceoldráma burletta dráma
fronsa nó geamaireacht dá luaitear anseo
roimhe seo nó ar aon chuid nó codanna díobh
den saghas nó den chineál sin a cheidh
modhúil chíúil agus nach mbeidh
naomhaithiseach diamhaslach mígheanasach
graosta ceannairceach ná gráiniúil ar chuma
eile ar feadh agus i rith téarma agus ré bliana
is fiche ón 24ú lá de Dheireadh Fómhair 1952
atá le caitheamh agus le criochnú go hiomlán
mura bhfoirceantar an téarma sin riomhe sin
mar fhoráiltear anseo ina dhiaidh seo AGUS
toirmisctear leis se ar GACH UILE DHUINE
ar feadh agus i rith an téarma na tréimhse agus
na ré a cheaptar anseo roimhe seo gabháil lena

is deposited with the Right Honourable the
Lord Mayor Aldermen and Burgesses of
Dublin and the third whereof is to be
deposited in the Central Office of the High
Court of Justice a well-regulated theatre or
playhouse and therein at all times (save when
a member of the Government shall see cause
to forbid the acting or performance of any
play or species of plays shows or theatrical
amusements) publicly to act represent or
perform or cause to be acted represented or
performed all interludes tragedies comedies
preludes operas burlettas plays farces
pantomimes or any part or parts thereof of
what kind or nature whatsoever PROVIDED
ALWAYS that all such interludes tragedies
comedies preludes operas burlettas plays
farces pantomimes and performances shall be
in every respect decent and becoming and not
profane blasphemous indecent obscene
seditious or otherwise obnoxious TO HAVE
AND TO HOLD the premises unto the said
Edward Arthur Henry Earl of Longford and
Louis Jammet their executors administrators
and assigns in trust for the said Dublin Gate
Theatre Company Limited their successors
and assigns to act represent or perform all
such hereinbefore mentioned interludes
tragedies comedies preludes operas burlettas
plays farces pantomimes or any part or parts
thereof of the said nature and kind decent and
becoming not profane blasphemous indecent
obscene seditious or otherwise obnoxious for
and during the term and space of twenty-one
years from the 24th day of October 1952 fully
to be completed and ended unless the said
term be sooner determined as hereinafter
provided AND ALL persons whatsoever are
hereby forbidden for and during the term
time and space hereinbefore limited from
presuming to erect build or keep open in any
manner whatsoever any theatre or theatres
stage or stages whatsoever within the City of
Dublin or County of Dublin or therein to act
represent or perform any interlude tragedy
comedy prelude opera burletta play farce
pantomime or any other exhibition such as
shall be authorised by these Letters Patent or
any part or parts thereof unless they have
already been or shall be thereunto duly
authorised and appointed in accordance with

ais aon amharclann nó amharclanna stáitse nó stáitsí a thógáil nó a dhéanamh nó a choimeád ar oscailt ar mhodh ar bith laistigh de Chathair Bhaile Átha Cliath nó de Chontae Bhaile Átha Cliath nó aithris nó léiriú nó taibhiú a dhéanamh ann ar aon idirdhréacht tragéide coiméide réamhdhréacht ceoldráma burletta dráma fronsa nó geamaireacht nó ar aon taispeántas eile de shórt a bheidh údaraithe leis na Litreacha Paitinne seo nó ar aon chuid nó codanna díobh mura bhfuil siad cheana nó mura mbeidh said údaraithe agus ceaptha chuige sin go cuí do réir dlí AGUS deonaíonn an Rialtas leis seo don Edward Arthur Henry Earl of Longford and don Louis Jammet a dúradh dá seiceadóirí dá riarthóirí agus dá sannaithe ar iontaobhas don *Dublin Gate Theatre Company Limited* dá gcomharbaí agus dá sannaithe lánchumhacht agus láncheadúnas agus lán-údarás chun cibé aisteorí nó daoine agus cibé méid díobh a chruínniú a choinneáil a rialú a phribhléidiú agus a choimeád ó am go ham chun cleachtadh nó aithris nó léiriú no taibhiú a dhéanamh are gach idirdhréacht traigéide coméide réamhdhréacht ceoldráma burletta dráma fronsa nó geamaireacht nó ar aon chuid nó codanna díobh mar a dúradh san áitreabh sin is dóigh ó am go ham leis an Edward Arthur Henry Earl of Longford agus leis an Louis Jammet a dúradh lena seiceadóirí lena riarthóiri agus lena sannaithe a bheith oriúnach agus riachtanach chun na críche sin agus sa Chomplact sin aisteoirí nó daoine beidh cibé líon aisteoirí nó daoine is dóigh ó am go ham leis an Edward Arthur Henry Earl of Longford agus leis an Louis Jammet a dúradh lena seiceadóirí lena riarthóiri agus lena sannaithe a bheith oriúnach agus riachtanach chun na críche sin agus na daoine sin do leanúint san amharclann sin fad is toil leis an *Dublin Gate Theatre Company Limited* a dúradh lena gcomharbaí nó lena sannaithe chun na siamsaí a luaitear anseo a thaibhiú go sitheach sítheoilte gan chosc gan bhac ó dhuine ná ó dhaoine ar bith chun áineas cóir a sholáthar do gach n-aon lenar mian an céanna a fheiceáil AGUS is dleatach agus bheadh sé dleathach don Edward Arthur Henry Earl of Longford agus don Louis Jammet a dúradh dá seiceadóiri dá

law AND the Government do hereby grant unto the said Edward Arthur Henry Earl of Longford and Louis Jammet their executors administrators and assigns in trust for the Dublin Gate Theatre Company Limited their successors and assigns full power and licence and authority from time to time to gather entertain govern privilege and keep such and so many players or persons to exercise and act represent or perform all such interludes tragedies comedies preludes operas burlettas plays farces or pantomimes or any part or parts thereof as aforesaid in the said premises as the said Edward Arthur Henry Earl of Longford and Louis Jammet their executors administrators and assigns shall from time to time think fit and requisite for that purpose which said Company of players or persons shall consist of such number of players or persons as the said Edward Arthur Henry Earl of Longford and Louis Jammet their executors administrators and assigns shall from time to time think fit and requisite for that purpose and such persons to continue in the said theatre during the pleasure of the said Dublin Gate Theatre Company Limited their successors or assigns for the performance of the entertainments stated herein peaceably and quietly without any impediment or interruption or any persons or persons whomsoever for the honest recreation of all such as shall desire to see the same AND it shall and may be lawful to and for the said Edward Arthur Henry Earl of Longford and Louis Jammet their executors administrators and assigns to take and receive of such persons as shall resort to hear or see any such plays and entertainments of the stage as aforesaid such sum or sums of money as have customarily been given or taken in the like kind or shall be thought reasonable by the patentees in regard to the expenses incurred in the improvement of the said theatre and for the scenes music decorations and other requisites AND the Government do hereby further give and grant unto the said Edward Arthur Henry Earl of Longford and Louis Jammet their executors administrators and assigns full power from time to time and at all times for and during the term time and space hereinbefore mentioned to make such allowance out of the moneys

riarthóiri agus dá sannaithe cibé suim nó
suimeanna airgid a thógáil agus a ghlacadh ó
na daoine a rachaidh ag éisteacht nó ag
féachaint aon chluichí agus siamsaí stáitse mar
a dúradh ba ghnáth a thabhairt nó a ghlacadh i
gcás den sórt céanna nó a mheasfaidh na
paitinnithe a bheith réasúnach ag féachaint do
na caiteachais faoin ndeacthas ag feabhsú na
hamharclainne sin agus leis na radharcanna
leis an gceol leis na hornáidí agus leis na
riachtanais eile AGUS bhéireann agus
deonaíonn an Rialtas leis seo freisin don
Edward Arthur Henry Earl of Longford agus
don Louis Jammet a dúradh dá seiceadóirí dá
riarthóirí agus dá sannaithe lán-chumhacht
chun go ndéanfaidís ó am go ham agus gach
am ar feadh agus i rith an téarma na tréimhse
agus na ré a luaitear anseo roimhe seo cibé
liúntas is oiriúnach leo as an airgead a
gheobhaidh siad amhlaidh de bharr na
dtaibhithe agus na siamsaí sin a dúradh a íoc
leis na taibheoirí agus leis na daoine eile a
bheidh ar fostú ag aithris nó ag léiriú nó ar
fostú i gcáil ar bith timpeall na hamharclainne
sin nó de réir mar is oiriúnach leo AGUS
déanfaidh an Edward Arthur Henry Earl of
Longford agus an Louis Jammet a dúradh a
seiceadóirí a riarthóirí agus a sannaithe ó am
go ham agus gach am gach duine scannalach
nó míordúil nó aon duine eile is cuí leo a
dhíbirt as an gComplacht sin agus beidh gach
duine agus aon duine nó daoine a dhíbreoidh
agus a scoirfidh siad amhlaidh faoi mhíchumas
chun imirt nó aisteoireacht a dhéanamh leis an
gComplacht sin san amharclann sin agus ó am
a dhíbeartha nó a scortha amhlaidh stopfaidh
agus stadfaidh ar fad de bheith ag fáil aon
choda nó cionúireachta nó tuarastail as
brabúis na léirthe san amharclann sin nó ón
Edward Arthur Henry Earl of Longford agus
ón Louis Jammet a dúradh nó óna siceadóirí
óna riarthóiri agus óna sannaithe.

AGUS DEARBHAÍTEAR LEIS SEO nach
gceadófar feasta ar an stáitse de bhua nó faoi
scáth an ghníomhais seo aon léiriú trína
dtabharfaí aithis in aon slí don Chreideamh
Críostaí nó d'aon Chreideamh eile atá
admhaithe ag an Stát de bhua Airteagal 44 den
Bhunreacht AGUS toirmisctear go docht leis
seo mí-úsáid nó mí-léiriú dá laghad a

which they shall so receive by such
performances and entertainments as aforesaid
to the performers and other persons employed
in acting or representing or in any quality
whatsoever about the said theatre or so as they
shall think fit AND the said Edward Arthur
Henry Earl of Longford and Louis Jammet
their executors administrators and assigns shall
from time to time and at all times eject out of
the said Company all scandalous disorderly or
other persons as they shall think meet and all
and every person or persons so by them
ejected and discharged shall be disabled from
playing or acting with the said Company in the
said theatre and shall from the time of such
ejectment or discharge stop and altogether
cease from receiving any part proportion or
salary out of the profits of the representations
in the said theatre or from the said Edward
Arthur Henry Earl of Longford and Louis
Jammet their executors administrators and
assigns.

AND IT IS HEREBY DECLARED that
henceforth no representation shall be admitted
on the stage by virtue or under cover of these
presents whereby the Christian Religion or any
other Religion recognised by the State by
virtue of Article 44 of the Constitution may in
any manner suffer reproach AND all and any
degree of abuse or misrepresentation of sacred

dhéanamh ar phearsana naofa a tharraingeodh nó a chaithfeadh drochmheas dá laghad ar chreideamh agus ní dhéanfar aon phearsa den sórt sin a thabhairt isteach ná a léiriú ach ar chuma a mbéadódh an meas is dual dóibh siúd a chomhlíonann críocha na bhfeidhmeanna naofa sin AGUS naisctear leis seo an aire is fearr a thabhairt i gcás léirithe a bhainfeadh in aon slí leis an mBeartas Sibhialta nó le Bunreacht an Stáit d'fhonn go mba chabhair iad chun tacú leis an ídarás dleathach agus le buan-choimeád na hordúlachta agus an dea-rialtais AGUS ionas go mbeidh an amharclann sin feasta ina meán chun an tsuáilce a chothú agus chun daoine a theagasc naisctear agus ordaítear leis seo gan aon siamsa ná taispeántas a aithris ná a léiriú faoin údarás a bheirtear leis seo má bhíonn aon abairt nó sliocht nó gotha ann a bheidh in aghaidh na modhúlachta nó na cráifeachta nó an dea-bhéasa go dtí go mbeidh sin ceartaithe nó glanta ag an mbainisteoir nó na bainisteoirí de thuras na huaire trí aon abairtí sleachta agus gothai den sórt sin a scriosadh amach as AGUS má cheadaíonn an Edward Arthur Henry Earl of Longford agus an Louis Jammet a dúradh a seiceadóirí a riarthóirí nó a sannaithe aon léiriú san amharclann a údaraitear leis seo a thuigfear nó a mheasfar a bheith mígheanasach diamhaslach mímhorálta nó ceannairceach agus mura stopfaidh agus mura scoirfidh siad láithreach dá léiriú nó dá aithris ar fhógra a fháil ó chomhalta den Rialtas nó in ainm agus ar údarás comhalta den Rialtas nó ó aon duine nó daoine a bheidh údaraithe go dleathach aige ansin agus sa chás sin tiocfaidh an gníomhas seo agus gach deonú agus pribhléid agus díolúine a bheirtear nó a dheonaítear leis seo chun bheith ar neamhní chun gach uile intinne agus críche

AR CHOINNÍOLL I gCÓNAI go mairfidh agus go bhfanfaidh an gníomhas seo ar an gcoinníoll má tharlaíonn aon am i gcaitheamh an téarma sin a dheonaítear leis seo go dtaispeánfar do chomhalta den Rialtas nach bhfuil an amharclann sin á haerú go cuí nó á coimeád i ndeisriocht cuí cóir nó nach bhfuil bealaí fairsinge oiriúnacha cearta isteach agus amach á gcothabháil agus ar fáil don mhuintir

characters which may in any degree tend to expose religion or bring it into contempt are hereby strictly prohibited and no such characters shall be introduced or played in any other light than such as may increase the just esteem of those who answer the end of those sacred functions AND the strictest regard to such representations as anywise concern the Civil Policy or the Constitution of the State is hereby enjoined that these may contribute to support lawful authority and to the preservation of order and good government AND so that for the future the said theatre may be instrumental in the promotion of virtue and instruction of human life it is hereby enjoined and commanded that no entertainment or exhibition whatsoever be acted or produced under the authority hereby granted which does or may contain any expression or passage or gesture offensive to decency piety or good manners until the same shall be corrected or purged by the Manager or Managers for the time being by expunging any such offensive expressions passages and gestures AND if the said Edward Arthur Henry Earl of Longford and Louis Jammet their executors administrators or assigns shall permit to be brought forward any representation at such theatre hereby authorised which shall be deemed or construed to be indecent blasphemous immoral or seditious and shall not forthwith discontinue and cease representing playing or acting the same on receiving notice from or in the name and by the authority of a member of the Government or by any persons or persons lawfully authorised by him then and in such case these presents and every grant privilege and immunity hereby given or granted shall become null and void to all intents and purposes whatsoever

PROVIDED ALWAYS that these presents shall be and remain upon the conditions that if at any time during the said term hereby granted it shall be made to appear to a member of the Government that the said theatre is not duly ventilated or kept in due and proper repair or that fit and proper commodious means of ingress and egress are not maintained and provided for those who frequent the same or

a thaithíonn an amharclann sin nó nach bhfuil na Rialacha na Rialacháin agus na Fodhlithe sin de chuid Bhardas Bhaile Átha Cliath atá i bhfeidhm i láthair na huaire á gcomhlíonadh go cuí agus go ceart nó mar gheall ar an saghas taibhithe a bhíonn ar siúl inti nó ar cháilíocht nó iompar aon lucht éisteachta nó aon duine a thaithíonn an amharclann sin nó ar aon chúis eile nach mbeadh an amharclann sin nó go scoirfidh sí de bheith ina háit siamsa phoiblí atá ordúil dea-rialaithe agus measúil ansin agus sa chás sin ar fhógra sin a thabairt chuige sin faoi láimh nó faoi shéala comhalta den Rialtas agus an fógra sin a fhoilsiú san *Iris Oifigiúil* so scoirfidh an gníomhas seo láithreach go bhfoirceannfar é agus go mbeidh ar neamhní chun gach intinne agus críche d'ainneoin aon ní atá in aon slí contrártha dó sin sa ghníomhas seo AGUS DEARBHAÍTEAR FREISIN LEIS SEO go ngabhann na coinníollacha breise seo a leanas leis na Litreacha Paitinne seo, is é sin le rá:-

1. Ni foláir an amharclann sin a bheith déanta agus í a chothabháil agus a stiúradh faoi réim agus de réir na bhFodhlithe a rinne Bardas Bhaile Átha Cliath an 7ú lá de Mhárta 1934 faoi Alt 55 den *Dublin Corporation Act, 1890*, agus faoi réim agus de réir na Rialacha na Rialachán agus na bhFodhlithe eile go léir atá déanta ag Ard-Mhéara Ró-Onórach, Seanóirí agus Buirgéisigh Bhaile Átha Cliath agus atá i bhfeidhm de thuras na huaire seo.
2. Ni foláir comhaltaí údaraithe den Gharda Síochána a ligean isteach tráth ar bith.
3. Ní ligfear insteach san amharclann ach an méid daoine a mbeidh suíocháin ann dóibh.
4. Ní cheadófar aon chaint naomhaithiseach ná aon mhíchuibheas cainte ar an stáitse.
5. Ní cheadófar aon mhígheannas éadaigh rince ná gotha ar an stáitse.
6. Ní cheadófar ar an stáitse aon mhaslú ná aon aithris tharcaisneach ar dhaoine atá ina mbeatha ná ba chúis oilbhéime ná a tharraingeodh ciréib nó briseadh síochána.
7. Ní dhéanfar aon mhná ná leanaí a chrochadh as na speireoga ná iad a shocrú i suíomh nach bhféadfaidis iad féin a scaoileadh as.

that the Rules Regulations and Bye-laws of the Dublin Corporation at the present time in force are not duly and properly observed or that owing to the character of the performance carried on therein or the class or conduct of any audience or persons frequenting the said theatre or from any other cause whatsoever the said theatre shall not be or shall cease to be an orderly well-conducted and respectable place of public entertainment then and in any such case upon signification in that behalf made under the hand or seal of a member of the Government and which signification shall be published in the *Iris Oifigiúil* these presents shall forthwith cease determine and be utterly void to all intents and purposes anything herein contained to the contrary thereof in anywise notwithstanding AND IT IS HEREBY FURTHER DECLARED that these Letters Patent are upon the further conditions following that is to say:-

1. The said theatre shall be constructed maintained and conducted subject to and in accordance with the Bye-laws made by the Dublin Corporation on the 7th day of March 1934 under Section 55 of the Dublin Corporation Act, 1890, and subject to and in accordance with all other Rules Regulations and Bye-laws at the present time in force of the Right Honourable the Lord Mayor Aldermen & Burgesses of Dublin.
2. Admission shall be given at all times to the authorised members of the Garda Síochána.
3. Admission to the interior of the theatre shall be given only to so many persons as there shall be seating accommodation for.
4. No profanity or impropriety of language shall be permitted on the stage.
5. No indecency of dress dance or gesture shall be permitted on the stage.
6. No offensive personalities or representations of living persons shall be permitted on the stage or anything calculated to give offence or to produce riot or breach of the peace.
7. No woman or children shall be hung from the flies nor fixed in positions from which they cannot release themselves.

8. Ní cheadófar aon mhasc poiblí san amharclann.

9. Ní thabharfar aon ugach do dhaoine mímhorálta teach le chéile ná a ngairm a chleachtadh san amharclann.

10. Ní dhíolfar son bhia ná deoch san amharclann ach in áiteanna nach gcuirfidh sin isteach ar chompord ná ar shábháltacht an lucht éisteachta.

11. Ní foláir seomraí gléasta agus cóiríocht a bheidh oiriúnach agus cuí a chur ar fáil d'aisteoirí idir fhir agus mhná in áitreabh na hamharclainne sin.

12. Ar chomhalta den Rialtas dá éileamh sin, bhéarfar cuntas cruinn iomlán ina dtaispeánfar méid agus cineál na dtaibhithe agus an fad aimsire a thóg gach taibhiú faoi leith acu sin san amharclann i gcaitheamh aon tréimhse áirithe.

13. Ní cheadófar aon deochanna meisciúla a dhíol ná a sholáthar ná ní cheadófar a ndíol ná a soláthar in aon chuid den áitreabh sin a ndeonaítear na Litreacha Paitinne seo ina leith.

AGUS má dhéantar tráth ar bith aon choinníoll acu sin a shárú ansin agus in aon chás den sórt sin má thugann comhalta den Rialtas fógra chuige sin faoina láimh nó faoina shéala agus go bhfoilseofar an fógra sin san *Iris Oifigiúil* scoirfidh an gníomhas seo láithreach forceannfar é agus beidh sé ar neamhní go hiomlán chun gach intinne agus críche d'ainneoin aon ní atá in aon slí contrártha dó sin anseo roimhe seo.

AR CHOINNÍOLL I gCÓNAÍ má iarrann an Edward Arthur Henry Earl of Longford agus an Louis Jammet a dúradh a seiceadóirí a riarthóirí nó a sannaithe tráth ar bith ar chomhalta den Rialtas aon choinníoll díobh sin darb uimhreacha 1 go 13 thuas a athrú nó a mhodhnu agus go gceadófar an t-athrú nó an modhnú sin ansin agus sa chás sin go measfar an coinníoll sin a bheith athraithe agus modhnaithe da réir sin ACH ní gá aon cheadú den sórt sin i gcás aon athrú a éileoidh Bardas Chathair Bhaile Átha Cliath de bhun na Rialacha na Rialachán agus na bhFodhlithe dá gcuid a dúradh.

8. No public masquerade shall be permitted in the theatre.

9. No encouragement shall be given to improper characters to assemble or ply their calling in the theatre.

10. All refreshments sold in the theatre shall be sold only in such positions as not to interfere with the convenience and safety of the audience.

11. All suitable and proper dressing rooms and accommodation shall be provided for male and female performers in the said theatre premises.

12. On demand being made in that behalf by a member of the Government a full and accurate return shall be made showing the number and character of the performances and the length of time occupied by each of such performances in the theatre during any specified period.

13. No intoxicating liquor shall be sold or served or permitted to be sold or served in any part of the said premises in respect whereof these Letters Patent are granted.

AND if at any time there shall be a breach or breaches or any of the said conditions then and in any such case upon signification in that behalf made by a member of the Government under his hand or seal and which signification shall be published in the *Iris Oifigiúil* these presents shall forthwith cease determine and be utterly void to all intents and purposes anything hereinbefore contained to the contrary thereof in anywise notwithstanding.

PROVIDED ALWAYS that if the said Edward Arthur Henry Earl of Longford and Louis Jammet their executors administrators or assigns shall at any time apply to a member of the Government to alter or modify any of the conditions numbered 1 to 13 above and such alteration or modification shall be permitted then and in such case the said conditions shall be deemed to be altered and modified accordingly PROVIDED that no such sanction shall be necessary to any alteration required by the Dublin Corporation in pursuance of their said Rules Regulations and Bye-laws

AGUS DEARBHAÍTEAR FÓS LEIS SEO go mbeidh na Litreacha Paitinne seo nó rollú nó eiseamlárú na Litreacha Paitinne seo slán agus bailí agus leordhóthanach agus éifeachtúil i ngach ní i láthair an dlí de réir intinn agus brí dhílis an chéanna agus go ndéanfar iad a ghlacadh agus a fhorléiriú agus a bhreithniú sa chéill is fabharaí agus is tairbhí chun leasa an Edward Arthur Henry Earl of Longford agus an Louis Jammet a dúradh a seiceadóirí a riarthóirí agus a sannaithe.

AND FURTHER IT IS HEREBY DECLARED that these Letters Patent or the enrolment or exemplification thereof shall be in all things good valid sufficient and effectual in law according to the true intent and meaning of the same and shall be taken and construed and adjudged in the most favourable and beneficial sense for the best advantage of the said Edward Arthur Henry Earl of Longford and Louis Jammet their executors administrators and assigns.

AR CHOINNÍOLL I gCÓNAÍ go rollófar na Litreacha Paitinne seo i bPríom-Oifig na hArd-Chúirte.

PROVIDED ALWAYS that these Letters Patent shall be enrolled in the Central Office of the High Court.

I bhFIANAISE AIR SIN chuir an Rialtas faoi deara Litreacha Paitinne a dhéanamh de na Litreacha seo, an dara lá seo de Dheireadh Fómhar, 1959.

IN WITNESS WHEREOF the Government have caused these Letters to be made Patent this second day of October, 1959.

L.S.

Sean F. Lemass,
Taoiseach.

Bibliography

MANUSCRIPT SOURCES

Office of the Attorney General
Files relating to the Dublin theatre patent regime.

Royal Irish Academy
Original correspondence of James, late earl of Charlemont.

PRINTED SOURCES

WORKS OF REFERENCE

Oxford dictionary of national biography, 60 vols (Oxford, Oxford Univ. Press, 2004).
Dictionary of Irish biography, 9 vols (Cambridge, Cambridge Univ. Press, 2009).
Lascelles, Rowley, *Liber munerum publicorum Hiberniae*, 2 vols (London, 1852).
E.M. Johnston-Liik, *History of the Irish Parliament*, 6 vols (Belfast, Ulster Historical Foundation, 2002).
Cotton, Henry, *Fasti ecclesiae Hibernicae: a succession of the prelates and members of cathedral bodies in Ireland. Vol. i: the province of Munster* (Dublin, Hedges & Smith, 1847).
An annual register of all the tragedies, comedies, farces that have been acted in the Theatre Royal in London from 1712 to 1760 (London, 1761).
Stanley Sadie, ed., *History of opera* (Houndsmills, Basingstoke, Hampshire, Macmillan, 1989).
A directory of Dublin for the year 1738 (Dublin, Dublin Corporation Public Libraries, 2000).

OFFICIAL PROCEEDINGS AND PUBLICATIONS

A collection of the parliamentary debates England from the year MDCLXVII to the present time. S. l. 1740.
Cobbett's parliamentary history of England from the earliest period to the year 1803, vol. 10 (London, Longman & Co., 1811).
Common's journal, Ireland.
Lords' journal, Ireland.
Proceedings of the Irish House of Lords, 1771–1800, ed. James Kelly, 3 vols (Dublin, Irish MSS Comm., 2008).

Parliamentary register of Ireland, 1781–1797, 17 vols (Dublin, 1782–1801. repr. with intro. by W.J. McCormack, Bristol and Tokyo 1999).

Hansard, 3rd series.

Hansard, 5th series (lords).

Hansard, 5th series (commons).

Dáil Debates, vols 142 and 199.

Calendar of State Papers, Ireland 1660–2, 1663–5, 1669–70 and addenda 1625–70.

Register of the privy council of Scotland, 3rd series vol. 7, 1681–2 (Edinburgh, HMSO, 1915).

Historical Manuscripts Commission, *Tenth report*, 1885, *Various Collections*, 1–8 (1901–13).

Calendar of the ancient records of Dublin, ed. Sir J.T. and Lady Gilbert, 19 vols (Dublin, 1889–1944).

Council Book of the Corporation of the city of Cork, from 1609 to 1643, and from 1690 to 1800, ed. Richard Caulfield (Guildford, J. Billing & Sons, 1876).

Report from the select committee on dramatic literature, HC 1831–2, iii, 1.

Memorandum by the Lord Chamberlain transmitted to managers of theatres, 1864, 1864 HC, l, 489.

Report from the select committee to inquire into the working of Acts of Parliament for licensing theatres, HC 1866, xvi, 1.

Report of the commissioners to make inquiry with regard to the laws and regulations relating to home, colonial and international copyright, HC 1878, xxiv.

Report from the select committee on theatres and places of entertainment, 1892, 1892 HC, xviii, 1.

Royal commission on liquor licensing laws, minutes of evidence with appendices and index (Ireland), 1898 HC, xxxviii, 527.

Report from the joint select committee on stage plays (censorship) 1909, 1909 HC, viii, 451.

Report of the joint committee on censorship of the theatre, with proceedings, evidence, appendices and index, HC 1966–7, x, 191.

Documents on Irish foreign policy, vol. 4: 1932–6. Ed. Catriona Crowe, Ronan Fanning, Michael Kennedy, Dermot Keogh and Eunan O'Halpin (Dublin, Royal Irish Academy 2002).

See, too, Index to Legislation and Index to Cases at Law.

GENERAL

Agate, James, *A shorter ego: second selection* (London, George G. Harrap & Co. Ltd, 1945).

Ackroyd, Peter, *Dickens* (London, Sinclair-Stevenson, 1990).

Anon., 'The Dublin drama and the old Theatre Royal', *Irish Builder*, 25 (1883), 16.

Anon., *The history of the Theatre Royal, Dublin, from its foundation in 1821 to the present time* (Dublin, Edward Ponsonby, 1870).

Anon., 'The law of the stage in Dublin', *ILT & SJ*, 43 (1909), 209.

Appleton, W.W., *Charles Macklin: an actor's life* (Cambridge, MA, Harvard Univ. Press, 1961).

Arrington, Lauren, '"I sing what was lost and dread what was won": W.B. Yeats and the legacy of censorship', *Irish University Review*, 38 (2008), 222.

Bartlett, Thomas, *Revolutionary Dublin, 1795–1801: the letters of Francis Higgins to Dublin Castle* (Dublin, Four Courts Press, 2004).

Bell, Sam Hanna, *The theatre in Ulster* (Dublin, Gill & Macmillan, 1972).

Bennett, Revd Dr John, *The evil of theatrical amusements, stated and illustrated in a sermon, preached in the Wesley-Methodist chapel, Lower Abbey Street, on Sunday, November 4, 1838* (Dublin, John Fannin, 1838).

Bold, Alan, *Modern Scottish literature* (London and New York, Longman, 1983).

Boswell, James, *The life of Samuel Johnson*, abridged ed. (London, Hutchinson & Co., 1906).

Brown, Michael, 'Farmer and fool: Henry Brooke and the late Irish Enlightenment' in Michael Brown and S.P. Donlan (eds), *The laws and other legalities of Ireland, 1689–1850* (Farnham, Surrey, Ashgate, 2011).

—, 'The location of learning in mid-eighteenth-century Ireland' in Muriel McCarthy and Ann Simmons (eds), *Marsh's Library: a mirror of the world: law, learning and libraries, 1650–1750* (Dublin, Four Courts Press, 2009).

— and S.P. Donlan (eds), *The laws and other legalities of Ireland* (Farnham, Surrey, Ashgate, 2011).

Burke, Helen M., *Riotous performances: the struggle for hegemony in the Irish theatre* (Notre Dame, IN, Univ. of Notre Dame Press, 2003).

Byron, George Gordon, Lord, *The poetical works of Lord Byron*, 7 vols, ed. E.H. Coleridge (London, John Murray, 1898–1904).

Calcraft, J.W. (pseudonym of J.W. Cole), *A defence of the stage, or an enquiry into the real qualities of theatrical entertainments, their scope and tendency, Being a reply to a sermon entitled 'The evil of theatrical amusements stated and illustrated' … by the Rev. Dr John B. Bennett, Including an examination of the authorities on which that sermon is founded* (Dublin, Milliken & Son, 1839).

Chanel (pseudo. of Clery, Arthur), *The idea of a nation* (Dublin, James Duffy & Co. Ltd, 1907).

Chetwood, W.R., *A general history of the stage (more particularly the Irish theatre) from its origin in Greece down to the present time* (Dublin, E. Rider, 1749).

Cibber, Colley, *An apology for the life of Mr Colley Cibber, comedian, and late patentee of the Theatre Royal, with a material view of the stage during his own time*, 4th ed. (Dublin, Geo. Faulkner, 1740).

Clark, W.S., *The early Irish stage: the beginnings to 1720* (Oxford, Clarendon Press, 1955).

—, *The Irish stage in the county towns* (Oxford, Clarendon Press, 1965).

Collier, Jeremy, *A short view of the immorality and profaneness of the English stage* (London, S. Keble et al., 1698).

Croker, J.W., *Familiar epistle to Frederick Jones, Esq. on the present state of the Irish stage* (Dublin, J. Barlow, 1804).

Curran, C.P., *Under the receding wave* (Dublin, Gill & Macmillan, 1970).

Dean, Joan Fitzpatrick, *Riot and great anger: stage censorship in twentieth-century Ireland* (Madison, WI, Univ. of Wisconsin Press, 2004).

de Burca, Seamus, 'The Queen's Royal Theatre, 1829–1960', *Dublin Historical Record*, 27 (1973–4), 10.

Devane, R.S., 'Suggested tariff on imported newspapers and magazines', *Studies*, 16 (1927), 552.

Dickson, David (ed.), *The gorgeous mask, Dublin, 1700–1850* (Dublin, Trinity History Workshop, 1987).

Donovan, K.J., '*Jack the Giant Queller*: political theater in Ascendancy Dublin', *Eire-Ireland*, 30:2 (Summer, 1995), 70.

Dryden, John, *The works of John Dryden, vol. 3: poems, 1685–1692* (Berkeley and Los Angeles, California, Univ. of California Press, 1969).

—, *The works of John Dryden, vol. 2: poems, 1681–1684* (Berkeley and Los Angeles, California and London, Univ. of California Press, 1972).

Dunton, John, *The Dublin Scuffle* (London, the author, 1699).

Ehrenpreis, Irvin, *Swift, the man, his work, and the age*, 3 vols (Cambridge, MA, Harvard Univ. Press, 1962–83).

Ellmann, Richard, *Oscar Wilde* (London, Penguin ed., 1988).

Faulks, Sebastian, *A possible life* (London, Vintage Books, 2013).

Fawkes, Richard, *Dion Boucicault: a biography* (London, Melbourne and New York, Quartet Books, 1979).

Fielding, Henry, *Plays, vol. 2*, ed. Thomas Lockwood (Oxford, Clarendon Press, 2007).

Fitzgibbon, John, '*A volley of execrations': the letters and papers of John Fitzgibbon, earl of Clare, 1772–1802*, ed. D.A. Fleming and A.P.W. Malcomson (Dublin, Irish MSS Comm., 2005).

Fletcher, Alan J., *Drama, performance and polity in pre-Cromwellian Ireland* (Cork, Cork Univ. Press, 2000).

Flood, W.H. Grattan, *A history of Irish music* (Dublin, Browne & Nolan, 1905).

Garrick, David, *The private correspondence of David Garrick with the most celebrated persons of his time*, 2 vols (London, H. Colburn and R. Bentley, 1835).

Gay, John, *Dramatic works, vol. 2*, ed. John Fuller (Oxford, Clarendon Press, 1983).

Geary, W.N.M., *The law of theatres and music-halls, including contracts and precedents of contracts* (London, Stevens & Sons, 1885).

Gilbert, J.T., *A history of the city of Dublin*, 3 vols (Dublin, McGlashan and McGlashan & Gill, 1854–9).

Gillespie, Raymond and Andrew Hadfield (eds), *The Irish book in English* (The Oxford History of the Irish Book) (Oxford, Oxford Univ. Press, 2006).

Gladstone diaries, The, vol. 1, ed. M.R.D. Foot (Oxford, Clarendon Press, 1988).

Greene, J.C., *Theatre in Belfast, 1736–1800* (Bethlehem, PA, Lehigh Univ. Press, London, Associated Univ. Presses, 2000).

—, 'The trials of Richard Daly and John Magee, involving the Sham Squire, the Lottery Swindle of 1788, the Billiard Marker's Ghost, and the Grand Olympic pig hunt', *Eighteenth-Century Ireland*, 24 (2009) 135.

— and G.L.H. Clark, *The Dublin stage, 1720–1745: a calendar of plays, entertainment and after pieces* (London and Toronto, Associated Univ. Presses, 1993).

Gregory, Augusta, *Our Irish theatre: a chapter of autobiography* (London and New York, G.P. Putnam's sons, 1913).

Greig, D.W., 'Condition – or warranty?', *Law Quarterly Review*, 89 (1973), 93.

Griffith, Eva, 'James Shirley and the earl of Kildare: speculating playhouses and dwarves à la mode' in Michael Potterton and Thomas Herron (eds), *Dublin and the Pale in the Renaissance, c.1540–1660* (Dublin, Four Courts Press, 2011).

Hall, Mr and Mrs S.C., *Ireland, its scenery, character, etc.* 3 vols (London, How & Parsons, Jeremiah How, 1841–3).

Healy, Maurice, *The old Munster Circuit* (London, Michael Joseph, 1948).

Hitchcock, Robert, *An historical view of the Irish stage from the earliest period ... with theatrical anecdotes*, 2 vols (Dublin, R. Marchbank, W. Folds, 1788–94).

Hogan, Robert and James Kilroy, *The Abbey Theatre: the years of Synge, 1905–1909* (Dublin, Dolmen Press, 1978).

Hume, R.D., *Henry Fielding and the London theatre, 1728–1737* (Oxford, Clarendon Press, 1988).

Ibsen, Henrik, *Ghosts*, transl. and introd. Michael Meyer (London, Eyre Methuen, 1973).

Inglis, Brian, *The freedom of the press in Ireland, 1784–1841* (London, Faber & Faber, 1954).

Jacobs, Arthur and Stanley Sadie, *Opera: a modern guide* (Newton Abbot, David & Charles, 1973).

James I, *ΒΑΣΙΛΙΚΟΝ ΔΩΡΟΝ, or his Maiesties Instructions to his Dearest Sonne, Henry the Prince* (London, E. Allde for E.W. and others of the company of Stationers, 1603).

Jennings, Gertrude, *Four one act plays* (London, Samuel French Ltd, Sidgwick & Jackson, Ltd, 1914).

Johnston, J., *The Lord Chamberlain's blue pencil* (London, Hodder & Stoughton, 1990).

Joyce, James, *Stephen Hero* (London, Paladin ed., 1991).

—, *Ulysses* (London, The Bodley Head, 1960).

Kapuściński, Ryszard, *Travels with Herodotus* (London, Penguin Books, 2008).

Kent, Brad, 'The banning of George Bernard Shaw's *The adventures of the black girl in her search for God* and the decline of the Irish Academy of Letters', *Irish University Review*, 38 (2008), 274.

Kwint, Marius, 'The legitimization of the circus in late Georgian England', *Past & Present*, 174 (2002), 72.

Lansdown, Richard, *Byron's historical drama* (Oxford, Clarendon Press, 1992).

Lawrence, W.J., 'New light on the old Dublin stage', *New Ireland Review*, 26 (1906–7), 156.

Lenihan, Maurice, *Limerick; its history and antiquities ecclesiastic, civil and military from the earliest ages* (Dublin, Hodges, Smith & Co., 186).

Lumley, Benjamin, *Reminiscences of the opera* (London, Hurst & Blackett, 1864).

McArdle, Grainne, 'Signora Violante and her troupe of dancers, 1729–32', *Eighteenth-Century Ireland*, 20 (2005), 55.

McBrien, E.J.D., *The liquor licensing laws of Northern Ireland* (Dublin, Gill & Macmillan, 1997)

McCarthy, Muriel and Ann Simmons (eds), *Marsh's Library, a mirror of the world: law, learning and libraries, 1650–1750* (Dublin, Four Courts Press, 2009).

McDonald, Frank, *The destruction of Dublin* (Dublin, Gill & MacMillan, 1985).

MacDonogh, Giles, *Berlin: a portrait of its history, architecture and society* (New York, St Martin's Press, London, Sinclair-Stevenson, 1997).

McFarlane, Gavin, *Copyright: the development and exercise of the performing right* (Eastbourne, John Offord, 1980).

Mann, Klaus, *Mephisto*, transl. Robin Smyth (Harmondsworth, Middlesex, Penguin Books, 1995).

Martin, Peter, *Censorship in the two Irelands, 1922–1939* (Dublin, Irish Academic Press, 2006).

Maume, Patrick, 'Nationalism and partition: the political thought of Arthur Clery', *Irish Historical Studies*, 31 (1998), 222.

Meenan, James (ed.), *Centenary history of the Literary and Historical Society of University College Dublin, 1855–1955* (Dublin, A & A Farmar, 2005).

Milton, John, *Complete prose works, vol. 4*, ed. D.M. Wolfe (New Haven, CT, Yale Univ. Press, London, Oxford UP, 1966).

Molière, J.B.P. *The Misanthrope, Tartuffe and other plays*, transl. and introd. Maya Slater (Oxford, Oxford UP, 2001).

Mooney, T. and F. White, 'The gentry's winter season' in David Dickson (eds), *The gorgeous mask: Dublin, 1700–1850* (Dublin, Trinity History Workshop, 1987).

Morash, Christopher, *A history of Irish theatre, 1601–2000* (Cambridge, Cambridge Univ. Press, 2002).

—, 'Theatre and print, 1550–1800' in Raymond Gillespie and Andrew Hadfield (eds), *The Irish book in English* (The Oxford History of the Irish Book, iii) (Oxford, Oxford UP, 2006).

Morrissey, T.J., *Towards a National University: William Delany SJ (1835–1924): an era of initiative in Irish education* (Dublin, Wolfhound Press, 1983).

Murray, Christopher, *Sean O'Casey: writer at work: a biography* (Dublin, Gill & Macmillan, 2004).

Nic Dháibhéid, Caoimhe. '"This is a case in which national considerations must be taken into account": the breakdown of the MacBride-Gonne marriage, 1908–9', *Irish Historical Studies*, 37 (2010), 241.

Norwich, John Julius, *A history of Venice* (London, Penguin Books, 1983).

Ó Faolain, Sean, *The collected stories of Sean Ó Faolain, vol. 1* (London, Constable, 1980).

O'Keeffe, John, *Recollection of the life of John O'Keeffe, written by himself*, 2 vols (London, Henry Colburn, 1826).

O'Malley, Conor, *A poet's theatre* (Dublin, Elo Press Ltd, 1981).

O'Neill, Michael, *The Abbey at the Queen's: the interregnum years, 1951–1966* (Nepean, Ontario, Borealis, 1999).

O'Neill, Michael J., *Lennox Robinson* (New York, Twayne Publishers Inc., 1964).

Osborough, W.N., *Literature, judges, and the law* (Dublin, Four Courts Press, 2008).

O'Shea, Mark, 'Morals of the people: the 1786 Dublin Theatres Act', *Irish Stage and Screen*, 12 (Aug./Sept. 1991).

O'Toole, Fintan, *A traitor's kiss: the life of Richard Brinsley Sheridan* (London, Granta Books, 1998).

Pepys, Samuel, *The diary of Samuel Pepys*, ed. Robert Latham and William Matthews, 11 vols (London, G. Bell, 1970–83).

Phillipson, N.T. and Rosalind Mitchinson (eds), *Scotland in the age of improvement* (Edinburgh, Edinburgh Univ. Press, 1970).

Potterton, Michael and Thomas Herron (eds), *Dublin and the Pale in the Renaissance, c.1540–1680* (Dublin, Four Courts Press, 2011).

Power, Frank and Peter Pearson (eds), *The Forty Foot: a monument to sea bathing* (Dublin, Environmental Publications, n.d.).

Power Victor, 'The Kelly theatre riot', *Eire-Ireland*, 7:1 (1972), 53.

The progresses and public processions of Queen Elizabeth. Among which are interspersed other solemnities, public expenditures, and remarkable events during the reign of that illustrious Princess, ed. John Nichols, 3 vols (London, J. Nichols, 1788–1805).

Prynne, William, *Histrio-Mastix* (London, E.A. & W.I. for Michael Sparke, 1631).

Reade, Charles and Dion Boucicault, *Foul Play* (London, Bradbury Evans & Co., 1869).

Reid, Desmond, 'Tennessee Williams', *Studies*, 46 (1957), 431.

Richards, Jeffrey. *Sir Henry Irving: a Victorian actor and his world* (London, Hambledon Continuum, 2005).

Rosenthal, Harold, 'Opera and music at Covent Garden' in Andrew Saint et al., *A history of the Royal Opera House, Covent Garden, 1732–1982* (London, Royal Opera House, 1982).

Rostand, Edmond, *Cyrano de Bergerac*, ed. Geoff Woollen (London, Bristol Classical Press, 1994).

Saint, Andrew, B.A. Young, Mary Clarke, Clement Crisp and Harold Rosenthal, *A history of the Royal Opera House, Covent Garden, 1732–1982* (London, Royal Opera House, 1982).

Scheijen, Sjeng, *Diaghilev: a life*, transl. Jane Hedley-Prôle and S.J. Leinbach (London, Profile Books, 2009).

Sheldon, E.K., *Thomas Sheridan of Smock Alley, recording his life as actor and theatre manager in both Dublin and London* (Princeton, NJ, Princeton Univ. Press, 1967).

Sheridan, Thomas, *A full vindication of the conduct of the manager of the Theatre Royal* (Dublin, S. Powell, 1747).

—, *An humble appeal to the publick, together with some considerations on the present critical and dangerous state of the stage in Ireland* (Dublin, G. Faulkner, 1758).

Shirley, James, *Dramatic works and poems ..., now first collected*, 6 vols (London, J. Murray, 1833).

Simpson, Alan, *Beckett, Behan and a theatre in Dublin* (London, Routledge Kegan & Paul, 1962).

Slowey, Desmond, *The radicalization of the Irish stage, 1600–1900* (Dublin and Portland, OR, Irish Academic Press, 2008).

Smith, Janet A., 'Some eighteenth-century ideas of Scotland' in N.T. Phillipson and Rosalind Mitchison (eds), *Scotland in the age of improvement* (Edinburgh, Edinburgh Univ. Press, 1970).

Stephens, J.R., *The profession of the playwright: British theatre, 1800–1900* (Cambridge, Cambridge Univ. Press, 1992).

Stephenson, P.J., 'The Abbey Theatre', *Dublin Historical Record*, 13 (1952), 22.

Stockwell, La Tourette, *Dublin theatres and theatre customs* (Kingsport, TX, Kingsport Press, 1938; repr. New York, B. Blom, 1968).

Swift, Carolyn, *Stage by stage* (Swords, Co. Dublin, Poolbeg Press, 1985).

Swift, Jonathan, *The correspondence of Jonathan Swift*, 5 vols, ed. Harold Williams (Oxford, Clarendon Press, 1963–5).

—, *Directions to servants and miscellaneous pieces*, ed. Herbert Davis (Oxford, Basil Blackwell, 1959).

—, *Poetical works*, ed. Herbert Davis, (London, Oxford UP, 1967).

—, *The complete poems*, ed. Pat Rogers (London, Penguin Books, 1983).

—, *The poems of Jonathan Swift*, ed. W.E. Browning (London, G. Bell & Son, 1910).

Thomas, David, David Carlton and Anne Etienne, *Theatre censorship: from Walpole to Wilson* (Oxford, Oxford Univ. Press, 2007).

Thomas, Keith, *Religion and the decline of the magic* (London, Penguin Books, 1978).

Tomalin, Claire, *Mrs Jordan's profession* (London, Penguin Books, 1995).

Victor, Benjamin, *The history of the theatres of London and Dublin, from the year 1730 to the present time*, 2 vols (London, T. Davies, 1761).

—, *A history of the theatres of London from 1760 to the present time* (London, T. Davies, 1771).

Von Eerde, K., *John Ogilby and the taste of his times* (Folkestone, Kent, Wm. Dawson & Son, 1976).

Waddams, Stephen, 'Johanna Wagner and the rival opera houses', *Law Quarterly Review*, 117 (2001), 431.

Walsh, T.J., *Opera in Dublin, 1705–1797* (Dublin, Allen Figgis, 1973).

—, *Opera in Dublin, 1798–1820: Frederick Jones and the Crow Street theatre* (Oxford, Oxford UP, 1993).

Whelan, Gerald and Carolyn Swift, *Spiked: Church-State intrigue and* The Rose Tattoo (Dublin, New Island, 2002).

Woods, J.V., *Liquor licensing laws of Ireland* (Castletroy, Limerick, the author, 1992).

Young, Arthur, *A tour in Ireland, 1776–1779*, ed. A.W. Hutton, 2 vols (London, Bohn's Library, 1892).

Young, B.A., 'From playhouse to opera house' in Andrew Saint et al., *A history of the Royal Opera House* (London, Royal Opera House, 1982).

Index of legislation, etc.

This inventory of legislation (interpreted broadly to include proclamations and subordinate legislation (or orders in council), aside from legislation properly so called, is arranged chronologically. The jurisdiction targeted is indicated by the appropriate abbreviation at the start of each entry (i.e., UK, GB, I, E, IFS, ROI, NI).

In the case of Acts of Parliament, for a number of early entries, the full title for the Act in question is given.

Index to cases of law

The arrangement here is alphabetically ordered

Index

compiled by Julitta Clancy

Note: plays cited are listed under 'dramatic works'

Old Curiosity Shop, The (Dickens), 91
Olivier, Lord, 225
Olympia Productions Ltd, 122
Olympia Theatre, Dublin, 121, 137
  collapse of proscenium arch (1974), 122–3, 129
  as Empire Palace, 138
  patent (1937), 122
Olympic Theatre, London, 135, 219
O'Malley, Conor, 178, 201
opera, 5, 6, 7, 16, 31, 33, 34, 88, 90, 92, 94, 111, 113, 146, 147, 148, 168, 169–71, 172, 173, 175, 177–8, 180, 197, 236n, 259; *see also* operatic works
  licensing, 61–2, 63, 95
  in Nazi Germany, 238–9
  performing rights, 249–50, 260, 261–2, 263
opera houses, 84, 145, 148–9, 186, 240; *see also* Cork Opera House; Covent Garden
operatic works
  Andrea Chenier (Giordano), 238–9
  Artaxerxes (Arne), 173, 196
  Beggar's Opera, The (Gay), 17, 31–2, 105, 216
  Beggar's Wedding, The, 167
  Bohemian Girl, The (Balfe), 261
  Castle of Andalusia, The (Arnold and O'Keeffe), 249–50, 255
  Don Juan (Gluck), 169
  Fidelio (Beethoven), 238
  Il Barbiere di Seviglia (Rossini), 76
  Inkle and Yarico (Arnold), 173, 195
  La Duenna (Sheridan), 249
  Le Prophète (Mayerbeer), 169
  Les Huguenots (Mayerbeer), 169
  Les Prés Saint Gervais (Lecocq), 175
  Lionel and Clauson (Dibdin), 196
  Lurline (Wallace), 261, 262
  Maritana (Wallace), 261
  Montecchi e Capuletti (Bellini), 169
  Robert le Diable (Mayerbeer), 169
  Salome (Strauss), 226
  Siege of Rhodes, The, 61
Orange Order, 197, 198
orange-sellers, 141, 142, 189
Orange Street theatre, Dublin, *see* Smock Alley
Orchard Street Theatre, Bath, 73
Ormond, dukes of, *see* Butler, James
Osbaldiston, David Webster, 38–9
Osborne, John, 225
Oscar Cinema, Sandymount, 120

O'Shaughnessy, Mr T.L., KC, 118
O'Shea, Bartholomew, 123
O'Shea, Mark, 150
Oslo (Norway), 180
O'Toole, Fintan, 36–7, 136
Otway, Thomas, 37, 161
Overstone and Sywell Dramatic Society, 269
Oxford Dictionary of National Biography, 23, 171, 262
Oxford, earl of, 248
Oxford University, 11, 32–3, 76

Paeton, Mr, 115
Paisley, Revd Ian, 205
Pakenham, Francis Aungier, earl of Longford, 123, 239
Palace Theatre, London, 206
Palmer, Mr (attorney), 165
Panormo, Percival, 171
pantomime, 16, 17, 26, 38, 112, 122, 135, 146, 197
  licensing, 61–2, 63, 88, 89, 90, 92, 95
  works: *Cinderella*, 38; *Old King Cole, or Harlequin and the Fiddlers Three*, 38; *Sorcerer* or *The Two Brothers of Catonia*, 38
Paris theatre, 43, 89, 181, 182
Parker, Sir James, 170
Parker, Mrs, 78
parliamentary select committees
  dramatic literature (1832), 252–61
  stage censorship (1909), 81, 201, 216, 217, 219, 220, 221–2, 223
  theatre censorship (1966), 226
  theatres and places of entertainment (1892), 79, 80–1, 82, 135, 218, 233–4
  theatrical licences and regulations (1866), 62, 63–4, 67, 70, 134–5, 137, 142, 187, 217–18, 219
Parsons, William, lord justice, 4
Patent Office, Dublin, 121
patents, *see* Dublin theatre patents; London theatre
Patrick's Close, Dublin, 13
Patti, Adelina, 111, 177
Pavilion Theatre, Kingstown, *see* Kingstown Pavilion (Dun Laoghaire)
Pavilion Theatre, Liverpool, 224
Pavilion Theatre, London, 135
Payne, Mr (court reporter), 187
Peacock Theatre, Dublin, 121, 126, 130n, 205
Pearse, Patrick, 231–2